Theories and Applications of Artificial Intelligence

Theories and Applications of Artificial Intelligence

Edited by
Mitch Hoppe

www.statesacademicpress.com

Published by States Academic Press,
109 South 5th Street,
Brooklyn, NY 11249, USA

ISBN: 978-1-63989-524-3

Cataloging-in-Publication Data

Theories and applications of artificial intelligence / edited by Mitch Hoppe.
    p. cm.
Includes bibliographical references and index.
ISBN 978-1-63989-524-3
1. Artificial intelligence. 2. Fifth generation computers.
3. Neural computers. I. Hoppe, Mitch.
Q335 .T44 2022
006.3--dc23

For information on all States Academic Press publications
visit our website at www.statesacademicpress.com

Contents

Preface

This book was inspired by the evolution of our times; to answer the curiosity of inquisitive minds. Many developments have occurred across the globe in the recent past which has transformed the progress in the field.

The intelligence demonstrated by machines, which is different from the natural intelligence displayed by humans and animals, is referred to as artificial intelligence. It encompasses the ability of a system to correctly interpret external data, to develop learning from that data and to use the learning for flexible adaptation to perform specific tasks. Artificial intelligence is a combination of deep learning and machine learning. Some of the examples of artificial intelligence include autonomous vehicles like self-driving cars and drones, online assistants, search engines, etc. It has applications in multiple industries such as healthcare, navigation, robotics, agriculture, automobiles, and marketing, etc. The various advancements in artificial intelligence are glanced at and their applications as well as ramifications are looked at in detail in this book. The ever growing need of advanced technology is the reason that has fueled the research in the field of artificial intelligence in recent times. Through this book, we attempt to further enlighten the readers about the new concepts in this field.

This book was developed from a mere concept to drafts to chapters and finally compiled together as a complete text to benefit the readers across all nations. To ensure the quality of the content we instilled two significant steps in our procedure. The first was to appoint an editorial team that would verify the data and statistics provided in the book and also select the most appropriate and valuable contributions from the plentiful contributions we received from authors worldwide. The next step was to appoint an expert of the topic as the Editor-in-Chief, who would head the project and finally make the necessary amendments and modifications to make the text reader-friendly. I was then commissioned to examine all the material to present the topics in the most comprehensible and productive format.

I would like to take this opportunity to thank all the contributing authors who were supportive enough to contribute their time and knowledge to this project. I also wish to convey my regards to my family who have been extremely supportive during the entire project.

Editor

English-persian plagiarism detection based on a semantic approach

F. Safi-Esfahani*, Sh. Rakian and M.-H. Nadimi-Shahraki

Faculty of Computer Engineering, Najafabad Branch, Islamic Azad University, Najafabad, Isfahan, Iran.

Corresponding author: fsafi@iaun.ac.ir (F. Safi-Esfahani).

Abstract

Plagiarism, defined as "the wrongful appropriation of other writers' or authors' works and ideas without citing or informing them", poses a major challenge to knowledge spread publication. Plagiarism has been placed in the four categories of direct, paraphrasing (re-writing), translation, and combinatory. This paper addresses the translational plagiarism, which is sometimes referred to as the cross-lingual plagiarism. In cross-lingual translation, writers meld a translation with their own words and ideas. Based on the monolingual plagiarism detection methods, this paper ultimately intends to find a way to detect the cross-lingual plagiarism. A framework called multi-lingual plagiarism detection (MLPD) has been presented for the cross-lingual plagiarism analysis with the ultimate objective of detection of plagiarism cases. English is the reference language, and Persian materials are back-translated using the translation tools. The data used for MLPD assessment is obtained from English-Persian Mizan parallel corpus. Apache's Solr is also applied to record the creep of the documents and their indexation. The accuracy mean of the proposed method was revealed to be 98.82% when employing highly accurate translation tools, which indicate the high accuracy of the method. Also the Google translation service showed the accuracy mean to be 56.9%. These tests demonstrate that the improved translation tools enhance the accuracy of the developed method.

Keywords: *Text Retrieval, Cross-lingual, Text Similarity, Translation, Plagiarism, Semantic-based Plagiarism Detection.*

1. Introduction

An easier access to digital information, particularly the internet, has exponentially increased the plagiarism cases. Plagiarism comes in different forms including direct copying of a text without giving credit to the original writer, misappropriation of other's ideas, resources and styles, translation, reproduction of the original works via different visual and audio media, and code plagiarism [1]. Ceska et al. (2008) [2] have produced a new taxonomy of plagiarism, which has been completed later that year by Alzahrani et al. [3], who categorized plagiarism into literal and intelligent based on the plagiarist's behavioral viewpoint, highlighting the differences between these two phenomena.

Figure 1 presents a simple categorization of plagiarism. While the software tools are the most effective ones when they come to detect plagiarism, the final decision should be made based on the manual handling of cases [4].

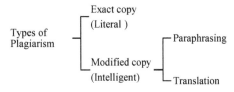

Figure 1: Taxonomy of plagiarism [6].

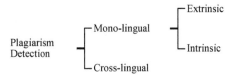

Figure 2. Plagiarism detection techniques.

Plagiarism detection could be categorized into monolingual and cross-lingual based on the varying degrees of homogeneity/heterogeneity of the language of documents (Figure 2).

Cross-lingual plagiarism refers to cases in which the writer melds a translation into his/her work without giving a proper reference to the original text. Cross-lingual plagiarism refers to the detection and identification of plagiarism in a multilingual environment. It should be noted that detection of translational plagiarism is more challenging than the other categories of plagiarism [3]. In this category, the retrieval of suspicious documents from a large corpus of multilingual documents is intended.

This paper puts forward a machine translation-based detection method in order to identify cases of cross-lingual plagiarism of documents based on the application of a semantic relatedness approach. Semantic similarity or semantic relatedness rates the likeness of words using (WUP) Wu-Palmer for detection of plagiarism. The detection of the cross-lingual plagiarism cases is generally the same as the external ways of detection, yet with some minor changes. Persian fuzzy plagiarism detection (PFPD) [5], which has been primarily designed to detect cases of paraphrasing monolingual texts, does not cover translational plagiarism. This paper attempts to add the capability of detection of translational plagiarism to the store of PFPD. As a matter of fact, we intend to cover translational plagiarism through the development of the PFPD technique to improve its precision. It is hypothesized that through integration of semantic approach with PFPD to measure the similarity of inter-lingual text, the precision of detection of translational plagiarism will improve. It should be noted that this paper does not apply to the detection of inherent plagiarism (changes in stylistics). Suspicious texts (target text) are in Persian, and the source language is English. Detection of cross-lingual plagiarism refers to cases of automatic detection of plagiarism between languages. The purpose of this work is the translational plagiarism detection between Persian and English texts.

Apache's Solr was applied to record the creep of the documents and their indexation. The accuracy mean of the proposed method was revealed to be 98.82%, while employing the highly accurate translation tools, which indicate the high accuracy of the proposed method. The Google translation service was also employed to translate suspicious documents from Persian to English in order to implement the proposed method, and showed 56.9% for the accuracy mean.

The rest of this paper is organized as follows. The second section will offer some explanations and concepts about the cross-lingual plagiarism. The third section reviews a number of relevant research works with accounts of their pros and

cons. The fourth section presents the methodology in detail. In the fifth section, we will deal with the implementation and analysis results. Finally, in the last part, we will review the conclusions made.

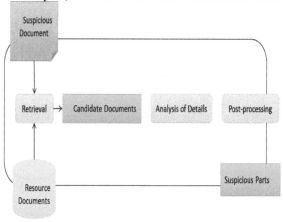

Figure 3. External plagiarism detection framework [6].

2. Concepts of cross-lingual plagiarism

Research on the detection of cross-lingual plagiarism has attracted many researches in the recent years, with a focus on the cross-lingual relatedness of the texts [2, 7-11]. The detection of the cross-lingual plagiarism cases is generally the same as the external ways of detection, yet with some minor changes. (The framework for the external detection methods is presented in Figure 3.) The differences are as follows:

(1) In the retrieval phase, it is required to write the suspicious texts in their source language.

(2) In the analysis of the details, the relatedness of the original and suspicious texts should be investigated. (It is also possible to back-translate the suspicious text, and then apply the monolingual plagiarism detection methods).

Query document and sets of documents serve as inputs in the operational framework of the cross-lingual plagiarism detection. Writing language, query document, and set of documents are not the same. Basically, there are three primary phases. In the first phase, a list of candidate documents is retrieved based on the CLIR models. If the suspicious document has been translated via a machine translation, it is possible to retrieve the candidate documents using IR models. In the second phase, a two-by-two study is conducted to find all suspicious parts of the query document that are similar to the candidate documents. In this phase, the language of the query and candidate texts is different. In the 3rd phase, post-processing is performed by a human agent to render the results obtained in a readable format [10].

The set of candidate texts is the distinguishing factor between the methods of cross-lingual plagiarism detection and external detection. While in cross-lingual plagiarism detection, the language of the suspicious and the original texts is heterogeneous and thus the comparison is made between other languages and the suspicious text, in the external plagiarism detection, the language of the suspicious and original texts is the same. The syntactical and lexical features are not sufficient to create a cross-lingual environment. To establish the relation between a cross-lingual text and detection of plagiarism, the syntactical features are usually combined with the semantic or statistical features [3].

Known methods for cross-lingual information retrieval (CLIR) may be applied to retrieve candidate documents; 1. Extracting the key words of the suspicious text to obtain a set of words to represent it, translating these words and searching them in the original text, 2. Back-translating the suspicious text, extracting the key words, and searching them in the original text [12].

The output of this stage is a set of documents that might have been plagiarized. It should be noted that it is possible to use various cross-lingual information retrieval techniques such as comparable corpus, parallel corpus, multi-lingual dictionary, and machine translation [13].

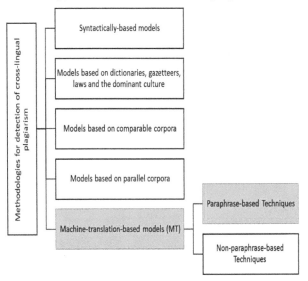

Figure 4. Taxonomy of different methodologies for detection of cross-lingual plagiarism.

3. Literature review

In the cross-lingual detail analysis phase, the similarity and relatedness of the suspicious documents and candidate documents are measured. For this, 5 models are available: 1. Syntactically-based models, 2. Models based on dictionaries, gazetteers, laws, and dominant culture, 3. Models based on comparable corpora, 4. Models based on parallel corpora, and 5.

Machine-translation-based models [12]. Figure 4 shows the taxonomy of different methodologies for the detection of cross-lingual plagiarism.

Machine-translation-based models were applied in the proposed method. Other methods utilize the machine translation principles as well, yet they do not cover translating suspicious documents. Many methods use machine translation for analyzing documents to detect cross-lingual re-use of documents. This turns the issue into detecting monolingual plagiarism, which has gained popularity in the recent years [12]. The proposed method falls in this category.

So far, few quantitative research works have been conducted about cross-lingual plagiarism. However, the interest is growing fast in this regard. According to [12], there was no technology available before 2008 to detect the cross-lingual plagiarism cases. However, detection of cross-lingual plagiarism may benefit from the research works carried out in the other fields [2,8,9,11,14,28].

In [11], the proposed method is based upon statistical bilingual dictionary, which is comprised of parallel corpora and a bilingual algorithm text. The authors have conducted a test on a 5-piece set of plagiarized documents. The results obtained have revealed that the similarity between the original source and the plagiarized texts is remarkably higher than the unaffected documents.

The research work [2] has suggested MLPlag as a cross-lingual analysis tool for the detection of plagiarism based on the positions of words. This tool uses European Word net TM to convert words into an independent format from the language in question. The authors have created two multilingual corpora: 1. Fairy-tale, made up of 400 legal texts of EU, which were randomly selected and included 200 reports in English and a corresponding number in Czech, 2. JRC-EU, a set of textual documents in simple English and their 27 Czech English. This method has revealed good results. However, the authors have stated that an incomplete Word net may result in difficulties in the detection of plagiarism, especially while dealing with the less common languages.

A number of research works have been carried out in the field of retrieval of multilingual documents, which may contribute to the detection of cases of plagiarism [15]. A system was proposed to identify the original source of a translated text among a large number of candidate texts. The content was represented with a vector of words using a comprehensive dictionary. The textual similarity was measured independent from the language of the documents. The writers conducted the test on a number of French and Spanish translated tests (from English) via a number of parallel corpora, which included 795 to 1130 pairs of texts and 1640 documents. The results obtained show that the system is capable of identifying the translation with an accuracy of 96%.

In [16], Kullback-Leibler have used divergence to reduce the number of documents to be compared with suspicious documents. In this study, a feature vector was created for each document of the reference set to be compared with the vector of the suspicious document. Ten documents with the lowest divergence with the vector of the suspicious documents were selected for the plagiarism analyses purposes.

Table 1. Comparison between Previous Research Works on Translational Plagiarism.

Reference/ Year/Authors	Method	Language	Main Features	Defects
[11] 2008 Barrón-Cedeno, A., et al.	Based on parallel corpora	Spanish-English	Based on a statistical dictionary created from parallel corpora and bilingual text document	Requires data for education
[2] 2008 Ceska, Z., M. Toman, and K. Jezek	Based on dictionaries, gazetteers, comprehensive laws	Czech-English	Analysis of word positions, European WordNet to convert words into formats independent of the target language	Incomplete WordNet may cause difficulties, especially while dealing with less common languages
[18] 2010 Kent, C.K. and N. Salim	MT- based	Malay-English	Analysis was based on three least-frequent 4-grams fingerprint matching	Fingerprint matching fails to identify cases where a word has been translated with its synonyms
[19] 2010 Muhr, M., et al.	Parallel corpora	European-English	Translation model output is used. Bekeley Aligner and EU corpora were employed to create a word-based model	Low accuracy
[17] 2011 Gupta, P., et al.	Vector Space Model (VSM)	German-Spanish & English	Analyze the monolingual paraphrases of English and cross-lingual paraphrases for German and Spanish languages	Low accuracy. This approach can be more effective by considering synonyms using thesauri, dictionary, and WordNet.
PFPD [5] 2015 Rakian, S., et al.	Fuzzy analysis in plagiarism detection and candidate documents retrieval	All Languages/ Tested for English/Persian Languages	Increasing precision and recall in candidate documents retrieval and in measuring the similarity. Avoid unnecessary comparisons	Paraphrasing detection monolingual texts
MLDP 2016 (Proposed Model)	MT-based	Persian-English	Promoting the fuzzy method to detect cases of rewriting of monolingual texts to help detect translational plagiarism cases	Extensive operations required

The research work [17] has focused on paraphrasing detection for both the monolingual and cross-lingual aspects applying Vector Space Model (VSM). The authors have considered English language for monolingual and German-Spanish languages for cross-lingual paraphrasing. This approach can be more effective by considering synonyms using thesauri, dictionary, and WordNet.

PFPD (Persian fuzzy plagiarism detection), presented in [5], is an approach to the external plagiarism detection in Persian texts. The aim of this framework is to make a compatible fuzzy method in Persian language. PFPD, which has been primarily designed to detect cases of paraphrasing monolingual texts, does not cover translational plagiarism either.

Normalizing language in the pre-processing phase is a common measure taken for the cross-lingual information retrieval techniques, in particular, the cross-lingual plagiarism detection. In [7], the authors have proposed using English as the source language for 2 reasons: 1. Most of the internet content is in English, 2. Non-English to English translation tools are easier to access. In the first phase, a language detector was employed to determine the language of the documents. If the language is shown to be other than English, it will be rendered into English. The second phase is dedicated to detection of monolingual cases of plagiarism. This method covers five phases: language normalization, retrieval of candidate documents, education of categorization, comprehensive analysis of plagiarism, and post-processing. This study has been used as an automatic translation tool to translate the texts into a single language. To detect the plagiarized texts form the unaffected ones, the researchers have turned to the categorization algorithm. In the retrieval phase, the documents that suspected to have been the subject of plagiarism will be extracted. This is a crucial phase as it is not possible to search such a large set of documents.

The research work [18] has suggested applications of API translation and Google search options. In the first phase, a suspicious text in Malay has been translated into English as the source language. The text has been entered in Google as a query after removal of stop and stemming words. Exact analysis was performed during the retrieval phase of the set of candidate documents. This analysis was based upon three least-frequent 4-grams fingerprint matching. The failure of fingerprint matching to detect words that were translated with synonyms is the main drawback of the method.

The research work [19] has attempted to utilize a partial machine translation process to detect the cross-lingual plagiarism cases. End translation has been replaced with the output of the translation model. The word-based model in this research work has been produced by Berkeley Aligner using the European parallel corpora. Each token has been substituted with five candidate translations, and if it was not possible to translate, the token would be directly used. Table 1 compares different plagiarism methods.

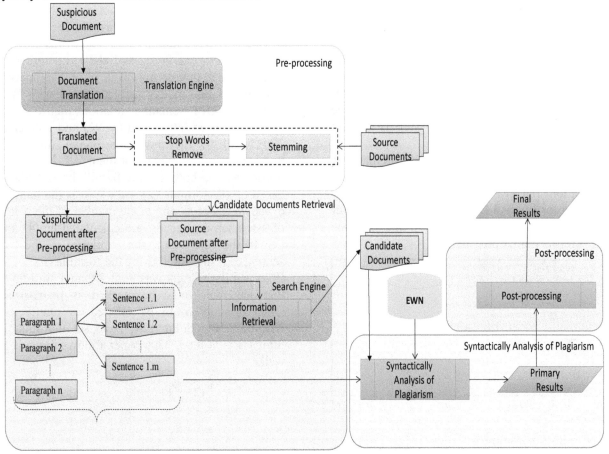

Figure 5. Recommended Framework- MLPD.

4. MLPD approach

This paper proposes MLPD (multi-lingual plagiarism detection) for a cross-lingual plagiarism analysis with the ultimate objective of detection of plagiarism cases. As the proposed model is designed to detect cross-lingual plagiarism, an automatic translation tool was employed to translate suspicious documents in English as the source language to make the analysis consistent. The proposed model intends to improve PFPD [5], a method used in detection of re-writing of monolingual texts that attempts to offer highly accurate detection results. It should be noted that methods of detection of monolingual plagiarism cannot be directly used for cases of

cross-lingual plagiarism due as the words of suspicious texts and source texts will fail to match. Even if the plagiarized text is the exact translation of the source text, there will be at least changes in order of the words. As a result, MLPD tries to overcome this problem via employing an automatic translation tool to translate suspicious documents in English as the source language in order to make the analysis consistent. The primary difference between MLPD and PFPD, which is a fuzzy method for monolingual plagiarism detection, lies in the fact that in the former, occurrences of cross-lingual plagiarism are revealed in the analysis phase. English is set as the default language as the primary objective is to detect cases of plagiarized cases of Persian texts translated from English, and the fact that most documents have been developed in English. The analysis will be performed after completion of the translations. The point is that even with employment of a superb translation tool, a partial content loss is inevitable. Figure 5 shoes how the proposed model works.

4.1. Text and word normalization

This phase includes translation of suspicious texts and removal of stop and stemming words. It is necessary to back-translate the suspicious texts before application of the plagiarism detection algorithms to detect potential cases of violation.

By stop words, we mean words that frequently occur in the texts without imparting any significant meaning [20]. Therefore, these words are removed for a faster analysis and shrinking the index store. The list of English stop words are available for processing.

Stemming removes suffixes and prefixes to produce word roots. Roots improve the information retrieval process. There are many stemmers for English language from which Porter and Kstem are very popular [21]. Here, we used Kstem for its higher precision.

```
   Input: candidateDocs[], susdoc
1   for each sentence i in susdocs
2    for each sentence j in docs
3     double similarity = compareSentences(sentence[i],
      sentence[j]);
4     if (similarity >=SIMTHRESHOLD)
5       result.add(sentence[j]);
6    Endfor
7    return result;
8   Endfor
   Output: result
```

Figure 6. Pseudo-code for measuring similarity of sentences.

4.2. Candidate documents retrieval

In this phase, a maximum of five documents with the highest frequency of suspicious sentences are selected from the source documents. This is done via the *Solr* search engine later.

4.3. Semantic analysis of plagiarism

In an attempt to detect monolingual plagiarism, Li et al. [22] have used the depth and length of the shortest route to the word in WorldNet synset. Similar to [22], our MLPD used the depth and length of the shortest route to the word in WordNet synset to detect monolingual plagiarism. WordNet is a lexical database for the English language that includes the lexical categories nouns, verbs, adjectives, and adverbs but ignores prepositions, determiners, and other function words. Sets of synonyms were linked to each

other through semantic-conceptual and lexical ties. WordNet structure has become very useful in the process of natural language, thanks to its structure.

This paper differs from [22], as it uses a different procedure for measurement of relatedness level.

The pseudo-code for this algorithm is presented in Figure 6. In this code, suspicious and candidate documents are used as input.

For each sentence of the suspicious paragraph, first a matrix is formed. This matrix is measured for different words of each pair of sentences. If the bigger sentence is called s_1 and the shorter one s_2, then the matrix (1) is measured for them. In this matrix, the columns represent words from s_1 that do not occur in s_2, and the rows represent words from s_2 that do not occur in s_1. The internal volumes of this matrix are calculated with Wu-Palmer (WUP) semantic relation metric. This metric has been introduced by Wu and Palmer in 1994 [23]. If the output is bigger than one, number one is designated for them.

Subsequently, both α and β will be calculated based on the formula (2) and (3) (n is the number of the words of s_1, and m the number of the words of s_2). Then δ_{12} and δ_{21} are calculated as (4) and (5). In the final stage, the similarity of the two sentences is measured using the formula (6).

If the similarity rank was higher than T threshold, that sentence would be marked as plagiarized. Otherwise, it would be labeled as unaffected. Alzahrani and Salim [24] have set the suitable limit for T at 0.65. This paper follows the suit as well.

$$\begin{array}{ccc} w_{11} & w_{12} & w_{13} \\ \end{array} \tag{1}$$
$$\begin{array}{c} w_{21} \\ w_{22} \end{array} \begin{bmatrix} s_{11} & s_{12} & s_{13} \\ s_{21} & s_{22} & s_{23} \end{bmatrix}$$

$$\alpha = \sum_{i=1}^{n} \max_{j=1}^{m} \left(w_{ij} \right) \tag{2}$$

$$\beta = \sum_{j=1}^{m} \max_{i=1}^{n} \left(w_{ij} \right) \tag{3}$$

$$\delta_{12} = (\alpha + \textit{Number of the same words}) / \#s_1 \tag{4}$$

$$\delta_{21} = (\beta + \textit{Number of the same words}) / \#s_2 \tag{5}$$

$$\gamma = \left| \delta_{12} - \delta_{21} \right| > 0.28 \text{ and } \max\left(\delta_{12}, \delta_{21}\right) < 0.83 \tag{6}$$

$$sim\left(s_1, s_2\right) = \begin{cases} min\left(\delta_{12}, \delta_{21}\right), \gamma \textit{ is TRUE} \\ max\left(\delta_{12}, \delta_{21}\right), \gamma \textit{ is FALSE} \end{cases}$$

Multi-Lingual Plagiarism Detection (MLPD)				
	W_{11} = various	W_{12} = carry	W_{13} = man	$\beta = \sum\limits_{j=1}^{m} \max\limits_{i=1}^{n}\left(w_{ij}\right) = 1.6$
W_{21} = person	0	0.31	0.8	0.8
W_{22} = case	0	0.57	0.8	0.8
$\alpha = \sum\limits_{i=1}^{n} \max\limits_{j=1}^{m}\left(w_{ij}\right) = 1.37$	0	0.57	0.8	

$$\delta_{12} = (\alpha + Number\ of\ the\ same\ words) / \#s_1 = (1.37+1)/4 = 0.59$$

$$\delta_{21} = (\beta + Number\ of\ the\ same\ words) / \#s_2 = (1.6+1)/3 = 0.86$$

$$(\gamma = \left|\delta_{12} - \delta_{21}\right| > 0.28)\ and\ (\max(\delta_{12}, \delta_{21}) < 0.83) = false$$

$$sim(s_1, s_2) = \begin{cases} min(\delta_{12}, \delta_{21}), \gamma\ is\ TRUE \\ max(\delta_{12}, \delta_{21}), \gamma\ is\ FALSE \end{cases}$$

$$sim_{MLPD}(s_1, s_2) = 0.86$$

Persian Fuzzy Plagiarism Detection (PFPD)

$$Same\ words\ (synonym): N/A$$

$$\delta = (0.5 \times Number\ of\ the\ same\ words) + (1 \times Number\ of\ the\ same\ words) = 0.5 \times 0 + 1 \times 1 = 1$$

$$\alpha = \frac{\delta}{|s_1|} = \frac{1}{4} = 0.25$$

$$\beta = \frac{\delta}{|s_2|} = \frac{1}{3} = 0.33$$

$$\gamma = \frac{\delta}{\left(|S_1| + |S_2| - \delta\right)} = \frac{1}{(4+3)-1} = 0.17$$

$$Sim_{PFPD}(S_1, S_2) = \frac{A.min(\alpha, \beta) + B.max(\alpha, \beta) + C.\gamma}{A+B+C} = \frac{20 \times 0.25 + 8 \times 0.33 + 3 \times 0.17}{20+8+3} = 0.26$$

Figure 7. Case study calculations.

4.4. Post-processing

Once the results are produced, a summary of the results of plagiarism detection including plagiarized parts, source of plagiarism, and similarity percentage are presented. Post-processing is used to report the results and integrate the plagiarized parts.

5. Case study

To shed light on how the similarity measurement method of the MLPD model works and highlight its differences with PFPD [5], an example is given.

Example: Imagine that two sentences to be compared have been represented with S_1 and S_2. S_3 is the translation of S_2, obtained from the Google translation engine.

S₁: Sometimes one man carried various names.

The words in S_1 after equalization of the text, removal of stop words, and stemming are:

[name, various, carry, man]; then $|S_1| = 4$

S2: در برخی موارد شخصی دارای چندین نام است

S3: In some cases, a person has several names.

The words in S3 after equalization of the text, removal of stop words, and stemming are:

[case, person, name]; then $|s_3| = 3$.

It should be noted that the word order is not important in measurement of similarity rate in [25], and the data structure used is a set. The same words in two sentences (shared points of S_1 and S_3): $S_1 \cap S_3 = [name]$.

The calculation of the formulas is illustrated in Figure 7. As the results indicate, while MLPD can detect the similarity of two sentences, PFPD fails to do so.

6. Assessment and trials

The dataset for assessment of MLPD were obtained from the standard English-Persian Mizan parallel corpus. This corpus is free for all, and has been used in the research works [26] and [27]. It contains one million parallel sentences of Gutenberg's novels along with their Persian translations that have been keyed in, spellchecked, and parallelized semi-automatically.

These trials attempt to prove the hypothesis of this research work and investigate the retrieval precision of the proposed model. A total of two sets of trial were conducted to test the hypothesis. First, each sentence is compared with its translation.

This reveals the accuracy of the proposed model when highly accurate translation tools are employed. In the second stage, the Google translation program translates the sentence, and then the results obtained are compared with the first phase.

Both trials were performed with MLPD and PFPD [5]. PFPD is a fuzzy method used in identification of re-writing. These trials were conducted to prove that the re-writing identification methods are not successful in detection of translational plagiarism.

6.1. Trial environment

In MLPD, first the Persian input is back-translated via the Google API free tool. In the retrieval phase, Apache's Solr was also applied to record the creep of the documents and their indexation. An HP Pavilion dv4-1515tx was used to complete the trials. Figure 8 gives a general scheme for the trial environment.

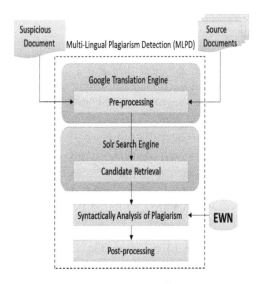

Figure 8. Experimental environment.

6.2. First set of trials

In the first set, each sentence is compared with its translation. This reveals the accuracy of the proposed model when highly accurate translation tools are employed. The trials were conducted on1021596 sentences. The results obtained are presented in Figure 9 and Table 2, respectively.

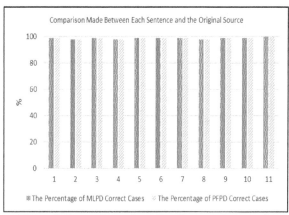

Figure 9. Percentage of results of comparison made between each sentence and original source.

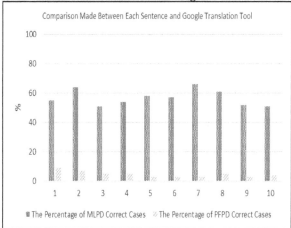

Figure 10. Percentage of results of comparison made between each sentence and google translation tool.

The results obtained reveal the accuracy mean of the proposed method to be 98.82% when employing highly accurate manually translated by an English expert, which indicate the high accuracy of the proposed method. This supports the idea that if suitable translation is used, the re-writing identification methods may contribute to the translational plagiarism detection.

6.3. Second set of trials

In the Second set, each sentence is translated by the Google translation program. The trials were conducted on 10000 sentences. The obtained results are presented in Figure 10 and Table 3. The results of the second trial indicate that when the Google translation program is employed, the accuracy mean is 56.9%, and the accuracy mean of PFPD is 4.7%. These tests demonstrate that the improved translation tools enhance the accuracy of the proposed method. Also after comparing the proposed method with PFPD, which is a method of monolingual plagiarism detection, it becomes obvious that the monolingual methods cannot be practiced for the cross-lingual plagiarism detection. This is because even if the plagiarized text is an exact translation of the original text, the word order will not be the same. As a result, the words of suspicious and original texts will not match.

Table 2. Results of comparison made between each sentence and original source.

No.	From Sentence:	To:	Correct Cases of MLPD	Mistakes of MLPD	Percentage of MLPD Correct Cases	Correct Cases of PFPD	Mistakes of PFPD	Percentage of PFPD Correct Cases
1	1	100001	98095	1905	99	98095	1905	99
2	100001	200000	97484	2516	98	97484	2516	98
3	200001	300000	98295	1705	99	98295	1705	99
4	300001	400000	97946	2054	98	97946	2054	98
5	400001	500000	98059	1941	99	98059	1941	99
6	500001	600000	98484	1516	99	98484	1516	99
7	600001	700000	98650	1350	99	98650	1350	99
8	700001	800000	97342	2658	98	97342	2658	98
9	800001	900000	98290	1710	99	98290	1710	99
10	900001	1000000	98627	1373	99	98627	1373	99
11	1000001	1021596	21447	149	100	21447	149	100

Table 3. Results of comparison made between each sentence and google translation tool.

No.	From Sentence	To Sentence	Correct Cases of MLPD	Mistakes of MLPD	Percentage of MLPD Correct Cases	Correct Cases of PFPD	Mistakes of PFPD	Percentage of PFPD Correct Cases
1	1	1000	550	450	55	84	916	9
2	1001	2000	632	368	64	70	930	7
3	2001	3000	501	499	51	48	952	5
4	3001	4000	537	463	54	43	957	5
5	4001	5000	574	426	58	30	970	3
6	5001	6000	564	436	57	25	975	3
7	6001	7000	651	349	66	24	976	3
8	7001	8000	605	395	61	41	959	5
9	8001	9000	511	489	52	27	973	3
10	9001	10000	504	496	51	33	967	4

7. Conclusion and future works

In this paper, we attempted to propose a method for a cross-lingual plagiarism detection based on a semantic approach. The accuracy mean of the proposed method when employing highly accurate translation tools was compared with the Google translation program. These tests demonstrate that the improved translation tools enhance the accuracy of the proposed method. In the first set, each sentence is compared with its translation. This reveals the accuracy of the proposed model when highly accurate translation tools are employed. The results obtained reveal the accuracy mean of the proposed method to be 98.82% when employing highly accurate translation tools, which indicate the high accuracy of the proposed method. The results of the second trial indicate that when the Google translation program is employed, the accuracy mean is 56.9%. These trials revealed that improving the existing translation tools would enhance the accuracy of the proposed method. Also they showed that monolingual methods could not be practiced for the cross-lingual plagiarism detection.

In the proposed MLPD, the Google translation machine was employed to translate suspicious texts. Other translation machines could be used to draw a comparison with the results of MLPD. Also the results obtained could be compared with the other translational plagiarism methods.

References

[1] Lukashenko, R., Graudina, V. & Grundspenkis, J. (2007). Computer-based plagiarism detection methods and tools: an overview, In: Proceedings of the international conference on Computer systems and technologies, Bulgaria, 2007.

[2] Ceska, Z., Toman, M. & Jezek, K. (2008). Multilingual plagiarism detection, Lecture Notes in Computer Science (including subseries Lecture Notes in Artificial Intelligence Lecture Notes in Bioinformatics), pp. 83-92.

[3] Alzahrani, S. M., Salim, N. & Abraham, A. (2012). Understanding Plagiarism linguistic patterns, textual features, and detection methods, IEEE Transactions on Systems, Man, and Cybernetics, Part C: Applications and Reviews, vol. 42, no. 2, pp. 133-149.

[4] Gruner, S. & Naven, S. (2005). Tool support for plagiarism detection in text documents, In: Proceedings of the ACM symposium on Applied computing, Santa Fe, New Mexico, 2005.

[5] Rakian, S., Safi-Esfahani, F. & Rastegari, H. (2015). A Persian Fuzzy Plagiarism Detection Approach, Journal of Information Systems and Telecommunication (JIST), vol. 3, no. 11.

[6] Stein, B., Meyer zu Eissen, S. & Potthast, M. (2007). Strategies for retrieving plagiarized documents,

In: Proceedings of the 30th annual international ACM SIGIR conference on Research and development in information retrieval, NY, USA, 2007.

[7] Corezola Pereira, R., Moreira, V. & Galante, R. (2010). A New Approach for Cross-Language Plagiarism Analysis, Multilingual and Multimodal Information Access Evaluation, pp. 15-26.

[8] Lee, C. H., Wu, C. H. & Yang, H. C. (2008). A Platform Framework for Cross-lingual Text Relatedness Evaluation and Plagiarism Detection, In: Innovative Computing Information and Control, ICICIC'08, IEEE, 2008.

[9] Pinto, D., Civera, J., Barrón-Cedeòo, A., Juan, A., & Rosso, P. (2009). A statistical approach to crosslingual natural language tasks, Journal of Algorithms, vol. 64, no. 1, pp. 51-60.

[10] Potthast, M., Barrón-Cedeño, A., Stein, B. & Rosso, P. (2010). Cross-language plagiarism detection. Language Resources and Evaluation, vol. 45, no. 1, pp. 45-62.

[11] Barrón-Cedeno, A., Rosso, P., Pinto, D. & Juan, A. (2008). In: Proceeding of PAN'2008, Greece, 2008.

[12] Cedeno, L. A. B. (2012). On the mono-and cross-language detection of text re-use and plagiarism, Universidad de La Rioja, 2012.

[13] He, D. & J. Wang. (2009). Cross-language information retrieval, Information Retrieval: Searching in the 21st Century, pp. 233-254.

[14] Potthast, M., Stein, B. & Anderka, M. (2008). A Wikipedia-based multilingual retrieval model, In: Advances in Information Retrieval. Springer, pp. 522-530.

[15] Pouliquen, B., Steinberger, R. & Ignat, C. (2006). Automatic identification of document translations in large multilingual document collections, arXiv preprint cs/0609060.

[16] Barrón-Cedeño, A., P. Rosso, & Benedí, J.M. (2009). Reducing the plagiarism detection search space on the basis of the kullback-leibler distance, Computational Linguistics and Intelligent Text Processing, pp. 523-534.

[17] Gupta, P., Singhal, K., Majumder, P. & Rosso, P. (2011). Detection of Paraphrastic Cases of Mono-lingual and Cross-lingual Plagiarism, In: Proceedings of ICON, Chennai, India, 2011.

[18] Kent, C. K. & Salim, N. (2010). Web based cross language plagiarism detection, In: Computational Intelligence, Modelling and Simulation (CIMSiM), Second International Conference on, IEEE, 2008.

[19] Muhr, M., Kern, R., Zechner, M. & Granitzer , M. (2010). External and Intrinsic Plagiarism Detection using a Cross-Lingual Retrieval and Segmentation System, Braschler and Harman.

[20] Van Rijsbergen, C.J. (1986). A new theoretical framework for information retrieval, In: Proceedings of the 9th annual international ACM SIGIR conference on Research and development in information retrieval. ACM, 1986.

[21] Scherbinin, V. & S. Butakov. (2008). Plagiarism Detection: The Tool and The Case Study. In e-Learning, 2008.

[22] Li, Y., McLean, D., Bandar, Z. A., O'Shea, J. D. & Crockett, K. (2006). Sentence similarity based on semantic nets and corpus statistics, IEEE Transactions on Knowledge and Data Engineering, vol. 18, no. 8, pp. 1138-1150.

[23] Palmer, Z. W. A. M. (1994). Verbs semantics and lexical selection, In: Proceedings of the 32nd annual meeting on Association for Computational Linguistics, pp. 133-138.

[24] Alzahrani, S. M. & Salim, N. (2010). Fuzzy semantic-based string similarity for extrinsic plagiarism detection: Lab report for PAN at CLEF'10, presented at the 4th International Workshop PAN'10, Padua, Italy, 2010.

[25] Meyer, D., Hornik, K. & Feinerer, I. (2008). Text mining infrastructure, Journal of Statistical Software, vol. 25, no. 5, pp. 1-54.

[26] Sarmad, M., IBM word-alignment model I for statistical machine translation.

[27] Azarbonyad, H. Shakery, A. & Faili, H. (2014). Learning to Exploit Different Translation Resources for Cross Language Information Retrieval, arXiv preprint arXiv:1405.5447.

[28] Rafieian, S. & Baraani-Dastjerdi, A. (2015). Plagiarism Checker for Persian (PCP) Texts Using Hash-based Tree Representative Fingerprinting, Journal of AI and Data Mining, vol. 4, no. 2, pp. 125-133.

2

Intrusion detection based on a novel hybrid learning approach

L. Khalvati[*], M. Keshtgary and N. Rikhtegar

Department of Computer & Information Technology, Shiraz University of Technology, Shiraz, Iran.

*Corresponding author: l.khalvati@sutech.ac.ir (L. Khalvati).

Abstract
The information security and the Intrusion Detection System (IDS) play a critical role in the internet. IDS is an essential tool for detecting different kinds of attacks in a network and maintaining data integrity, confidentiality, and system availability against possible threats. In this paper, a hybrid approach is proposed towards achieving a high performance. In fact, the important goal of this paper is to generate an efficient training dataset. In order to exploit the strength of clustering and feature selection, an intensive focus on intrusion detection combines the two, so the proposed method is using these techniques as well. At first, a new training dataset is created by K-Medoids clustering and Selecting Feature using the SVM method. Then Naïve Bayes classifier is used for evaluation. The proposed method is compared with another mentioned hybrid algorithm and also 10-fold cross validation. The experimental results based on the KDD CUP'99 dataset show that the proposed method has a better accuracy and detection rate and also false alarm rate than the others.

Keywords: *Intrusion Detection System, K-Medoids, Feature Selection, Naïve Bayes, Hybrid Learning Approach.*

1. Introduction

Today, internet access has become an important part of our daily life but the huge worldwide connections have caused security issues [1]. A secure network must have three features: confidentiality, integrity, and availability. Confidentiality means that accessing the network's data should be allowed only for the authorized people; integrity means that data should not be distorted during its transmission through the network; and availability means that whenever the information is required, it should be available to the authorized people.

Intrusion detection system (IDS) is a defensive system whose main goal is to detect actions that attempt to deny the network security features. Generally, there are two main types of intrusion detection systems: Signature-based Intrusion Detection System (SIDS) and Anomaly-Based Intrusion Detection System (AIDS) [2]. SIDS is the process of detecting harmful activities based upon known patterns of previous attacks, whereas AIDS is the process of detecting detrimental activities whenever the behavior of the system deviates from the normal behavior. AIDS can be executed by different techniques such as Naïve Bayes classifier, which is used in this paper, to improve the accuracy of IDS.

In the present work, we propose a multi-level approach through a combination of K-Medoids clustering, Selecting Feature using SVM algorithm and also Naïve Bayes classifier to improve the performance of IDS. First of all, K-Medoids clustering and Selecting Feature using the SVM algorithms are used to construct a new training dataset. Then the new training dataset is utilized to train the Naïve Bayes classifier. The results obtained demonstrate that the proposed method performs better in terms of accuracy, detection rate, and also false alarm rate.

The remainder of this paper is organized as what follows. Related work is discussed in Section 2. Section 3 represents the materials and methods that are used in this work. Section 4 describes the evaluation metrics. Our experiments are represented in Section 5. Finally, the paper is concluded in Section 6.

2. Related work

In the recent years, various hybrid IDS systems have been developed to achieve the best possible performance. In this section, we will review some of these methods that did not pay attention to building an efficient training dataset and normalization or made it by the K-Means algorithm.

Aslahi-Shahri et al. [3] have proposed a hybrid method that integrates SVM and genetic algorithm (GA). The experimental results on the KDDCUP'99 dataset have shown that this method is capable of achieving the good true-positive and also false-positive values.

Ravale et al. [4] have presented a hybrid approach based upon combining K-Means clustering algorithm and RBF kernel function of SVM method for IDS. The evaluation results show that their method performs better in terms of detection rate and accuracy when applied to the KDDCUP'99 dataset.

Esmaily et al. [5] have introduced a method based upon the integration of Decision Tree (DT) algorithm and Multi-Layer Perception (MLP) Artificial Neural Network (ANN). The results obtained reveal that the hybrid method is able to identify the attacks with high accuracy and reliability.

Anita et al. [6] have applied a hybrid approach based upon the K-Nearest Neighbor, K-Means, and Decision Table Majority rule based on the KDDCUP'99 dataset. The important achievement of this paper was the reduction of false alarm rate in the intrusion detection system and improving its efficiency.

Guo et al. [7] have proposed a new and easy-to-implement hybrid learning method named distance sum-based support vector machine (DSSVM). By applying DSSVM to the KDDCUP'99 dataset, the results obtained show that the proposed method performs well in both the detection rate and the computational costs.

Moussaid et al. [8], firstly, did a pre-processing phase for normalizing each TCP connection, and then the SVM technique was applied to the KDD KDDCUP'99 dataset to reduce the number of features. Finally, the K-Means algorithm was used to test the performance of the chosen attributes. The results obtained showed that choosing 10 features by SVM had a better performance.

Aziz et al. [9] have developed a multi-layer hybrid machine-learning method. This method consists of three layers: at first, the principal component analysis (PCA) is used for feature selection; and then the genetic algorithm (GA) is used for generating the anomaly detectors; and finally,

several different classifiers including Naïve Bayes, multi-layer perceptron neural network, and decision trees are used. The results obtained demonstrated that the Naïve Bayes classifier had a better accuracy in the case of the U2R and R2L attacks, while the j48 decision tree classifier had a better accuracy in detecting the DOS and Probe attacks.

Ihsan et al. [10] have discussed different normalization techniques and their effect on different classifiers such as the Naïve Bayes classifier. The results obtained illustrate that the hybrid normalization performs better than the conventional normalization techniques.

Xia et al. [11], at first, created an efficient train dataset using the K-Means and Ant Colony algorithms, and then the effectiveness of four different feature selection methods including Feature removal method, Sole feature method, hybrid method for feature selection, and Gradually Feature Removal method (GFR) by the SVM classifier was evaluated. The results obtained showed that the GFR method performed better than the others.

Mukherjee et al. [12] have investigated the performance of four different feature selection methods using Correlation-based Feature Selection, Information Gain, Gain Ratio, and Feature Vitality-Based Reduction Method by performing the Naïve Bayes classifier on the reduced dataset. The results of this research work show that the selected attributes by Feature Vitality Based Reduction Method gives a better intrusion detection performance.

3. Materials and methods

In this section, we describe the dataset and algorithms used in this research work.

3.1. Dataset and data pre-processing

Since KDD CUP'99 is the most commonly used dataset for simulating intrusion detection [1], we will use 10% of it in our experiments. Each record in this dataset includes 41 features and a class label. The features are listed in table 1, and the class labels can be categorized into 5 classes: normal, Denial of Service (DOS), unauthorized access from a remote machine (R2L), User to Root (U2R), and probe. Data pre-processing is the first step in the data analyzing procedure. This phase includes different methods like removing repeated data, normalization, and discretization. Here, we will describe the pre-processing methods that are used in this paper, as what follow.

What one notes is that there are a lot of duplicate records in the KDD cup99 dataset that may cause biased results of classifiers towards more frequent records, and so their elimination is a necessity for achieving more accurate results. By removing duplicate records, the size of dataset is reduced from 494,021 to 145,586 records. Furthermore, each dataset consists of different attributes

describing records. These features are qualitative or quantitative with different ranges of values and influence on the data analysis process. However, normalization can eliminate this effect by scaling data into a specific range.

Table 1. Network data features.

#	Network data feature	#	Network data feature	#	Network data feature
1	Duration	15	su_attempted	29	same srv rate
2	protocol type	16	num_root	30	diff srv rate
3	Service	17	num_file creations	31	srv diff host rate
4	Flag	18	num shells	32	dst host count
5	src_byte	19	num_access_files	33	dst_host_srv_count
6	dst_byte	20	num_outbound_cmds	34	dst_host_same_srv_rate
7	Land	21	is_host_login	35	dst_host_diff_srv_rate
8	wrong_fragment	22	is_guest_login	36	dst_host_same_src_port_rate
9	Urgent	23	Count	37	dst_host_srv_diff_host_rate
10	Hot	24	srv_count	38	dst_host_serror_rate
11	num_failed_login	25	serror_rate	39	dst_host_srv_serror_rate
12	logged_in	26	srv_serror_rate	40	dst_host_rerror_rate
13	num_compromised	27	rerror_rate	41	dst_host_srv_rerror_rate
14	root_shell	28	srv_rerror_rate	42	Class label

In this paper, a hybrid normalization technique combining a probability function for qualitative attributes and Mean Range Normalization for quantitative attributes is used to transform their values in the range of [0-1]. (For more details, see [10].) In order to illustrate this technique, suppose that X, which is a qualitative attribute, takes on the {a, b, a, a, b, a, b} values, where N = 7. The probability function for the values of X is known as follows [10]:

$$f_x(x) = \Pr(X = x) = \Pr(\{s \in S : X(s) = x\}) \quad (1)$$

Thus for instance, f_x (a) = 4/7 and f_x (b) = 3/7. Moreover, Mean Range Normalization is used for the quantitative attributes [10]. It is defined as (2):

$$x_i = \frac{v_i - \min(v_i)}{\max(v_i) - \min(v_i)} \quad (2)$$

- v_i : current value of an attribute
- $\mathbf{Min(v_i)}$: minimum value of that attribute
- $\mathbf{Max(v_i)}$: maximum value of that attribute

Therefore, all the qualitative and quantitative attributes values would be in the range of [0-1].

3.2. Construction of small training dataset
This paper aims to make an efficient train dataset using clustering and feature selection algorithms, as discussed in the following sub-sections.

3.2.1. K-Medoids clustering
Due to the fact that the K-Medoids algorithm is robust and not sensitive to noise and outlier values [13], we employed it to create a new train dataset. K-Medoids is a famous clustering algorithm, which is used to break the dataset up into the groups based on what follows [13]:

- Select k of the n instances randomly as the medoids for the initial clusters.
- Assign each data instances to the closest medoid to generate the initial clusters.
- Repeat the following steps until the cluster membership stabilizes.
- Find the most central point of each cluster.
- Re-assign each data to the closest medoid selected in the earlier step.

In this work, since the U2R and R2L attack patterns are so similar to normal instances, we elected k = 3 to cluster the dataset into three groups. Then we selected the most similar data in each cluster.

3.2.2 Feature reduction strategy

Feature reduction strategy is the process of finding and choosing a useful subset of features. Finding an optimal feature selection method is so important [14]. In this paper, to make an efficient dataset, Selecting Feature using SVM [8] algorithm performs on the new dataset created by the above steps. Table 2 also shows the selected features by this algorithm.

Table 2. Selected features by Feature selection using SVM method.

Method	Features
Feature selection using SVM	2, 3, 4, 5, 6, 8, 13, 22, 23, 24.

3.4. Naïve Bayes Classifier

Naïve Bayes classifier, known as a conditional probability model, is one of the most useful and efficient learning algorithms. This method works based on the Baye's theorem and also a strong assumption that is defined as Conditional Independence and supposes that the probability of one feature does not have any effect on the probability of the other ones [15].

4. Performance evaluation Metrics

There are three performance metrics that were utilized for measuring the efficiency of algorithms in this work.

$$Accuracy = \frac{(TP+TN)}{(TP+TN+FP+FN)} \qquad (3)$$

$$Detection\ Rate = \frac{TP}{(TP+FP)} \qquad (4)$$

$$False\ Alarm\ Rate = \frac{FP}{(FP+TN)} \qquad (5)$$

- True positive (**TP**): Number of samples that are correctly classified as attacks.
- True negative (**TN**): Number of normal samples that are correctly classified as normal.
- False positive (**FP**): Number of normal samples that are incorrectly classified as attacks.
- False negative (**FN**): Number of attack samples that are incorrectly classified as normal.

5. Results and discussion

The total procedure of our work is illustrated in figure 1. All the experiments were produced WEKA 3.6 toolkit. We created a train dataset by K-Medoids clustering and Feature selection using the SVM method. Subsequently, its performance was measured by the Naïve Bayes classifier. In order to evaluate the proposed hybrid method, it

was compared with three other methods based on K-Medoids and GFR feature selection method, K-Medoids without feature selection, and the most famous method namely 10-fold cross-validation. Tables 3 and 4 show confusion matrices associated with them, respectively.

As depicted in table 3, the proposed method obtains better results in detecting the DOS attack and also a normal behavior.

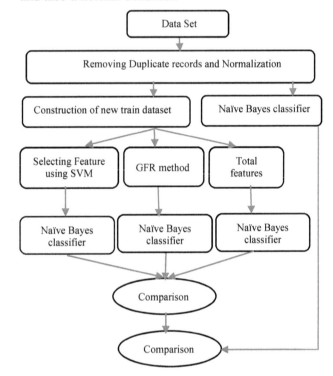

Figure 1. Proposed method procedure.

Table 3. Confusion matrix obtained by proposed method.

	DOS	Normal	Probe	U2R	R2L	Accuracy
DOS	49380	2232	2920	0	40	**90.5**
Normal	113	82242	4881	499	97	**93.6**
Probe	26	878	1224	0	3	57.4
U2R	0	561	56	378	4	37.8
R2L	0	27	0	0	25	48.1

Table 4 represents the confusion matrix obtained by K-Medoids, GFR, and the Naïve Bayes classifier. It can be observed that this method performs better in terms of detecting Probe U2R and also the R2L attacks.

Table 4. Confusion matrix obtained by utilizing K-Medoids, GFR and Naïve Bayes classifier.

	DOS	Normal	Probe	U2R	R2L	Accuracy
DOS	41968	1396	9909	873	426	76.9
Normal	2	80867	3029	1525	2409	92.1
Probe	0	253	1247	388	243	**58.5**
U2R	0	52	49	860	38	**86.1**
R2L	0	10	0	13	29	**55.8**

Various algorithms have different abilities in detection of normal and abnormal behaviours. Table 5 shows the performance of the mentioned methods regarding the accuracy and detection rate. As shown in table 5 and also figure 2, the proposed method outperforms the others in terms of accuracy, detection rate, and false alarm rate.

Table 5. Comparison between accuracy and detection rate.

	Accuracy (%)	Detection rate (%)	False alarm rate
Proposed method	**91.5**	**90.1**	**6.36**
K-Medoids+ GFR+Naïe Bayes	85.8	86.36	7.92
K-Medoids+Total features+Naïve Bayes	85.1	85.05	8.76

As shown in table 5, the proposed method is superior to the others.

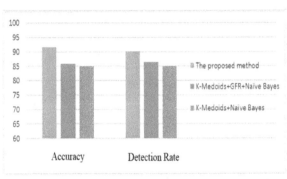

Figure 2. Comparison between detection rate and accuracy among proposed method, K-Medoids+GFR+Naïve Bayes, and K-Medoids+Naïve Bayes.

Table 6 represents the results across accuracy, detection rate, and also false alarm rate, which are obtained from 10-fold cross-validation Naïve Bayes classifier and our proposed hybrid learning approach. It can be found that the proposed method performs better in relation to accuracy, detection rate, and false alarm rate.

Table 6. Comparison between accuracy and detection rate.

	Proposed hybrid learning approach	10-fold cross-validation+Naïve Bayes
Accuracy (%)	91.5	90.3
Detection rate	90.1	82.7
False alarm rate	6.36	13.13

And finally, in table 7, the improvement in our method is specified.

6. Conclusion and future work

In this paper, we proposed a hybrid learning approach through a combination of K-Medoids clustering, Selecting Feature using SVM, and also Naïve Bayes classifier. The KDD CUP'99 benchmark dataset was used for evaluation. The experimental results obtained showed that our proposed approach was an efficient one. In this method, a new training dataset is created by K-Medoids clustering and Selecting Feature using SVM. Then its performance is evaluated by the Naïve Bayes classifier. The results obtained showed that the proposed method performed well in terms of accuracy, detection rate, and also false alarm rate. An interesting aspect that can be developed in the future is to consider a hybrid approach that performs better in detecting the R2L, U2R, and Probe attacks. Another emphasis to put on the research work was to find a new way to choose the number of clusters and also the initial cluster medoids.

Table 7. Improvement of proposed method in comparison with others.

	K-Medoids + GFR + Naïve Bayes	K-Medoids + total features + Naïve Bayes	10-fold cross-validation + Naïve Bayes
Accuracy (%)	5.7	6.4	1.2
Detection rate (%)	3.74	5.05	7.4
False alarm rate (%)	1.56	2.4	6.77

References

[1] Lin, W.-C., Ke, S.-W. & Tsai, C.-F. (2015). CANN: An intrusion detection system based on combining cluster centers and nearest neighbors. Knowledge-based systems, vol. 78, pp. 13-21.

[2] Elejla, O. E., Belaton, B., Anbar, M. & Alnajjar, A. (2016). Intrusion Detection Systems of ICMPv6-based DDOS attacks, Neural Computing and Applications, pp. 1-12.

[3] Aslahi-Shahri, B., Rahmani, R., Chizari, M., Maralani, A., Eslami, M., Golkar, M., et al. (2015). A hybrid method consisting of GA and SVM for intrusion detection system, Neural Computing and Applications, vol. 27, no. 6, pp. 1669-1676.

[4] Ravale, U., Marathe, N. & Padiya, P. (2015). Feature selection based hybrid anomaly intrusion detection system using K means and RBF kernel function, Procedia Computer Science, vol. 45, pp. 428-435.

[5] Esmaily, J., Moradinezhad, R. & Ghasemi, J. (2015). Intrusion detection system based on Multi-Layer Perceptron Neural Networks and Decision Tree. 7th Conference on Information and Knowledge Technology (IKT), Urmia, Iran 2015.

[6] Anita, S. C., & Gupta, S. (2015). An effective model for anomaly IDS to improve the efficiency. International Conference on Green Computing and Internet of Things (ICGCIoT), Noida, India, 2015.

[7] Guo, C., Zhou, Y., Ping, Y., Zhang, Z., Liu, G. & Yang, Y. (2014). A distance sum-based hybrid method for intrusion detection, Applied intelligence, vol. 40, no. 1, pp. 178-188.

[8] El Moussaid, N. & Toumanari, A. (2014). Overview of intrusion detection using data-mining and the features selection. International Conference on Multimedia Computing and Systems (ICMCS), Marrakech, Morocco, 2014.

[9] Aziz, A. S. A., Hassanien, A. E., Hanaf, S. E.-O. & Tolba, M. F. (2013). Multi-layer hybrid machine learning techniques for anomalies detection and classification approach, 13th International Conference on Hybrid Intelligent Systems (HIS), Gammarth, Tunisia, 2013.

[10] Ihsan, Z., Idris, M. Y. & Abdullah, A. H. (2013). Attribute Normalization Techniques and Performance of Intrusion Classifiers: A Comparative Analysis, Life Science Journal, vol. 10, no. 4, pp. 2568-2576.

[11] Li, Y., Xia, J., Zhang, S., Yan, J., Ai, X. & Dai, K. (2012). An efficient intrusion detection system based on support vector machines and gradually feature removal method, Expert Systems with Applications, vol. 39, no.1, pp. 424-430.

[12] Mukherjee, S. & Sharma, N. (2012). Intrusion detection using naive Bayes classifier with feature reduction, Procedia Technology, vol. 4, pp. 119-128.

[13] Murty, P. S. R., Murty, R. K. & Sailaja, M. (2016). Exploring the Similarity/Dissimilarity measures for unsupervised IDS. International Conference on Data Mining and Advanced Computing (SAPIENCE), Ernakulam, India, 2016.

[14] Shahamat, H. & Pouyan, A. A. (2015). Feature selection using genetic algorithm for classification of schizophrenia using fMRI data, Journal of AI and Data Mining, vol. 3, no. 1, pp. 30-37.

[15] Kaur, R., Kumar, G. & Kumar, K. (2015). A comparative study of feature selection techniques for intrusion detection. 2nd International Conference on Computing for Sustainable Global Development (INDIACom), New Delhi, India, 2015.

3

Prioritizing the ordering of URL queue in focused crawler

D. Koundal

University Institute of Engineering and Technology, Panjab University, Chandigarh, India

Corresponding author: koundal@gmail.com (D. Koundal)

Abstract

The enormous growth of the World Wide Web in recent years has made it necessary to perform resource discovery efficiently. For a crawler, it is not a simple task to download the domain specific web pages. This unfocused approach often shows undesired results. Therefore, several new ideas have been proposed, and crawling is a key technique, which is able to crawl particular topical portions of the World Wide Web quickly without having to explore all web pages. Focused crawling is a technique, which is able to crawl particular topics quickly and efficiently without exploring all WebPages. The proposed approach does not only use keywords for the crawl, but also rely on high-level background knowledge with concepts and relations, which are compared with the texts of the searched page.

In this paper, a combined crawling strategy is proposed that integrates the link analysis algorithm with association metric. An approach is followed to find out the relevant pages before the process of crawling and to prioritize the URL queue from downloading higher relevant pages to an optimal level based on domain dependent ontology. This strategy makes use of ontology to estimate the semantic contents of the URL without exploring which in turn strengthen the ordering metric for URL queue and leads to the retrieval of most relevant pages.

Keywords: *WebCrawler, Importance-metrics, Association - metric, Ontology.*

1. Introduction

A crawler is a constituent of search engine that retrieves Web pages by strolling around the Internet following one link to another. A focused crawling algorithm weights a page and extracts the URLs. By rating the URLs, the crawler decides which page to retrieve next. A focused crawler fetches the page that locates on the head of its queue, examines the page and assigns a score to each URL. According to the scores inserted into the queue, the queue will organize itself in order to place URLs with higher scores in the queue head so that they first will be processed. Again, the crawler will fetch the URL on the head of the queue for new processing [1].

Intuitively, the term in-links refers to the hyperlinks pointing to a page. Usually, the larger the number of in-links, the higher a page will be rated. The assumption is made that if two pages are linked to each other, they are likely to be on the same topic. Anchor text can provide a good source of information about a target page, because it signifies how people linking to the page actually describe it. Several studies have tried to use either the anchor text or the text close to it to predict a target page's content. Researchers have developed several link-analysis algorithms over the past few years [2-11]. The most popular link-based Web analysis algorithm includes Page Rank.

A major problem of a focused crawler is to effectively order the links at the crawl frontier so that a maximum number of relevant pages are loaded, while loading only a minimum number of irrelevant pages. This is a challenging task because most of the existing focused crawlers use local search algorithms in Web searching. This may miss a relevant page if there does not exist a chain of hyperlinks that connects one of the seed pages to that relevant page.

The whole paper divides into the following sections: The section 2 discusses the related work done so far on this challenge. Section 3 gives various prioritizing algorithms. Section 4 tells about association metric based on ontology. Section 5 deals with proposed work on this challenge. The results of experimental evaluation presented in section 6. The implementation details are given in section 7. The section 8 covers conclusion.

2. Related work

Most of the focused crawling techniques use link-structures of the web to improve ordering of URLs in priority queue. A recurring problem in a focused crawling is finding relevant page that is surrounded by non-relevant pages. One remedy presented in [12] by Aggarwal et al. uses the characteristics of the linkage structure of the web while performing the crawl by introducing a concept of "intelligent crawling" where the user can specify an arbitrary predicate (e.g. keywords, document similarity, anything that can be implemented as a function which determines documents relevance to the crawl based on URL and page content) and the system adapts itself in order to maximize the harvest rate. Ehrig et al. in [13] in another approach named as CATYRPEL consider an ontology-based algorithm for page relevance computation. After preprocessing, entities (words occurring in the ontology) are extracted from the page and counted. Relevance of the page with regard to user selected entities of interest is then computed by using several measures on ontology graph (e.g. direct match, taxonomic and more complex relationships). The evaluation of the importance of the page P as I (P) uses some metrics [14]. Cho et al. proposed an approach calculating the PageRank score on the graph induced by pages downloaded and then using this score as a priority of URLs extracted from a page. This may be due to the fact that the PageRank score is calculated on a very small, non-random subset of the web and also that the PageRank algorithm is too general for use in topic-driven tasks. L. page et al. in [15] proposed an approach for calculating the PageRank score on the graph induced by pages downloaded so far and then using this score as a priority of URLs extracted from a page. They show some improvement over the standard Breadth-first algorithm. Ontology based web crawler [16] estimates the semantic content of the link of the URL in a given set of documents based on the domain dependent ontology, which in turn reinforces the metric that is used for prioritizing the URL queue. The link representing concepts in the ontology knowledge path is given higher priority. However in this work, the content of the page based on the concepts is also used for

determining the relevancy of the page. An approach presented by [17] is used to prioritize the ordering of URLs through using association metric along with other importance metric. The rank or relevancy score of the URL is calculated based on the division score with respect to topic keywords available in a division i.e., finding out how many topic keywords there are in a division in which this particular URL exists and calculates the total relevancy of parent page of the relevancy score of the URL page [18]. The maximal set of relevant and quality page is to be retrieved [19].

In this proposed approach, a combination of importance metric and association metric are presented in order to obtain ordering metric for prioritizing the URLs in queue on the basis of syntactic as well as semantic nature of URL.

3. Importance Metric

For a given Webpage p, there are different types of importance metrics, which are as follow:

Back link Count

$I(p)$ is the number of links to page p that seem over the entire Web. Intuitively, a page p that is linked by many pages is more important than one that is rarely referenced. This type of "citation count" has been used widely to evaluate the impact of published papers.

Page Rank

Page Rank is the connectivity-based page quality metric suggested by Page et al. [15]. It is a static measure to rank pages in the absence of any queries. That is, PageRank computes the "global worth" of each page. Intuitively, the Page Rank measure of a page is similar to its in-degree, which is a possible measure of the significance of a page. The PageRank of a page will be high, if many pages with a high PageRank have links to it, and a page having few outgoing links contributes more weight to the pages, it links to a page containing many outgoing links. Thus, a link from the Yahoo home page counts the same as a link from some individual's home page. However, since the Yahoo home page is more important (it has a much higher IB count), it would make sense to value that link more highly. The weighted back link count of page p is given by

$$IR(p) = (1-d) + d[IR(t1)/c1 + \dots + IR(tn)/cn]$$

4. Association metric with Ontology

Ontology serves as metadata schemas, providing a controlled vocabulary of concepts, each with unambiguously defined and machine-process able semantics. By defining shared and common domain theories, ontologies help people and machines to communicate succinctly - supporting semantics exchange, not merely syntax.

Ontology is a description (like a formal specification of a program) of the concepts and relationships that can be for an agent or a community of agents. The essential of an ontology is *"is-a"* hierarchy. The Reference Ontology thus created would have the following associations like "is a", "part of", "has" relationships.

The *association metric* for the URL u is estimated based on its relevancy with the reference ontology using proper text classification algorithms. Once the page p of the URL u is downloaded, the association metric for this page p is also calculated and preserved, as it will be a parent page for many links to be crawled. $AS(p)$ is the same as all links from that page p but it utilizes the Web's hyperlink structure to retrieve new pages by traversing links from previously retrieve ones.

Here an ontology-based strategy is taken into account for page relevance computation. After preprocessing, entities (words occurring in the ontology) are extracted from the page and counted and weight of the page is then calculated. With this, a candidate list of Web pages in order of increasing a priority is maintained. In next section, the core elements of proposed work are discussed in detail.

5. Proposed Work
A. System Overview

The focused crawling method consists of two interconnected cycles. The *first cycle* is ontology cycle that defines the crawling target in the form of instantiated ontology. This cycle also presents the output of the crawling process to the user in the form of a document list and proposals for enhancement of the already existing ontology to the user. The *second cycle* comprises the Internet crawler. It intermingles automatically with the data contained on the Web and retrieves them then it connects to the ontology to determine relevance. The relevance computation is used to select relevant documents for the user and to focus on links for the further search for relevant documents and metadata available on the Web. Our proposed focused crawler is based on domain dependent ontology has following components:

All_URLs queue is employed for storing the list of URLs to download.

Metric Module persistently scans through *All_URLs* to make the refinement decision. It

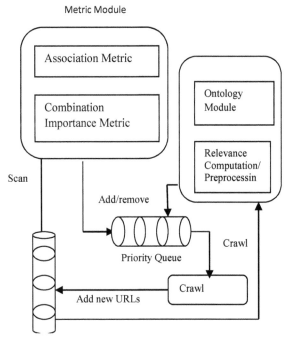

Figure 2. Prototype architecture of ontology based focused crawler

schedules for replacement of the less-important pages in priority queue with the more important page. Metric Module is a collection of Association metric and Combination Metric.

Ontology module works as background knowledge for a crawler to search in the web. It has been widely accepted that ontology is the core ingredient for the Semantic Web. This will have to be extended for the relevance measure of focused crawler. For this purpose, it is a formal and declarative representation, which includes the vocabulary (or names) for referring to the terms in that subject area and the logical statements that describe what the terms are, how they are related to each other, and how they can or cannot be related to each other. Ontology therefore provides a vocabulary for representing and communicating knowledge about some topics and a set of relationships that hold among the terms in the vocabulary. After preprocessing like HTML tag removal, stemming, lexical entries of the ontology are matched against the URLs and a relevance score is computed.

Relevance computation is a function, which tries to map the content (e.g. natural language text, hyperlinks) of a Web document against the accessible ontology to gain an overall relevance-score.

Crawl Module is started with a given set of links. The links are retrieved according to their rank.

Priority queue is used for placing the URLs to be crawled in the front. The URLs in priority queue is chosen by metric module. The processed web resources are indexed and stored in a database and then stored resources are being semantically analyzed and rated in the context of a given ontology. The crawl frontier is implemented by a standard DBMS system.

All crawling modules share the data structures needed for the interaction with the crawler. The prototype maintains a list of unvisited URLs called the frontier. This is initialized with the seed URLs specified at the configuration file. Besides the frontier, the simulator contains a queue. The scheduling algorithm fills it with the first k URLs of the frontier, where k is the size of the queue mentioned above, once the scheduling algorithm has been applied to the frontier. Each crawling loop involves picking the next URL from the queue, fetching the page corresponding to the URL from the local database that simulates the Web and determining whether the page is relevant or not. If the page is not in the database, the simulation tool can fetch this page from the real Web and store it into the local repository. If the page is relevant, the outgoing links of this page are extracted and added to the frontier, as long as they are not already in it. The crawling process stops once a certain end condition is fulfilled, usually when a certain number of pages have been crawled or when the simulator is ready to crawl another page and the frontier is empty. If the queue is empty, the scheduling algorithm is applied and fills the queue with the first k URLs of the frontier, as long as the frontier contains k URLs. If the frontier doesn't contain k URLs, the queue is filled with all the URLs of the frontier.

B. Proposed Prioritizing Algorithm:
The proposed crawler will work according to the following segment of code.
Input: seed URLs: *start_urls*
Assumption: Initially form beginning assumes Priority queue is full.
Output: Replacing "less important" pages with "more important pages" in a priority queue based on domain specific ontology.
enqueue (url_queue, start_urls);
While (not empty (url_queue) and not termination)
{
url = **dequeue** (url_queue);
page = crawl_page (url);
enqueue (crawled_pages, (url, page));
url_list = extract_urls (page);
For each page p in crawled_pages

Association_weight_page = *AS(p); // compute association weight (metric) of page*
End loop

For each u in url_list
enqueue (links, (url, u));
If [u not in url_queue] and [(u ,-) not in crawled_pages]
enqueue (url_queue, u);
Association_Weight_URL = *AS(u); //compute association weight of URL*
Combination_Importance = *CI(u); //CI(u)= pagerank[u]+ backlink[p]*
End loop

Ordering_metric = O (u);
//
$$O[u] = b_1 CI(u) + b_2 AS(u) + b_3[AS(p_1) + AS(p_2) + ... + AS(p_n)] + b_4 TD[u]$$
where p1, p2 ...pn are the parent pages to this url u
reorder_queue (url_queue); *//based on O[u]*

}

C. Ordering Metric O (u)
The ordering metric O is used by the crawler for this selection, i.e., it selects the URL u such that $O(u)$ has the highest value among all URLs in the queue. In our experiments, we explore the types of ordering metrics that are best suited for either IB (p) or IR (p). The Ordering Metric O(u) used for reordering the URL queue in our crawler is a composite metric defined as follows:
CI (u) = Page Rank[u]
$$O[u] = b_1 CI(u) + b_2 AS(u) + b_3[AS(p_1) + AS(p_2) + ... + AS(p_n)] + b_4 TD[u]$$
Where, p_i is the i_{th} Parent page of URL u to be crawled and $b_1, b2, b_3, b_4$ are real constants to be evaluated from the results of our crawl.

The proposed new ordering metric will solve the major problem of finding the relevancy of the pages before the process of crawling, as well as plays an important role in estimating the relevancy of the links in the page to an optimal level.

6. Implementation details
The implementation of our ontology embedded crawler is an application with in the KAON, the Karlsruhe Ontology and Semantic Web tool suite. The underlying data structure is provided by KAON-API. The crawler is designed with the TextToOnto tool i.e. KAON Workbench. The tight integration of the crawler with the ontology and metadata management component is also important to allow for quick adaption and extension of the

structures. The proposed framework for focused crawling has been implemented in KAON framework and is written in Java.

7. Experimental Results

The results of this paper are the relevant web pages obtained from crawled pages for the different three seed URLs. The resulting comparison charts are drawn using Microsoft Excel software. Graphical interpretations of these results are also shown here.

Performance Metrics

In order to evaluate the performance of a given scheduling algorithm, the metric used is:

Harvest rate

Harvest rate is a common measure on how well a focused crawler performs. It is expressed as

$$HR = r/p,$$

Where,

HR is the harvest rate,

r is the number of relevant pages found and

p is the number of pages downloaded.

Seed URLs

For the crawler to start crawling we provide some seed URLs.

http://www.puchd.ac.in (Panjab University),

http://www.du.ac.in (Delhi university),

http://www.ignou.ac.in/ (Indra Gandhi National Open University).

Scenario

1. http://www.puchd.ac.in/

In first experimental run, total 1000 pages were crawled from which 478 relevant pages were obtained. Therefore, the harvest ratio obtained for this crawler run is 48%. The harvest ratio for seed URL **http://www.puchd.ac.in:80/** is shown in Figure 4.

From first crawler run, the sample of top ten URLs of

obtained results set is shown in Table 1 as:

2. http://www.du.ac.in/

In second experimental run, 464 relevant pages were obtained from total crawled pages i.e. 1,000.

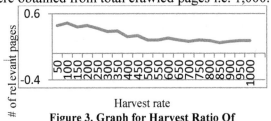

Harvest rate

Figure 3. Graph for Harvest Ratio Of
http://www.puchd.ac.in/

Table 1. Top 10 results for Panjab University

rank	Web Page
1	http://directory.puchd.ac.in:80/
2	http://exams.puchd.ac.in:80/
3	http://uiet.puchd.ac.in:80/
4	http://puchd.ac.in:80/prospectus.php
5	http://punet.puchd.ac.in:80/
6	http://forms.puchd.ac.in:80/
7	http://admissions.puchd.ac.in:80/
8	http://results.puchd.ac.in:80/
9	http://tenders.puchd.ac.in:80/
10	http://alumni.puchd.ac.in:80/

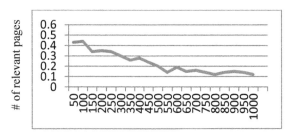

Harvest rate

Figure 5. Graph for Harvest Ratio of
http://www.du.ac.in/

Therefore, the harvest ratio obtained in this second run is 46% which is shown in Figure 5.

1. http://www.ignou.ac.in/

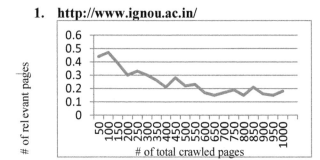

Figure 6. Graph of harvest ratio of
http://www.ignou.ac.in/

In the third experimental run, 496 relevant pages are obtained from 1000 crawled pages. Therefore, the harvest ratio obtained in this third run is .49% as shown in Figure 6.

A. Average Harvest Rate Of Three Experimental Run

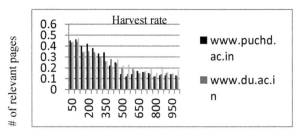

# of total crawled pages

Figure 7. Average Harvest ratio of above three URLs

In above three experimental runs, total 3,000 webpages were crawled from which total of 1,434 pages were obtained. The above results show that our ontology-based focused crawler is better than standard crawler and having average harvest ratio of 48%.

B. Comparison Of Unfocused Crawler And Ontology-Based Crawler:

The literature analysis shows that unfocused crawler with link analysis algorithm crawled 350 pages out of 1000 pages i.e. the obtained harvest ratio is 35% as shown in Table 2.

Table 2. Simulation results of different algorithm

Strategy	# of pages visited	# of relevant pages visited	Harvest Ratio
Breadth First	1,000	287	28%
PageRank	1,000	350	35%
Ontology based crawler	1,000	478	48%

Another evaluation run shows that more relevant pages were` obtained using ontology-based crawler rather than unfocused crawler is given in Figure 8. With the help of ontology-based crawler using link analysis algorithm, the harvest ratio obtained is 48%, while with unfocused crawler having link analysis algorithm, the harvest ratio obtained is 35%. This shows that more relevant pages can be retrieved by using ontology with our proposed combined strategy.

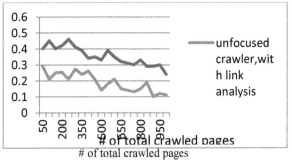

# of total crawled pages

Figure 8. Comparison of unfocused crawler, with link analysis and ontology-based crawler, with link analysis algorithm

8. Conclusion

In this paper, a combined strategy of link analysis algorithm guided by topic ontology is proposed in order to efficiently discover pages relevant to the domain of interest. The prototype uses the

structured information in the ontology to guide the crawler in its search for web pages that are relevant to the topic specified in the ontology. The test results show that the use of link analysis in our prototype gives a slight increase in the harvest rate. Our crawler depends on rating the links which in turn enhance the discovery mechanism, with the introduction of combination of importance metric, this distinguishes our approach from existing approaches as the link with the higher calculated rank will be visited next. A final conclusion of this work is the realization that it is definitely worth using advanced knowledge structures when searching a specific domain on the Internet and it is possible to extract much more information from the large distributed database Internet as today's applications allow. This makes it an effective tool for the Semantic Web environment. This may result in improving the performance in the area of focused crawling and overcomes the various drawbacks of the current approaches.

References

[1] Blaz Novak, "A Survey of Focused Web Crawling Algorithms" SIKDD 2004 multi conference IS2004, 12-15 Oct 2004.

[2] Hiep Phuc Luong, Susan Gauch, Qiang Wang, 2009. Ontology-based Focused Crawling, International Conference on Information, Process, and Knowledge Management, pp. 123-128.

[3] Li, H., Peng, Q. Q., Du, Y. J., Zhao, Y., Chen, S. M., Gao, Z. Q. (2009). Focused web crawling strategy based on web semantics analysis and web links analysis. Journal of Computational Information Systems, 5(6), 1793-1800

[4] Batsakisa S, Petrakisa EGM, Milios E. Improving the performance of focused web crawlers. Data Knowl Eng 2009;68(10):1001–13

[5] Chakrabarti S, van den Berg M, Dom B. Focused crawling: a new approach to topic-specific web resource discovery. Comput Netw 1999;31(11–16):1623–40.

[6] Chakrabarti, S., M. Berg, B. Dom, Fo cused crawling: A new approach to topic-sp ecific web resource discovery, Computer Networks and ISDN Systems, 31 (11-16), 1999, 1623-1640

[7] S´anchez, D., M. Batet, D. Isern. Ontology-based information content computation. Knowledge-Based Systems, 24 (2011), 297-303

[8] Mohen Jamali, Hassan Sayyadi, Babak Bagheri, Hariri and Hassan Abolhassani, 2006. A method of focused crawling using combination of link structure and content similarity, Proceedings of the International Conference on Web Intelligence.

[9] Kozanidis L. An ontology-based focused crawler. In: LNCS 5039. Springer; 2008. p. 376–9.

[10] Liu Z, Du Y, Zhao Y. Focused crawler based on domain ontology and FCA. J Inform Comput Sci 2011;8(10):1909–17

[11] Ester M., Gro M. and Kriegel H.-P.: 2001, Focused Web crawling: A generic framework for specifying the user interest and for adaptive crawling strategies, Technical report, Institute for Computer Science, University of Munich.

[12] Aggarwal, C., F. Al-Garawi and P. Yu. "Intelligent Crawling on the World Wide Web with Arbitrary Predicates", In Proceedings of the 10th International WWW Conference, Hong Kong, May 2001.

[13] Ehrig M. and A. Maedche "Ontology-Focused Crawling of Web Documents" Proc. the 2003 ACM symposium on applied computing.

[14] Cho, J., H.Garcia - Molina, and L. Page. Efficient crawling through URL ordering. Computer Networks, 30(17):161172, 1998.

[15] Page, L., S. Brin, R. Motwani, T. Winograd. "The PageRank Citation Ranking: Bringing Order to the Web", Stanford Digital Library Technologies Project.

[16] Ganesh, S., M. Jayaraj, V. Kalyan, and G. Aghila,"Ontology-based Web Crawler," Proc. of the International Conference on Information Technology: Coding and Computing, Las Vegas, NV, USA, pp.337-341, 2004.

[17] Deepika Koundal, Mukesh Kumar, Renu Vig, "Prioritizing the URLs in Ontology based Crawler" published and presented at International Conference of IEEE- AICC '2009 at Thapar University, Patiala.

[18] Debashis Hati, Amritesh kumar, 2010. An approach for identifying URLs based on Division score and link score in focused crawler, International journal of computer applications, Volume 2 – No.3.

[19] Debashis Hati, Amritesh Kumar, Lizashree Mishra, 2010. Unvisited URL Relevancy Calculation in Focused Crawling Based on Naïve Bayesian Classification, International Journal of Computer Applications, Volume 3- No.9.

Designing stable neural identifier based on Lyapunov method

F. Alibakhshi[1*], M. Teshnehlab[2], M. Alibakhshi[3] and M. Mansouri[4]

1. Control Department, Islamic Azad University South Tehran Branch, Tehran, Iran.
2. Center of Excellence in Industrial Control, K.N. Toosi University, Tehran, Iran.
3. Young Researchers & Elite Club, Borujerd Branch, Islamic Azad University, Borujerd, Iran.
4. Intelligent System Laboratory (ISLAB), Electrical & Computer engineering department, K.N. Toosi University, Tehran, Iran.

*Corresponding author: Alibakhshi.fatemeh@gmail.com (F. Alibakhshi)

Abstract

The stability of learning rate in neural network identifiers and controllers is one of the challenging issues, which attract many researchers' interest in neural networks. This paper suggests adaptive gradient descent algorithm with stable learning laws for modified dynamic neural network (MDNN) and studies the stability of this algorithm. Also, stable learning algorithm for parameters of MDNN is proposed. By the proposed method, some constraints are obtained for learning rate. Lyapunov stability theory is applied to study the stability of the proposed algorithm. The Lyapunov stability theory guaranteed the stability of the learning algorithm. In the proposed method, the learning rate can be calculated online and will provide an adaptive learning rate for the MDNN structure. Simulation results are given to validate the results.

Keywords: *Gradient Descent Algorithm, Identifier, Learning Rate, Lyapunov Stability Theory.*

1. Introduction

In recent decades, soft computing is frequently used in business and industry. Artificial neural networks are essential parts of any computing software [4]. The most widely used neural network architecture is the multilayer feed forward neural network. The most popular approach for training the multilayer feed-forward neural network (FNN) is the backpropagation (BP) algorithm based on gradient descent (GD) method. Determining an appropriate learning rate for this algorithm is important. The training algorithms (learning rules) could be defined as "a procedure for modifying the weights and biases of a network in order to train the network to perform some tasks" [6,11]. The network model having a good function approximation capability through the training samples can well reflect the complex nonlinear relationship between objects [17]. However, one problem inherent within them is their convergence to local minima and the user set acceleration rates and inertia factor parameters that are sensitive to the learning process [1–3]. The FNNs with the BP learning algorithm have been used successfully in pattern recognition, optimization, classification, modeling,

identification and controlling [13,31]. However, the problems of the slow convergence rate, local minimum and instability are the most challenging issues in this algorithm.

In recent decades, many efforts have been made to improve the convergence of the BP algorithm. There are some works to improve BP algorithm in order to have online training [9,19-21]. For this algorithm determining, an appropriate learning rate is necessary, so that the learning process become stable. If the learning rate is large, learning may happen rapidly, but it may also become unstable. To ensure stable learning, the learning rate is small enough. Small learning rate may also lead to a long training time. These problems are inherent to the basic learning rule of FNN that are based on GD optimization methods [15,30]. The convergence properties of such algorithms are discussed in [5,7,12,15,16,18], and [22]. Learning algorithms based on GD includes real-time recurrent learning (RTRL), ordered derivative learning and so on [1]. Derivative-based methods have the advantage of fast convergence, but they tend to converge to local minima [2]. In addition, due to their dependence on the analytical derivatives, they are limited to specific objective functions, inferences, and MFs [2].

Some papers [1-3,25,26] have investigated the stability of fuzzy neural networks. The popular method for stability analysis is Lyapunov stability. Also, in [8,10,27,28] Lyapunov stability theorem is considered.

The learning algorithm in neural and fuzzy neural networks not only has the role of updating parameters but also has influence on stability and convergence. The stability and convergence of learning algorithms are rarely investigated in the papers. In this study, the stability of learning algorithm is addressed in dynamic neural networks.

In this paper, the main concern is using Lyapunov stability approach for determining stable learning rate in system identification via modified dynamic neural network. The GD training the parameters of update rule for MDNN is considered.

The rest of article is organized as follows: in section 2, the structure of the dynamic neural network is discussed. In section 3, MDNN learning algorithm applied to process. Simulations and results for three nonlinear systems are presented in section 4. Section 5 presents conclusions.

2. Dynamic neural network

In the feed forward artificial neural, a neuron receives its inputs from other neurons. The weight sum of these signals is the input to the activation function. The resulting value of the activation function is the output of a neuron. This output is branched out to other processing units. This simple model of the artificial neuron ignores many of the characteristics of its biological counterpart. For example, it does not take into account time delays that affect the dynamics of the system [23]. The dynamic neural network (DNN) for the first time proposed by Gupta [24]. The basic structure of dynamic neuron (DN) is shown in figure 1.

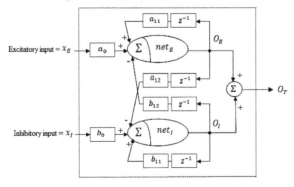

Figure 1. Structure of dynamic neuron [29].

Each neuron composed of two units: the inhibitory (negative) unit and excitatory (positive) unit. The inhibitory units received the summation of positive inputs, a delay of own outputs and abstraction a delay of excitatory outputs by multiple to determined weights. The excitatory units received the summation of negative inputs, a delay of own outputs and abstraction a delay of initiatory outputs by multiple to the determined weights [29].

The final output of the neuron can be written as follow:

$$O_T(t) = O_E(t) + O_I(t) \qquad (1)$$

where, O_E, O_I are represent the output of excitatory (net_E) and inhibitory units (net_I), respectively and can be written as:

$$net_E(t) = a_0 X_E(t) + a_{11} net_E(t-1) - b_{12} net_I(t-1) \quad (2)$$

$$net_I(t) = b_0 X_I(t) + b_{11} net_I(t-1) - a_{12} net_E(t-1) \quad (3)$$

And:

$$net_T(t) = net_E(t) + net_I(t) \qquad (4)$$

where, X_E, X_I are the positive and negative inputs, respectively and the parameters of a_0, a_{11}, a_{12}, b_0, b_{11}, b_{12} are the weights of DN.

3. Stability analysis of learning algorithm

Suppose an MDNN as an identifier shown in figure 2.

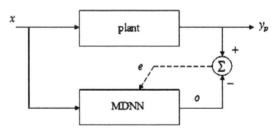

Figure 2. Modified dynamic neural network as the identifier.

Details of the MDNN network are illustrated in the figure 3.

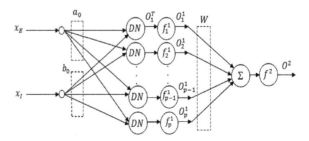

Figure 3. Modified dynamic neural network architecture.

Assume that the parameters of the MDNN are changed with time. In figure 3, $W(k) = [w_1(k), w_2(k), \ldots, w_p(k)]^T$ the is the weight vector of the MDNN output layer, $O^2(k)$ is the final output of MDNN and $O^1(k)$ is the output of hidden layer of MDNN, $O^T(k)$ is the output of DN neuron. DN structure of neurons is shown in figure 1. This network has n inputs in the input layer, p DN in the hidden layer and one conventional neuron in the output layer. $f^1(.)$ and $f^2(.)$ are nonlinear activation functions. According to figure 3 it is obvious that:

$$O^1(k) = f^1(net_T(k)), \quad O^2(k) = f^2(WO^1(k)) \quad (5)$$

$$O(k) = O^2(k) = f^2(Wf^1(net_T(k))) \quad (6)$$

The cost function for the training algorithm is defined as:

$$e(k) = y_p(k) - O(k), \quad E(k) = \frac{1}{2}e^2(k) \quad (7)$$

where, $e(k)$ is real output error, $y_p(k)$ is the output of plant, $O(k)$ is the final output of MDNN. Weights of output layer are updated by GD method as follows:

$$W(k+1) = W(k) + \eta^o(k)\left(-\frac{\partial E(k)}{\partial W(k)}\right) \quad (8)$$

where, $\eta^o(k)$ is the learning rate parameters of the output layer, and we have:

$$\frac{\partial E(k)}{\partial W(k)} = \left(\frac{\partial E(k)}{\partial e(k)}\right) \times \left(\frac{\partial e(k)}{\partial O(k)}\right) \times \left(\frac{\partial O(k)}{\partial W(k)}\right) \quad (9)$$

$$= -e(k)\left(\frac{\partial O(k)}{\partial W(k)}\right)$$

From (8) and (9), it will be inferred that:

$$W(k+1) = W(k) + \eta^o(k)e(k)\left(\frac{\partial O(k)}{\partial W(k)}\right) \quad (10)$$

$$\Delta W(k) = \eta^o(k)e(k)\left(\frac{\partial O(k)}{\partial W(k)}\right)$$

$$D_W(k) = \frac{\partial O(k)}{\partial W(k)} \quad (11)$$

And the updating rule for hidden layer parameters by GD method is as follows:

$$\Gamma(k+1) = \Gamma(k) + \eta^h(k)\left(-\frac{\partial E(k)}{\partial \Gamma(k)}\right) \quad (12)$$

where, $\Gamma = [a_0 \, a_{11} \, a_{12} \, b_0 \, b_{11} \, b_{12}]$ is the weight

vector and, $\eta^h(k)$ is the learning rate of DN. Assuming $\Delta\Gamma(k) = \Gamma(k+1) - \Gamma(k)$ the weights are updated as follows:

$$a_0(k+1) = a_0(k) + \eta^h(k)\left(-\frac{\partial E(k)}{\partial a_0(k)}\right) \quad (13)$$

$$\frac{\partial E(k)}{\partial a_0(k)} = \left(\frac{\partial E(k)}{\partial e(k)}\right) \times \left(\frac{\partial e(k)}{\partial O(k)}\right) \times \left(\frac{\partial O(k)}{\partial a_0(k)}\right) \quad (14)$$

$$= -e(k)\left(\frac{\partial O(k)}{\partial a_0(k)}\right)$$

From (13) and (14), it will be inferred that:

$$\Delta a_0(k) = \eta^h(k)e(k)\left(\frac{\partial O(k)}{\partial a_0(k)}\right) \quad (15)$$

It can also be written as:

$$\Delta a_{11}(k) = \eta^h(k)e(k)\left(\frac{\partial O(k)}{\partial a_{11}(k)}\right) \quad (16)$$

$$\Delta a_{12}(k) = \eta^h(k)e(k)\left(\frac{\partial O(k)}{\partial a_{12}(k)}\right) \quad (17)$$

$$\Delta b_0(k) = \eta^h(k)e(k)\left(\frac{\partial O(k)}{\partial b_0(k)}\right) \quad (18)$$

$$\Delta b_{11}(k) = \eta^h(k)e(k)\left(\frac{\partial O(k)}{\partial b_{11}(k)}\right) \quad (19)$$

$$\Delta b_{12}(k) = \eta^h(k)e(k)\left(\frac{\partial O(k)}{\partial b_{12}(k)}\right) \quad (20)$$

$$D_\Gamma(k) = \frac{\partial O(k)}{\partial \Gamma(k)} \quad \Gamma = [a_0 \, a_{11} \, a_{12} \, b_0 \, b_{11} \, b_{12}] \quad (21)$$

In this paper, candidate Lyapunov function is a function of error which is associated with GD based learning algorithms. This means when Lyapunov function converges to zero GD based learning algorithm is converged to zero too. Now a discrete Lyapunov function is considered as follows:

$$V(k) = \frac{1}{2}e^2(k) \quad (22)$$

Then, the variation of Lyapunov function on each iteration will be:

$$\Delta V(k) = V(k+1) - V(k) \quad (23)$$

$$= \frac{1}{2}\left(e^2(k+1) - e^2(k)\right)$$

$$= \frac{1}{2}\left(e(k+1) - e(k)\right)\left(e(k+1) + e(k)\right)$$

$$= \frac{1}{2}\Delta e(k)\left(2e(k) + \Delta e(k)\right)$$

The variation of error can be approximated by:

$$\Delta e\left(k\right)=\left\{\left(\frac{\partial e\left(k\right)}{\partial W\left(k\right)}\right)^{T}\Delta W\left(k\right)+\overbrace{tr\left[\left(\frac{\partial e\left(k\right)}{\partial a_{0}\left(k\right)}\right)^{T}\Delta a_{0}\left(k\right)\right]}^{\alpha_{1}}+\overbrace{tr\left[\left(\frac{\partial e\left(k\right)}{\partial a_{11}\left(k\right)}\right)^{T}\Delta a_{11}\left(k\right)\right]}^{\alpha_{2}}+\overbrace{tr\left[\left(\frac{\partial e\left(k\right)}{\partial a_{12}\left(k\right)}\right)^{T}\Delta a_{12}\left(k\right)\right]}^{\alpha_{3}}\right.$$

$$\left.+\overbrace{tr\left[\left(\frac{\partial e\left(k\right)}{\partial b_{0}\left(k\right)}\right)^{T}\Delta b_{0}\left(k\right)\right]}^{\alpha_{4}}+\overbrace{tr\left[\left(\frac{\partial e\left(k\right)}{\partial b_{11}\left(k\right)}\right)^{T}\Delta b_{11}\left(k\right)\right]}^{\alpha_{5}}+\overbrace{tr\left[\left(\frac{\partial e\left(k\right)}{\partial b_{12}\left(k\right)}\right)^{T}\Delta b_{12}\left(k\right)\right]}^{\alpha_{6}}\right\} \tag{24}$$

where, the $tr\left(.\right)$ is the trace of matrices. From (10) it will be concluded that:

$$\left(\frac{\partial e\left(k\right)}{\partial W\left(k\right)}\right)^{T}\Delta W\left(k\right)=\left(\frac{\partial e\left(k\right)}{\partial O\left(k\right)}\right)^{T} \tag{25}$$

$$\times\left(\frac{\partial O\left(k\right)}{\partial W\left(k\right)}\right)^{T}\times\eta^{o}\left(k\right)e\left(k\right)\left(\frac{\partial O\left(k\right)}{\partial W\left(k\right)}\right)$$

$$=-\eta^{o}\left(k\right)e\left(k\right)\left(\frac{\partial O\left(k\right)}{\partial W\left(k\right)}\right)^{T}\times\left(\frac{\partial O\left(k\right)}{\partial W\left(k\right)}\right)$$

$$=-\eta^{o}\left(k\right)e\left(k\right)\left\|D_{W}\left(k\right)\right\|^{2}$$

From (15) and (21), α_{1} obtained as follows:

$$\alpha_{1}=tr\left[\left(\frac{\partial e\left(k\right)}{\partial a_{0}\left(k\right)}\right)^{T}\Delta a_{0}\left(k\right)\right] \tag{26}$$

$$=tr\left[\left(\frac{\partial e\left(k\right)}{\partial O\left(k\right)}\right)^{T}\times\left(\frac{\partial O\left(k\right)}{\partial a_{0}\left(k\right)}\right)^{T}\right.$$

$$\left.\times\;\eta^{h}\left(k\right)e\left(k\right)\left(\frac{\partial O\left(k\right)}{\partial a_{0}\left(k\right)}\right)\right]$$

$$=tr\left[-\eta^{h}\left(k\right)e\left(k\right)\left(\frac{\partial O\left(k\right)}{\partial a_{0}\left(k\right)}\right)^{T}\times\left(\frac{\partial O\left(k\right)}{\partial a_{0}\left(k\right)}\right)\right]$$

$$=-\eta^{h}\left(k\right)e\left(k\right)tr\left[\left(\frac{\partial O\left(k\right)}{\partial a_{0}\left(k\right)}\right)^{T}\times\left(\frac{\partial O\left(k\right)}{\partial a_{0}\left(k\right)}\right)\right]$$

$$=-\eta^{h}\left(k\right)e\left(k\right)\left\|D_{a_{0}}\left(k\right)\right\|_{F}^{2}$$

Let $\left\|.\right\|_{F}$ be Frobenius norm. Thus, using (16) to (20) and (21), the following equations are obtained:

$$\alpha_{2}=-\eta^{h}\left(k\right)e\left(k\right)\left\|D_{a_{11}}\left(k\right)\right\|_{F}^{2} \tag{27}$$

$$\alpha_{3}=-\eta^{h}\left(k\right)e\left(k\right)\left\|D_{a_{12}}\left(k\right)\right\|_{F}^{2} \tag{28}$$

$$\alpha_{4}=-\eta^{h}\left(k\right)e\left(k\right)\left\|D_{b_{0}}\left(k\right)\right\|_{F}^{2} \tag{29}$$

$$\alpha_{5}=-\eta^{h}\left(k\right)e\left(k\right)\left\|D_{b_{11}}\left(k\right)\right\|_{F}^{2} \tag{30}$$

$$\alpha_{6}=-\eta^{h}\left(k\right)e\left(k\right)\left\|D_{b_{12}}\left(k\right)\right\|_{F}^{2} \tag{31}$$

So, it can be written as:

$$\Delta e\left(k\right)=-\eta^{o}\left(k\right)e\left(k\right)\left\|D_{W}\left(k\right)\right\|^{2} \tag{32}$$

$$-\eta^{h}\left(k\right)e\left(k\right)\left\{\left\|D_{a_{0}}\left(k\right)\right\|_{F}^{2}+\left\|D_{a_{11}}\left(k\right)\right\|_{F}^{2}\right.$$

$$+\left\|D_{a_{12}}\left(k\right)\right\|_{F}^{2}+\left\|D_{b_{0}}\left(k\right)\right\|_{F}^{2}$$

$$\left.+\left\|D_{b_{11}}\left(k\right)\right\|_{F}^{2}+\left\|D_{b_{12}}\left(k\right)\right\|_{F}^{2}\right\}$$

From (23) and (32), it will be inferred that:

$$\Delta V\left(k\right)=\frac{1}{2}\Delta e\left(k\right)\left(2e\left(k\right)+\Delta e\left(k\right)\right) \tag{33}$$

$$=\frac{1}{2}\left(-\eta^{o}\left(k\right)e\left(k\right)\left\|D_{W}\left(k\right)\right\|^{2}-\eta^{h}\left(k\right)e\left(k\right)\left\{\left\|D_{a_{0}}\left(k\right)\right\|_{F}^{2}+\left\|D_{a_{11}}\left(k\right)\right\|_{F}^{2}+\left\|D_{a_{12}}\left(k\right)\right\|_{F}^{2}+\left\|D_{b_{0}}\left(k\right)\right\|_{F}^{2}+\left\|D_{b_{11}}\left(k\right)\right\|_{F}^{2}+\left\|D_{b_{12}}\left(k\right)\right\|_{F}^{2}\right\}\right)$$

$$\times\left(2e\left(k\right)-\eta^{o}\left(k\right)e\left(k\right)\left\|D_{W}\left(k\right)\right\|^{2}-\eta^{h}\left(k\right)e\left(k\right)\left\{\left\|D_{a_{0}}\left(k\right)\right\|_{F}^{2}+\left\|D_{a_{11}}\left(k\right)\right\|_{F}^{2}+\left\|D_{a_{12}}\left(k\right)\right\|_{F}^{2}+\left\|D_{b_{0}}\left(k\right)\right\|_{F}^{2}+\left\|D_{b_{11}}\left(k\right)\right\|_{F}^{2}+\left\|D_{b_{12}}\left(k\right)\right\|_{F}^{2}\right\}\right)$$

$$=-\frac{1}{2}e^{2}\left(k\right)\left(\eta^{o}\left(k\right)\left\|D_{W}\left(k\right)\right\|^{2}+\eta^{h}\left(k\right)\left\{\left\|D_{a_{0}}\left(k\right)\right\|_{F}^{2}+\left\|D_{a_{11}}\left(k\right)\right\|_{F}^{2}+\left\|D_{a_{12}}\left(k\right)\right\|_{F}^{2}+\left\|D_{b_{0}}\left(k\right)\right\|_{F}^{2}+\left\|D_{b_{11}}\left(k\right)\right\|_{F}^{2}+\left\|D_{b_{12}}\left(k\right)\right\|_{F}^{2}\right\}\right)$$

$$\times\left(2-\eta^{o}\left(k\right)\left\|D_{W}\left(k\right)\right\|^{2}-\eta^{h}\left(k\right)\left\{\left\|D_{a_{0}}\left(k\right)\right\|_{F}^{2}+\left\|D_{a_{11}}\left(k\right)\right\|_{F}^{2}+\left\|D_{a_{12}}\left(k\right)\right\|_{F}^{2}+\left\|D_{b_{0}}\left(k\right)\right\|_{F}^{2}+\left\|D_{b_{11}}\left(k\right)\right\|_{F}^{2}+\left\|D_{b_{12}}\left(k\right)\right\|_{F}^{2}\right\}\right)<0$$

Then:

$$\Delta V\left(k\right)<0\Rightarrow 0<\eta^{o}\left(k\right)\left\|D_{W}\left(k\right)\right\|^{2}+\eta^{h}\left(k\right) \tag{34}$$

$$\left\{\left\|D_{a_{0}}\left(k\right)\right\|_{F}^{2}+\left\|D_{a_{11}}\left(k\right)\right\|_{F}^{2}+\left\|D_{a_{12}}\left(k\right)\right\|_{F}^{2}+\left\|D_{b_{0}}\left(k\right)\right\|_{F}^{2}+\left\|D_{b_{11}}\left(k\right)\right\|_{F}^{2}+\left\|D_{b_{12}}\left(k\right)\right\|_{F}^{2}\right\}<2$$

If we choose $\eta^o(k) = \eta^h(k)$ then:

$$0 < \eta^o(k) = \eta^h(k) < \frac{2}{\left\|D_W(k)\right\|^2 + \left\|D_{a_0}(k)\right\|_F^2 + \left\|D_{a_{11}}(k)\right\|_F^2 + \left\|D_{a_{12}}(k)\right\|_F^2 + \left\|D_{b_0}(k)\right\|_F^2 + \left\|D_{b_{11}}(k)\right\|_F^2 + \left\|D_{b_{12}}(k)\right\|_F^2} \tag{35}$$

From (35) we choose the learning rates as follows:

$$0 < \eta^o(k) < \frac{2}{\left\|D_W(k)\right\|^2} \tag{36}$$

$$0 < \eta^h(k) < \frac{2}{6\left(\left\|D_W(k)\right\|^2 + \left\|D_{a_0}(k)\right\|_F^2 + \left\|D_{a_{11}}(k)\right\|_F^2 + \left\|D_{a_{12}}(k)\right\|_F^2 + \left\|D_{b_0}(k)\right\|_F^2 + \left\|D_{b_{11}}(k)\right\|_F^2 + \left\|D_{b_{12}}(k)\right\|_F^2\right)} \tag{37}$$

4. Simulation and results

In this section, the proposed algorithm in sections 3 is simulated on three nonlinear systems as examples 1, 2 and 3.

In each example, there are 1000 random numbers which divide to training and test data sets. Dynamic neural network is used as identifier as illustrated in figure 2.

Example 1: Identification of a nonlinear dynamical system. In this example, the nonlinear plant with multiple time-delays is described as [3]:

$$y(k+1) = f\big(y(k), y(k-1), y(k-2), \tag{38}$$
$$u(k), u(k-1)\big)$$

where, $u(k)$ and $y(k)$ are the system input and output, respectively.

Where:

$$f(x_1, x_2, x_3, x_4, x_5) = \frac{x_1 x_2 x_3 x_5 (x_3 - 1) + x_4}{1 + x_2^2 + x_3^2} \tag{39}$$

For simulation of this nonlinear system, a neural network with the structure depicted in figure 2 is employed, where n is assumed to be 5, and p is taken as 15. In this neural network, it has been assumed that f^2 is a linear function, and f^1 is a symmetric sigmoid function defined as below:

$$f^1(net) = \frac{1 - e^{-net}}{1 + e^{-net}} \tag{40}$$

where, net is the weighted sum of the inputs. For comparison, the mean square error (MSE) criterion has been used.

In the simulation results, figure 4 indicates convergence with fulfillment of the stability conditions.

Example 2: This system of equation is as follows [14]:

$$y(k+1) = \frac{y(k)}{1 + y^2(k)} + u^2(k) \tag{41}$$

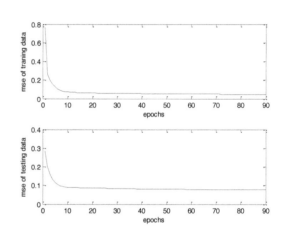

Figure 4. Learning rate is smaller than the upper limit bound.

where, $u(k)$ and $y(k)$ are the system input and output, respectively.

For simulation of this nonlinear system, a neural network with the structure depicted in figure 2 is employed, where n is assumed to be 2, and p is taken as 10.

In the simulation results, figure 5 indicates convergence with fulfillment of the stability conditions.

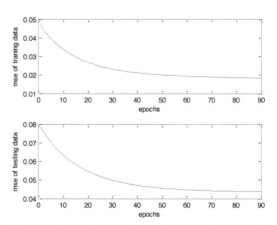

Figure 5. Learning rate is smaller than the upper limit bound.

Example 3: This system of equation is as follows [1-3]:

$$y\left(k+1\right)=0.3y\left(k\right)+0.6y\left(k-1\right)+f\left(u\left(k\right)\right) \quad (42)$$

where, $u(k)$ and $y(k)$ are the system input and output, respectively. The unknown function $f(.)$ is described as follows:

$$f\left(u\right)=0.6\sin\left(\pi u\right)+0.3\sin\left(3\pi u\right)+0.1\sin\left(3\pi u\right) \quad (43)$$

For simulation of this nonlinear system, a neural network with the structure depicted in figure 2 is employed, where n is assumed to be 3, and p is taken as 15. In the simulation results, figure 6 indicates convergence with fulfillment of the stability conditions.

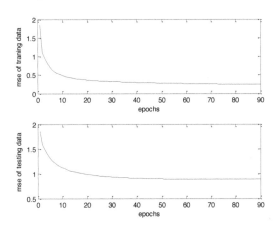

Figure 6. Learning rate is smaller than the upper limit bound.

5. Conclusions

In this paper, for permanent learning of modified dynamic neural network parameters online, Lyapunov stability theory is employed. In this learning algorithm, the associated parameters are trained according to descending gradient. Taking advantage of Lyapunov stability theory, some regions are defined, and through selection of the permanent training rate out of these regions, it can be guaranteed that the learning algorithm is stable throughout the identification process. The results of the obtained theory have been simulated for three examples. The simulation results suggest that in the training process, the system is stable and the convergence rate is desirable. This procedure can be employed in neural controllers.

References

[1] AliyariShoorehdeli, M., Teshnehlab, M., KhakiSedigh, A. & AhmadiehKhanesar M. (2009). Identification using ANFIS with intelligent hybrid stable learning algorithm approaches and stability analysis of training methods. Elsevier, Applied Soft Computing 9, pp. 833–850.

[2] AliyariShoorehdeli, M., Teshnehlab, M. & KhakiSedigh, A. (2009). Training ANFIS as an identifier with intelligent hybrid stable learning algorithm based on particle swarm optimization and extended Kalman filter. Elsevier, Fuzzy SetsandSystems160, pp. 922 –948.

[3] AliyariShoorehdeli, M., Teshnehlab, M. & KhakiSedigh, A. (2009). Identification using ANFIS with intelligent hybrid stable learning algorithm approaches. Springer, Neural Comput & Applic 18, pp. 157–174.

[4] Bonissone, P. P., Goebl, K. Y. T. & khedkar, P. S. (1999). Parameter convergence and learning curves for neural networks. Proc, of IEEE, vol. 87, no. 9, pp. 1641-1667.

[5] Fine, T. L., Goebl, S. & khedkar, P. S. (1997). Hybrid Soft Computing System: Industrial and Commercial Application. Neural Computation, pp. 747-769.

[6] Hagan, M. T., Demuth, H. B. & Beale, M. (1996). Neural network design, McGraw – Hill publishing company. First edition.

[7] Hagan, M. T. & Menhaj, M. (1994). Training feedforward networks with Marquardt algorithm. IEEE Transactions on Neural Networks, vol. 5, no. 6, pp. 989-993.

[8] Zhang, T., Ge, S. S. & Hang, C. C. (May 2000). Adaptive neural network control for strict-feedback nonlinear systems using back stepping design. Elsevier Science Ltd., pp. 1835-1846.

[9] Hedjar, R. (2007). Online Adaptive Control of Non-linear Plants Using Neural Networks with Application to Temperature Control System. J. King Saud Univ., vol. 19, Comp. & Info. Sci, pp. 75-94.

[10] Ge, S. S., Hang, C. C. & Zhang, T. (June 2000). Stable Adaptive Control for Nonlinear Multivariable Systems with a Triangular Control Structure. IEEE Transactions on Automatic Control, vol. 45, no. 6.

[11] Kazem, B. I. & Zangana, N. F. H. (2007). A Neural Network Based Real Time Controller for Turning Process. Jordan Journal of Mechanical and Industrial Engineering, ISSN 1995-6665, pp 43 – 55.

[12] Kuan, C. M. & Hornik, K. (1991). Dynamical systems using neural networks. IEEE Transactions on Neural Networks, vol. 1, no. 1, pp. 4-27.

[13] Meireles, M. R. G., Almeida, P. E. M. & Simões, M .G. (2003). A Comrehensive Review For Industrial Applicability Of Artifical Neural Networks. IEEE Trans. Ind. Electron, vol. 50, no. 3, pp. 585 – 601.

[14] Mandic, D. P., Hanna, A. I. & Razaz, Moe. (2001). A Normalized GraDient Descent Algorithm For Nonlinear Adaptive Filters Using A Gradient Adaptive Step Size. IEEE Signal Processing, Letters . vol. 1, no. 1.

[15] Sha, D. & Bajic, V. B. (2011). An Optimized Recursive Learning Algorithm for Three-Layer Feed forward Neural Networks For MIMO Nonlinear System Identifications. Intelligent Automation and Soft Computing, vol. 17, no. x, pp. 1-15.

[16] Song, Q. & Xiao, J. (1997). On the Convergence Performance of Multilayered NN Tracking Controller. Neural & Parallel Computation, vol. 5, no. 3, pp. 461-470.

[17] Sun, X., Liu, Q. & Zhang, L. (2011). A BP Neural Network Model Based on Genetic Algorithm for Comprehensive Evaluation. IEEE, 978-1-4577-0856.

[18] Torii, M. & Hagan, M. T. (2002). Stability of steepest descent with momentum for quadratic functions. IEEE Trans. On Neural Networks, vol. 13, no. 3, pp. 752-756.

[19] Velagic, J., Osmic N. & Lacevic, B. (2008). Neural Network Controller for Mobile Robot Motion Control, World Academy of Science. Engineering and Technology 47.

[20] Velagic, J. & Hebibovic, M. (2004). Neuro-Fuzzy Architecture for Identification and Tracking Control of a Robot. In Proc, The World Automation Congress - 5th International Symposium on Soft Computing for Industry ISSCI2004, June 28 - July 1, Sevilla Spain, paper no. ISSCI-032, pp. 1-9.

[21] Velagic, J., Lacevic, B. & Hebibovic, M. (2005). On-Line Identification of a Robot Manipulator Using Neural Network with an Adaptive Learning Rate. in Proc. 16th IFAC World Congress, 03-08 June, Prague, Czech Republic, no. 2684, pp. 1-6.

[22] Wu, W., Feng, G. R., Li, Z. X. & Xu, Y. S. (2005). Deterministic Convergence of an Online Gradient Method for BP Neural Networks. IEEE Transaction on Neural Networks, vol. 16, no. 3, pp. 533-540.

[23] Wasserman, P. D. (1989). Neural Computing: Theory and Practice, Van Nostrand, New York.

[24] Gupta, M. M. & Rae, D. H. (1993). Dynamic Neural Units with Applications to the Control of Unknown Nonlinear Systems. 7th Journal of intelligent and Fuzzy Systems, vol. 1, no. 1, pp. 73-92, Jan.

[25] Kim, W. C., Ahn, S. C. & Kwon, W. H. (1995). Stability Analysis and Stabilization of Fuzzy State Space Models. Fuzzy Sets Syst. 71 (April (1)), pp.131–142.

[26] Yu, W. & Li, X. (June 2003), Fuzzy neural modeling using stable learning algorithm. In: Proceedings of the American Control Conference, pp. 4542–4547.

[27] Jafarov, E. M. (August 2013). On Stability Delay Bounds of Simple Input-delayed Linear and Non-Linear systems: Computational Results. International Journal of Automation and Computing (IJAC), vol. 10, no. 4, pp. 327–334.

[28] Sun, H. Y., Li, N., Zhao, De. P. & Zhang, Q. L. (August 2013). Synchronization of Complex Networks with Coupling Delays via Adaptive Pinning Intermittent Control. International Journal of Automation and Computing (IJAC), vol. 10, no. 4, pp. 312–318.

[29] Sabahi, K., Nekoui, M. A., Teshnehlab, M., Aliyari M. & Mansouri, M. (July 2007). Load Frequency Control in Interconnected Power System Using Modified Dynamic Neural Networks. Proceedings of the 15th Mediterranean Conference on Control & Automation, Athens - Greece.

[30] Widrow, B. & Lehr, M. A. (1990). Adaptive Neural Networks: Perceptron, Madaline, and Back propagation. Proceedings of the IEEE, Special Issue on Neural Networks, I: Theory & Modeling; 78(9), pp.1415-1442.

[31] Heydari, A. & Balakrishnan, S. N. (2014). Optimal Switching and Control of Nonlinear Switching Systems Using Approximate Dynamic Programming. IEEE Transactions on Neural Networks and Learning Systems, vol. 25, no. 6, pp. 1106-1117.

5

A graph search algorithm: Optimal placement of passive harmonic filters in a power system

M. Aghaei and A. Dastfan[*]

Electrical Engineering Department, University of Shahrood, Shahrood, Iran.

*Corresponding author: dastfan@shahroodut.ac.ir (A. Dastfan).

Abstract

The harmonic in distribution systems becomes an important problem due to an increase in nonlinear loads. This paper presents a new approach based on a graph algorithm for optimum placement of passive harmonic filters in a multi-bus system, which suffers from harmonic current sources. The objective of this paper is to minimize the network loss, the cost of the filter and the total harmonic distortion of voltage, and also enhances voltage profile at each bus effectively. Four types of sub-graph have been used for search space of optimization. The method handles standard capacitor sizes in planning filters and associated costs. In this paper, objective function is not differential but eases solving process. The IEEE 30 bus test system is used for the placement of passive filter. The simulation has been done to show applicability of the proposed method. Simulation results prove that the method is effective and suitable for the passive filter planning in a power system.

Keywords: *Harmonics, Passive Filter, Optimization, Graph Algorithm.*

1. Introduction

The increase of current and voltage harmonics levels in power systems is caused through a growth in nonlinear loads. The harmonic of voltages and currents in power system are generated mainly due to the application of power electronic convertor, switching devices, and transformer's saturation [1]. Power electronic devices show nonlinear load features and thus they create distorted currents even when supplied with a purely sinusoidal voltage. These distorted currents cause current and voltage distortion throughout the power system. To improve power quality, several methods exist such as the use of higher-pulse converters, the choice of transformer connections, the modification of electric circuit configuration, and the application of active and passive harmonic filters [1]. Among them, passive harmonic filters (PHF) cause low impedance shunt paths for harmonic currents and compensate reactive power through its capacitor at the fundamental frequency. Low maintenance, cost, and complexity are the main advantages of PHF compare to other solutions such as active power filter. The PHFs have several disadvantages such

as parallel and series resonances, aging of passive components, and dependency on the source impedance, which should be considered in PHF designing [2].

Since the PHF planning is a nonlinear programming problem, it is difficult to solve by conventional approaches such as a blind search. Many methods have been devised for an optimal PHF planning in the literature. Conventional methods of search and optimization are slow in finding a solution in a very complex search space [3, 4]. Hence, some methods such as artificial neural networks (ANNs) [5] or genetic algorithms (GAs) [6,7] are widely applied for searching an optimal solution of locating and sizing passive filters. In many cases, the difficulties of GA method are the computing of efficiency and convergence because it contains selection, copy, crossover and mutation and so on. For instance, Eberhart and Kennedy recently suggested a particle swarm optimization (PSO) based on the analogy of swarm of bird and school of fish [8]. PSO algorithm uses as a branch of stochastic techniques to explore the search space for optimization. In [9,10] a probabilistic approach is used for filter planning that requires stochastic calculation in a large range. Reference [11] presents a method which combines the orthogonal array experiment technique and an ant direction hybrid differential evolution algorithm for optimal passive harmonic filter planning.

This paper presents a practical technique based on a graph search method for filter placement problem.

The proposed algorithm determines the number, sizes, and locations of filters to be placed on a distribution system in order to minimize cost. The optimization algorithm treats capacitor sizes as discrete variables and uses standard sizes and exact capacitor costs.

2. Problem formulation

The main objectives are to minimize the filter cost, the network power losses and total harmonic distortion of voltages while satisfying the harmonic standard and improving voltage profile.

In this paper, the following assumptions have been made:

• Rated voltage will not be affected by the addition of filters,

• consider linear and nonlinear loads in a balanced three-phase system.

2.1. Constraints

Voltage constraints will be considered by specifying upper and lower bounds of rms voltage. (e.g., v^{min} =0.9 pu, v^{max} =1.1 pu)

$$V^{min} \leq \sqrt{\sum_h \left(V_i^{(h)}\right)^2} \leq V^{max}, for \quad i=1,...,n \qquad (1)$$

Where i, h denotes bus number and harmonic order, respectively.

The distortion of voltage is considered through specifying maximum total harmonic distortion ($THD_{v,i}$), voltages and currents at system bus:

$$THD_{v,i} = \left(\frac{\left[\sqrt{\sum_{h \neq 1}\left(v_i^{(h)}\right)^2}\right]}{v_i^{(1)}}\right) \times 100\% \leq THD_v^{max} \qquad (2)$$

$, for \quad i=1,...,n$

Bounds of values for (1) and (2) are specified by the IEEE-519 standard limits [16].

2.2. Objective Function

The problem of optimization can be stated as follows:

$$\min f = (KVTHD) + (K_A Ploss) \qquad (3)$$
$$+ (k_v profv) + (k_{cfp} Q)$$

where, $VTHD$ sum of voltage total harmonic distortion deviation from standard limits,
$Ploss$ Total network losses,
$profv$ Sum of voltages deviation from 1 per unit at each bus,
Q Size of filter capacitor in kVAR,
K_A Cost per MW (e.g., K_A=120 $/MW, [14])
K_{cfp} Cost per kVAR of fixed capacitance
K_V a factor to convert voltages deviation from 1 per unit to dollars;
K a factor to convert THD deviation from standards to dollars.

Network losses consist of two parts. The first part is computed by differencing between generated and loaded power at fundamental frequency and the second part is computed through using harmonic power flow outputs as follows:

$$P_{loss} = \sum_{h=1}^{L}\left[\sum_{i=1}^{n}\sum_{j=1(j<i)}^{n} V_i^{(h)}V_j^{(h)}Y_{ij}^{(h)} \times \cos(\theta_i^{(h)} - \theta_j^{(h)} - \delta_{ij}^{(h)})\right] \qquad (4)$$

where, $V_i^{(h)}$ and $\theta_i^{(h)}$ are magnitude and phase of hth harmonic voltage at bus i and $Y_{ij}^{(h)}$ and $\delta_{ij}^{(h)}$ are magnitude and phase of hth harmonic line admittance between buses i and j, respectively.

3. The graph search algorithm

A graph is made of a set of nodes that are connected by arcs. Each node corresponds to a possible combination of the size of filters capacitor and locations of filters for a given number of filters to be placed. A specific graph is used for each possible number of filters to be placed. The proposed algorithm searches the nodes of graph in an attempt to determine the optimal solution. Beginning with minimum number of filters to be placed (a user-specified parameter); a search is performed to locate the node in that graph which produces minimum cost. If the determined maximum number of filters (a user-specified parameter) has not been reached, the number of filters to be placed is incremented by one and the next graph is searched. Values of costs for every node are determined on each graph, and another filter will increase overall cost. Then, the process is terminated.

3.1. Definition of the graph nodes and arcs

A complete graph for a given number of filters contains several nodes from which each one corresponds to a possible combination of filter capacitor sizes and locations of filters. In the huge power networks, the number of nodes that must be examined can be very large, and an effective procedure was developed to allow only a relatively small percentage of nodes to be evaluated to determine a near-optimal solution. Thus, the following four different types of arcs have been defined so the algorithm can move from one node to another based on the rules of these four types of arcs in search of the optimal solution.

3.1.1. Type I arcs
This type of arcs changing one filter capacitor size only with locations remaining unchanged and moving from one node to another is defined as "Type I" move.

3.1.2. Type II arcs
Type II represents a change of one filter location only. These arcs require the nodes on both sides that have the same capacitor size. In addition, the buses specified must be electrically adjacent to another. Move from one node to another using this type of arc is referred to as "Type II" move.

Since in both Types I and II moves, there is only a change in one decision variable; therefore, these moves can be considered as "local variations". For example, suppose that two single-tune filters are to be placed on two buses in a distribution system. Assume the initial node corresponds to a solution that places at buses 5, 14 with capacitor sizes 600 kVAR. Standard capacitor sizes in use are 150, 300, 450, 600, 750 kVAR, and so on. Possible Types I and II moves from this initial node are shown in figure 1. These "adjacent" moves would be evaluated in a systematic manner until a decrease in costs is determined. Once this occurs, the new node will be center node for starting possible moves.

3.1.3. Type III arcs
An arc of this type represents a simultaneous change in the size and location of a single filter. These changes are allowed to electrically adjacent busses at the location of filter and capacitor size only changes by one step according to a typical capacitor size in use. This move type is referred to as "Type III" move. For the initial node, possible Type III moves from this node are shown in figure 2.

3.1.4. Type IV arcs
This type of arcs location of filter changes to another bus that is not necessarily adjacent to the existing location. This arcs type connects all nodes that differ only in the location of a single filter, with all sizes of capacitors and all other locations of filters unchanged. Moves of this type

are referred to as "Type IV" moves. For the initial node, all possible moves of this type are shown in figure 3.

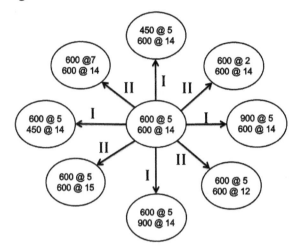

Figure 1. Possible types I and II moves.

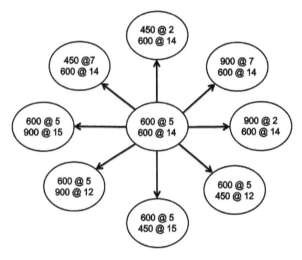

Figure 2. Possible type III moves.

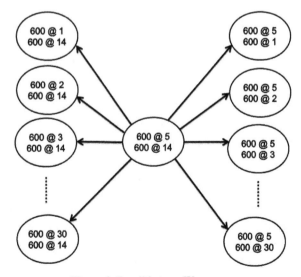

Figure 3. Possible type IV moves.

The purpose of Types III and IV moves is to allow the algorithm to escape from local minimums that may be encountered in search of the global optimum. These moves were found to produce good results, often allowing escape from a local minimum. This algorithm implemented allows the user to specify the moves to be considered.

3.2. The overall solution procedure

Step 1: Consider the user specified minimum number of filters to be placed in network.

Step 2: Choose an initial solution for these numbers of filters, or let the computer randomly select one creating the initial node in the graph.

Step 3: Evaluate Types I and II moves in a systematic manner. Any move, which causes a decrease in objective function, is immediately accepted and creates new node in our graph and other possible arcs from this node are denied. Then, a new node is centered for evaluating Types I and II moves. This process should be continued until no further improvements in costs can be made. At this point, a local optimum solution for the network has been obtained.

Step 4: Evaluate Type III moves in a systematic manner after no further improvement can be made with Type I or II moves. If any Type III move is accepted, again Types I and II moves should be returned to Step 3 for evaluation. If all Type III moves fail, go to next Step.

Step 5: Ultimately evaluate Type IV moves. Once any Type IV move is accepted, return to Step 3 for evaluation of Types I and II moves. If all moves of Type IV fail, the near-optimal solution for these numbers of filters has been found. Go to Step 6.

Step 6: Compare the objective function resulting from this solution to the objective function with the previous number of filters. If the new objective function is decreased, increase the number of filters and return to Step 2. Otherwise, the algorithm terminates. The solution corresponding to the previous number of filters is the overall near-optimal solution.

4. Test case system

In order to test and validate our method for planning passive filter, the IEEE 30 bus test system from [15] was implemented and is showed in figure 4. The system data is shown in tables A.1 and A.2 (see Appendix). All loads in the network are linear except for, four nonlinear loads, which are located at busses 5, 14, 21 and 30. These nonlinear loads are 6-pulses diode rectifiers. Due to the existence of these power electronic devices,

considerable harmonic currents are injected into the system. Harmonic currents in per unit are shown in table 1. Simulation result shows about 24.1052 MW losses without the presence of filters. The voltages profile and total harmonic voltage distortion (THD$_v$) at each bus are determined through no passive filter in the system. In order to compensate harmonics, single-tune passive filter for low order harmonics and high pass filter for higher order harmonics are used in this network that is most common shunt filter types.

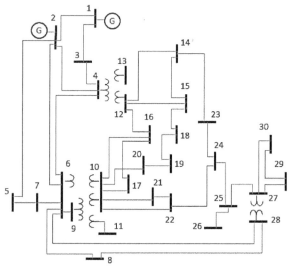

Figure 4. The IEEE 30 bus test system.

Table 1. Harmonic currents in per unit for IEEE 30 bus test system.

Bus	5	14	21	30
h=5	0.0072	0.0128	0.0416	0.0082
h=7	0.0051	0.0091	0.0297	0.0059
h=11	0.0033	0.0058	0.0189	0.0037
h=13	0.0028	0.0049	0.0160	0.0032
h=17	0.0021	0.0038	0.0122	0.0024
h=19	0.0019	0.0034	0.0109	0.0022
h=23	0.0016	0.0028	0.0090	0.0018
h=25	0.0014	0.0026	0.0083	0.0016

4.1. Simulation results

To determine the global optimum solution for locating passive filters, the graph search algorithm is used. Two passive filter packs are placed at buses 2, 21 with capacitor size 600 KVAR, and this state is considered as initial node for starting our approach. By processing algorithm, the number of filters is increased and results related to each stage are obtained. The first stage of optimization is to find optimum location and capacitor size for two filter packs. Graph algorithm offers an optimum solution based on locating these filter packs at busses 1 and 9 with capacitor sizes of 0.6, 3.6 KVAR, respectively. By increasing the number of filters to 3, and finding optimum location and capacitor size for those filters, the objective function shows an improvement to this change, and so the process continues. The decrement of objective function goes on until there are six filter packs in the network. However, on this stage, objective function shows an increasing trend against previous stages. This increase is a sufficient reason to terminate the optimization process. Therefore, this algorithm suggests five filter packs to be located at this test system for mitigation harmonics. The final result is to locate five filter packs at busses 1, 5, 8, 21 and 30 with capacitor sizes 0.45, 3.6, 3.6, 3.6 and 0.6, respectively. Results from graph algorithm for two to six filter packs are presented in table 2. Network losses are included losses in fundamental frequency and harmonic frequency. Figures 5 shows the voltages profile and figure 6 shows THD_v before and after installing passive filters at each bus. It shows that the THD_v is well controlled and voltage profile is improved after the placement of the filters so that values of THD_v satisfy the standard limits. Minimum voltage occurs in bus 7 with value 0.945 per unit and maximum voltage at bus 1 with value 1.06 per unit. Also all of the values of THD_v are below 4.5%.

improved but increased the number of filters to six. However, no improvement has been seen in results but the algorithm suggests five filter branches as problem global solution.

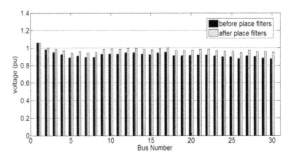

Figure 5. Voltage profile before and after placing filters.

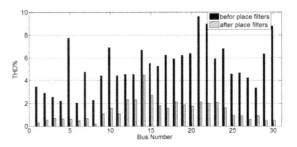

Figure 6. THDV before and after placing filters.

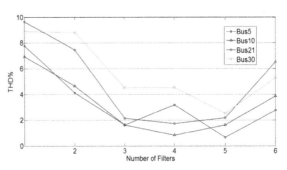

Figure 7. THD of voltage in each stage for four network buses.

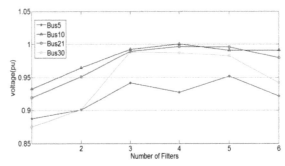

Figure 8. Voltage in each stage for four network buses.

Table 2. Results on test system.

#filter	location	Capacitor size(MVAR)	Network losses (MWATT)
2	1	0.60	2.8572
	9	3.6	
3	5	3.9	2.6284
	21	3.6	
	27	3.6	
4	1	0.45	2.6196
	10	3.6	
	21	3.6	
	27	3.6	
5	1	0.45	2.5252
	5	0.36	
	8	0.36	
	21	0.36	
	30	0.60	
6	2	0.36	2.9412
	3	0.60	
	7	0.60	
	9	0.36	
	15	0.36	
	29	0.45	

Figures 7 and 8 show THD of voltage and voltage profile at buses 5, 10, 21 and 30 on each stage of graph algorithm process for different number of filters. As can be indicated, results show that five filter branches located at network buses have

In order to demonstrate the performance of the proposed graph algorithm, some performance comparisons with well-known genetic algorithm (GA) are made. For this purpose, the realistic 18 bus system [17] is used. In [18] the GA is utilized for solving the same problem in 18-bus system.

Also, we plan passive filters through the graph algorithm in this network. Figures 9 and 10 illustrate the 5th and 7th harmonic voltages in p.u., respectively before and after filter placement using the proposed method and GA.

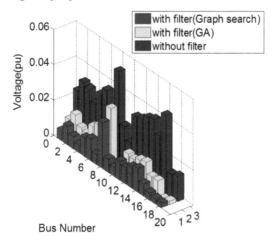

Figure 9. Fifth harmonic voltages before and after filter installation.

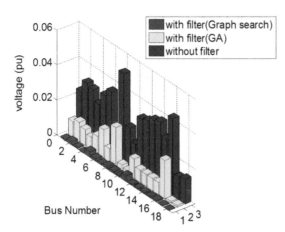

Figure 10. Seventh harmonic voltages before and after filter installation.

These figures show that the proposed this method is very efficient for optimization problems and suitable for planning passive filters in power networks.

In this method, there is no complex calculation for obtaining results on each step of optimization. The only calculation is related to get values of objective function. Because of arcs and nodes are graphical tools to describe space of problem, this method has a good visual comprehension. In this paper, a graph algorithm is applied on two power networks for finding optimum placement of filters and the simulation results show satisfaction of problems, which indicate the graph algorithm is a practical method for the optimization problem.

Using four move types in the proposed method is not necessary for testing all possible states and therefore this algorithm requires less time to

converge. Since the more time in this method is spent for doing power flow with using fast power flow methods, this time is decreased. In addition to the optimum placement of filters in power networks, another optimization includes filter parameters optimization, which is studied in [19]. Therefore, these two optimization problems can be focused in future studies.

5. Conclusion
This paper has presented a new method for mitigation harmonic with passive harmonic filters design. The approach is a graph search algorithm. It can handle standard capacitor sizes and associated costs. This algorithm does not use a differential objective function which eases solving process. Mathematical simplicity of the method makes it possible to include many features in the algorithm that would be rather difficult with previous solution methods (e.g., the user can constrain the filter locations). The IEEE 30 bus test system is used for placement passive filter for showing the applicability of the proposed method. The simulation results verify the feasibility and the validity of the proposed graph search algorithm in the design of optimal passive harmonic filter of a multi-bus system.

References
[1] Arrillaga, J. & Watson, N. R. (2003). Power system harmonics. Second Edition, In: Wiley, J. & Sons (Eds.), ltd.

[2] Massoud, A. M., Finney, S. J. & Williams, B.W. (2004). Review of harmonic current extraction techniques for an active power filter, in: 11th International Conference on Harmonics and Quality of Power, pp. 154–159, 2004.

[3] Yan, Y. H., Chen, C. S., Moo, C. S. & Hsu, C. T. (1994). Harmonic analysis for industrial customers. IEEE Trans. Ind. Applicat. , vol. 30, pp. 462–468.

[4] Makram, E. B., Subramaniam, E. V., Girgis, A. A. & Catoe, R. (1993). Harmonic filter design actual recorded data. IEEE Trans. Ind. Applicat. , vol. 29, pp. 1176–1182.

[5] Chang, Y-P., Low, Ch. & Wu, Ch-J. (2007). Optimal design of discrete-value passive harmonic filters using sequential neural-network approximation and orthogonal array. IEEE Transactions On Power Delivery. vol. 22, no. 3, pp. 1813-1821.

[6] Chang, G., Wang, H-L. & Chu, Sh-Y. (2004). Strategic placement and sizing of passive filters in a power system for controlling voltage distortion. IEEE Transactions on Power Delivery, vol. 19, no. 3, pp. 1204-1211.

[7] Chang, G., Chu, Sh-Y. & wang, H-L. (2006). A new method of passive harmonic filter planning for

controlling voltage distortion in a power system. IEEE Transactions on Power Delivery, vol. 21, no. 1, pp. 305-312.

[8] Ko, Ch-N., Chang, Y-P. & Wu, Ch-J. (2009). A pso method with nonlinear time-varying evolution for optimal design of harmonic filters. IEEE Transactions on Power Systems, vol. 24, no. 1, pp. 437-444.

[9] Chang, G., Wang, H-L. & Chu, Sh-Y. (2007). A probabilistic approach for optimal passive harmonic filter planning. IEEE Transactions On Power Delivery, vol. 22, no. 3, pp. 1790-1798.

[10] Chang, G., Wang, H-L., Chuang, G-Sh. & Chu, Sh-Y. (2009). Passive harmonic filter planning in a power system with considering probabilistic constraints. IEEE Transactions on Power Delivery, vol. 24, no. 1, pp. 208-217.

[11] Chang, Y-P., & Low, Ch. (2008). An ant direction hybrid differential evolution heuristic for the large-scale passive harmonic filters planning problem. Expert Systems with Applications. vol. 35, pp. 894–904.

[12] Carlisle, J. C. & El-Keib, A. A. (2000). A graph search algorithm for optimal placement of fixed and switched capacitors on radial distribution systems. IEEE Transactions on Power Delivery, vol. 15, no. 1, pp.423-428.

[13] Baghzouz, Y. & Ertem, S. (1990). Shunt capacitor sizing for radial distribution feeders with distorted substation voltage. IEEE Trans. Power Delivery, vol. 5, pp. 650–657.

[14] Wu, Z. Q. & Lo, K. L. (1995). Optimal choice of fixed and switched capacitors in radial distributions with distorted substation voltage. Proc. Inst.Elect. Eng., Gen., Transm. Distrib, vol. 142, no. 1, pp. 24 –28.

[15] Saadat, H. Power system analysis. (2002). 2nd edition, E-Publishing Inc, New York. vol. 1, pp. 289-298.

[16] IEEE Recommended Practices and Requirements for Harmonics Control in Electric Power Systems. (1992). IEEE Std. 519.

[17] Yan, Y. H., Chen, C. S., Moo, C. S., & Hsu, C. T. (1994). Harmonic analysis for industrial customers. IEEE Trans. Ind. Appl., vol. 30, no. 3, pp. 462–468.

[18] Hong, Ying-Yi., & Chiu, Ching-Sheng. (2010). Passive filter planning using simultaneous perturbation stochastic approximation. IEEE Transactions on Power Delivery, vol. 25, no. 2, pp. 939-946.

[19] Dastfan, A., Yassami, H., & Rafiei, M. R. (2014). Optimum design of passive harmonic filter by using game theory concepts. Intelligence Systems in Electrical Engineering Journal, vol. 4, no. 4, pp. 13-22.

Appendix.

Table A.1.

Bus	Type	Load (MW)	Load (MVAR)
1	PV	0	0
2	PV	21.7	12.7
3	PQ	2.4	1.2
4	PQ	7.6	1.6
5	PQ	94.2	19
6	PQ	0	0
7	PQ	22.8	10.9
8	PQ	30	30
9	PQ	0	0
10	PQ	5.8	2
11	PQ	0	0
12	PQ	11.2	7.5
13	PQ	0	0
14	PQ	6.2	1.6
15	PQ	8.2	2.5
16	PQ	3.5	1.8
17	PQ	9	5.8
18	PQ	3.2	0.9
19	PQ	9.5	3.4
20	PQ	2.2	0.7
21	PQ	17.5	11.2
22	PQ	0	0
23	PQ	3.2	1.6
24	PQ	8.7	6.7
25	PQ	0	0
26	PQ	3.5	2.3
27	PQ	0	0
28	PQ	0	0
29	PQ	2.4	0.9
30	PQ	10.6	1.9

BUS DATA

Table A.2.

			Branch Data		
From	To	Type	R(pu)	X(pu)	B(pu)
1	2	Transmission Line	0.0192	0.0575	0.0264
1	3	Transmission Line	0.0452	0.1852	0.0204
2	4	Transmission Line	0.057	0.1737	0.0184
3	4	Transmission Line	0.0132	0.0379	0.0042
2	5	Transmission Line	0.0472	0.1983	0.0209
2	6	Transmission Line	0.0581	0.1763	0.0187
4	6	Transmission Line	0.0119	0.0414	0.0045
5	7	Transmission Line	0.046	0.116	0.0102
6	7	Transmission Line	0.0267	0.082	0.0085
6	8	Transmission Line	0.012	0.042	0.0045
6	9	Transformer	0	0.208	0
6	10	Transformer	0	0.556	0
9	11	Transmission Line	0	0.208	0
9	10	Transmission Line	0	0.11	0
4	12	Transformer	0	0.256	0
12	13	Transmission Line	0	0.14	0
12	14	Transmission Line	0.1231	0.2559	0
12	15	Transmission Line	0.0662	0.1304	0
12	16	Transmission Line	0.0945	0.1987	0
14	15	Transmission Line	0.221	0.1997	0
16	17	Transmission Line	0.0824	0.1923	0
15	18	Transmission Line	0.107	0.2185	0
18	19	Transmission Line	0.0639	0.1292	0
19	20	Transmission Line	0.034	0.068	0
10	20	Transmission Line	0.0936	0.209	0
10	17	Transmission Line	0.0324	0.0845	0
10	21	Transmission Line	0.0348	0.0749	0
10	22	Transmission Line	0.0727	0.1499	0
21	22	Transmission Line	0.0116	0.0236	0
15	23	Transmission Line	0.1	0.202	0
22	24	Transmission Line	0.115	0.179	0
23	24	Transmission Line	0.132	0.27	0
24	25	Transmission Line	0.1885	0.3292	0
25	26	Transmission Line	0.2544	0.38	0
25	27	Transmission Line	0.1093	0.2087	0
28	27	Transformer	0	0.396	0
27	29	Transmission Line	0.2198	0.4153	0
27	30	Transmission Line	0.3202	0.6027	0
29	30	Transmission Line	0.3399	0.4533	0
8	28	Transmission Line	0.0636	0.2	0.0214
6	28	Transmission Line	0.0169	0.0599	0.0065

A new model for Persian multi-part words edition based on statistical machine translation

M. Zahedi* and A. Arjomandzadeh

School of Computer Engineering & Information Technology, University of Shahrood, Shahrood,Iran.

Corresponding author: zahedi@shahroodut.ac.ir (M. Zahedi).

Abstract
Multi-part words in English language are hyphenated and hyphen is used to separate different parts. Persian language consists of multi-part words as well. Based on Persian morphology, half-space character is needed to separate parts of multi-part words where in many cases people incorrectly use space character instead of half-space character. This common incorrectly use of space leads to some serious issues in Persian text processing and text readability. In order to cope with the issues, this work proposes a new model to correct spacing in multi-part words. The proposed method is based on statistical machine translation paradigm. In machine translation paradigm, text in source language is translated into a text in destination language on the basis of statistical models whose parameters are derived from the analysis of bilingual text corpora. The proposed method uses statistical machine translation techniques considering unedited multi-part words as a source language and the space-edited multi-part words as a destination language. The results show that the proposed method can edit and improve spacing correction process of Persian multi-part words with a statistically significant accuracy rate.

Keywords: *Persian Multi-Part Words, Spacing Rules, Statistical Machine Translation, Parallel Corpora, Hierarchical Phrase-based, Fertility-based IBM Model, Syntax-Based Decoder.*

1. Introduction

Persian text consists of words which are made of multiple parts and they are called multi-part words. An important key note in multi-part words is that the parts of multi-part words must be separated while whole multi-part word must be distinguished as an integrated word; To achieve this goal, the parts of multi-part words must be separated by half-space character to keep the integrity of whole multi-part word. Half-space is a character with zero-width non-joiner length which is actually used to prevent joining the characters of the multi-part words and keep the parts of multi-part word as close as possible.

One of the most common problems in Persian text is incorrectly use of spaces between multi-part words which leads to non-integrity of multi-part words and it also leads to incorrect word boundary detection that can be solved by replacing spaces with half-spaces. Based on Persian language spacing rules which specify where space or half-space is needed, half-spaces must be inserted between parts of multi-part words. If space character is used between the parts of multi-part words, the word doses not obey standard word form and each part will be incorrectly considered as a separate word such as, "هیچ گاه", "بی شمار" and "حاصل ضرب". It is important to be noticed that the spell checker algorithms concentrate on the spelling errors which are often caused by operational and cognitive mistakes [1], thus the errors occurring due to the usage of space and half-space in a wrong manner are usually ignored by spell checker algorithms.

Few researchers have worked on editing the spacing in Persian words [2-4]. A toolkit is presented by Shamsfard et al. [2] to detect boundaries of words, phrases and sentences, check and correct the spelling, do morphological analysis and Part-Of-Speech (POS) tagging. The approach finds the stems and affixes of words with Finite State Automaton (FSA) and tags them with the part of speech tags. Mahmoudi et al. [3] focused only on modeling Persian verb morphology. The method detects six morphological features of a given verb and generates a verb form using a FSA. These features consist of several language-specific features such as POS of a given verb, dependency relationships of the verb and POS of subject of the verb. Consequently, unsupervised clustering is used to identify compound verbs with their corresponding morphological features in the training step. In this approach POS taggers are used by a statistical method in order to extract some features and FSA is employed to generate an inflected verb form using these morphological features. Rasooli et al. [4] provide a lexicon which consists of space-separated multi-part words that are mapped to half-space separated multi-part words. The approach identifies all the space-separated multi-part words that can be mapped to half-space separated multi-part words. An expanded lattice version of the sentence including both forms is then decoded with a language model to select the path with the highest probability. This approach relies on a lexicon which consists of all kinds of Persian multi-part words such as verb inflections. Therefore, if the lexicon lacks in multi-part words, the approach cannot edit spaces between the parts of word efficiently. The aforementioned approaches rely on lexicon. So, if the lexicon lacks in multi-part words, the approach cannot edit spacing in multi-part words.

The main issue in POS tagger approach is lexicon that must cover all the variety of the multi-part words in which all the parts of the multi-part words are tagged. On the other hand, the lack of the tagging especially in half-space rule leaves more unedited multi-part words in evaluation step. Moreover, available Persian tagged corpus such as Peykare [5] does not comply with half-space character.

In this paper, we propose a different statistical approach which uses a fertility-based IBM Model [6] as word alignment by employing a parallel corpus which is created for the special purpose of Persian multi-part word edition. In the next step, Synchronous Context-Free Grammar (SCFG) for hierarchical phrase-based translation [7] is employed. In decoding step, the extracted grammars and weights assigned to each grammar are employed to decode the word with a syntax-based decoder.

This paper is organized as follows. In section 2, the problems and challenges of Persian text space rules and machine translation theory are reviewed. Section 3 describes fertility-based IBM model and

hierarchical phrase-based and utilizes the proposed method in order to edit spacing in Persian text. The next section discusses experimental results and finally the paper ends with conclusion section.

2. Preliminaries
2.1. Spacing issues
In the standard morphology of Persian text, parts of multi-part words should be separated with zero-width non-joiner length character. Therefore, if space character is used in multi-part words, the parts are incorrectly considered as separate words. Space character specifies boundaries of words and half-space character is used for separating the parts in multi-part words.

Based on standard morphology of Persian text, there are two types of spacing between words:

- Spacing between words in a sentence, which is called "space".
- Spacing between the parts of multi-part words which is called "half-space". Some words are made up of several parts, but the parts make up a single word which are called multi-part words, such as:

غیرقابل،   بی‌حوصله،   پائین‌تر،   جریمه‌های،   رقابت‌های،

ازدست نمی‌دهد، می‌شود، تصور نموده‌اند، می‌بایست

Half-space is a character with zero-width non-joiner length which is actually used to prevent joining the parts in multi-part words and keep the parts of multi-part word as close as possible. The terms "زبان‌شناسی" and "می‌شود" are made up of two parts in which half-space maintains word integrity in these multi-part words.

Correct word spacing specifies correct word boundaries which is denoted by spaces in Natural Language Processing (NLP) and clears ambiguity of text. Word boundary detection is considered as an important first step in Persian natural language processing tasks. Half-space character is important in word boundary detection in cases where Persian words are made up of multiple parts.

2.2. Basic theory of statistical machine translation
In Statistical Machine Translation (SMT) theory, every word in source language has many translations and highest probability in corpora (which is defined by (1)) is assigned to the most appropriate translation. Due to Bayes theorem (which is defined by (2)) and since the denominator here is independent of e, finding $\hat{e}$ is the same as finding e. So, to make the product

$P(e)P(f\,|e)$ as large as possible, equation (3) is presented [6,8,9].

$$\hat{e} = \underset{e}{\operatorname{argmax}} P(e|f) \qquad (1)$$

$$P(e\,|f) = (P(e)\,P(f|e))/(P(f)) \qquad (2)$$

$$\hat{e} = \operatorname{argmax}_e P(e)\,P(f|e) \qquad (3)$$

$P(e)$ is the prior probability and $P(f\,|e)$ is the conditional probability of target language word with given the source language word and $\hat{e}$ is the maximum probability product of $P(f)P(e|f)$.

SMT requires a parallel corpus to extract linguistic information for each language pair. In first step, SMT assigns translation probability for each parallel word with aid of the IBM model [6] which is used as the word alignment method in this paper. Brown et al. [6] proposes five statistical models for the translation process and the computational complexity increases through going from Model 1 to Model 5 while it is closer to human language and requires additional parameters [10].

3. Materials and methods
3.1. Fertility-based IBM model and hierarchical phrase-based model

IBM Model 3 [6] consists of three parameters: lexicon model parameter, fertility model parameter and distortion model parameter. The generative story of the IBM model 3 focuses on training which is based on the concept of fertilities:

Given a vector alignment of a source sentence $\mathbf{a}_1^J$, the fertility of target word i expresses the number of source words aligned to it [11].

$$\Phi_i\left(\mathbf{a}_1^J\right) = \sum_{j:a_j=i} 1 \qquad (4)$$

It omits the dependency on $\mathbf{a}_1^J$ (and defining $P(j\,|\,0)=1$), the probability is expressed as follows.

$$P(f_1^J, a_1^J | e_1^I) = P(\Phi_0 | J) \cdot \prod_{i=1}^{I}[\Phi_i! \, P(\Phi_i | e_i)] \qquad (5)$$
$$\cdot \prod_j \left[P\left(f_i | e_{a_j}\right) \cdot P(j\,|\,a_j) \right]$$

For each foreign input word f, it factors on the fertility probability $P(\Phi_i\,|f_i)$. The factorial $\Phi_i!$ stems from the multiple tableaux for one alignment, if $\Phi_i > 1$.

To compute the translation model probability, a fertility-based IBM Model is employed as insertion words (NULL insertion) and dropping of words (words with fertility 0) to edit the multi-part words spacing.

Sentence alignment in figure 1 is shorthand for a theoretical stochastic process by which unedited words would be changed into edited words. There are a few sets of decisions to be made. As an example, the word "محمدزاده", is a multi-part word which consists of "محمد" and "زاده". So, the space character between the two parts must be edited into half-space character.

Figure1. Word alignment in Persian language.

The proposed method employs hierarchical phrase-based translation to model half-space in phrases. Hierarchical phrase-based translation is a translation model based on synchronous context-free grammars that models translation as phrase pairs. The translation rules are extracted from parallel aligned sentences [7]. On the other hand, hierarchical phrase-based translation employed IBM Model word alignment to extract hierarchical phrase pairs. Therefore, it extracts structure of multi-part words and employs the extracted grammars to edit the multi-part words.

3.2. Proposed method
The general procedure of proposed approach consists of accompanying general methodology of SMT; word alignment, build hierarchical phrase-based model using Synchronous Context-Free Grammar (SCFG), Training phase for weighting extracted features in log-linear model with minimum error rate training and decoding.

In the first phase, words are aligned based on IBM model. In the second phase of the proposed approach hierarchical phrase-based model is employed to extract synchronous context-free grammar. Grammar extraction needs a symbol character to extract linguistic information of space and half-space while space character and half-space character are not considered as symbol characters. In the proposed approach token "*" and token "&" are chosen to denote space character and half-space character, respectively. Therefore, grammar extraction extracts linguistic information of space character between the distinct words and half-space character between the parts of multi-part words. In the third phase, Log-linear model is trained with MERT. MERT determines weights which denote the importance level of grammars. The proposed approach uses a log-linear model with seven features.

To avoid trying to support all the multi-part words in dataset, the structure of multi-part words is trained by the training dataset. To do this, the approach needs linguistic information about space character between the distinct words and half-space character between the parts of multi-part words. The created parallel corpora contain 30000 words which contains various multi-part words with different number of occurrences. A sample of created parallel corpora is presented in table 1. As shown in table 1, the structure of parallel corpora consists of unedited multi-part words in source side and the edited one in the target side in which token "*" denotes space character and token "&" denotes half-space character.

Table 1. a sample of created parallel corpus. The left side is unedited corpus and the right side is edited corpus.

unedited corpus	edited corpus
به ٭ گوشش ٭ خورد:٭«هر کس ٭از ٭ ما ٭ کمکی ٭ بخواهد ٭ ما ٭ به ٭ او ٭ کمک ٭ می ٭ کنیم،٭ ولی ٭ اگر ٭ کسی ٭ بی ٭ نیازی ٭ بورزد ٭ و ٭ دست ٭ حاجت ٭ پیش ٭ مخلوقی ٭ دراز ٭ نکند،٭ خداوند ٭ او ٭ را ٭ بی ٭ نیاز ٭ می ٭ کند. ٭ آن ٭ روز ٭ چیزی ٭ نگفت. ٭ و ٭ به ٭ خانه ٭ خویش ٭ برگشت.٭	به ٭ گوشش ٭ خورد:٭«هر کس ٭از ٭ ما ٭ کمکی ٭ بخواهد ٭ ما ٭ به ٭ او ٭ کمک ٭ می&کنیم،٭ ولی ٭ اگر ٭ کسی ٭ بی&نیازی ٭ بورزد ٭ و ٭ دست ٭ حاجت ٭ پیش ٭ مخلوقی ٭ دراز ٭ نکند،٭ خداوند ٭ او ٭ را ٭ بی&نیاز ٭ می&کند. ٭ آن ٭ روز ٭ چیزی ٭ نگفت. ٭ و ٭ به ٭ خانه ٭ خویش ٭ برگشت.٭
باز ٭ با ٭ هیولای ٭ مهیب ٭ فقر ٭ که ٭ هم ٭ چنان ٭ بر ٭ خانه ٭ اش ٭ سایه ٭ افکنده ٭ بود ٭ روبرو ٭ شد، ٭ ناچار ٭ روز ٭ دیگر ٭ به ٭ همان ٭ نیت ٭ به ٭ مجلس ٭ رسول ٭ اکرم ٭ حاضر ٭ شد، ٭ آن ٭ روز ٭ هم ٭ همان ٭ جمله ٭ را ٭ از ٭ رسول ٭ اکرم ٭ شنید:«هر کس ٭از ٭ ما ٭ کمکی ٭ بخواهد ٭ ما ٭ به ٭ او ٭ کمک ٭ می ٭ کنیم، ٭ ولی ٭ اگر ٭ کسی ٭ بی ٭ نیازی ٭ بورزد، ٭ خداوند ٭ او ٭ را ٭ بی ٭ نیاز ٭ می ٭ کند. این ٭ دفعه ٭ نیز ٭ بدون ٭ این ٭ که ٭ حاجت ٭ خود ٭ را ٭ بگوید، ٭ به ٭ خانه ٭ خویش ٭ برگشت، ٭ چون ٭ خود ٭ را ٭ هم ٭ چنان ٭ در ٭ چنگال ٭ فقر ٭ ضعیف ٭ و ٭ بیچاره ٭ و ٭ ناتوان ٭ می ٭ دید، ٭ برای ٭ سومین ٭ بار ٭ به ٭ همان ٭ نیت ٭ به ٭ مجلس ٭ رسول ٭ اکرم ٭ رفت، ٭ باز ٭ هم ٭ لب ٭ های ٭ رسول ٭ اکرم ٭ به ٭ حرکت ٭ آمد ٭ و ٭ با ٭ همان ٭ آهنگ ٭ که ٭ به ٭ دل ٭ قوت ٭ و ٭ به ٭ روح ٭ اطمینان ٭ می ٭ بخشید همان ٭ جمله ٭ را ٭ تکرار ٭ کرد٭ .	باز ٭ با ٭ هیولای ٭ مهیب ٭ فقر ٭ که ٭ هم&چنان ٭ بر ٭ خانه&اش ٭ سایه ٭ افکنده ٭ بود ٭ روبرو ٭ شد، ٭ ناچار ٭ روز ٭ دیگر ٭ به ٭ همان ٭ نیت ٭ به ٭ مجلس ٭ رسول ٭ اکرم ٭ حاضر ٭ شد، ٭ آن ٭ روز ٭ هم ٭ همان ٭ جمله ٭ را ٭ از ٭ رسول ٭ اکرم ٭ شنید:«هر کس ٭از ٭ ما ٭ کمکی ٭ بخواهد ٭ ما ٭ به ٭ او ٭ کمک ٭ می&کنیم، ٭ ولی ٭ اگر ٭ کسی ٭ بی&نیازی ٭ بورزد، ٭ خداوند ٭ او ٭ را ٭ بی&نیاز ٭ می&کند. این ٭ دفعه ٭ نیز ٭ بدون ٭ این ٭ که ٭ حاجت ٭ خود ٭ را ٭ بگوید، ٭ به ٭ خانه ٭ خویش ٭ برگشت، ٭ چون ٭ خود ٭ را ٭ هم&چنان ٭ در ٭ چنگال ٭ فقر ٭ ضعیف ٭ و ٭ بیچاره ٭ و ٭ ناتوان ٭ می&دید، ٭ برای ٭ سومین ٭ بار ٭ به ٭ همان ٭ نیت ٭ به ٭ مجلس ٭ رسول ٭ اکرم ٭ رفت، ٭ باز ٭ هم ٭ لب&های ٭ رسول ٭ اکرم ٭ به ٭ حرکت ٭ آمد ٭ و ٭ با ٭ همان ٭ آهنگ ٭ که ٭ به ٭ دل ٭ قوت ٭ و ٭ به ٭ روح ٭ اطمینان ٭ می&بخشید همان ٭ جمله ٭ را ٭ تکرار ٭ کرد٭ .

Figure 2 shows an overview of the proposed method. In the first phase, words are aligned based on IBM model. The standard way of aligning word is the method implemented in GIZA++ [12, 13]; In the next phase, Thrax grammar extractor is used to extract SCFGs with the aid of Hadoop method that is applicable to large datasets [14]. It also supports extraction of both Hiero [7] and SAMT grammars [15] with extraction heuristics.

The last phase includes training and testing. Z-MERT [16] is used in training step to extract K-best candidate translation. Log-linear employed Minimum Error Rate Training (MERT) [17] method with Z-MERT toolkit in the training step to tune parameters. Seven parameters are tuned in this step:

N-gram language model $P_{LM}(t)$ parameter, lexical translation model $P_w(\gamma|\alpha)$ parameter and $P_w(\alpha|\gamma)$ parameter, rule translation model $P(\gamma|\alpha)$ parameter and $P(\alpha|\gamma)$ parameter, word penalty parameter and the arity of word parameter. Regarding rules of the form $X \rightarrow <\gamma, \alpha, \sim, w>$ in hierarchical phrase-based model, X is a non-terminal symbol, γ is a sequence of non-terminals and source terminals and α is a sequence of non-terminals and target terminals. Symbol $\sim$ is a one-to-one correspondence for the non-terminals appeared in γ and α. To build an interpolated Kneser-Ney language model [18] on the target side of the training data, SRILM [19] toolkit is used. Parameters are initialized as follows: language model parameter is initialized to 1, word penalty is initialized to -2.8 and the other parameters are initialized to 0. All the parameters have default values in Joshua decoder. Finally Joshua decoder [20] decodes the best translation with the log-linear method. Joshua decoder is used to decode the test set. Joshua decoder is an implementation of the CKY+ algorithm [21] and implements scope-3 filtering [22] and uses cube pruning [23] to reduce parsing complexity [20] when filtering grammars to test sets. The decoder is employed to produce the k-best translations for each sentence of the test set. Decoding algorithm maintains cubic time parsing complexity (in the sentence length).

4. Results and discussion

This section presents the experiments and the

results of created test sets. The model needs parallel corpus which consists of unedited corpus and the edited one. A dataset with these aligned corpora is not available for Persian language. Two criteria are specified for creating a dataset for this special purpose: First criterion states that space and half-space characters must be denoted as two different symbol characters in the corpora. The second criterion is to create a dataset of parallel corpora in which unedited multi-part words are placed in one side and edited multi-part words are placed in the other side. In the edited side of parallel corpora, spaces between the parts of the multi-part words are replaced by half-spaces.

Therefore, a dataset is created based on the two criteria and it is publicly available for other researchers. The model needs dataset especially for evaluation step.

The evaluation set must consist of two sets: one for tuning parameters of the model, and the other one for validation experiments. A tuning set is created and used to set the parameters of model in order to use minimum error rate training in the training step.

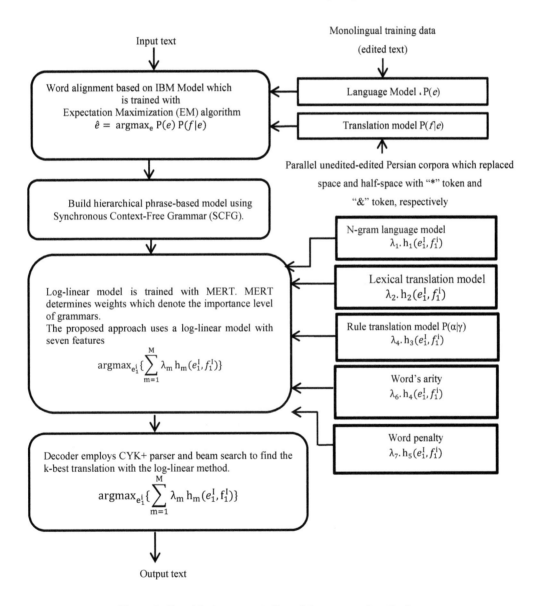

Figure 2. Graphical representation of the proposed method.

As shown in table 2, the words such as "وقتی‌که", "گونه‌ای", "می‌شود", "لب‌ها", "زمانی‌که", "می‌دهد" are edited successfully, because the training set includes these words. As it is shown in table 2, the words like "می‌خندیم" is edited successfully,

however, it is not exactly included in the training set. This is the ability of the proposed method to edit the words which are not exactly included in the training dataset. The training dataset contains the words with similar structure with sufficient frequency. Therefore, the proposed method can model the co-occurrence of parts of the multi-part words. In more details, one can see that the word "بی‌حوصله" is not edited. As shown in table 3, by

increasing the frequency of similar words like "بی‌همتا" and "بی‌امان", "بی‌دغدغه" makes it possible for the proposed method to edit "بی‌حوصله" correctly.

Table 2. A sample of evaluation output.

Input	Output
وقتی که واقعا می خندیم عضله گونه ای بزرگ و منقبض می شود و	وقتی‌که واقعا می‌خندیم عضله گونه‌ای بزرگ و منقبض می‌شود و
لب ها رو به سمت بالا کشیده می شود که این نشان می دهد، فرد	لب‌ها رو به سمت بالا کشیده می‌شود که این نشان می دهد، فرد
واقعا خوشحال است. زمانی که از دیدن فردی خوشحالیم، سرمان	واقعا خوشحال است. زمانی‌که از دیدن فردی خوشحالیم، سرمان
را بالا می گیریم و برعکس سر پایین نشان از ناراحتی از حضور	را بالا می‌گیریم و برعکس سر پایین نشان از ناراحتی از حضور
اوست وتکان دادن سر نمادی از فرد بی حوصله است.	اوست و تکان‌دادن سر نمادی از فرد بی حوصله است .

Table 3. Evaluation in the case of increasing the frequency of words with the same structure in the training dataset.
("بی‌حوصله")

Input	Output
وقتی که واقعا می خندیم عضله گونه ای بزرگ و منقبض می شود و	وقتی‌که واقعا می‌خندیم عضله گونه‌ای بزرگ و منقبض می‌شود و
لب ها رو به سمت بالا کشیده می شود که این نشان می دهد، فرد	لب‌ها رو به سمت بالا کشیده می‌شود که این نشان می‌دهد، فرد
واقعا خوشحال است. زمانی که از دیدن فردی خوشحالیم، سرمان را	واقعا خوشحال است. زمانی که از دیدن فردی خوشحالیم، سرمان را
بالا می گیریم و برعکس سر پایین نشان از ناراحتی از حضور اوست	بالا می‌گیریم و برعکس سر پایین نشان از ناراحتی از حضور اوست و
وتکان دادن سر نمادی از فرد بی حوصله است.	تکان دادن سر نمادی از فرد بی‌حوصله است .

Therefore, if the sufficient number of the multi-part words with the similar structure exist in the training set, the multi-part word would be edited even the word is unseen in the training set.

There are some multi-part words, where each part can be considered as an independent word such as "به" and "ویژه" in "به‌ویژه". If maximum entropy POS tagger [24] is used to train the tags, it cannot perform efficiently. Since maximum entropy approach edits the spacing by using maximum co-occurrence of space and half-space between the parts and since the maximum co-occurrence does not have linguistic information to edit spacing, the approach is not efficient to edit spacing. If the co-occurrence of half-space after "به" is more than the co-occurrence of space, the space is edited to half-space while the word "به" can be considered as an independent word. Therefore, correct spacing would not be achieved by just relying on the co-occurrence of space and half-space characters between the parts of multi-part words, while in the proposed approach, spacing in multi-part words can be edited successfully because of using linguistic information.

The approach is evaluated using False Positive (FP), False Negative (FN), Precision (P) and Recall (R) measures. Recall (R) and Precision (P) are calculated using the following equations.

Recall(R)= (Number of correct edited multi-part words)/(Total number of multi-part words in the text)   (6)

Precision (P)= (Number of correct edited multi-part words)/(Number of edited words)   (7)

Recall is also considered to be the accuracy score of the approach by calculating number of correct edited multipart words against the total number of multi-part words in the corpus. Precision is also considered to be the accuracy score of the approach by calculating number of correct edited multi-part words against the total number of edited words which are edited by the approach. The accuracy rate is computed with the average of four different created test sets. In the proposed approach, recall and precision are obtained 92% and 98%, respectively. The score of false positive and false negative are 1.8% and 3%, respectively. Another measure used to evaluate the efficiency of the proposed method is BLEU [25]. BLEU is not an error rate but an accuracy measure [26] and it discovers the best scoring result as follows.

$$P(w_1, w_2, \ldots, w_T) = \qquad (8)$$
$$P(w_1)\, P(w_2|w_1) P(w_3|w_1 w_2) \ldots P(w_T|w_1, \ldots, w_{T-1})$$

where, $w_1, \ldots, w_T$ is a sentence and w_i is the i-th word of sentence.
BLEU score of the proposed method reaches 0.91.

5. Conclusion

In this paper, a statistical approach is introduced to edit Persian text focusing on spacing in Persian multi-part words. The paper employs statistical machine translation which translates one language into another. The proposed approach utilizes this ability to edit Persian text. Thus, the proposed approach employs parallel corpora in which unedited multi-part words are considered as source language and space-edited multi-part words are considered as destination language. Since no standard dataset exists in literature, three Persian parallel corpora is prepared to meet the needs; one for train, one for tune and one for test. To align the created parallel corpora, the proposed method employs a fertility-based IBM model and calculates the parameters of probabilistic distributions and extracts linguistic information with Synchronous Context-Free Grammars (SCFG) of hierarchical phrase-based model. In evaluation phase, a syntax-based decoder is used to decode different created test sets in this paper. Based on this model, multi-part words are edited efficiently even the words are not exactly trained in the training set provided that the same word structure is trained in the training set. Furthermore, the experimental validation shows that the proposed method can edit spacing in multi-part words with a desired result.

References

[1] Kashefi, O., Sharifi, M. & Minaei-Bidgoli, B. (2012). A Novel String Distance Metric for Ranking Persian Respelling Suggestions. Natural Language Engineering (NLE), Cambridge University Press, United Kingdom, vol. 2, no. 19, pp.259–284.

[2] Shamsfard, M., Sadat Jafari, H. & Ilbeygi, M. (2010). STeP-1: A Set of Fundamental Tools for Persian Text Processing. The 7th International Conference on Language Resources and Evaluation, Valletta, Malta, 2010.

[3] Mahmoudi, A., Faili, H. & Arabsorkhi, M. (2013). Modeling Persian Verb Morphology to Improve English-Persian Machine Translation. The 12th Mexican International Conference on Artificial Intelligence, Mexico City, Mexico, 2013.

[4] Rasooli, M. S., Kholy, A. E. & Habash, N. (2013). Orthographic and Morphological Processing for Persian to English Statistical Machine Translation. The 6th International Joint Conference on Natural Language Processing, Nagoya, Japan, 2013.

[5] Bijankhan, M., Sheykhzadegan, J., Bhrani, M. & Ghayoomi, M. (2010). Lessons from Building a Persian Written Corpus: Peykare. Language Resources and Evaluation, vol. 54, no. 2, pp. 143-164.

[6] Brown, P .E., Della Pietra, S. A., Della Pietra, V. J. & Mercer, R.L. (1993). The Mathematics of Statistical Machine Translation: Parameter Estimation. Computational Linguistics - Special Issue on Using Large Corpora: II, vol. 19, no. 2, pp. 263-311.

[7] Chiang, D. (2005). A Hierarchical Phrase-based Model for Statistical Machine Translation. Proceedings of the 43rd Annual Meeting of the Association for Computational Linguistics, Ann Arbor, Michigan, 2005.

[8] Brown, P. F., Cocke, J., Della Pietra, S. A., Della Pietra, V. J., Jelinek, F., Mercer, R. L. & Roossin, P. S. (1990). A Statistical Approach to Machine Translation. Computational Linguistics, vol. 16, no. 2, pp. 79-85.

[9] Berger, A. L., Brown, P. F., Della Pietra, S. A., Della Pietra, V. J., Gillett, J. R., Lafferty, J. D., Mercer, R. L., Printz, H. & Ures, L. (1994). The Candide System for Machine Translation. The workshop on Human Language Technology, Stroudsburg, USA, 1994.

[10] Kohen, Ph. (2010). Statistical Machine Translation. Cambridge, New York, Melbourne, Madrid, Cape Town, Singapore, Sao Paulo, Delhi, Dubai, Tokyo: Cambridge University Press.

[11] Schoenemann, T. (2010). Computing Optimal Alignments for the IBM-3 Translation Model. The 14th Conference on Computational Natural Language Learning, Uppsala, Sweden, 2010.

[12] Och, F. J. & Ney, H. (2000). Improved Statistical Alignment Models. The 38th Annual Meeting on Association for Computational Linguistics, Stroudsburg, PA, USA, 2000.

[13] Och, F. J. & Ney, H. (2003). A Systematic Comparison of Various Statistical Alignment Models. Computational Linguistics, vol. 29, no. 1, pp. 19-51.

[14] Weese, J., Ganitkevitch, J., Callison-Burch, Ch., Post, M. & Lopez, A. (2011). Joshua 3.0: Syntax-based Machine Translation with the Thrax Grammar Extractor. The 6th Workshop on Statistical Machine Translation, Stroudsburg, PA, USA, 2011.

[15] Zollmann, A. & Venugopal, A. (2006). Syntax Augmented Machine Translation via Chart Parsing. The Workshop on Statistical Machine Translation, Stroudsburg, USA, 2006.

[16] Zaidan, O. F. (2009). Z-MERT: A Fully Configurable Open Source Tool for Minimum Error Rate Training of Machine Translation Systems. The Prague Bulletin of Mathematical Linguistics, Czech Republic, 2009.

[17] Och, F. J. (2003). Minimum Error Rate Training for Statistical Machine Translation. The 41st Annual Meeting on Association for Computational Linguistics, Stroudsburg, USA, 2003.

[18] Heafield, K., Pouzyrevsky, I., Clark, J. H. & Kohen, Ph. (2013). Scalable Modified Kneser-Ney Language Model Estimation. The 51st Annual Meeting on Association for Computational Linguistics, Sofia, Bulgaria, 2013.

[19] Stolcke, A. (2002). SRILM - An Extensible Language Modeling Toolkit. The 7th International

Conference on Spoken Language Processing, Denver, Colorado, USA, 2002.

[20] Post, M., Ganitkevitch, J., Orland, L., Weese, J. & Cao, Y. (2013). Joshua 5.0: Sparser, Better, Faster, Server. The Eighth Workshop on Statistical Machine Translation, Sofia, Bulgaria, 2013.

[21] Chappelier, J. & Rajman, M. (1998). A Generalized CYK Algorithm for Parsing Stochastic CFG. The 1st Workshop on Tabulation in Parsing and Deduction, Paris, France, 1998.

[22] Hopkins, M. & Langmead, G. (2010). SCFG Decoding without Binarization. The 2010 Conference on Empirical Methods in Natural Language Processing, Association for Computational Linguistics, Cambridge, USA, 2010.

[23] Chiang, D. (2007). Hierarchical Phrase-based

Translation. Computational Linguistics, vol. 33, no. 2, pp. 201–228.

[24] Ratnaparkhi, A. (1996). A Maximum Entropy Model for Part-Of-Speech Tagging. The 1996 Conference on Empirical Methods in Natural Language Processing, Association for Computational Linguistics, Philadelphia, USA, 1996.

[25] Papineni, K., Roukos, S., Ward, T. & Wei-Jing Zhu (2002). Bleu: A Method for Automatic Evaluation of Machine Translation. The 40th Annual Meeting of the Association for Computational Linguistics, Philadelphia, USA, 2002.

[26] Gonzalez, J. (2012). A Finite State Approach to Phrase-based Statistical Machine Translation. The 10th International Workshop on Finite State Methods and Natural Language Processing, Spain, 2012.

7

An improved joint model: POS tagging and dependency parsing

A. Pakzad and B. Minaei Bidgoli[*]

Department of Computer Engineering, Iran University of Science & Technology, Tehran, Iran.

*Corresponding author: b_minaei@iust.ac.ir (B. Minaei).

Abstract

Dependency parsing is a way of syntactic parsing and a natural language that automatically analyzes the dependency structure of sentences, and the input for each sentence creates a dependency graph. Part-Of-Speech (POS) tagging is a prerequisite for dependency parsing. Generally, dependency parsers do the POS tagging task along with dependency parsing in a pipeline mode. Unfortunately, in pipeline models, a tagging error propagates, but the model is not able to apply useful syntactic information. The goal of joint models simultaneously reduce errors of POS tagging and dependency parsing tasks. In this research, we attempted to utilize the joint model on the Persian and English language using Corbit software. We optimized the model's features and improved its accuracy concurrently. Corbit software is an implementation of a transition-based approach for word segmentation, POS tagging and dependency parsing. In this research, the joint accuracy of POS tagging and dependency parsing over the test data on Persian, reached 85.59% for coarse-grained and 84.24% for fine-grained POS. Also, we attained 76.01% for coarse-grained and 74.34% for fine-grained POS on English.

Keywords: *Joint model, Part-Of-Speech, Dependency Parsing, Persian Language.*

1. Introduction

POS tagging and dependency parsing are two important tasks in natural language processing. POS tagging is a preliminary step in the dependency-parsing task. An incorrect POS tag propagates errors in dependency parsing, but POS tagging is unable to use syntactic information.

A POS tagging and dependency parsing system for the Persian language suffers from error propagation, but it cannot use syntactic information for POS tagging. Hatori et al. (2012) presented an incremental joint model for POS tagging and dependency parsing on the Chinese language using Corbit software [1]. However, in this research, we reconciled the joint model of the Chinese language to the Persian language; the model's features were also optimized for Persian and English. Further, the joint accuracy for POS tagging and unlabeled dependency parsing for coarse-grained POS and fine-grained POS on Persian were 85.59% and 84.24%, respectively. Also, we reached 76.01% for coarse-grained and 74.34% for fine-grained POS on English. Experimental results on the Persian Syntactic Dependency Treebank1.0 and Universal Dependencies English Web Treebank v1.0 showed that our improved joint model significantly improved both POS tagging and dependency parsing accuracies compared to the pipeline model.

2. Related work

Bohnet and Nivre (2012) proposes a transition-based model for joint POS tagging and labeled dependency parsing with non-projective trees on the Chinese language [2]. This joint model uses beam search inference and global structure learning. Globally learned models can use richer feature space than locally trained models.

Hatori et al. (2011) presents the first incremental approach to the task of joint POS tagging and dependency parsing on Chinese [3]. We used this method in our research. In this approach, given a segmented sentence the model simultaneously considers POS tags and dependency relations within the given beam, and outputs the best parse along with POS tags. This incremental joint model has two problems: First, since the combined search space is huge, efficient decoding is difficult and naïve use of the beam is probable contributing to a decline in the search quality. Second, since the suggested model performs joint POS tagging and dependency parsing from left to right of the sentence, the model cannot exploit look-ahead POS tags to decide the next action. To deal with a huge search space, the model uses a dynamic programming (DP) extension for shift-reduce parsing, which allows the model to merge equal parser states and increases speed and accuracy. The model solves the lack of look-ahead POS information problem by delayed features. The delayed features include undetermined POS tags which are evaluated when the look-ahead POS tags are specified. This joint model is language-independent. Li et al. (2011) proposes graph-based joint models according to syntactic features. It defines first-, second-, and third-order joint models [4].

Li et al. (2012) presents a graph-based joint model. The POS tagging task does not profit much from a joint model because on average the POS features score is only 1/50 of the syntactic features in the joint results [5]. In other words, the POS features do not have much effect on determining the best joint result. The proposed model separately updates the POS features weights and the syntactic feature weights, and increases the weights of POS features in the joint optimization framework. This model improves POS tagging and dependency parsing accuracies. Being available on the Persian language, first the data has been tagged and then has been used for dependency parsing. Seraji et al. (2012) presents two dependency parsers for the Persian language [6]. MaltParser and MSTParser are transition-based and graph-based dependency parsers, respectively. Both parsers are trained on the Uppsala Persian Dependency Treebank. The unlabeled attachment score for MaltParser and MSTParser are 74.81% and 71.08%, respectively. Those results are not comparable with our joint model results because the dataset is different. Khallash et al. (2013) studies the effect of morphological and lexical features on dependency parsing for Persian [7]. It studies the effect of features on the transition-based dependency parser MaltParser and the graph-based dependency parser MSTParser. Labeled attachment score with gold POS tags for MaltParser and MSTParser are 86.98% and 86.81%, respectively. Unlabeled attachment scores are not reported.

3. Baseline models
First, we introduce both a baseline POS tagger and a dependency parser. A combination of baseline models make-up the pipeline model. Then we describe the joint model and its default features. Added and subtracted features of the model and the logic behind each are discussed in the section 4.1.2. The dataset is divided into train, validation and test sets. Train and validation sets are used to determine the model's parameters for intermediate experiments, train and test sets are used for the final experiments. Corbit software is an unlabeled dependency parser. All of accuracies, which are reported in this article, are unlabeled attachment scores. Corbit reports POS tagging and dependency parsing accuracies with DEP and POS, respectively. We added a new DepPos accuracy measure, which shows the correctness of the POS tag and the dependency relation and the word's head simultaneously.

3.1. Baseline POS tagger
The Stanford Log-linear Part-Of-Speech Tagger was used in this research. This software is an implementation of Log-Linear POS Taggers with java as described in [8].

3.2. Baseline dependency parser
Corbit software has several different run modes [1]:
1- SegTag: Joint segmentation and POS tagging model.
2- Dep': dependency parser.
3- Dep: Dep' without look-ahead features.
4- TagDep: joint POS tagger and dependency parser .
5- SegTag+Dep/SegTag+ Dep': a pipeline combination of SegTag and Dep or Dep'.
6- SegTagDep: joint segmentation and POS tagging and dependency parsing model.

In this research, we used the Dep' mode which uses the shift-reduce parsing method as a baseline dependency parser.

3.3. Pipeline POS tagging and dependency parsing model
First, the data was tagged, and then we used the tagged data for dependency parsing with baseline dependency parsing.

4. Joint POS tagging and dependency parsing model
In this research, we used a joint POS tagging and dependency parsing model proposed by Jun Hatori [1] as a base model. We reconciled the

model for Persian and English, and then we optimized the model's features.

4.1. Features
4.1.1. Default model's features
The joint POS tagging and dependency parsing model uses baseline dependency parser features represented in figure 1. In addition to these features, it uses syntactic features for POS tagging and delayed features. Figures 2(a) and 2(b) show the delayed features and syntactic features lists of a joint model.

$$w_j \quad t_{j-1} \quad t_{j-1} \circ t_{j-2} \quad w_{j+1}{}^{1)}$$
$$w_j \circ E(w_{j-1}){}^{2)} \qquad w_j \circ E(w_{j+1}){}^{2)}$$
$$E(w_j) \circ w_j \circ E(w_{j+1}){}^{3)}$$
$$B(w_j) \quad E(w_j) \quad P(B(w_j)) \quad P(E(w_j))$$
$$C_n(w_j) \quad (n \in \{2, \ldots, len(w_j) - 1\})$$
$$B(w_j) \circ C_n(w_j) \quad (n \in \{2, \ldots len(w_j)\})$$
$$E(w_j) \circ C_n(w_j) \quad (n \in \{2, \ldots len(w_j) - 1\})$$
$$C_n(w_j) \quad (if \; C_n(w_j) \; equals \; to \; C_{n+1}(w_j))$$
$$1) \; if \; len(w_{j+1}) < 3; \quad 2) if \; len(w_j) < 3;$$
$$3) \; if \; len(w_j) = 1$$

Figure 1. Feature templates for baseline POS tagger, where t_i is the tag assigned to the i-th word w_i, B(w) and E(w) is the beginning and the ending character of word w, $C_n(w)$ is the n-th character of w, P(c) is the set of tags associated with the single-character word c based on the dictionary [3].

$$(a) \quad q_0.t \quad q_0.w \circ q_0.t \qquad s_0.t \circ q_0.t$$
$$s_0.t \circ q_0.t \circ q_1.t \qquad s_1.t \circ s_0.t \circ q_0.t$$
$$s_0.w \circ q_0.t \circ q_1.t \qquad s_1.t \circ s_0.w \circ q_0.t$$

$$(b) \quad t \circ s_0.w \qquad\qquad t \circ s_0.t$$
$$t \circ s_0.w \circ q_0.w \qquad t \circ s_0.t \circ q_0.w$$
$$t \circ B(s_0.w) \circ q_0.w \qquad t \circ E(s_0.w) \circ q_0.w$$
$$t \circ s_0.t \circ s_0.rc.t \qquad t \circ s_0.t \circ s_0.lc.t$$
$$t \circ s_0.w \circ s_0.t \circ s_0.rc.t \quad t \circ s_0.w \circ s_0.t \circ s_0.lc.t$$

Figure 2. (a) List of delayed features for joint parser; (b) Syntactic features for the joint parser, where t is the POS tag to be assigned to q0 [3].

4.1.2. Features optimization
POS's are classifications of words based on their functions in sentences for purposes of grammatical analysis. Each coarse-grained POS is divided into a number of fine-grained POS's. In cases where no fine-grained POS has been recognized, the fine-grained POS is the same as the coarse grained one, for example, ADJ is CPOS and its FPOS are AJP, AJCM, and AJSUP. In this research, we considered lemma as a basic feature for the joint model, and tried to improve Corbit's performance with a combination of this basic feature and Corbit default features. Corbit gets CTB file as an input file. This file includes the

word's index, word, POS tag, head and dependency relation columns. First, we changed the input format to Conll. Conll format includes Coarse-grained POS tag, Fine-grained POS tag, lemma and Feats columns not found in the CTB format. The software did not exploit lemma, Feats and deprel features in the default version. Therefore, we added some new features to the software. The main research goal was POS tagging and dependency parsing on raw texts, so we chose the lemma feature, since there are lemmatizer tools for Persian and English, which can provide the required information for the software. Also, experiments and their analysis showed that some features were insufficient, and thus they were removed. Accuracy improved for both Corse-grained and Fine-grained POS tags.

- **Added features**

We tried 66 different combinations of features with lemma on Persian, and we obtained 26 features which improved accuracies. Table 1 shows the features that increased accuracies for both Coarse-grained and Fine-grained POS on Persian. Then, we tried Corbit with added features on English and accuracies, which were improved.

- **Reduced features**

We tried 66 feature combinations, and some of which reduced accuracy for both Coarse-grained POS and Fine-grained POS on Persian. It seemed these default features without lemma did not have a positive impact on accuracies. Thus, we removed these features one by one. According to the results, two Corbit default features reduced joint model accuracy for Persian; consequently, we eliminated these two features from the joint model features. Then, we tried Corbit with reduced features on English Treebank. The results showed improvement.

5. Experiments
In this research, we evaluated both the pipeline model and the joint model performance on the Persian Syntactic Dependency Treebank 1.0 and Universal Dependencies English Web Treebank v1.0. The model was trained several times, and model parameters were set. The POS tagging accuracy, dependency-parsing accuracy, and joint accuracy have been reported.

5.1. Data
We conducted experiments on the Persian Syntactic Dependency Treebank as well as Universal Dependencies English Web Treebank

v1.0 for Persian and English Treebanks, respectively. Here we introduce both Treebanks briefly.

5.1.1. Persian syntactic dependency treebank

This Treebank is the first Persian dependency Treebank, and includes 29,982 sentences and 498,081 words. Its sentences have syntactic relations (based on dependency grammar) like subject, object, predicate … and POS tags like verb, noun, adjective…. Following standard practice, we adopted training, validation and test datasets. The Persian dependency Treebank was randomly split into three sets 80%, 10%, and another 10% were allocated for training, validation and test datasets, respectively. A unique feature of this Treebank is that there are 4,800 distinct verb lemmas in its sentences making it a valuable resource for educational goals [9].

5.1.2. Universal dependencies English web Treebank v1.0

Corpus consists of over 250,000 words of English weblogs, newsgroups, emails, reviews and question-answers manually annotated for syntactic structure and are designed to allow language technology researchers to develop and evaluate the robustness of parsing methods in those web domains. It contains 254,830 word-level tokens and 16,624 sentence-level tokens of webtext in 1,174 files annotated for sentence- and word-level tokenization, part-of-speech, and syntactic structure. The data is roughly evenly divided across five genres: weblogs, newsgroups, emails, reviews, and question-answers. The files were manually annotated following the sentence-level tokenization guidelines for web text and the word-level tokenization guidelines developed for English treebanks in the DARPA GALE project.

5.2. Default joint model performance

The joint model has two important parameters, beam size and iteration number. As shown in figures 3, 4, 5 and 6 increasing the iteration number and beam size improves the model for both of Persian and English. An increase in beam size of 16 to 32 and 64 significantly increases run time with little improvement in accuracy. Thus, we consider 16 for the beam size. Final results were estimated with 10 iterations, because more iterations increased run time and the accuracy improvement was not significant.

Only text from the subject line and message body of posts, articles, messages and question-answers were collected and annotated [10].

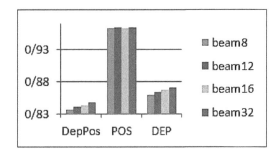

Figure 3. Study of relationship between beam size and accuracy on Persian.

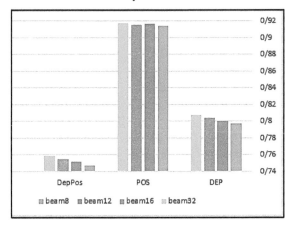

Figure 4. Study of relationship between beam size and accuracy on English.

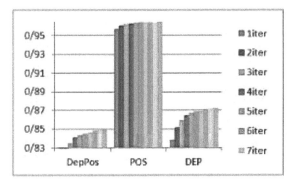

Figure 5. Study of relationship between iteration on Persian.

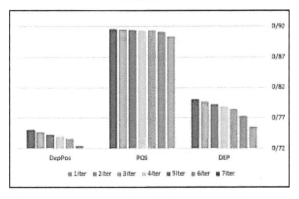

Figure 6. Study of relationship between iteration on English.

Table 1. Added Features- Lm denotes Lemma, s.w. and s.t. are the Form and Tag of the Root Word of Tree s, s.rc and s.lc are the Right- and Left-most Children of s, and ∘ Denotes the conjunction of Features.

Added Features	
1-Lm(q_0)	2-Lm(s_0)
3-Lm(s_1)	4-Lm($s_0.rc$)
5-Lm($s_1.lc$)	6-$s_0.w$ ∘ Lm(s_0)
7-$s_1.w$ ∘ Lm(s_0)	8-$s_1.w$ ∘ Lm(s_1)
9-$q_0.w$ ∘ Lm(q_0)	10-$s_0.w$ ∘ $s_1.w$ ∘ Lm(s_0) ∘ Lm(s_1)
11-$s_0.w$ ∘ $s_0.t$ ∘ $s_1.w$ ∘ Lm(s_0) ∘ Lm(s_1)	12-$s_0.t$ ∘ $s_1.w$ ∘ $s_1.t$ ∘ Lm(s_0) ∘ Lm(s_1)
13-$s_0.w$ ∘ $s_0.t$ ∘ $s_1.w$ ∘ $s_1.t$ ∘ Lm(s_0) ∘ Lm(s_1)	14-$s_0.t$ ∘ $q_0.t$ ∘ Lm(s_0)
15-$s_0.t$ ∘ $s_1.t$ ∘ $q_0.t$ ∘ Lm(s_0) ∘ Lm(s_1)	16-1$s_0.w$ ∘ $s_1.t$ ∘ $q_0.t$ ∘ Lm(s_0)
17-$s_0.t$ ∘ $q_0.t$ ∘ $q_1.t$ ∘ Lm(s_0) ∘ Lm(q_0)	18-$s_0.t$ ∘ $s_1.t$ ∘ $s_1.lc.t$ ∘ Lm(s_0)
19-$s_0.t$ ∘ $s_1.t$ ∘ $s_1.rc.t$ ∘ Lm(s_0)	20-$s_0.t$ ∘ $s_0.rc.t$ ∘ $s_1.t$ ∘ Lm(s_0)
21-$s_0.t$ ∘ $s_1.t$ ∘ $s_1.lc.t$ ∘ Lm(s_0) ∘Lm(s_1) ∘ m($s_1.lc$)	22-$s_0.t$ ∘ $s_0.lc.t$ ∘ $s_1.t$ ∘ Lm(s_0)
23-$s_0.t$ ∘ $s_0.rc.t$ ∘ $s_1.t$ ∘ Lm(s_0) ∘ Lm($s_0.rc$) ∘ Lm(s_1)	24-$s_0.w$ ∘ $s_1.t$ ∘ $s_1.rc.t$ ∘ Lm(s_0) ∘ Lm(s_1) ∘ Lm($s_1.rc$)
25-$s_0.w$ ∘ $s_1.t$ ∘ $s_0.lc.t$ ∘ Lm(s_0) ∘ Lm(s_1) ∘ Lm($s_0.lc$)	26-$s_0.t$ ∘ $s_1.t$ ∘ $s_2.t$ ∘ Lm(s_0) ∘ Lm(s_1)

Table 2. Reduced features.

Reduced Features	
1) $s_0.t$ ∘ $s_1.t$ ∘ $s_2.t$	2) $s_0.w$ ∘ $s_0.t$ ∘ $s_1.t$

Table 3. Pipeline model results.

Pipeline Model	Lang.	Tag Acc	DepPos
CPOS	Persian	0.9742	0.766494
	English	0.9468	0.747097
FPOS	Persian	0.9611	0.860225
	English	0.9458	0.734691

5.3. Pipeline model performance

Data has been tagged with the Stanford tagger, and then the tagged data was parsed with a baseline dependency parser. In the pipeline method, Corbit software just does the dependency parsing task using gold POS tags. POS tagging and dependency parsing for Coarse-grained and Fine-grained POS tags are shown in table 3.

Table 4 shows that the default joint model has a better performance than the pipeline model for Coarse-grained POS (8% and 0.73% improvement for Persian and English, respectively).

Table 5 shows that the accuracy of the joint model for Fine-grained POS on Persian was 2.4% less than the pipeline model. For English, the results of Joint model and pipeline model are almost equal.

Table 4. Model First Result for CPOS.

Model	Lang.	DepPos	POS	DEP
Joint model	Persian	0.849489	0.964459	0.872165
Baseline	Persian	0.766494	0.9742	0.766494
Joint model	English	0.754374	0.915063	0.803961
Baseline	English	0.747097	0.911404	0.797360

Table 5. Model first result for FPOS.

model	Language	DepPos	POS	DEP
Joint model	Persian	0.836072	0.949871	0.872363
Baseline	Persian	0.860225	0.9611	0.860225
Joint model	English	0.735049	0.901781	0.789367
Baseline	English	0.734691	0.899833	0.791117

5.4. Joint model performance with gold POS tag

We ran Corbit software with the gold POS tag on dependency parsing mode, and the best dependency result obtained for the default joint model is shown in table 6.

Table 6. Dependency parsing results with gold.

model	Lang.	DepPos
CPOS	Persian	0.893478
	English	0.764374
FPOS	Persian	0.896646
	English	0.755049

- **Improved joint model performance**

The effect of each added feature on Corbit software accuracy for Coarse-grained and Fine-grained POS is shown in table 7. A positive number means an increase and negative number means a decrease in accuracy. We tried to choose features that improved both Coarse-grained and Fine-grained POS accuracies. The other features that significantly reduced either CPOS or FPOS or both accuracies were not included in the features list. A 0.03% increase in accuracy for both CPOS and FPOS meant improvement, but in the case where only one of the POS increased and the other decreased, the feature was considered useful only if the sum of the increase and decrease was more than 0.04%; otherwise, this feature added significantly to the run time. As mentioned in section 5.1, an increase in iteration number increased accuracy. Results showed that a gradient shift of accuracy in the 1st to 5th iterations was more than in the 6th to 10th iterations. Therefore, we used 5th iteration results. It is clear that if features show improvement in 5 iterations, they have improvement with fewer gradients in 6 to 10 iterations. Added features are listed in table 1. In each step, we add one feature to the other features, and measure the changes in accuracy for both CPOS and FPOS.

Default joint model accuracy (*), joint model accuracy after adding features (**) and reducing features (***) with 5 iterations and a beam size of 16 on the validation dataset is shown in table 8. Joint model accuracy by adding features on Persian has improved 0.7% for CPOS and 0.8% for FPOS. After reducing 2 default features, the joint model accuracy increased 0.3% for CPOS and 0.2% for FPOS on Persian.

Totally, For Persian, the joint model accuracy increased 1% for CPOS and 1% for FPOS. Corbit's accuracy with added features had 0.29% improvement for CPOS and 33% improvement for FPOS on English. The joint model accuracy with reduced features improved CPOS and FPOS 0.24% and 0.31%, respectively. Therefore, Corbit's accuracy for English improved 0.53% and

0.64% for CPOS and FPOS in order. As we mentioned in section 5.1, the Persian dependency Treebank includes 29,982 sentences and 498,081 words but Universal Dependencies English Web Treebank contains 254,830 word-level tokens and 16,624 sentence-level tokens of web texts. It shows that Persian Treebank's sentences and words are almost twice, so we achieved higher improvement for Persian comparing to English.

The default joint model and joint model accuracy after optimization on test data is shown in table 9. As can be seen, the joint model accuracy improved 0.83% for CPOS and 0.49% for FPOS on Persian and 0.40% for CPOS and 0.53% for FPOS on English after feature optimization. The DEP for CPOS increased 0.81% and 0.37% for Persian and English, respectively. The FPOS improved 0.4% for Persian and 0.53% for English.

Table 7. Added features effect on increase and decrease of accuracy for Persian.

#	CPOS	FPOS	#	CPOS	FPOS
1	0.2	0.4	2	0.2	-0.03
3	0.04	0.08	4	-0.02	0.16
5	0.27	0	6	-0.02	0.08
7	0.12	0.08	8	-0.05	0.11
9	-0.08	0.28	10	0.18	0.16
11	0.16	0.34	12	0.03	0.01
13	-0.01	0.06	14	0.11	0.19
15	0.22	0.14	16	-0.04	0.13
17	0.01	0.21	18	0.11	0.09
19	0.03	0.26	20	0.28	0.26
21	0.13	0.13	22	0.06	0.12
23	0.13	0.14	24	0.07	-0.01
25	0.3	0.04	26	0.05	0.4

6. Conclusion

This research is based on a joint POS tagging and dependency-parsing model used on the Chinese language. POS tag and dependency relationship are language-specific features called morphological features [11]. First, we reconciled the model with Persian and English. In experiments, the default joint model had improvement over the pipeline model for CPOS. Then, we considered lemma as a key feature for feature optimization on Persian and English. We studied different combinations of lemma with default features. The combinations that had a subtractive effect were removed.

Finally, a 1% improvement for Persian and almost 0.5% for English was obtained for CPOS and FPOS.

In this research, we focused on Persian and English but adding lemma is possible for other languages and the improved joint model is language-independent.

Table 8. Joint model accuracy on validation dataset with 5 iterations, before adding features of table 3, after adding features of table 3, after adding features of table 3 and reducing features of table 4.

POS	Lang.		DepPos	POS	DEP
CPOS	Persian	*	0.843418	0.963179	0.867129
		**	0.850632	0.96554	0.872671
		***	0.853404	0.96624	0.875069
	English	*	0.754374	0.915063	0.803961
		**	0.757220	0.914506	0.806285
		***	0.759609	0.914864	0.808465
FPOS	Persian	*	0.829847	0.949251	0.866359
		**	0.837963	0.952532	0.872561
		***	0.839965	0.952913	0.874497
	English	*	0.735049	0.901781	0.789367
		**	0.738349	0.901543	0.794457
		***	0.741441	0.902100	0.797610

Table 9. Joint model accuracy on test dataset with 10 iterations before and after features optimization.

POS	Lang.		DepPos	POS	DEP
CPOS	Persian	*	0.847674	0.964827	0.868994
		**	0.855900	0.966992	0.877040
	English	*	0.756136	0.917278	0.802518
		**	0.760179	0.917085	0.806239
FPOS	Persian	*	0.837532	0.950018	0.873023
		**	0.842490	0.953348	0.877034
	English	*	0.738126	0.904686	0.790883
		**	0.743433	0.903812	0.795509

Acknowledgment

This study has been supported by Iran University of Science and Technology of Iran. We gratefully acknowledge the support of the research department.

References

[1] Hatori, J. Matsuzaki, T., Miyao, Y. & Tsujii, J. I. (2012). Incremental joint approach to word segmentation, pos tagging, and dependency parsing in chinese. In Proceedings of the 50th Annual Meeting of the Association for Computational Linguistics, vol. 1, pp. 1045-1053.

[2] Bohnet, B. & Nivre, J. (2012). A transition-based system for joint part-of-speech tagging and labeled non-projective dependency parsing. In Proceedings of the 2012 Joint Conference on Empirical Methods in Natural Language Processing and Computational Natural Language Learning, pp. 1455-1465.

[3] Hatori, J., Matsuzaki, T., Miyao, Y. & Jun'ichiTsujii. (2011). Incremental Joint POS Tagging and Dependency Parsing in Chinese. In IJCNLP, pp. 1216-1224.

[4] Li, Z., Zhang, M., Che, W., Liu, T., Chen, W. & Li, H. (2011). Joint models for Chinese POS tagging and dependency parsing. In Proceedings of the Conference on Empirical Methods in Natural Language Processing, pp. 1180-1191.

[5] Li, Z., Zhang, M., Che, W., Liu, T. & Chen, W. (2012). A Separately Passive-Aggressive Training Algorithm for Joint POS Tagging and Dependency Parsing. In COLING, pp. 1681-1698.

[6] Seraji, M., Megyesi, B. & Nivre, J. (2012). Dependency parsers for Persian. In COLING, pp. 35-44.

[7] Khallash, M., Hadian, A. & Minaei-Bidgoli, B. (2013). An Empirical Study on the Effect of Morphological and Lexical Features in Persian Dependency Parsing. In Fourth Workshop on Statistical Parsing of Morphologically Rich Languages, pp. 97-107.

[8] Toutanova, K., Klein, D., Manning, C. D. & Singer, Y. (2003). Feature-rich part-of-speech tagging with a cyclic dependency network. In Proceedings of the 2003 Conference of the North American Chapter of the Association for Computational Linguistics on Human Language Technology, vol. 1, pp. 173-180.

[9] Rasooli, M. S., Kouhestani, M. & Moloodi, A. (2013). Development of a Persian syntactic dependency treebank. In Proceedings of the 2013 Conference of the North American Chapter of the Association for Computational Linguistics on Human Language Technologies, pp. 306-314.

[10] Bies, A., Mott, J., Warner, C. & Kulick, S. (2012). English Web Treebank. Technical Report LDC2012T13, Linguistic Data Consortium, Philadelphia, PA.

[11] Zahedi, M. & Arjomandzadeh, A. (2015). A new model for Persian multi-part words edition based on statistical machine translation. Journal of AI and Data Mining, vol. 4, no. 1, pp. 27-34.

8

Speech enhancement based on hidden Markov model using sparse code shrinkage

E. Golrasan[*] and H. Sameti

Department of Computer Engineering, Sharif University of Technology, Tehran, Iran.

*Corresponding author: egolrasan@yahoo.com (E. Golrasan).

Abstract

This paper presents a new hidden Markov model-based (HMM-based) speech enhancement framework based on the independent component analysis (ICA). We propose analytical procedures for training clean speech and noise models using the Baum re-estimation algorithm, and present a maximum a posteriori (MAP) estimator based on the Laplace-Gaussian (for clean speech and noise, respectively) combination in the HMM framework, namely sparse code shrinkage-HMM (SCS-HMM).

The proposed method on the TIMIT database in the presence of three noise types at three SNR levels in terms of PESQ and SNR are evaluated and compared with Auto-Regressive HMM (AR-HMM) and speech enhancement based on HMM with discrete cosine transform (DCT) coefficients using the Laplace and Gaussian distributions (LaGa-HMM$_{DCT}$). The results obtained confirm the superiority of the SCS-HMM method in the presence of non-stationary noises compared to LaGa-HMM$_{DCT}$. The results of the SCS-HMM method represent a better performance of this method compared to AR-HMM in the presence of white noise based on the PESQ measure.

Keywords: *Speech Enhancement, HMM-based Speech Enhancement, Multivariate Laplace Distribution, Independent Component Analysis (ICA transform), Sparse Code Shrinkage Enhancement Method.*

1. Introduction

Speech enhancement aims to improve speech quality using various algorithms. Enhancing speech degraded by noise, or noise reduction, is the most important field of speech enhancement, and is used for many applications such as mobile phones, VoIP, teleconferencing systems, speech recognition, and hearing aids.

Among the different proposed solutions, the statistical approach in speech enhancement is often preferred due to the stochastic nature of speech signals [1]. Generally, the statistical methods are divided into the model-based [2, 3] and non-model-based [4, 5] techniques. In the model-based procedures, the clean speech and noise models are first generated in a training phase, and then the clean speech is estimated based on this prior information in a test phase. The non-model-based procedures only consist of the test phase, and the required information is estimated using the noisy speech. Under the non-stationary noisy conditions, the model-based

techniques have advantages over the non-model-based techniques through prior information [3].

Hidden Markov Model (HMM) is one of the powerful model-based methods applied to speech enhancement and has resulted in high efficiency, especially under non-stationary noisy conditions [2]. One of the most important factors that influences the model precision of an HMM is the probability density function (pdf) of clean speech, noise, and noisy speech. In the HHM-based speech enhancement, the Gaussian pdf is used to model clean speech and noise, while the recent studies [4,6,7] have shown that clean speech and noise pdf are non-Gaussian distributions. The multivariate Laplace distribution has been recommended for modeling HMM as a non-Gaussian distribution [8]. In this modeling, using multivariate Laplace distribution causes a non-closed form formula. To solve this problem, it was assumed that the DCT coefficients were statistically independent, whereas DCT only reduces the correlation between the coefficients, and they are not completely uncorrelated to each other. If we assume that the DCT coefficients are uncorrelated to each other and that the distribution of coefficients is Laplace, we cannot assume that the coefficients are statistically independent. If we use independent component analysis (ICA) instead of DCT, whose coefficients are greatly statistically independent from each other, we can do a more accurate statistical modeling.

We modeled the clean speech signal using HMM in ICA domain with Laplace distribution, while doing the noise modeling only by assuming Gaussian pdf for noises. In this work, we propose a novel MAP HMM-based speech enhancement algorithm that uses the ICA transformation. Our theoretical analysis shows that under the assumption of Laplace clean speech and Gaussian noise, the proposed algorithm leads to a well-known enhancement technique, sparse code shrinkage. This paper is organized as follows. In Section 2, the HMM training methods are reviewed. In Section 3, the MAP estimator is derived based on HMM in the ICA space. In Section 4, a summary of the proposed algorithm is given. In Section 5, we present the experimental evaluation and results, and in Section 6, the conclusions are given.

2. Signal model

Assume a time-domain noisy speech vector y_n at time n that is composed of a clean speech vector s_n and an additive noise vector d_n given as (1). Taking the independent component analysis (ICA) of y_n, we get (2) in this equation. We assumed that noise is independent from clean speech, and that the vectors have the length L and a zero mean. The AR features of Pth order $a_n=[1,a(1),...,a(p)]$ for $s_n=[s(0),s(1),...,s(L-1)]$ could be derived by the linear predictive coefficient approach [9], and the AR coefficients of other signals are obtained analogously.

$$y_n = s_n + d_n \tag{1}$$

$$Y_{ICA} = S_{ICA} + D_{ICA} \tag{2}$$

An HMM with M states and N mixtures is defined as $\lambda = (\pi_{1 \times M}, a_{M \times M}, c_{M \times N}, \delta_{M \times N \times L})$, where π is the initial state distribution, a denotes the state transition probability distribution, c is the probability distribution for each mixture in each state, and $\delta_{M \times N \times L}$ is the matrix of pdf parameters in each mixture. The parameters of λ are estimated by the Baum re-estimation formulas

[10]. In order to estimate clean speech from noisy signal, it is necessary to construct the HMM models for clean speech (λ_S) and noise (λ_D) separately, and then combine them to create the noisy HMM (λ_Y).

2.1. Speech model

Based on the central limit theorem, we can assume that S_{ICA} has a multivariate Gaussian pdf with independent coefficients according to (3) and (5). In these equations, index k shows the kth ICA coefficient of an L-dimensional vector.

As shown in [6], the Laplace distribution function, compared to the Gaussian distribution function, is closer to the speech signal distribution in different domains, and thus we can consider the distribution of vector S_{ICA} as a multivariate Laplace pdf. We know that the ICA coefficients are independent. Therefore, the multivariate Laplace pdf of S_{ICA} is derived by (4) and (5), where b_k is the scale parameter of the kth coefficient. In these equations, it is assumed that S_{ICA} has a zero mean.

$$p(S_{ICA}(k)) = \frac{1}{\sqrt{2\pi}\sigma_k} \exp(-\frac{(S_{ICA}(k))^2}{2\sigma_k^2}) \tag{3}$$

$$p(S_{ICA}(k)) = \frac{1}{2b_k} \exp(-\frac{|S_{ICA}(k)|}{b_k}) \tag{4}$$

$$p(S_{ICA}) = \prod_{k=0}^{L-1} p(S_{ICA}(k)) \tag{5}$$

We used (4) and (5) for each mixture in each state, and estimated the model parameters of λ_S in closed form using the Baum's auxiliary function. In fact, changing Gaussian pdf to Laplace pdf in each HMM mixture modifies the equations for parameter estimation of δ_S (the Laplace scale parameter estimation in each mixture in each state). Estimation of the Laplace scale parameter can be derived by differentiating the auxiliary function of (6) with respect to scale parameter resulting in (7).

$$Q(\lambda_s, \lambda_s^{old}) = \sum_{j=1}^{M} \gamma_1(j) \ln(\pi_j) + \sum_{n=1}^{T-1} \sum_{i=1}^{M} \sum_{j=1}^{M} \varepsilon_n(i,j) \ln(a_{ij})$$
$$+ \sum_{n=1}^{T-1} \sum_{j=1}^{M} \gamma_n(j) \ln(p(S_{ICA} | \varphi_j)) \tag{6}$$

$$\bar{b}_{j,k} = \frac{\partial Q}{\partial b_{j,k}} = \frac{\sum_{n=1}^{T-1} \gamma_n(j) | S_{ICA} |}{\sum_{n=1}^{T-1} \gamma_n(j)} \tag{7}$$

In the above-mentioned equations, $\gamma_n(j)$ is the probability of being in state j at time n, $\varepsilon_n(i,j)$ is the transition probability of state i at time n to state j at time $n+1$, and $p(S_{ICA} | \varphi_j)$ is obtained using (4) and (5), where $\varphi_j(k)$ equals the scale parameter of the kth dimension in state j ($\varphi_j(k) = b_{j,k}$).

2.2. Noise model

In this work, we assumed that D_{ICA} had a multivariate Gaussian distribution. In other words, if we use (3) and (5) for each mixture in each state, then we can estimate the model parameters of λ_D using the Baum's auxiliary function. Therefore, estimation of $\delta_{D,M \times N \times L}$ in model λ_D, can be interpreted as estimation of the diagonal covariance matrix (Σ_D) for each mixture in each state. This means that the main diagonal of the covariance matrix contains the variances for each independent dimension.

3. Map estimation

In this section, we present the MAP estimation based on the Hidden Markov model that in the ICA space. We assumed, that the speech distribution was non-Gaussian, and that the noise distribution was Gaussian. Studies have shown that the proposed framework under the assumption that the signal is non-Gaussian and the noise is Gaussian leads to a sparse code shrinkage [11], which we called the SCS-HMM technique.

Let s_t be an L-dimensional vector of the clean speech. Similarly, let d_t be an L-dimensional vector of the noise. Assume that the noise is additive and statistically independent of the speech. Let $y_t = s_t + d_t$ be an L-dimensional vector of the noisy speech. Let $s_0^T = \{s_t; t = 1:T\}$, $d_0^T = \{d_t; t = 1:T\}$, and $y_0^T = \{y_t; t = 1:T\}$. The MAP estimation of clean speech s_t, given as y_0^T, is obtained by maximizing $\mathrm{p}(s_t | y_0^T)$ over s_t. Therefore, we applied the EM algorithm for the iterative local maximization of $\mathrm{p}(s_t | y_0^T)$.

In this method, at each iteration, the auxiliary function is maximized in (8),

$$Q(s_t^{k+1}) = \sum_{q,u} p_\lambda(q,u | s_t^k) \ln p_\lambda(q,u,s_t^{k+1} | y_t) \quad (8)$$

where, s_t^k and s_t^{k+1} denote the estimate of s_t as obtained in the kth and $k+1th$ iteration, respectively. Maximization of $Q(s_t^{k+1})$ over s_t^{k+1} results in an estimate for which

$\ln p(s_t^{k+1} | y_t) \geq \ln p(s_t^k | y_t)$, where equality holds if and only if $s_t^{k+1} = s_t^k$.

Maximization of (8) results in the following signal re-estimation formula:

$$s_t^{k+1} = \arg\max_{s_t^{k+1}} \sum_{q,u} p_\lambda(q,u | s_t^k) \ln p_\lambda(q,u,s_t^{k+1} | y_t) \quad (9)$$

$$= \sum_{q,u} p_\lambda(q,u | s_t^k) \arg\max_{s_t^{k+1}} (\ln p_\lambda(q,u,s_t^{k+1},y_t))$$

$$= \sum_{q,u} p_\lambda(q,u | s_t^k) \arg\max_{s_t^{k+1}} (\ln p_\lambda(q,u,s_t^{k+1} | y_t))$$

where,

$$p_{\lambda_s \lambda_d}(q,u,s_t^{k+1},y_t) = p_{\lambda_s \lambda_d}(y_t | q,u,s_t^{k+1}) p_{\lambda_s}(q,u,s_t^{k+1}) \quad (10)$$
$$= p_{\lambda_d}(y_t | s_t^{k+1}) p_{\lambda_s}(q,u,s_t^{k+1}) = p_{\lambda_d}(y_t - s_t^{k+1}) p_{\lambda_s}(q,u,s_t^{k+1})$$

On substituting (10) into (9), we obtained the following formula:

$$s_t^{k+1} = \sum_{q,u} p_\lambda(q,u | s_t^k). \quad (11)$$

$$\arg\max_{s_t^{k+1}} (\ln p_{\lambda_d}(y_t - s_t^{k+1}) + \ln p_{\lambda_s}(q,u,s_t^{k+1}))$$

For a Gaussian distributed noise, the term $\ln p_{\lambda_d}(y_t - s_t^{k+1})$ in (11) has no extremum. Therefore, the maximization in (11) is decided only by the term $\ln p_{\lambda_s}(q,u,s_t^{k+1})$. In order to estimate the clean signal in the ICA space, we used the ICA unmixing matrix w_s, obtained from the training phase. Thus, the estimate of signal s can be obtained by letting $w_d = w_s$. For clarity of presentation, we denoted w_s by w. In this case, the MAP estimation rule from (11) can be expressed in the form of:

$$s_t^{k+1} = \sum_{q,u} p_\lambda(q,u | w s_t^k) \arg\max(\sum_{l=1}^{L} (\ln p_{\lambda_d}(w_{l.}(y_t - s_t^{k+1})) \quad (12)$$
$$+ \ln p_{\lambda_s}(q,u,w_{l.}(s_t^{k+1}))) + 2\ln|\det(w)|)$$

where, $w_{l.} = w(l,:)$ denotes the lth row of matrix w. In (12), the conditional probability $p_\lambda(q,u | w.s_t^k)$ is calculated by the forward-backward algorithm [12], and the second term of the above equation is calculated as follows:

$$s_t = \arg\max_{s_t}(\sum_{l=1}^{L} \ln p_{\lambda_d}(w_{l.}(y_t - s_t)) \quad (13)$$
$$+ \ln p_{\lambda_s}(q,u,w_{l.}(s_t))) + 2\ln|\det(w)|)$$

We can perform the estimation in the independent space first, and then transform the estimate obtained into the original space. Denote $w_{l.}y_t$ as $z_t(l)$ and $w_{l.}s_t$ as $x_t(l)$. Thus the components of vector x_t can be calculated by the equations (14) and (15):

$$x_t = \begin{bmatrix} x_t(1) \\ \vdots \\ x_t(l) \\ \vdots \\ x_t(L) \end{bmatrix} \qquad (14)$$

$$x_t(l) = \arg\max_x (\ln p_{\lambda_d}(z_t(l) - x_t(l)) + \ln p_{\lambda_s}(x_t(l)\,|\,q,u)) \quad (15)$$

$$\Leftrightarrow \arg\min_x (\frac{1}{2\sigma^2}(z_t(l) - x_t(l))^2 + f^{u|q}(x_t(l)))$$

where, $f^{u|q}(x_t(l)) = -\ln p_{\lambda_s}(x_t(l)\,|\,q,u)$. The minimization is equivalent to solving the following equation:

$$\frac{1}{\sigma^2}(x_t(l) - z_t(l)) + f'^{u|q}(x_t(l)) = 0 \qquad (16)$$

Although (16) may not have a closed form solution, the estimation function can be approximated as follows [13]:

$$x_t(l) = sign(z_t(l))\max(0,|z_t(l)| - \sigma^2 \frac{1}{b_{u|q}}) \qquad (17)$$

In the above equation, $b_{u|q}$ is the scale parameter of the fourth mixture in the qth state. The estimation rule in (17) is known as the sparse code shrinkage estimation [11]. Given the two words $p_\lambda(q,u\,|\,w.s_t^k)$ and

$$\sum_{l=1}^{L} \arg\max_x (\ln p_{\lambda_d}(w_l(y_t - s_t)) + \ln p_{\lambda_s}(w_l(s_t)\,|\,q,u)),$$

we can estimate the clean signal component by (11).

4. Summary of the proposed SCS-HMM algorithm

This section provides a summary of the steps involved in the proposed SCS-HMM enhancement algorithm, as described in Sections 2 and 3.

1. First, using two sets of data $\tilde{s}$ and $\tilde{d}$, which should have the same statistical properties as the noise d and signal s, calculate the ICA transformation matrices w_d and w_s. This can be performed using any of the existing ICA algorithms.
2. Train HMM using the independent components $S_{ICA} = w_s\tilde{s}$ and $D_{ICA} = w_d\tilde{d}$, as described in Sections 2.1 and 2.2, respectively.

3. To perform the enhancement process of the observed noisy signal y, we applied the estimation rule (11) to estimate the clean speech $\hat{s}$.

5. Experimental evaluation

The objective evaluation of AR-HMM, LaGa-HMM, and the proposed algorithm was performed in terms of the SNR and PESQ measures. The experimental evaluation was performed using the speech signals selected from the TIMIT database, separately for each gender. The training set contained 100 sentences for each gender, and the testing set contained the sentences of the speaker female and male. There were no common sentences between the training and test sets. The noisy speech signals were created by adding different noises such as the white, babble, and machinegun noises at 0 db, 5 db, and 10 db. All of the signals were sampled at 8 kHz. The signals were split into frames of 64 samples using the rectangular window. The fast-ICA algorithm [14] was employed to estimate the ICA basis functions based on the training set. In the training phases of the various models, there was no inter-frame overlap. The clean speech models were generated using 10 states and 30 mixtures. In AR-HMM and LaGa-HMM, the noise models were constructed based on 4 states and 4 mixtures. Due to the use of MAP estimation in the SCS-HMM method, the noise model was generated using 1 state and 1 mixture. In AR-HMM, we used an AR-order of 10 for a clean speech and noise. The fast-ICA algorithm was employed to estimate the ICA basis functions based on the training data. The performance of the proposed algorithm SCS-HMM was compared with AR-HMM in [12], and LaGa-HMM$_{DCT}$ in [8]. Tables 1 and 2, respectively, demonstrate the SNR and PESQ values achieved by AR-HMM, LaGa-HMM$_{DCT}$, and SCS-HMM. The results obtained confirm the superiority of the SCS-HMM method in the presence of non-stationary noises compared to LaGa-HMM$_{DCT}$ based on the SNR measure. The results of the SCS-HMM method represent a better performance of this method, compared to AR-HMM, in the presence of white noise based on the PESQ measure.

This result is expected, because the MAP method is constructed based on stationary noises such as the white noise. For this reason, the performance of the SCS-HMM method is better than AR-HMM in the presence of white noise based on the PESQ measure. However, improvements in SNR results were not observed. An example of clean, noisy, and enhanced speech spectrograms are depicted in figure 1. Using the spectrogram representation, it can be seen that the SCS-HMM result is close to the original clean signal.

Table 1. Comparative performance in terms of SNR.

Enhancement algorithm		Babble noise			White noise			Machinegun noise		
		0dB	5dB	10dB	0dB	5dB	10dB	0dB	5dB	10dB
Male	AR-HMM	8.73	11.34	14.53	5.42	8.60	11.56	8.73	11.34	14.23
	LaGa-HMM$_{DCT}$	7.96	10.55	13.67	4.24	7.17	10.70	7.63	9.08	10.93
	SCS-HMM	8.59	10.89	13.79	5.34	8.34	11.49	7.36	9.24	11.53
Female	AR-HMM	6.37	9.44	12.87	7.29	9.74	12.43	10.35	13.34	16.14
	LaGa-HMM$_{DCT}$	5.41	7.75	11.57	6.93	9.06	11.16	7.92	9.63	12.10
	SCS-HMM	6.22	8.42	12.20	7.22	9.56	12.03	8.91	10.29	12.58

Table 2. Comparative performance in terms of PESQ.

Enhancement algorithm		Babble noise			White noise			Machinegun noise		
		0dB	5dB	10dB	0dB	5dB	10dB	0dB	5dB	10dB
Male	AR-HMM	2.05	2.41	2.73	1.79	2.08	2.33	2.80	3.01	3.25
	LaGa-HMM$_{DCT}$	1.75	2.24	2.59	1.76	2.03	2.30	2.62	2.93	3.08
	SCS-HMM	1.92	2.29	2.70	2.01	2.20	2.41	2.49	2.78	3.05
Female	AR-HMM	1.86	2.13	2.46	1.66	1.90	2.15	2.72	3.02	3.31
	LaGa-HMM$_{DCT}$	1.64	2.08	2.38	1.56	1.85	2.09	2.60	2.85	3.23
	SCS-HMM	1.71	2.10	2.44	1.70	1.90	2.23	2.47	2.80	3.14

6. Conclusion

In this paper, we presented a new HMM-based speech enhancement framework based on the independent component analysis (ICA). Furthermore, a MAP estimator was derived for the ICA coefficients of a clean speech. It was also shown that the proposed framework under the assumption of the signal being Laplace distribution and noise being Gaussian distribution led to sparse code shrinkage, called the SCS-HMM technique. The evaluation results, in terms of SNR and PESQ, indicated the superiority of the SCS-HMM method in the presence of non-stationary noises, compared to LaGa-HMM$_{DCT}$. The results of the SCS-HMM method represented a better performance of this measure. The performance of SCS-HMM in the presence of other noise types based on PESQ and in the presence of all noises based on SNR showed slightly inferior performance of this method.

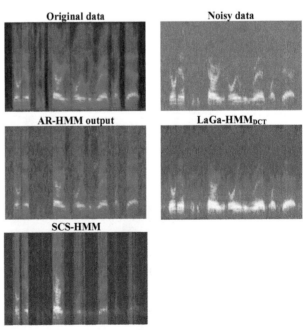

Figure 1. Spectrograms of female speech corrupted by white noise at SNR=5 dB.

References

[1] Zhao, D. Y. & Kleijn, W. B. (2007). HMM-Based Gain Modeling for Enhancement of Speech in Noise. IEEE Transactions on Audio, Speech and Language Processing, vol. 15, pp. 882-892.

[2] Sameti, H. & Deng, L. (2002). Nonstationary-state hidden Markov model representation of speech signals for speech enhancement. Signal Process., vol. 82, pp. 205-227.

[3] Srinivasan, S., Samuelsson, J. & Kleijn, W. B. (2006). Codebook Driven Short-Term Predictor Parameter Estimation for Speech Enhancement. IEEE Trans. on Audio, Speech & Language Processing, vol. 14, no. 1, pp.163-176.

[4] Martin, R. (2005). Speech Enhancement Based on Minimum Mean-Square Error Estimation and Super-Gaussian Priors. IEEE Trans. on Speech Audio Proc., vol. 13, no. 5, pp. 845–856.

[5] Lotter, T. & Vary, P. (2005). Speech Enhancement by MAP Spectral Amplitude Estimation Using a Super-Gaussian Speech Model. EURASIP Journal Appl. Signal Proc., vol. 2005, pp. 1110–1126.

[6] Gazor, S. & Zhang, W. (2003). Speech probability distribution. IEEE Signal Processing Letters, vol. 10, no. 7, pp. 204-207.

[7] Chen, B. & Loizou, P. (2007). A Laplacian-Based MMSE Estimator for Speech Enhancement. Speech Communication, vol. 49, no. 2, pp. 134-143.

[8] Aroudi, A., Veisi, H. & Sameti, H. (2012). Speech Enhancement Based on Hidden Markov Model with Discrete Cosine Transform Coefficients Using Laplace and Gaussian Distributions. in ISSPA, Conference on Information Science, Signal Processing and their Application, Montreal, Canada, pp 304-309.

[9] MARKEL, J. D., & GRAY, A. H. (2013). Linear Prediction of Speech, Springer-Verlag, New York.

[10] Bishop, C. M. (2006). Pattern Recognition and Machine Learning, Springer-Verlag New York.

[11] Wipf, D. (2006). Bayesian methods for finding sparse representations, Ph.D. Thesis, University of California, San Diego.

[12] Ephraim, Y., Malah, D. & Juang, B. H. (1989). On the Application of Hidden Markov Models for Enhancing Noisy Speech. IEEE Transactions on Acoustics, Speech, and Signal Processing, Vol. 37, No. 12, pp. 1846-56.

[13] Zou, X., Jancovic, P., Liu, J. & Köküer, M. (2008). Speech Signal Enhancement Based on MAP Algorithm in the ICA Space. IEEE Transactions on Signal Processing, vol. 56, no. 5, pp. 1812-1820.

[14] Langlois, D., Chartier, S. & Gosselin, D. (2010). independent component analysis: InfoMax and FastICA algorithms. Tutorials in Quantitative Methods for Psychology, vol. 6, no. 1, pp. 31–38.

9

Improving the performance of MFCC for Persian robust speech recognition

D. Darabian*, H. Marvi and M. Sharif Noughabi

Department of Electrical Engineering, University of Shahrood, Shahrood, Iran.

* Corresponding author:danial.darabian1@gmail.com (D. Darabian).

Abstract

The Mel Frequency cepstral coefficients are the most widely used feature in speech recognition but they are very sensitive to noise. In this paper to achieve a satisfactorily performance in Automatic Speech Recognition (ASR) applications we introduce a noise robust new set of MFCC vector estimated through following steps. First, spectral mean normalization is a pre-processing which applies to the noisy original speech signal. The pre-emphasized original speech segmented into overlapping time frames, then it is windowed by a modified hamming window .Higher order autocorrelation coefficients are extracted. The next step is to eliminate the lower order of the autocorrelation coefficients. The consequence pass from FFT block and then power spectrum of output is calculated. A Gaussian shape filter bank is applied to the results. Logarithm and two compensator blocks form which one is mean subtraction and the other one are root block applied to the results and DCT transformation is the last step. We use MLP neural network to evaluate the performance of proposed MFCC method and to classify the results. Some speech recognition experiments for various tasks indicate that the proposed algorithm is more robust than traditional ones in noisy condition.

Keywords: *MFCC, Autocorrelation, Gaussian Filter Bank, Root, Mean Normalization.*

1. Introduction

Today speech technologies are commercially available for an unlimited range of tasks. The historical background of this technology indicates that the first speech recognition systems were built at Bell's lab in 1950. Improvement in ASR systems capabilities with respect to speech variability factors typically noise was at 1980 - 1990. Nevertheless, it is still a challenge to use ASR systems in real world environment because they are exposed to significant level of noise and it makes mismatch in training and testing conditions in real world applications. Recent research concentrates on developing ASR systems that would be much more robust against factors which make variability in the speech in real world environment.

The mismatch between training and testing condition can be reduced at several levels of ASR system's speech processing chain. Approaches against speech variability factors can be classified in three different groups: 1. Speech enhancement, 2. Speech model adaptation, 3. Robust feature extraction. In this paper, we concentrate on robust feature extraction typically the Mel-frequency cepstral coefficients (MFCCs).

2. Recent methods to improve MFCC

Block diagram of the standard MFCC which includes fundamental steps to derive MFCC from an original input speech shown in figure 1.

Various approaches have been proposed to improve the tolerance of an ASR system with respect to noise and a great deal of work has been done for robust feature extraction typically MFCC.

In some cases, which make significant changes in MFCC the autocorrelation coefficient was mentioned to improve MFCC algorithm in 1999 [1]. The idea was to use one-sided autocorrelation sequences of speech instead of original speech because autocorrelation of the noise in many cases could be considered relatively constant over time so a high pass filtering could lead to suppress the noise furthermore (RAS-MFCC).

The technique mentioned above was used again in 2006 called AMFCC [2]. Since the background noise corrupts the autocorrelation coefficients of the speech signal mostly at lower time lags while the higher-lag autocorrelation coefficients are least affected, this method uses only the higher-lag autocorrelation coefficients. Eliminating the lower order of the noisy speech signal autocorrelations coefficients should lead to removal of the main noise components .The maximum autocorrelation index to be removed is usually found experimentally [3].

Spectral differentiation was applied on the higher-lag autocorrelation coefficients algorithm in 2010 (DRHOASS-MFCC).

Another research was done over log compression in 2001. Results showed that root compression is better than logarithm compression for noise robustness (ROOT-MFCC) [4,5].

In another paper published in 2009, a Gaussian shape filter bank in place of triangular shaped bins was introduced (GMFCC) [6]. The objective was to make a higher amount of correlations between sub-bands outputs. It was shown that the inverted Mel-frequency cepstral coefficients is useful feature set for ASR systems which contain complementary information presented in high frequency region individually as well as in combination with the conventional triangular filter based (IMFCC & IGMFCC)[6].

Cepstral mean normalization and spectral mean normalization technique called SMN-CMN MFCC was another method [7,8].

MFCC standard algorithm was improved in the implementation aspects in 2012[9] because it has a large amount of computation and this is disadvantage in real time applications. An improved MFCC algorithm called MFCC-E was introduced that it reduced computations by 50% and made hardware implementations easy.

In [10] the AGC-MFCC has been used to improve MFCC algorithm.

Improvement in this algorithm is progressing rapidly and the development mentioned above was just only some limited cases. This paper is the complementary efforts, which follow previous work.

According to the recent methods mentioned above MFCC can be classified in three different groups:

1. Modifications in the standard blocks.
2. Modification includes adding some complementary blocks to the standard algorithm.
3. Modification includes reduce in hardware implementation.

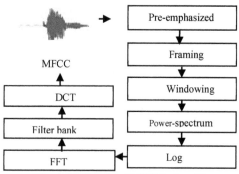

Figure 1. Standard MFCC algorithm.

In this paper, the aim is to improve MFCC algorithm with respect to adding complementary blocks and modification in the standard block.

In the next section, the proposed method is described.

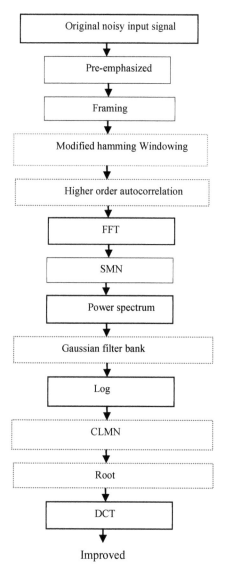

Figure 2. Proposed robust feature extraction algorithm (AGCR-MFCC).

3. Proposed method
This section describes our novel method to obtain new set of MFCC feature vector.

As mentioned in the recent methods section to improve MFCC algorithm, we introduce some methods used previously such as Gaussian filter banks, Modified hamming window, Higher order autocorrelation, Root method, Modified hamming window they are used separately in the standard algorithm without modifying other standard block but no one tried to combine all these advantages together but we try to do and to find out a way to combine last proposed methods: furthermore, we introduce new compensator blocks which they will improve recognition rate.

As illustrated in Figure 2 at the first step the input original noisy speech signal pass through pre-emphasized block using pre-emphasis filter in (1):

$$P(z) = 1\text{-}\alpha z^{-1} \qquad (1)$$

Then frame blocking is performed and the modified hamming window is applied to the each frame.

3.1. Modified hamming window
In this paper, we use a family of hamming window, which is introduced in a paper in 2012[11].
If w (n) be a simple hamming window, our using window is in (2):

$$w_{new}(n) = n\, w\,(n) \qquad (2)$$

The changes applied to the simple hamming window are in three different aspects:
1. Spectral leakage factor
2. Relative side lobe attenuation
3. Main lobe width
It can be observed that the spectral leakage increases and side lobe attenuation decreases to some extent which they have minor effect in recognition performance but considerably increase in main lobe width and will help to improve recognition performance. The changes in simple hamming window illustrated in figure 3.

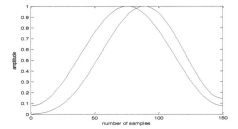

Figure 3. Hamming window (----) and modified hamming window (----).

3.2. Higher order autocorrelation
One-sided autocorrelation sequences of the framed signal passed from modified hamming window, which are obtained, and the lower lags of the autocorrelation sequences are removed [3]. It can further suppress the noise.

If d(m,k) is additive noise and s(m,k) is noise-free speech signal which m is number of frames and k is samples number then :

$$X(m,k) = s(m,k) + d(m,k) \qquad (3)$$

If the noise is uncorrelated with the speech it follows that the autocorrelation of the noisy speech is the sum of autocorrelation of clean speech and autocorrelation of the noise:

$$R_{xx(m,k)} = R_{ss(m,k)} + R_{dd(m,k)} \qquad (4)$$

If the additive noise is assumed to be stationary the autocorrelation sequences of noise can be considered to be identical for all frames and eliminating the lower order of the noisy speech signal autocorrelation coefficients should lead to removal of the main noise components. The maximum autocorrelation index to be removed is usually found experimentally which is selected in the following experiments section.

$$R_{xx(m,k)} = R_{ss(m,k)} + R_{dd(m)} \qquad (5)$$

Then Fourier transform is calculated and power spectrum is found. Next step is SMN block which we use it to suppress the additive noise furthermore. Then we apply a Gaussian shape filter bank.

3.3. Gaussian shape filter bank
Triangular shape filter bank is used in the standard algorithm. A triangular shape filter bank is a symmetric tapered but does not provide any weight outside the sub bands that it covers (Figure 4). As a result, the correlation between a sub band and its nearby spectral component from adjacent sub bands is lost. It is proposed here a Gaussian shape filter bank[6] which provides gradually decaying weights at it's both ends for compensating possible loss of correlation the expression for GF can be written as:

$$\varphi_i = e^{\frac{-(k-kb_i)}{2\sigma_i^2}} \qquad (6)$$

$$kbi = (i+1)\,.\,\Delta_{mel} \qquad (7)$$

where, in (6) and (7) sigma is variance of any sub bands and kb is boundary points in triangular filter bank derived from equations below (i, is the number of Gaussian):

$$\Delta_{mel} = \frac{f_{max(mel)}}{i+1} \qquad (8)$$

In (8) f_{max} is maximum sampling frequency rate and it is calculated in Mel-Scale through (9):

$$f_{mel}=2595 \log (1+\frac{f}{700}) \qquad (9)$$

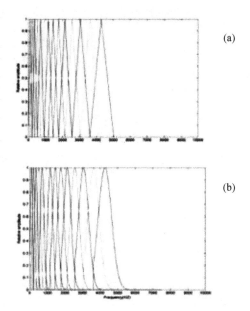

(a)

(b)

Figure 4. a: Triangular filter bank , b: Gaussian filter.

3.3. CLMN and root blocks

The proposed algorithm uses spectral mean normalization to suppress the additive noise and uses cepstral log mean normalization after logarithm to remove the effect of convolution noise. Combination of CLMN and SMN can inhibit additive and convolution noise at the same time. In this paper SMN block applies after FFT block and CLMN applies after logarithm function to compensate vulnerability of logarithm to convolution noise we name that CLMN (cepstral logarithm mean normalization).

The calculations of SMN and CLMN are based on this fact that expectation of noisy part is constant so it can be removed in CLMN and SMN process which is shown in equations below:

$$X(m,k) = S(m,k) + d(m,k) \qquad (10)$$

$$\hat{x}(m, k) = x(m, k)-E[x(m, k)]$$

$$= \{s(m, k)+d(k)\}-\{E[s(m, k)+d(k)]\} \qquad (11)$$

$$= s(m, k)-E[s(m, k)] = \hat{s}(m, k)$$

Logarithm function in the MFCC generation is very sensitive to noise and is one reason for poor noise performance of MFCC. After logarithm function CLMN is used. The root compression block is the next block in our proposed algorithm due to generating values close to zero after CLMN [4,5]. The log function gives large negative values for input close to zero and this leads to spreading of the energy. CLMN doesn't change

these values and its task is just to suppress convolution noise and they are still close to zero (furthermore CLMN makes data more close to zero). So root compression is used and followed by DCT leads to better compaction of the energy. The large negative excursion of CLMN outputs for values close to zero leads to a splattering of energy whereas root compression, which express as $(.)^{\alpha}$ with $0 <\alpha< 1$ leads to better compaction of energy. Algorithm uses root block after CLMN to achieve this aim. The application of CLMN is defined in the following equations:

$$X(m,k) = s(m,k) * d(k) \qquad (12)$$

$$X(m,k) = s(m.k) . d(k) \qquad (13)$$

$$LogX(m,k)=log(S(m,k).H(k))=logS(m,k)+logH(k) \qquad (14)$$

$$Log X(m,k)-E(Log X(m,k)) =$$

$$logS(m,k)+logH(k)–E(logS(m,k))-logH(k)= \qquad (15)$$

$$log S(m,k) –E(log S(m,k))$$

In (13) the original signal is under convolution noise then the FFT applied and (14) is resulted then logarithm performance make the conversion of multiplying to the adding and expectation function suppress the noise according to (15).

We call our proposed method as AGCR-MFCC which A stands for "Autocorrelation" G stands for "Gaussian shape filter bank" and C stands for "CLMN" and R stands for "Root".

4. Experimental setup

In order to evaluate the performance of proposed algorithm and to classify, we use MLP neural network with one input layer, two hidden layer and one output layer. We experiment some other hidden layer values but the results show that it has the best results. Number of neurons in the two hidden layer can be chosen by a user in the MATLAB code. We spot them both 50 because at this value network has the best response.

60 words which are chosen through 10 different speakers with 15 repetition in each word have been chosen so we have 60 classes (and so 60 output neurons), and 900 words.

70% of the entire data (630 words) is used for training and 30% (270 words) is used for testing.

The proposed approach was implemented on Farsdat speech data base. Frame length is appropriate to speech length but the number of frames is constant 60 and length of window is 50ms and sampling frequency is 22000.

To obtain the noisy speeches the clean speech corrupted by artificial white Gaussian noise (WGN) in four different signals to noise ratio (SNR) levels. Silence speech parts are removed using a general silence detection technique. Figure 5 illustrates a general form of MLP neural network, which is used to classify in this paper.

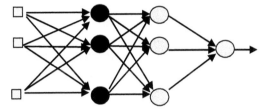

Figure 5. Neural network with two hidden layer [12].

As mentioned the Data base is divided into training set and testing set. Features vector sets of size 14 are extracted using different family of MFCC: standard MFCC, RAS-MFCC, AMFCC, ROOT-MFCC, GMFCC, AGMFCC and AGCR-MFCC (proposed method) and their performances are compared. As describe above, adding the artificial Gaussian noise at four SNR levels generate the polluted testing utterances. Using a random number generation program generates the white noise.

4.1. Experimental results

As described in the section 3.2, the maximum autocorrelation index to be removed is usually found experimentally, Table 1 shows experiment results which lead to selecting the best index to be removed .

Table 1. Various index was experimented to select the best and appropriate index (T: threshold) to be removed at autocorrelation segment in AGCR-MFCC. Experiment results show that the highest noisy average recognition ratio belong to T=100.

Index	20dB	10dB	5dB	0dB	Noisy average recognition ratio
T=10	77	72	65.6	55	67.4
T=30	75.3	73.2	67.5	64.6	70.15
T=50	73.5	73	72.5	40	64.75
T=70	77.3	77	61.6	55.5	67.85
T=100	83.5	80.8	77.7	76.91	78.91

In the Table 1 variable T (threshold) is the index whose experiments are performed on it and the results show that when T=100 is selected the best speech recognition occurred.

Figure 6 and Figure 7 shows a comparative results to select the best index to be removed as it is shown in the T=100 the best speech recognition rate is achieved. The process of experiments is explained at experimental setup and the other details are explained in the following section.

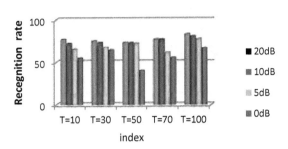

Figure 6. A comparative results to select the best index to be removed as it is shown T=100 has the best recognition rate.

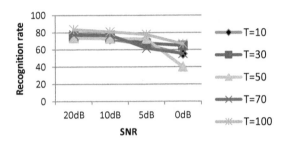

Figure 7. Results which depict that T=100 has the best speech recognition rate.

In order to use the root compression block in the modified algorithm it should be determined variable α.

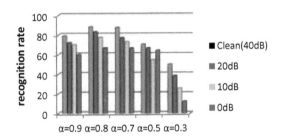

Figure 8. Various α values was experimented and α=0.8 was selected because of better recognition rate in some certain SNR.

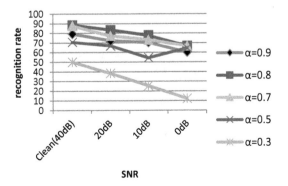

Figure 9. Results which depict that α=0.8 has the best speech recognition rate.

We study some various α rates and choose the best one in noisy condition. We tried various α rates .Some experiments were done to select the best value of α for the best speech recognition application. The results of corresponding experiments α sets 0.8. Table 2 includes the experiment results to select the best root value to use after CLMN block.

Table 2. The experiments to select the best root for using after CLMN block was performed. Results show that α=0.8 yields better speech recognition accuracy in noisy condition. The highest noisy average recognition ratio occurred in α=0.8.

α values	Clean (40dB)	20dB	10dB	0dB	Noisy average recognition ratio
0.9	79.2	72.2	70.2	60.1	67.5
0.8	88.3	83.2	77.7	76.91	78.91
0.7	87.7	77.2	73.2	66.6	72.3
0.5	70.5	66.6	54.4	64.3	61.7
0.3	50	38.3	25.5	12.2	25.3

Results show that α=0.8 yields better speech recognition accuracy in noisy condition. The highest noisy average recognition ratio occurred in α=0.8. Figure 8 and 9 indicate that α=0.8 is an appropriate value in our Farsi speech recognition experiments. Then the general experiments performed to evaluate the performance of our novel method to obtain a new set of MFCC feature vectors with these determined values.

We compare the performance of MFCC, AMFCC, GMFCC, ROOT MFCC, CMN-SMN MFCC, AGMFCC, and AGCR-MFCC (proposed method) when training data and testing data are in clean (40dB) environment and after adding artificial noise at 4 SNR levels. The noises are added to the clean speech signal at 20,10,5 and 0dB SNRs table 3 indicates the results obtained using MFCC, AMFCC, GMFCC, ROOT MFCC, CMN-SMN MFCC, AGMFCC, AGCR-MFCC (proposed method) front-ends. For the case of speech sounds corrupted by white noise shown in Figure 10 and table 3 the performance of MFCC degrade most significantly among all features in presence of the noise and it was found to be worse among other robust features. Evidence depicts that the performance of MFCC degrades significantly compared with other feature vectors when added noise increases. It is due to standard MFCC is sensitive to noise and it was not an unexpected result whereas in the clean environment standard MFCC has still the best application than other suggested methods. Figure 10 shows a remarkable improvement especially in noisy condition (5dB, 0dB) for our proposed method. The best

performance comes from AGCR-MFCC with improvement in recognition score of %3.3 at 20dB %7.2 at 10dB 17.6% at 5dB and 27.41 % at 0dB in comparison with standard MFCC due to variations applied to the standard algorithm which makes it robust to noise such as including SMN block, Gaussian shape filter instead of triangular shape filter, autocorrelation and removing the lower orders. CLMN and ROOT compression block to compensate logarithm function but in clean condition the standard algorithm has still the best results and this is obvious because we know that standard MFCC feature has no problem in clean condition and its application degrade in the noisy condition and our proposed method has been organized to overcome this problem therefore we don't expect our proposed algorithm be better in clean condition. Our proposed algorithm running duration is more than standard algorithm but it is ignored. In the standard algorithm, the average of processing time is less than 1 minute but in our proposed one is less than 1.30 minutes to extract features.

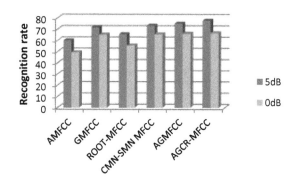

Figure 10. This figure shows that the results of experiments in the two noisy condition and as it is shown AGCR-MFCC has better recognition rate at noisy condition in comparative with other extracting MFCCs methods.

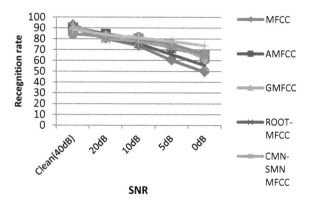

Figure 11. AGCR-MFCC has the best speech recognition especially in noisy condition such as 5dB and 0Db which the results are clearer in these SNRs.

Table 3. The entire training and testing data was used for experiments. Results for AGCR-MFCC show improvement in comparison with other traditional method in recognition rate when artificial white Gaussian additive noise increase. Noisy average recognition ratio proves that proposed method is more robust to noise than traditional methods.

SNR/feature	MFCC	AMFCC	GMFCC	ROOT-MFCC	CMN-SMN MFCC	AGMFCC	AGCR-MFCC (proposed method)
Clean(40dB)	93.2	90.2	91.5	89.9	91.2	84.4	88.8
20dB	80.2	84.4	82	80.1	80	82.3	83.5
10dB	73.6	80.1	81.3	75.5	77.7	81.5	80.8
5dB	60.1	71.6	74.6	65.55	72.2	75.09	77.7
0dB	49.5	65.2	62.2	55.6	65.6	66.08	76.91
Noisy average recognition ratio	65.85	75.32	75.02	69.18	73.87	76.24	78.91

5. Conclusion and future work

This paper modified one of the most common features for robust speech recognition application to improve ASR accuracy under noisy condition.

To evaluate the experiments, we use the MLP neural network for classification. In proposed method triangular, filter bank has been replaced by Gaussian shape filter bank then to compensate the undesirable effect of the noise and we use the CLMN and root compression blocks. Spectral mean normalization (SMN), Autocorrelation and eliminating the lower Order was other works which all made improve the noise-robustness of MFCC standard blocks.

Although these variations make computational costs because we will have more multiplying and adding computations typically in the autocorrelation, eliminating the lower order and Root block, Consequently more hardware logical gate is needed in hardware implementation but we pay these costs and certainly it is reasonable because the powerful application of MFCC algorithm is undeniable and as we know the standard algorithm degrade in presence of Noise drastically. If we Pay the computational and implementations costs, we can impart this feature even in presence of noise and we can keep it as a powerful feature in the future works [13,14].

Our research improvement model contains complementary blocks and modifications in the standard blocks were performed but there are still some blocks which were not examined and the question which has been still remained is that: is there any better replacement blocks for them?

Future works would involve these examinations. Further studding about hardware implementation which is an important necessity should be conducted.

References

[1] You, K. H. & wang, H. C. (1999). Robust features for noisy speech recognition based on temporal trajectory filtering of short time autocorrelation sequences. Speech communication, vol. 28, pp. 13-24.

[2] Shannon, B. J. & Paliwal, K. K. (2006). Feature extraction from higher lag autocorrelation coefficient for robust speech recognition, vol. 48, no. 11, pp. 1458-1481.

[3] Devand, A. & bansal, P. (2010). Robust feature extraction for noisy speech recognition from magnitude spectrum of higher order autocorrelation coefficients. International journal of computer application(0975-8887), vol. 10, no. 8.

[4] Lim, J. S. (1979). Spectral root holomorphic deconvolution system, IEEE Trans. ASSP, vol. 27, no. 3, pp. 223–233.

[5] Alexandre, P. & Lockwood, P. (1993). Root cepstral analysis: A unified view. Speech Communication, vol. 12, no. 3, pp 277–288.

[6] Chakroborty, S. & Saha, G. (2009). Improved Text-Independent Speaker Identification using Fused MFCC & IMFCC Feature Sets based on Gaussian Filter. International Journal of Signal Processing, vol. 5, no. 1, pp. 11-19.

[7] Sarikaya, R. & John, H. L. H. (2001). Analysis of the root-cepstrum for acoustic modeling and fast decoding in speech recognition. In: Euro speech, Aalborg, Denmark.

[8] Liu, F. H., Acero, A. & Stern, R. (1992). Efficient joint compensation of speech for the effects of additive noise and linear filtering. Proc. Of IEEE ICASP, vol. 1, pp. 257–260.

[9] Xie, C., Cao, X. & Lingling, H. (2012). Algorithm of Abnormal Audio Recognition Based on Improved MFCC. International workshop on information and electronic engineering (IWIEE), pp 731-737.

[10] Marvi, H., Darabian, D. & Sharif Noughabi, M. (2013). Robust speech recognition using modified MFCC and neural network. 11th ICIS conference Tehran.

[11] Sahidullah, M. D. & Saha, G. (2012). A novel windowing technique for efficient computation of MFCC for speaker recognition. Signal Processing Letters, IEEE, vol. 20, no. 2, pp. 149 – 152.

[12] Xiong, X. PhD thesis. (2009). Robust Speech Features and acoustic Models for Speech Recognition. Computer engineering Department, Nanina's Technological University.

[13] Zunjing, W. & Zhigang, C. (2005). Improved MFCC-Based Feature for Robust Speaker Identification. Identification Tsinghua Science and Technology ISSN, vol. 10, no. 2, pp.158-161.

10

Solution of multi-objective optimal reactive power dispatch using pareto optimality particle swarm optimization method

S.A. Taher, M. Pakdel

Department of Electrical Engineering, University of Kashan, Kashan, Iran

*Corresponding author: sataher@kashanu.ac.ir (S.A. Taher).).

Abstract

For Multi-Objective Optimal Reactive Power Dispatch (MORPD), a new approach is proposed as a simultaneous minimization of the active power transmission loss, the bus voltage deviation and the voltage stability index of a power system are obtained. Optimal settings of continuous and discrete control variables (e.g., generator voltages, tap positions of tap changing transformers and the number of shunt reactive compensation devices to be switched) are determined. MORPD is solved using Particle Swarm Optimization (PSO). Also, Pareto Optimality PSO (POPSO) is proposed to improve the performance of the multi-objective optimization task defined with competing and non-commensurable objectives. The decision maker requires to manage a representative Pareto-optimal set provided by imposition of a hierarchical clustering algorithm. The proposed approach was tested using IEEE 30-bus and IEEE 118-bus test systems. When simulation results are compared with several commonly used algorithms, they indicate better performance and good potential for their efficient applications in solving MORPD problems.

Keywords: *Optimal reactive power dispatch, Particle swarm optimization, Multi-objective, Pareto optimality, Voltage profile, Voltage stability.*

1. Introduction

The Optimal Reactive Power Dispatch (ORPD) has played significant roles in the security and economics of power systems. Using this, the operators can select a number of control tools such as switching reactive power compensators, changing generator voltages and adjusting transformer tap settings, and achieving the Optimal Power Flow (OPF). Considering the given set of physical and operating constraints involved, the equality constraints include power flow equations and the inequality restrictions in various reactive power sources. ORPD objective is to minimize the transmission loss of the power system, keep the voltage profiles within acceptable range and improve the voltage security while satisfying certain operation constraints. However, as the transmission networks have tended to become stressed in a large number of utilities across the globe due to a variety of reasons, many voltage collapse accidents have occurred over the last few

decades. Hence, voltage security has been considered in ORPD. The generator voltages are continuous variables, and the transformer ratios and shunt capacitors/inductors are discrete ones. The problem, therefore, has been defined as a non-linear, multi-uncertainty, multi-constraint, multi-minimum and multi-objective optimization (MOO) problem with a mixture of discrete and continuous variables.

A number of mathematical models for ORPD have been proposed in the literature [1–6]. Most of them adopt single-objective function and minimize it including transmission loss of the power system. Recently, minimizing voltage deviation from the desired values and improving voltage stability margin are considered as the objective function, making ORPD therefore, a MOO exercise [7–10]. In previous works, power losses and voltage deviation have received comparatively more attention than improving voltage stability. In this study, ORPD is similarly formulated as a MOO exercise with the objectives containing all three indices mentioned above as well as the operating constraints and load constraints.

Mathematical optimization techniques used to solve ORPD [1, 2, 7, 8] include gradient-based algorithms, linear programming, non-linear programming, Newton method and interior point methods. These conventional techniques require many mathematical assumptions, and hence, for problems involving non-continuous and non-linear functions, these techniques become less effective and are hardly ever used in recent years.

In recent decades, stochastic and heuristic optimization techniques, such as Evolutionary Algorithms (EAs), have emerged as efficient optimization tools [11]. EAs however, have been extensively employed for solving reactive power optimization [3–6, 9–10, 12-13]. Some of the prominent ones include Genetic Algorithm (GA) [14], particle swarm optimization (PSO) [15–19], differential evolution (DE) [20–22], seeker optimization algorithm (SOA) [23] and non-dominated sorting genetic algorithm-II (NSAGA-II) [24–25]. Theoretically, these techniques are able to converge to the near global optimum solution. PSO [26] was first suggested by Kennedy and Eberhart in 1995, and was subsequently employed successfully in power system studies for such applications as reactive power, voltage control, OPF, dynamic security border identification and state estimation [27–30].

Reviewing most studies to date, seems interesting to note that ORPD is not treated as a true multi-objective problem [18–19, 23], but instead, by linear combination of different objectives as a weighted sum, ORPD in effect has been often converted to a single objective problem. This unfortunately, requires multiple runs, as many times as the number of desired Pareto-optimal solutions. Furthermore, this method cannot be used to find Pareto-optimal solutions in problems having a non-convex Pareto-optimal front. In addition, there is no rational basis of determining adequate weights and the objective function formed might lose the significance due to combining non-commensurable objectives. To avoid this difficulty, in this study, the concept of Pareto-optimal set or Pareto-optimal front for MOO was presented as adopted in several works presented in the literature [9, 24–25]. This method is based on optimization of the most preferred objective while considering the other objectives as constraints bounded by some allowable levels. These levels are then altered to generate the entire Pareto-optimal

set. The most obvious weaknesses of this approach are time-consuming and finding weakly non-dominated solutions [31]. There are reports of Pareto optimization method being used to solve the reactive power optimization problem [9, 32], or to design the power system stabilizer [33].

In this paper, an approach is proposed based on Pareto Optimality PSO (POPSO) whose effectiveness is verified in solving a multi-objective ORPD (MORPD) by simulating results of two standard test systems, including IEEE 30-bus and IEEE 118-bus power systems. When comparing the study results with previous works, POPSO was shown to perform well in both test systems by showing the solutions near global optima.

2. Problem formulation
2.1. Objective functions
The objective functions for both ORPD and voltage control problem comprise three important terms in which technical and economic goals are considered. The economic goal is mainly to minimize the active power transmission loss. The technical goals are to minimize the load bus voltage deviation from the desired voltage and also the L-index to improve the voltage security [18].

2.1.1. Power loss
Minimizing the active power transmission loss can be described as follows [18]:

$$\textbf{Min} \quad P_{loss} = \sum_{k=1}^{N_E} Loss_k \tag{1}$$

Where, P_{loss} is the active power transmission loss of the power system, N_E is the number of branches and $Loss_k$ is the power losses of the kth branch.

2.1.2. Voltage deviation
An effective way to improve voltage profile is to minimize the selected deviation of voltage from the desired value as follow [18]:

$$\textbf{Min} \quad \sum \Delta V = \sum_{i=1}^{N_L} \left| V_i - V_i^{ref} \right| \tag{2}$$

Where, $\sum \Delta V$ is the sum of load bus voltage deviation, N_L is the total number of the system load buses, Vi and V_i^{ref} are actual and desired voltage magnitudes at bus i, respectively. In general, V_i^{ref} is set to be 1.0 pu.

2.1.3. Voltage stability index
There are several indices proposed for voltage stability and voltage collapse prediction, including:

voltage collapse proximity indicator (*VCPI*) [34] or voltage stability margin (*VSM*) [35]. However, *L*-index is a faster one presented by Kessel and Glavitsch [36] and developed further by Tuan et al [37]. In this paper, *L*-index is selected as the objective function for voltage stability index to improve the voltage security and keeps the operating system as far as possible from the voltage collapse point. Apart from the speedy calculation time needed to evaluate each load bus steady state voltage stability level, the chosen index can also take into account generator buses reaching reactive power limits. The *L*-index value ranges from zero to one; zero indicating a stable voltage condition (i.e. no system load) and one indicates voltage collapse. The bus with the highest *L*-index value will be the most vulnerable bus and hence, this method helps identifying the weakest areas needing critical reactive power support in the system. A summary of how *L*-index algorithm is evaluated is given below [18, 36]:

The transmission system itself is linear and allows a representation in terms of the node admittance matrix (*Y*). The network equations in this terms is:

$$\begin{bmatrix} I^L \\ I^G \end{bmatrix} = \begin{bmatrix} Y_1 & Y_2 \\ Y_3 & Y_4 \end{bmatrix} \cdot \begin{bmatrix} V^L \\ V^G \end{bmatrix} \tag{3}$$

Two categories of nodes are recognized: the load bus (PQ) set α_L and the generator bus (PV) set α_G. The hybrid matrix (*H*) can be generated from admittance matrix (*Y*) by a partial inversion as below:

$$\begin{bmatrix} V^L \\ I^G \end{bmatrix} = H \cdot \begin{bmatrix} I^L \\ V^G \end{bmatrix} = \begin{bmatrix} Z^{LL} & F^{LG} \\ K^{GL} & Y^{GG} \end{bmatrix} \cdot \begin{bmatrix} I^L \\ V^G \end{bmatrix}, \tag{4}$$

Where, V^L and I^L are vectors of voltages and currents at PQ buses; V^G and I^G are vectors of voltages and currents at PV buses; Z^{LL}, F^{LG}, K^{GL}, Y^{GG} are sub-matrices.

For any consumer node *j*, *j* v α_L, the following equation for V_j can be derived from the *H*-matrix:

$$V_j = \sum_{i \in \alpha_L} Z_{ji} . I_i + \sum_{i \in \alpha_G} F_{ji} V_i . \tag{5}$$

Voltage V_{oj} however, is been defined as:

$$V_{oj} = -\sum_{i \in \alpha_G} F_{ji} V_i . \tag{6}$$

Hence, the local indicator Lj becomes [36]:

$$L_j = \left| 1 - \frac{V_{oj}}{V_j} \right| = \left| 1 - \frac{\sum_{i \in \alpha_G} F_{ji} V_i}{V_j} \right| \tag{7}$$

Where, V_i and V_j are the complex voltages, and F_{ji} are the coefficients taken from a so-called *H* matrix, generated by a partial inversion of the nodal

admittance matrix and the coefficients describe the system structure.

For stable situations the condition $0 \leq L_j \leq 1$ must not be violated for any of the nodes *j*. Hence, a global indicator *L* describing the stability of the whole system may be described as:

$$L = \max_{j \in \alpha_L} (L_j) \tag{8}$$

The *L* value for the best individual is compared with the threshold value and if the value is less than that, it indicates a voltage secure condition. The threshold value is fixed by conducting off-line study on the system for different operating conditions, thereby, minimizing the system voltage indicator [18] that is:

$$\text{Min} f_3 = L \tag{9}$$

2.2. Constraints

Minimizing the said objective functions is subjected to a number of equality and inequality constraints as outlined below.

2.2.1. Equality constraint

This is essentially the load constraint, i.e. the active and reactive power balance described by the following set of power flow equations [18, 19]:

$$\begin{cases} 0 = P_i - V_i \sum_{j \in N_L} V_j (G_{ij} \cos \theta_{ij} + B_{ij} \sin \theta_{ij}), & i = 1, ..., N_{B-1} \\ 0 = Q_i - V_i \sum_{j \in N_L} V_j (G_{ij} \sin \theta_{ij} - B_{ij} \cos \theta_{ij}), & i = 1, ..., N_{PQ} \end{cases} \tag{10}$$

Where, V_i is the voltage magnitude at i^{th} bus, P_i and Q_i are net active and reactive power injection at bus *i*, G_{ij} and B_{ij} are the mutual conductance and susceptance between bus *i* and *j* respectively, θ_{ij} is the voltage angle difference between bus *i* and *j*, N_{B-1} is the total number of buses excluding slack bus, N_{PQ} is the set of *PQ* buses and N_L is the number of load buses.

2.2.2. Inequality constraint

Sometimes referred to as the operational constraint, this includes the generator voltages V_G, shunt compensations Q_C, transformer tap settings *T*, generator reactive power outputs Q_G and load bus voltages V_L defined as [18, 19]:

$$\begin{cases} V_{Gi\min} \leq V_{Gi} \leq V_{Gi\max}, & i = 1, ..., N_G \\ Q_{Ci\min} \leq Q_{Ci} \leq Q_{Ci\max}, & i = 1, ..., N_C \\ T_{i\min} \leq T_i \leq T_{i\max}, & i = 1, ..., N_T \\ Q_{Gi\min} \leq Q_{Gi} \leq Q_{Gi\max}, & i = 1, ..., N_G \\ V_{Li\min} \leq V_{Li} \leq V_{Li\max}, & i = 1, ..., N_L \end{cases} \tag{11}$$

Where, N_G, N_C, N_T and N_L are the total number of generators, shunt compensations, transformer taps and load buses, respectively.

2.3. Problem statement

In general, considering aggregation of objectives and constraints, power loss, voltage control and voltage stability index could be mathematically formulated as a non-linear constrained MOO as described below [18]:

$$
\left.
\begin{array}{ll}
Min & P_{loss}(x\,u) \\
Min & \sum \Delta V(x,u) \\
Min & L(x,u) \\
s\,t. & \\
& H(x,u) = 0 \\
& G_{min}(x,u) \leq G(x,u) \leq G_{max}(x,u)
\end{array}
\right\}
\quad (12)
$$

Where, x is the state variable vector, consisting of load bus voltages V_L and generator reactive power outputs Q_G; u is the control variable vector including generator voltages V_G, shunt compensations Q_C and transformer tap settings T. $H(x,u)$ and $G(x,u)$ are the compact forms of Eqs. (10) and (11), respectively.

3. Pareto Optimality Particle Swarm Optimization (POPSO)

3.1. Classical particle swarm optimization

PSO is a stochastic evolutionary computation optimization technique based on the movement of swarms [26]. It was inspired by social behavior of bird flocking or fish schooling. The population is considered as swarm, and each individual is called a particle randomly initialized. Each of these particles traverses the search space looking for the global minimum or maximum. The position of each particle corresponds to a candidate solution for the optimization problem, and is treated as a point in a D-dimensional space. For a given particle P_i, its position and velocity are represented as $x_i(t)=(x_{i,1}(t),...,x_{i,d}(t),...,x_{i,D}(t))$ and $v_i(t)=(v_{i,1}(t),...,v_{i,d}(t),...,v_{i,D}(t))$, respectively. The particles have memory and each particle keeps track of its previous best position. The best previous position (the position giving the best fitness value) found so far by particle P_i is recorded as $pbest_i=(p_{i,1},...,p_{i,d}...,p_{i,D})$. The swarm remembers another value which is the best position discovered by the swarm, The best previous position among all the particles in the population (or in the neighborhood) is represented as $gbest=(g_{i,1},...,g_{i,d},...,g_{i,D})$. The velocity for particle and the their positions are updated by the following two equations [18, 26]:

$$
v_{i,d}(t+1) = w \times v_{i,d}(t) + c_1 \times rand_1 \times (pbest_{i,d}(t) - x_{i,d}(t)) + c_2 \times rand_2 \times (gbest_d(t) - x_{i,d}(t)) \quad (13)
$$

$$
x_{i,d}(t+1) = x_{i,d}(t) + v_{i,d}(t+1) \quad (14)
$$

Where, w is the inertia weight, c_1 and c_2 are learning factors, $rand_1$ and $rand_2$ are two random functions in the range [0, 1]. The Eq. (13) is used to calculate the ith particle's velocity by taking three terms into consideration: the particle's previous velocity, the distance between the particle's best previous and current positions, and, finally, the distance between the position of the best particle in the swarm and the ith particle's current position. The ith particle flies toward a new searching point according to Eq. (14). In general, the performance of each particle is measured by a predefined problem-dependent fitness function.

PSO has three tuning parameters and the performance of its algorithm is influence by them. The parameters are w, c_1 and c_2 shown in Eq. (13). w is the inertia weight employed to control the impact of the previous history of velocities on the current one. Suitable selection of the inertia weight w can provide a balance between global and local exploration abilities, consequently on average less iteration is needed to find a sufficiently optimal solution [38]. The linearly decreasing w-strategy [39] decreases from w_{max} to w_{min}, according to the following equation:

$$
w = w_{max} - \frac{w_{max} - w_{min}}{iter_{max}} \times iter \quad (15)
$$

Where, $iter$ is the current iteration number and $iter_{max}$ is the maximum iteration number, w_{max} and w_{min} often set to 0.9 and 0.4, also c_1 and c_2 are the learning factors and determine the influence of personal best $pbest_i$ and global best $gbest$, respectively shown in Eq. (13). Most implementations [26–30] use a setting with $c_1 = c_2 = 2$, which means each particle will be attracted to the average of $pbest_i$ and $gbest$. Recently, reports show that it might be even better to choose a larger cognitive parameter c_1 than a social parameter c_2, but with this constraint $c_1 + c_2 \leq 4$ [40].

The number of particles or swarm size N_{pop} is one of the most important parameters that influence results of PSO. Too few particles will cause the algorithm to become stuck in a local minimum, while too many particles will slow down the algorithm. The algorithm performance depends therefore, on the parameters and the functions being optimized, so it is important to find a set of parameters that work well in all cases [18].

3.2. Pareto optimality concept

Optimization of several objective functions simultaneously, takes place frequently in power system studies. Generally, these functions are non-commensurable and often have conflicting objectives. There are two approaches for solving MOO problems. First, is the application of the traditional algorithms aiming to convert the multi-objective to a single objective optimization problem, often carried out by aggregating all objectives in a weighted function, or simply transforming all but one of the objectives into constraints. The advantage of such an approach is application existing single-objective optimization algorithms to solve problem directly and the limitations include: 1) requiring a pre-knowledge on the relative importance of the objectives and their limitations which are being converted into constraints; 2) inability to find multiple solutions in a single run, thereby requiring it to be applied as often as the number of desired Pareto optimal solutions; 3) difficulty in evaluating the trade-off between objectives and 4) search space should be convex, otherwise the solution may not be attainable. The second approach is based on Pareto optimality (PO) concept, where a set of optimal solutions is found, instead of one optimal solution. The reason for the optimality of many solutions is that no one can be considered to be better than any other with respect to all objective functions. Compared with traditional algorithms, PO is more suitable for solving MOO not only due to the ability to obtain multiple solutions in a single run, but, a good spread of the non-dominated solutions can also be obtained [41].

The following definitions describe concept of Pareto-optimal mathematically [41]:

Def. 1 The general MOO problem consists of a number of objectives to be optimized simultaneously and is associated with a number of equality and inequality constraints. It can be formulated as follows:

$$
\begin{aligned}
Min \quad & \vec{y} = \vec{F}(\vec{x}) = [\vec{f}_1(\vec{x}), \vec{f}_2(\vec{x}), \dots \vec{f}_{N_{obj}}(\vec{x})]^T \\
s.t. \quad & \vec{H}_j(\vec{x}) = 0 \\
& \vec{G}_j(\vec{x}) \le 0, j = 1, 2, \dots, M
\end{aligned} \right\} \quad (16)
$$

Where, $\vec{x}^* = [\vec{x}_1^*, \vec{x}_2^*, \dots, \vec{x}_D^*] \in \Omega$ and $\vec{y}$ is the objective vector. Here, three functions are considered including: $\vec{f}_1(\vec{x}) = P_{Loss}(x, u)$, $\vec{f}_2(\vec{x}) = \sum \Delta V(x, u)$ and $\vec{f}_3(\vec{x}) = L(x, u)$.

$\vec{H}_j(\vec{x})$ is equality constraint including active and reactive power balance. $\vec{G}_j(\vec{x})$ are un-equality constraints, includes the generator voltages, shunt compensations, transformer tap settings, generator reactive power outputs and load bus voltages. $\vec{x}^*$ is a D-dimensional vector representing the decision variables within a parameter space Ω and N_{obj} is the number of objectives. The space spanned by the objective vectors is called the objective space. The subspace of the objective vectors satisfying the constraints is called the feasible space.

Def. 2 For a MOO problem, any two solutions can have one of two possibilities, one covers or dominates the other or none dominates the other. In a minimization problem, without loss of generality, a decision vector $\vec{x}_1 \in \Omega$ is said to dominate the decision vector $\vec{x}_2 \in \Omega$ (denoted by $\vec{x}_1 \prec \vec{x}_2$), if the decision vector $\vec{x}_1$ is not worse than $\vec{x}_2$ in all objectives and strictly better than $\vec{x}_2$ in at least one objective. Therefore, a solution $\vec{x}_1$ dominates $\vec{x}_2$ if the following conditions are satisfied:

$$
\begin{cases}
\forall i \in \{1, 2, \dots, N_{obj}\} : \vec{f}_i(\vec{x}_1) \le \vec{f}_i(\vec{x}_2) \\
\exists j \in \{1, 2, \dots, N_{obj}\} : \vec{f}_j(\vec{x}_1) < \vec{f}_j(\vec{x}_2)
\end{cases} \quad (17)
$$

Def. 3 A decision vector $\vec{x}_1 \in \Omega$ is called Pareto-optimal, if there does not exist another $\vec{x}_2 \in \Omega$ that dominates it. An objective vector is called Pareto-optimal, if the corresponding decision vector is Pareto-optimal.

Def. 4 The set of all non-dominated solutions is called Pareto optimal set (POS) and the set of the corresponding values of the objective functions is called Pareto optimal front (POF) or simply Pareto front. In case of no non-dominated solution, Pareto optimal front would be non-convex.

PO is shown graphically in Figure 1 for an arbitrary two-objective minimization problem. It is apparent that for solutions contained in dominated regions, there exists at least one solution in the non-dominated region that is strictly better in terms of both objectives. Furthermore, each non-dominated solution is obviously not inferior to any solution within the entire search space.

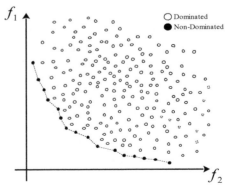

Figure 1. Depiction of domination using a two-objective minimization case

3.2.1. Best compromise solution (BCS)

From the Pareto-optimal set of non-dominated solutions, the proposed POPSO selects one solution for the decision maker as the best compromise solution. For this optimization, due to the imprecise nature of the decision making process involved, the ith objective function F_i is represented by a membership function μ_i defined as [9, 42]:

$$\mu_i = \begin{cases} 1 & F_i \leq F_{i,min} \\ \dfrac{F_{i,max} - F_i}{F_{i,max} - F_{i,min}} & F_{i,min} < F_i < F_{i,max} \\ 0 & F_i \geq F_{i,max} \end{cases} \qquad (18)$$

Where, $F_{i,min}$ and $F_{i,max}$ are the minimum and maximum value of the ith objective function among all non-dominated solutions, respectively. For each non-dominated solution k, the normalized membership function μ^k is calculated as:

$$\mu^k = \frac{\sum_{i=1}^{N_{obj}} \mu_i^k}{\sum_{k=1}^{M} \sum_{i=1}^{N_{obj}} \mu_i^k} \qquad (19)$$

Where, M is the number of non-dominated solutions. Here, the best compromise solution is the one with the maximum μ^k.

4. Solution algorithm

The difficulty in extending the original PSO to POPSO is the selection of *pbest* and *gbest* for each particle, since no single optimum solution in Pareto optimal set exist. The algorithm uses an archive, which is in essence an external repository of the population, storing non-dominated solutions. Initializing randomly the population starts the algorithm. All particles are initially compared with each other in order to store the non-dominated ones in the archive. Particles velocity and positions are updated using Eqs. (13-14) for which $gbest_d$ is randomly selected from the global Pareto archive for each particle, therefore $gbest_d$ is transformed to $gbest_{i,d}$. It means that *gbest* is exclusive for each particle. As for the $pbest_{i,d}$, the first value is set equal to the initial position of particle. In the subsequent iterations, $pbest_{i,d}$ is updated in the following stages:

    (I)   if the current $pbest_{i,d}(t)$ dominates the new position $x_{i,d}(t+1)$ then $pbest_{i,d}(t+1) = pbest_{i,d}(t)$,

    (II)   if the new position $x_{i,d}(t+1)$ dominates $pbest_{i,d}(t)$ then $pbest_{i,d}(t+1) = x_{i,d}(t+1)$,

    (III)   if no one dominates the other, then, one of them is randomly selected to be the $pbest_{i,d}(t+1)$.

Contrary to standard PSO, where a best solution is obtained, there are several equally good non-dominated solutions stored in the POPSO archive. In every iteration t, the new positions of all particles are compared to identify the non-dominated ones, which are then compared further with all solutions stored in the archive. Following updating the archive, new non-dominated solutions are added and old solutions that have become dominated are eliminated. The size of the archive is therefore, an important parameter, which needs to be determined accordingly. Once the archive becomes full, a new non-dominated solution is found. Then this new solution replaces another non-dominated solution randomly selected in the archive. In this article, no limit has been considered for the archive size. The algorithm runs until the maximum number of iterations is reached. Below, the proposed POPSO algorithm for solving the MORPD is discretely described in steps:

Step 1: Input data

    Input power system data and parameter values such as inertia weight w and learning factors c_1 and c_2 in the appropriate equations.

Step 2: Initialization

    (I) Initialize randomly the position and initial velocity of the particles. Each particle in the population consists of D component, where D is the number of space dimensions indicating the number of control variables such as generator voltages, transformer taps and shunt reactive compensations. Select and verify each particle for constraints; if the particle doesn't satisfy the relevant constraints, then regenerate another one.

    (II) Compute the multi-objective functions (P_{loss}, $\sum \Delta V$ and L-index) for each particle and its relevant constrains using power flow algorithm such as Newton Raphson method; then save this in a vector form.

    (III) Check the PO of each particle, and store non-dominated particles in Pareto archive. If the specific constraint doesn't exist for archive, the size of the archive is assumed unlimited.

Step 3: Updating

    (I) Update velocity and positions of particles according to Eqs. (13-14); $gbest_{i,d}(t)$ is randomly selected from the Pareto archive for each particle.

(II) Update $pbest_{i,d}(t+1)$ for each particle according to checking the PO of $pbest_{i,d}(t)$ and $x_{i,d}(t+1)$. If no one dominates the other, then, one of them is randomly selected to be the $pbest_{i,d}(t+1)$.

(III) If the particle doesn't remain within the feasible solution region, discard it and mutate again.

Step 4: Evaluation

Evaluate the multi-objective functions for each particle by power flow; and save it in a vector form.

Step 5: Selection and update the archive

(I) Check the PO of each particle. If the fitness value of the particle is non-dominated (compared to the Pareto optimal front in the archive), save it into the archive.

(II) If a particle is dominated from the new one in the Pareto archive, then discard it.

Step 6: Repeat

Repeat step 3 to step 5 until the maximum number of iterations is reached. The flowchart for the MORPD solution using POPSO is illustrated in Figure 2.

5. Simulation results

The proposed approach was tested with two non-linear test systems (IEEE 30-Bus and IEEE 118-Bus power system) for validation [43]. Basic information for test systems as well as control variable settings and limits are elaborated in Tables 1 and 2. The algorithm implemented in MATLAB and executed on a PC with a Pentium IV 2.1G CPU.

The following parameters are adopted in POPSO: population size = 100; inertia weight w which linearly decreases from 1 to 0.5; initial learning factors $c_1 = 2.0$ and $c_2 = 1.6$; desired number of generations = 50.

Table 1. Control variables of IEEE 30-bus and IEEE 118-bus test systems

Test system	Number of bus	Number of branch	Number of control variables		
			V_G	T	Q_C
IEEE 30-bus	30	41	6	4	4
IEEE 118-bus	118	186	54	9	14

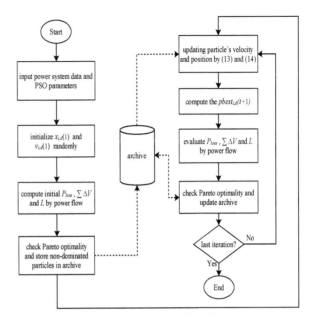

Figure 2. Flowchart for solving MORPD problem using POPSO.

Table 2. Control variable settings IEEE 30-bus and IEEE 118-bus test systems

Control variable	Control variable limits		Step
	Min (p.u.)	Max (p.u.)	
V_G	0.9	1.1	-
T	0.9	1.1	0.01
Q_C	0	0.5	0.01

5.1. Simulation of the IEEE 30-bus test system

The proposed POPSO method was tested on the standard IEEE 30-bus system shown in Figure 3. It consists of six generator buses (bus 1 being the slack bus, while buses number 2, 5, 8, 11 and 13 are PV buses with continuous operating values), 24 load buses and 41 branches in which four branches (4–12, 6–9, 6–10 and 27–28) are tap changing transformers with discrete operating values. In addition, buses 10, 15, 19 and 24 are taken as shunt compensation buses with discrete operating values. Therefore, in total, 14 control variables are taken for MORPD in this test system. Table 3 illustrates the simulation results for the IEEE 30-bus test system, where Pareto optimal front and Pareto optimal set are listed for 36 rows of non-dominated solutions. Table 4 shows the best compromise solution (BCS) and 3 solutions in Pareto optimal front that have minimum value for each objective function individually and are similar to single objective functions (Min P_{loss}, Min $\sum \Delta V$ and Min L-index). The diversity of the Pareto optimal front over the trade-off surface is also shown in Figure 4.

The variation of best compromise solution power loss, voltage deviation and voltage stability index versus the number of iterations are presented in Figures. 5-7, respectively. As can be seen, the convergence characteristics are not monotonic most likely due to the existence of best compromise solution (BCS). In the each iteration, there are several non-dominated solutions and one of them has been selected as BCS considering Eqs. (18-19). In the following iteration, however, one other solutions might be selected as BCS, therefore a non-monotonic convergence may occur. Pre and post optimization for bus voltage profiles are shown in Figure 8. As can be seen after optimization, the voltage profiles are greatly improved, and voltage deviations are reduced.

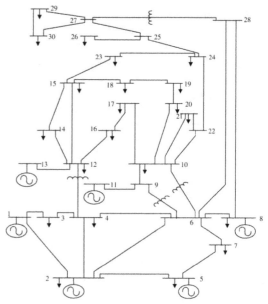

Figure 3. IEEE 30-bus test system

Table 3.The results of IEEE 30-bus test system

Pareto optimal front			Pareto optimal set													
P_{loss}	$\sum \Delta V$	L	V_{G1}	V_{G2}	V_{G5}	V_{G8}	V_{G11}	V_{G13}	T_{4-12}	T_{6-9}	T_{6-10}	T_{27-28}	Q_{C10}	Q_{C15}	Q_{C19}	Q_{C24}
5.1542	0.1080	0.1281	1.0446	1.0262	1.0190	1.0000	1.0293	0.9983	1.00	0.98	1.02	0.97	0.13	0.08	0.09	0.16
5.3292	0.0888	0.1296	1.0325	1.0400	1.0117	0.9855	1.0302	1.0024	0.99	0.98	1.04	0.95	0.10	0.09	0.09	0.20
4.5374	0.4512	0.1237	1.0974	1.0682	1.0784	1.0890	1.0154	1.0198	1.02	1.02	1.01	1.02	0.16	0.07	0.00	0.10
4.6244	0.3048	0.1207	1.0783	1.0683	1.0511	1.0502	1.0307	1.0252	1.04	1.00	1.03	1.00	0.15	0.07	0.04	0.07
4.6654	0.4320	0.1185	1.0819	1.0617	1.0757	1.0481	1.0433	1.0179	1.03	0.99	1.03	0.99	0.16	0.15	0.07	0.06
4.5190	**0.7968**	**0.1161**	**1.1000**	**1.0772**	**1.0712**	**1.0761**	**1.0499**	**1.0322**	**1.01**	**1.01**	**1.05**	**0.98**	**0.23**	**0.12**	**0.12**	**0.04**
4.9474	0.1776	0.1225	1.0542	1.0459	1.0365	1.0214	1.0283	1.0002	1.04	0.98	1.01	0.97	0.14	0.12	0.07	0.09
4.7983	0.2472	0.1216	1.0671	1.0414	1.0702	1.0545	1.0297	1.0012	1.01	1.00	1.00	0.98	0.17	0.05	0.06	0.08
5.2205	**0.0768**	**0.1339**	**1.0227**	**1.0339**	**1.0130**	**0.9977**	**1.0007**	**1.0021**	**1.02**	**1.00**	**1.00**	**0.95**	**0.21**	**0.13**	**0.07**	**0.13**
4.9473	0.1608	0.1237	1.0557	1.0304	1.0342	1.0166	1.0177	0.9889	1.00	0.99	1.02	0.97	0.12	0.10	0.09	0.15
5.1051	0.1056	0.1348	1.0430	1.0260	1.0410	1.0016	1.0257	0.9806	1.00	1.01	1.02	0.96	0.16	0.08	0.10	0.16
4.9142	0.1608	0.1247	1.0501	1.0382	1.0537	1.0197	1.0156	0.9846	1.00	1.01	1.01	0.97	0.15	0.12	0.05	0.16
4.8736	0.2472	0.1201	1.0756	1.0603	1.0543	1.0490	1.0347	1.0009	1.02	0.97	1.05	0.97	0.10	0.01	0.09	0.07
4.8666	0.1824	0.1247	1.0579	1.0360	1.0648	1.0368	1.0134	1.0027	1.02	1.00	1.02	0.99	0.16	0.14	0.01	0.12
4.8522	0.1968	0.1234	1.0541	1.0520	1.0382	1.0306	1.0217	1.0035	1.02	1.00	1.03	0.99	0.18	0.10	0.07	0.09
4.6820	0.3000	0.1210	1.0800	1.0462	1.0741	1.0494	1.0292	1.0114	1.03	1.00	1.05	1.00	0.21	0.04	0.05	0.10
4.5216	0.6048	0.1173	1.0966	1.0754	1.0952	1.0819	1.0381	1.0272	1.03	0.99	1.04	1.01	0.17	0.05	0.06	0.10
4.9216	0.1848	0.1222	1.0594	1.0522	1.0532	1.0259	1.0239	0.9950	1.03	0.98	1.03	0.98	0.12	0.11	0.08	0.10
4.6692	0.3696	0.1185	1.0779	1.0723	1.0409	1.0485	1.0474	1.0150	1.02	0.99	1.03	0.99	0.18	0.05	0.05	0.09
4.6820	0.3336	0.1207	1.0884	1.0632	1.0736	1.0517	1.0321	1.0067	1.03	1.01	1.04	1.02	0.21	0.11	0.03	0.07
4.6423	0.3888	0.1201	1.0813	1.0763	1.0448	1.0631	1.0367	1.0124	1.02	1.01	1.04	1.01	0.20	0.14	0.03	0.04
4.6362	0.3576	0.1207	1.0771	1.0536	1.0480	1.0579	1.0325	1.0391	1.00	1.00	1.03	1.00	0.13	0.07	0.03	0.08
4.7256	0.3168	0.1191	1.0854	1.0475	1.0742	1.0576	1.0505	1.0114	1.00	0.98	1.04	1.00	0.14	0.08	0.00	0.06
4.6664	0.2808	0.1225	1.0783	1.0726	1.0711	1.0498	1.0291	1.0147	1.01	1.02	1.06	1.00	0.19	0.07	0.01	0.07
4.6828	0.4200	0.1179	1.0830	1.0807	1.0668	1.0500	1.0422	1.0195	1.02	0.99	1.05	1.01	0.20	0.13	0.02	0.06
4.6703	**0.2458**	**0.1192**	**1.0713**	**1.0372**	**1.0386**	**1.0433**	**1.0318**	**1.0301**	**1.04**	**0.99**	**1.01**	**1.00**	**0.10**	**0.04**	**0.05**	**0.08**
4.6917	0.4416	0.1164	1.0808	1.0756	1.0913	1.0694	1.0557	1.0223	1.02	0.97	1.04	0.97	0.11	0.06	0.07	0.03
4.6995	0.2400	0.1250	1.0712	1.0609	1.0445	1.0482	1.0140	1.0121	1.02	1.01	1.03	0.99	0.18	0.09	0.04	0.07
4.6090	**0.5208**	**0.1151**	**1.0864**	**1.0542**	**1.0698**	**1.0695**	**1.0587**	**1.0016**	**1.02**	**0.98**	**1.04**	**1.02**	**0.14**	**0.09**	**0.07**	**0.11**
4.7586	0.2520	0.1207	1.0784	1.0632	1.0459	1.0513	1.0327	0.9987	1.04	0.99	1.02	0.99	0.14	0.10	0.07	0.09
4.6423	0.3888	0.1201	1.0813	1.0763	1.0448	1.0631	1.0367	1.0124	1.01	1.01	1.04	1.01	0.20	0.14	0.03	0.04
4.7006	0.3288	0.1179	1.0868	1.0700	1.0652	1.0430	1.0452	1.0200	1.04	0.98	1.05	1.00	0.16	0.07	0.03	0.09
4.6882	0.2880	0.1222	1.0902	1.0726	1.0711	1.0498	1.0291	1.0147	1.01	1.01	1.06	1.00	0.19	0.07	0.01	0.06
4.7531	0.3048	0.1194	1.0800	1.0740	1.0692	1.0404	1.0363	1.0095	1.03	0.99	1.05	0.99	0.21	0.05	0.01	0.12
4.7257	0.2184	0.1247	1.0677	1.0568	1.0629	1.0329	1.0157	1.0226	1.02	1.02	1.04	1.00	0.20	0.05	0.04	0.11
4.6669	0.3648	0.1191	1.0800	1.0722	1.0750	1.0743	1.0272	1.0163	1.03	0.99	1.03	1.01	0.17	0.10	0.03	0.08

Table 4. Best compromise solution (BCS) and minimum value for each objective function

	P_{loss} (MW)	$\sum \Delta V$	L
BCS	4.6703	0.2458	0.1192
Min P_{loss}	**4.5190**	0.7968	0.1161
Min $\sum \Delta V$	5.2205	**0.0768**	0.1339
Min L	4.6090	0.5208	**0.1151**

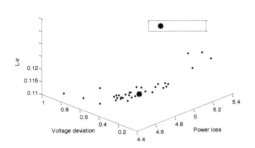

Figure 4. Pareto optimal front of the proposed approach

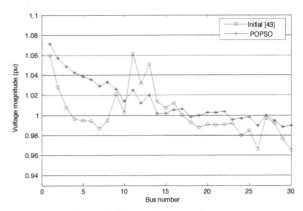

Figure 8. Bus voltage profiles

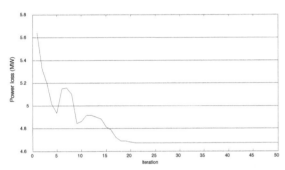

Figure 5. Convergence of best compromise solution power loss

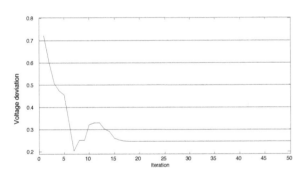

Figure 6. Convergence of best compromise solution voltage deviation

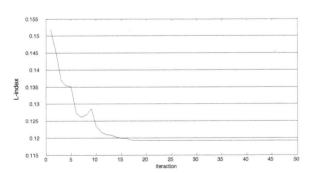

Figure 7. Convergence of best compromise solution voltage stability index

To evaluate the performance of proposed POPSO approach, the simulation results are compared with other listed algorithms in Table 5 as discussed below:

Comparing POPSO with initial case
The following points are noted: a) Active power losses before and after proposed POPSO optimization are 5.7213 (column 2 Table 5) and 4.6703 (column 11 Table 5), respectively, indicating a power loss reduction of 18.37%. b) Voltage deviation is also reduced from 0.7656 in the initial case to 0.2458, i.e. a reduction of 67.89%. c) Voltage stability index, too is reduced from 0.1563 to 0.1192 (i.e. 23.74%, improvement).

Comparing POPSO with PSO and FAPSO
The numerical results from Table 5 indicate that in the same test system, the BCS determined by POPSO is better than both PSO and FAPSO [18]. Here, the least improvement (reduction) achieved in power loss, voltage deviation and voltage stability index are 5.65%, 6.89% and 3.72%, respectively.

Comparing POPSO with CLPSO
In CLPSO technique, three cases with different objectives are considered [19]: Case 1, a single objective is defined to minimize the real power loss; Case 2, two objectives are defined in order to minimize the power loss and voltage deviation; and Case 3, where two objectives of minimizing the power loss and voltage stability index are defined. The best candidate in Pareto optimal front for comparing POPSO with CLPSO-Case 1 is Min P_{loss} in Table 4, where the solution for P_{loss} is 4.519 which compared to the latter (i.e. 4.5615) indicates slight improvement in working with POPSO. BCS is chosen in this study for comparing POPSO and CLPSO-Case 2 and CLPSO-Case 3. Only voltage

deviation in CLPSO-Case 2 is slightly less than POPSO, but POPSO still illustrates better results with respect to other specification. Comparing CLPSO-Case 3 with POPSO, P_{loss} and voltage deviation are still inferior for the former. It is worth mentioning that in [19], the number of shunt compensations employed in CLPSO's is 9, while in this paper we have used 4. This may cause L index to be less than the case considered for POPSO comparisons (in CLPSO-Case 3, L index is 0.0866 against 0.1192 for POPSO).

Comparing POPSO with DE
In DE algorithm [22], three cases (Case 1: minimization of system power loss, Case 2: improvement of voltage profile and Case 3: enhancement of voltage stability) with different objectives are considered as follows: for minimizing real power loss, the best candidate at Pareto optimal front for comparison is for Min P_{Loss} in POPSO is 4.519 (column 2, Table 4) against 4.555 for DE (0.036 MW loss reduction) and as can be seen POPSO shows improvement over DE in all other specs, too (at least 78.38% improvement in $\sum \Delta V$ and L). Also, the best candidate at Pareto optimal front for comparison with DE-Case 2 and DE-Case 3 (Min $\sum \Delta V$ and Min L) are 0.0768 (column 3, Table 4) against 0.0911 for voltage deviation, and 0.1151 (column 4, Table 4) against 0.1246 for voltage stability, respectively (at least 15.69% and 7.62% improvement are observed in voltage profile and voltage stability index, respectively).

Comparing POPSO with NSGA-II and MNSGA-II
NSGA-II and MNSGA-II are algorithms that use Pareto optimality for MOO. Minimizing the power loss and voltage stability index could be defined as the two objectives of ORPD [25]. Best P_{Loss} and best L are Pareto optimal front solutions, each representing a minimum objective function for power loss and voltage stability index. The best candidates at Pareto optimal front for comparing POPSO with NSGA-II and MNSGA-II are Min P_{loss} for Best P_{Loss} and Min L for Best L. Advantage of POPSO with respect to NSGA-II and MNSGA-II are expressed in Table 5, where BCS indicate improvement in power loss and voltage stability index of at least 5.69% and 13.75%, respectively. Figures 9-11, clearly compares the results of proposed POPSO with other methods for IEEE 30-bus test system. Therefore, as can be seen, the proposed POPSO method yields nearer global

optimal solution for both single and multi-objectives.

5.2. Simulation of the IEEE 118-bus test system
In order to evaluate the applicability of the proposed method to bigger systems, IEEE 118-bus power system is employed which consists of 54 generator buses, 64 load buses and 186 branches in which 14 branches are tap changing transformers with discrete operating values. In addition, 9 buses are taken as shunt compensation buses with discrete operating values. In this system, a total of 77 control variables are taken for MORPD.

Table 6 and Figures 12-15 show the results obtained by the proposed POPSO when compared with other methods [18, 19, 25, 43] where improvement in power loss, voltage deviation and voltage stability index are at least 1.26%, 3.3% and 8.27%, respectively, and can therefore be efficiently used for the MORPD problem. Again, it is worth noting that in [19], the number of shunt compensations employed in CLPSO's is 14, and in this paper we have used 9. The same argument for L index as outlined above applies here too (in CLPSO-Case 3, L index is 0.0965 against 0.1087 for POPSO).

6. Conclusion
In this paper, a new approach based on POPSO has been proposed and applied to MORPD problem. The problem has been formulated as MOO problem with competing power loss, bus voltage deviation and voltage stability index. A hierarchical clustering technique is implemented to provide the operator with a representative and manageable Pareto optimal set without destroying the characteristics of the trade-off front. Moreover, a proposed mechanism is employed to extract the best compromise solution over the trade-off curve. The Pareto multi-objective algorithms here implemented have the advantage of including multiple criteria without the need for introducing weights in a simple aggregating function. The results show that the proposed approach is efficient for solving MORPD problem where multiple Pareto optimal solutions can be found in one simulation run. The algorithms have been tested for standard IEEE 30-bus and 118-bus test systems and results are compared with others commonly used algorithms in the literature. Comparison shows that the proposed approach performed better than the other algorithms and can be efficiently used for the MORPD problem as near global optimum solutions reached in this study. The comparison seems to dominate other algorithms results.

Table 5. Comparison of POPSO with other techniques on IEEE 30-bus test system

	Initial [43]	PSO [18]	FAPSO [18]	CLPSO [19]			DE [22]			NSGA-II [25]		MNSGA-II [25]		POPSO (BCS)
				Case 1	Case 2	Case 3	Case 1	Case 2	Case 3	Best P_{loss}	Best L	Best P_{loss}	Best L	
P_{loss}(MW)	5.7213	5.1600[a]	4.9500[a]	4.5615	4.6969	4.6760	4.555	6.4755	7.0733	4.952	5.128	4.9454	5.102	**4.6703**
$\sum \Delta V$	0.7656	0.3840[b]	0.2640[b]	0.4773	0.2450	0.5171	1.9589	0.0911	1.4191	-	-	-	-	**0.2458**
L	0.1563	0.1307	0.1238	0.1230	0.1247	0.0866	0.5513	0.5734	0.1246	0.1393	0.1382	0.13940	0.1382	**0.1192**

[a] P_{loss}(p.u.) $\times 100 = P_{loss}$ (MW)
[b] ΔV(p.u.) $\times N_L = \sum \Delta V$

Table 6. The results of POPSO and comparison with other methods on IEEE 118-bus test system

	Initial [43]	PSO [18]	FAPSO [18]	CLPSO [19]			NSGA-II [25]		MNSGA-II [25]		POPSO (BCS)
				Case 1	Case 2	Case 3	Best P_{loss}	Best L	Best P_{loss}	Best L	
P_{loss}(MW)	133.14	117.81	115.37	130.96	132.06	132.08	119.57	132.21	119.279	132.17	**113.92**
$\sum \Delta V$	2.0150	0.7488	0.7744	1.8525	1.6177	2.8863	-	-	-	-	**0.7241**
L	0.1497	0.1295	0.1185	0.1461	0.1210	0.0965	0.4553	0.4113	0.4553	0.4074	**0.1087**

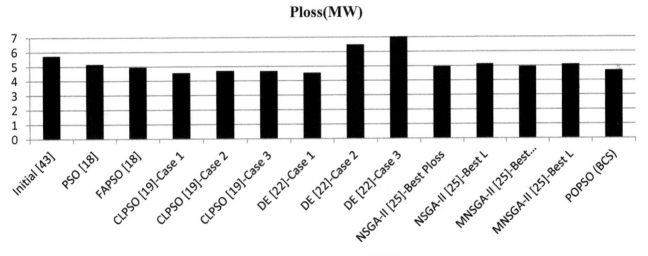

Figure 9. Comparison results of power loss in IEEE 30-bus test system

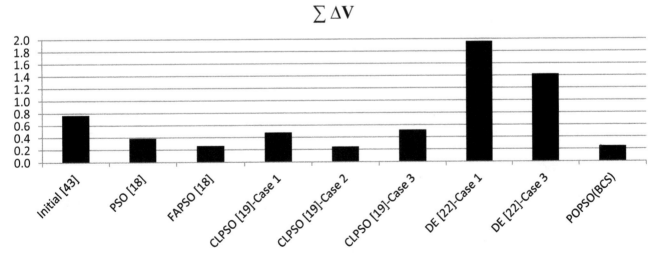

Figure 10. Comparison results of voltage deviation in IEEE 30-bus test system

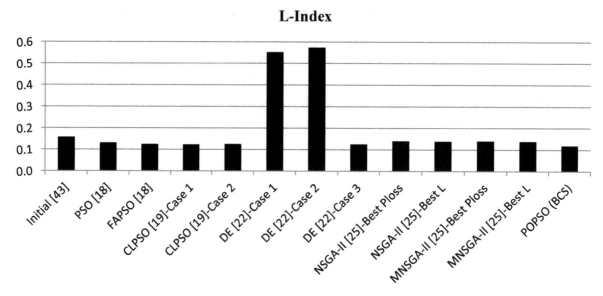

Figure 11. Comparison results of *L*-index in IEEE 30-bus test system

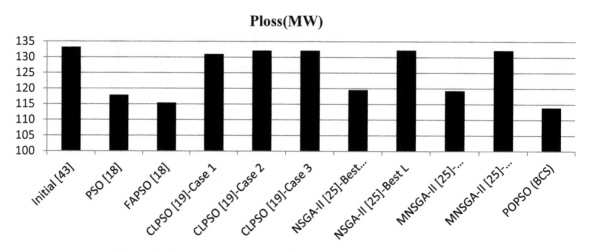

Figure 12. Comparison results of power loss in IEEE 118-bus test system

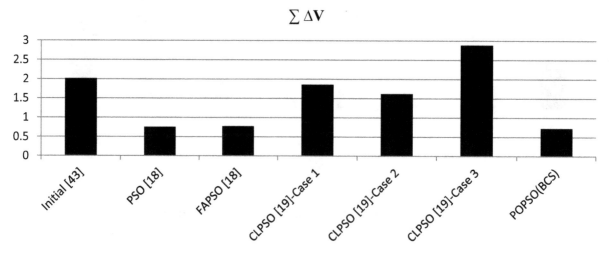

Figure 13. Comparison results of voltage deviation in IEEE 118-bus test system

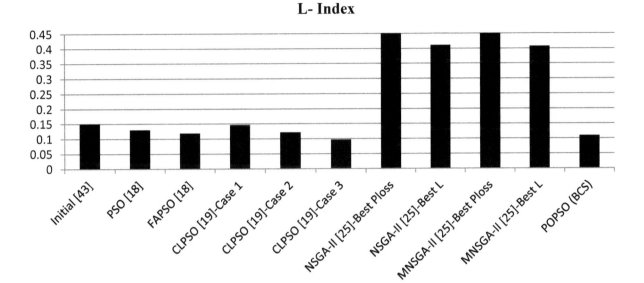

Figure 14. Comparison results of *L*-index in IEEE 118-bus test system

References

[1] Deeb, N., S. M. Shaidepour, "Linear reactive power optimization in a large power network using the decomposition approach", IEEE Trans. Power System, vol. 5, no. 2, pp. 428–35, 1990.

[2] Granville, S. "Optimal reactive dispatch through interior point methods", IEEE Trans. Power System, vol. 9, no. 1, pp. 136–46, 1994.

[3] Gomes, J. R, O. R. Saavedra, "A Cauchy-based evolution strategy for solving the reactive power dispatch problem", International Journal Electrical Power and Energy System, vol. 24, no. 4, pp. 277–83, 2002.

[4] Bhagwan, D. D., C. Patvardhan, "Reactive power dispatch with a hybrid stochastic search technique", International Journal Electrical Power and Energy System, vol. 24, no. 9, pp. 731–6, 2002.

[5] Devaraj, D., "Improved genetic algorithm for multi-objective reactive power dispatch problem", European Trans. on Electrical Power, vol. 17, no. 6, pp. 569-581, 2007.

[6] Liu, Y. T., L. Ma, J.J. Zhang, "Reactive power optimization by GA/SA/TS combined algorithms", International Journal Electrical Power and Energy System, vol. 24, no. 9, pp. 765–9, 2002.

[7] Tomsovic, K., "A fuzzy linear programming approach to the reactive power/ voltage control problem", IEEE Trans. Power System, vol. 7, no. 1, pp. 287–93, 1992.

[8] Grudinin, N. "Reactive power optimization using successive quadratic programming method", IEEE Trans Power System, vol. 13, no. 4, pp. 1219–25, 1998.

[9] Abido, M. A., J.M. Bakhashwain, "Optimal VAR dispatch using a multi-objective evolutionary algorithm", International Journal Electrical Power and Energy System, vol. 27, no. 1, pp. 13-20, 2005.

[10] Jiang, C., C. Wang, "Improved evolutionary programming with dynamic mutation and metropolis criteria for multi-objective reactive power optimization", IEE Proc Generation Transmission Distribution, vol. 152, no. 2, pp. 291–4, 2005.

[11] Zhou, A., B-Y. Qu, H. Li, S-Z. Zhao, P. N. Suganthan, Q. Zhang, "Multiobjective Evolutionary Algorithms: A Survey of the State-of-the-art", Swarm and Evolutionary Computation, vol. 1, no. 1, pp. 32-49, 2011.

[12] Aribia, H. B., N. Derbel, H.H. Abdallah, "The active–reactive – complete dispatch of an electrical network", International Journal of Electrical Power and Energy Systems, vol. 44, no. 1, pp. 236-248, 2013.

[13] Pires, D. F., C. H. Antunes, A. G. Martins, "NSGA-II with local search for a multi-objective reactive power compensation problem", International Journal of Electrical Power and Energy Systems, vol. 43, no. 1, pp. 313-324, 2012.

[14] Wu, Q. H. , Y.J. Cao, J.Y. Wen, "Optimal reactive power dispatch using an adaptive genetic algorithm", International Journal Electrical Power and Energy System, vol. 20, no. 8, pp. 563–569, 1998.

[15] del Valle, Y. et al., "Particle swarm optimization: basic concepts, variants and applications in power systems", IEEE Trans. Evol. Comput., vol. 12, no. 2, pp. 171–195, 2008.

[16] Esmin, A. A. A., G. Lambert-Torres, A. C. Zambroni de Souza, "A hybrid particle swarm optimization applied to loss power minimization", IEEE Trans. Power System, vol. 20, no. 2, pp. 859–869, 2005.

[17] Vlachogiannis, J. G., K. Y. Lee, "A comparative study on particle swarm optimization for optimal steady-state performance of power systems", IEEE Trans. Power System, vol. 21, no. 4, pp. 1718–1728, 2006.

[18] Zhang, W., Y. Liu, "Multi-objective reactive power and voltage control based on fuzzy optimization strategy and fuzzy adaptive particle swarm", International

Journal Electrical Power and Energy System, vol. 30, no. 9, pp. 525–532, 2008.

[19] Mahadevan, K., P. S. Kannan, "Comprehensive learning particle swarm optimization for reactive power dispatch", International Journal Applied Soft Computing, vol. 10, no. 2, pp. 641–652, 2010.

[20] Varadarajan, M., K. S. Swarup, "Network loss minimization with voltage security using differential evolution", Electric Power System Res., vol. 78, no. 5, pp. 815–823, 2008.

[21] Varadarajan, M., K. S. Swarup, "Differential evolutionary algorithm for optimal reactive power dispatch", International Journal Electrical Power and Energy System, vol. 30, no. 8, pp. 435–441, 2008.

[22] Abou El Ela, A. A., M. A. Abido, S.R. Spea, "Differential evolution algorithm for optimal reactive power dispatch", Electric Power System Research, vol. 81, no. 2, pp. 458-464, 2011.

[23] Dai, Ch., W. Chen, Y. Zhu, X. Zhang "Reactive power dispatch considering voltage stability with seeker optimization algorithm" International Journal of Electrical Power & Energy Systems, vol. 79, no. 10, pp. 1462-1471, 2009.

[24] Zhihuan, L., L. Yinhong, D. Xianzhong, "Non-dominated sorting genetic algorithm-II for robust multi-objective optimal reactive power dispatch", IET Generation, Transmission & Distribution, vol. 4, no. 9, pp. 1000 – 1008, 2010.

[25] Jeyadevi, S., S. Baskar, C. K. Babulal, M. Willjuice Iruthayarajan, "Solving multi-objective optimal reactive power dispatch using modified NSGA-II", International Journal of Electrical Power and Energy Systems, vol. 33, no. 2, pp. 219-228, 2011.

[26] Kennedy, J., R.C. Eberhart, "Particle swarm optimization", Proc IEEE Int. Conf. Neural Networks, vol. 4, pp. 1942–8, 1995.

[27] Yoshida, H., K. Kawata, Y. Fukuyama, S. Takayama, Y. Nakanishi, "A particle swarm optimization for reactive power and voltage control considering voltage security assessment", IEEE Trans. Power System, vol. 15, no. 4, pp. 1232–9, 2000.

[28] Abido, M. A., "Optimal power flow using particle swarm optimization", International Journal Electrical Power and Energy System, vol. 24, no. 7, pp. 563–71, 2002.

[29] Kassabalidis, I. N., M. A. El-Sharkawi, R. Marks, L.S. Moulin, A.P. Alves da Silva, "Dynamic security border identification using enhanced particle swarm optimization", IEEE Trans. Power System, vol. 17, no. 3, pp. 723–9, 2002.

[30] Naka, S., T. Genji, T. Yura, Y. Fukuyama, "A hybrid particle swarm optimization for distribution state estimation", IEEE Trans. Power System, vol. 18, no. 1, pp. 60–68, 2003.

[31] Ngatchou, P., A. Zarei, A. El-Sharkawi, "Pareto multi objective optimization", Intelligent Systems Application to Power Systems, Proceedings of the 13th International Conference on 6-10 Nov. 2005, pp. 84 – 91.

[32] Montoya, F. G., et al., "Minimization of voltage deviation and power losses in power networks using Pareto optimization methods", Engineering Applications of Artificial Intelligence, vol. 23, no. 5, pp. 695-703, 2010.

[33] Yassami, H., A. Darabi, S. M. R. Rafiei, "Power system stabilizer design using Strength Pareto multi-objective optimization approach", Electric Power Systems Research, vol. 80, no. 7, pp. 838–846, 2010.

[34] Balamourougan, V., T.S. Sidhu, M. S. Sachdev, "Technique for online prediction of voltage collapse", IEE Proc. Gen. Trans. Distrib., vol. 151, no. 4, pp. 453-460, 2004.

[35] Hugang, X., C. Haozhong, L. Haiyu, "Optimal reactive power flow incorporating static voltage stability based on multi-objective adaptive immune algorithm", Energy Conversion and Management, vol. 49, no. 5, pp. 1175–1181, 2008.

[36] Kessel, P., H.Glavitsch, "Estimating the voltage stability of a power system", IEEE Trans Power Del., vol. 1, no. 3, pp. 346–54, 1986.

[37] Tuan, T. Q., J. Fandino, N. Hadjsaid, J.C. Sabonnadiere, H. Vu, "Emergency load shedding to avoid risk of voltage instability using indicators", IEEE Trans Power System, vol. 9, no. 1, pp. 341–8, 1994.

[38] Kennedy, J., "The particle swarm: Social adaptation of knowledge," in Proc. IEEE Int. Conf. Evolutionary Comp., Indianapolis, IN, pp. 303–308, 1997.

[39] Shi, Y., R.C. Eberhart, "A modified particle swarm optimizer", In: Proceedings of the IEEE international Conference Evolutionary Computation, pp. 69–73, 1998.

[40] Carlisle, A., G. Dozier, "An off-the-shelf PSO", In: Proceedings of the IEEE International Workshop Particle Swarm Optimization, USA, pp. 1–6, 2001.

[41] Sharaf, A. M., A.A.A. El-Gammal, "A multi objective multi-stage particle swarm optimization MOPSO search scheme for power quality and loss reduction on radial distribution system", International Conference on Renewable Energies and Power Quality, 2009.

[42] Dhillon, J. S., S.C. Parti, D.P. Kothari, "Stochastic economic emission load dispatch", Electric Power System Research, vol. 26, no. 3, pp. 179–86, 1993.

[43] Power System Test Case Archive, December [Online], Available: http://www.ee.washington.edu/research/pstca/, 2006.

11

Estimation of parameters of metal-oxide surge arrester models using Big Bang-Big Crunch and Hybrid Big Bang-Big Crunch algorithms

M. M. Abravesh[1*], A. Sheikholeslami[2], H. Abravesh[1] and M. Yazdani Asrami[2]

1. Department of Electrical Engineering, Hadaf Institute of Higher Education, Sari, Iran.
2. Department of Electrical Engineering, Noshirvani University of Technology, Babol, Iran.

*Corresponding author: mohammadabravesh@yahoo.com (M.M. Abravesh).

Abstract
Metal oxide surge arrester accurate modeling and its parameter identification are very important for insulation coordination studies, arrester allocation, and system reliability since quality and reliability of lightning performance studies can be improved with the more efficient representation of the arresters´ dynamic behavior. In this work, the Big Bang - Big Crunch (BB-BC) and Hybrid Big Bang - Big Crunch (HBB-BC) optimization algorithms were used to select the optimum surge arrester model equivalent circuit parameter values, minimizing the error between the simulated peak residual voltage value and that given by the manufacturer. The proposed algorithms were applied to 63 kV and 230 kV metal oxide surge arresters. The results obtained showed that by using this method, the maximum percentage error was below 1.5%.

Keywords: *Surge Arresters, Residual Voltage, Big Bang – Big Crunch (BB-BC) Algorithm, Hybrid Big Bang – Big Crunch (HBB-BC) Algorithm, Parameter Estimation, EMTP.*

1. Introduction

Internal and external overvoltages on high voltage transmission lines are very common causes of interruptions. In order to protect them against overvoltages, surge arresters are implemented to divert the overvoltage current to the ground. Metal oxide surge arresters (MOSAs), due to their good performances, are extensively used in power systems [1]. Proper voltage-current characteristics, low power losses, high-level reliability in the operation time, high-speed response to overvoltages and long lifetime are some advantages of MOSAs [2].

The adequate circuit representation of metal oxide surge arrester characteristics is very important for insulation coordination studies and system reliability. In the case of switching surge studies, the surge arresters can be represented with their non-linear V–I characteristic. However, such a practice would not be suitable for lightning surge studies with fast front waves [3]. This is due to the fact that the surge arresters behave differently in the presence of a fast disturbance. Typically, the predicted residual voltage for an impulse current

with the time to peak of 1 μs is about 8-12% higher than that with the time to peak of 8μs.
Also with further increase in the time to peak between 45 and 60 μs, the residual voltage is 2-4% lower than that for the 8μs current impulse [1].
In order to obtain more accurate results and reliable estimation in insulation coordination studies, several frequent dependent models of metal oxide surge arresters such as the IEEE and Pinceti models have been proposed [4,5].
A comparative study of the various existing models in the literature showed that the difficulties with these models reside essentially in the calculation and the adjustment of their parameters. The parameter determinations of each model, in a way that the model simulation results, correspond to the actual behavior of the arrester. Thus many researchers have paid attention to using an appropriate optimization algorithm. This was used to minimize the error between the computed and manufacturer's residual voltage curves [6-10].
In the present work, the transient models of MOSA are simulated using EMTP. The method is based on the use of the measured MOSA terminal

voltage obtained from the following injection of the 10 kA, 8/20 μs impulse current. The main issue for the suggested models is the determination of the parameters for each model, in a way that the simulated curve has a good agreement with the real recorded waveform. The simulation results are applied to the Big Bang-Big Crunch (BB-BC) and Hybrid Big Bang-Big Crunch (HBB-BC) algorithms to determine the parameters of different models. The validity and accuracy of the estimated parameters are assessed by comparing the predicted residual voltage with the manufacturer's experimental results [11,12,16,18]. Good agreement of results verifies the ability of the proposed algorithm for estimating the surge arrester parameters.

2. Surge arrester models

Many different models have been presented to describe the transient behavior of surge arresters. IEEE has proposed a model, that shown in figure 1. In the IEEE model, two non-linear resistance of A_0 and A_1 have been separated using R_1L_1 filter [4]. For waves with slow front time, the equivalent impedance of the filter is insignificant, and A_0 and A_1 are parallel. However, in the case of the waves with fast front time, the equivalent impedance is significant, and most of the current passes through the non-linear resistance of A_0.

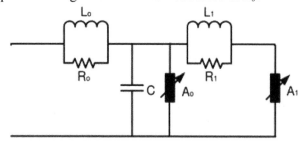

Figure 1. IEEE model.

The non-linear V-I characteristics of A_0 and A_1 are plotted in percent of guaranteed residual voltage at 10 kA, 8/20 μs current impulse in figure 2 [11].

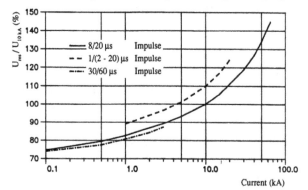

Figure 2. Non-linear characteristics of A_0 and A_1.

The model presented in figure 3 has been presented by Pinceti, and is derived from the IEEE model. In this model, the definition of V-I characteristic of A_0 and A_1 non-linear resistances is based on the curves shown in figure 2. The capacitance effect is negligible. The two resistances in parallel with the inductances are replaced by one resistance to avoid numerical troubles. The values for L_0 and L_1 are presented in table 1 [5].

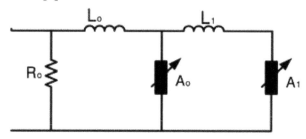

Figure 3. Pinceti model.

The parameters of each model are computed using the electrical characteristic data, obtained from the manufacturers' datasheet. The equations for the parameter computations of the IEEE and Pinceti models are presented in table 1 [4,5].

Table1. Model parameter computations.

	IEEE	Pinceti
R_0	$(100d)/n$ Ω	1 M Ω
R_1	$(65d)/n$ Ω	-
L_0	$(0.2d)/n$ μH	$\frac{1}{12} \cdot \frac{V_{r(1/T2)}-V_{r(8/20)}}{V_{r(8/20)}} \cdot V_n$ μH
L_1	$(15d)/n$ μH	$\frac{1}{4} \cdot \frac{V_{r(1/T2)}-V_{r(8/20)}}{V_{r(8/20)}} \cdot V_n$ μH
C	$(100n)/d$ pF	-

V_n is the arrester's rated voltage, $V_{r(8/20)}$ is the residual voltage for a 10 kA, 8/20 μs lightning current, $V_{r(1/T2)}$ is the residual voltage for a 1/T_2 10 kA lightning current, n is a scale factor and d is the length of arrester column in meters. Table 2 and 3 present the electrical and physical characteristic data for the examined surge arrester.

3. Objective function

The surge arrester models were simulated using the EMTP software. The initial parameters for each surge arrester models were calculated. The impulse current of 10 kA, 8/20 μs was applied to the simulated models. Using the BB-BC and HBB-BC algorithms, the residual voltages obtained from the simulation of each model were compared with the measured voltage. The parameters of the MOSA models could be determined by minimizing the following objective function.

Table 2. Electrical and insulation data of arrester for 63 kV [11].

MCOV	48 kV
Rated Voltage	60 kV
Maximum Residual Voltage with lightening current 8/20 µs	137 kV
Height	996 mm
Insulation Material	Porcelain
Creepage	3285 mm

Table 3. Electrical and insulation data of arrester for 230 kV [11].

MCOV	160 kV
Rated Voltage	198 kV
Maximum Residual Voltage with lightening current 8/20 µs	451 kV
Height	1625 mm
Insulation Material	Porcelain
Creepage	6570 mm

The proposed algorithm in this work for the surge arrester models is based upon the experimental data [12]. The following equation shows the objective function [15]:

$$F = \int_0^T [V(T, \bar{X}) - Vm(t)]^2 dt \qquad (1)$$

where,

F : sum of the quadratic errors;

T : duration of the impulse current injected;

$V(t, x)$: the residual voltage obtained from simulation results;

$V_m(t)$: measured residual voltage;

x : state variable vector (model parameters).

If the function and variables are discrete, the objective function will be presented as follows:

$$F = \sum_{j=1}^N [V(j\Delta t, x) - V_m(j\Delta t)]^2 \, \Delta t \qquad (2)$$

where,

N : Number of discrete points;

$\Delta t = T / N$: computing time step.

The *V-I* characteristic of the surge arrester can be assumed by a non-linear resistance whose variation is exponential, as follows [13]:

$$I = P \left(\frac{V}{V_{ref}} \right)^q \qquad (3)$$

where, V and I are the voltage and current of the surge arrester, respectively, p and q are constant values, and V_{ref} is an arbitrary reference voltage.

4. Big Bang-Big Crunch algorithm

The BB-BC optimization method is one of the evolutionary algorithms presented as a solution for solving an optimization problem. This algorithm is composed of two stages, and is the same as the other evolutionary algorithms from the aspect of population production. The creation of the initial population randomly is called the Big Bang phase. In this stage, the population spreads all over the whole search space randomly and uniformly. The second stage is Big Crunch, which is actually a convergence operator. This operator has a many input but just one output, which is named as the center of mass, since the only output has been derived by calculating the center of mass. The center of mass is calculated using the following formula:

$$X_j^{c(k)} = \frac{\sum_{i=1}^{Np} \frac{1}{f^i} x_j^{(k,i)}}{\sum_{i=1}^{N} \frac{1}{f^i}} \qquad j = 1, 2, \ldots, D \qquad (4)$$

where, $X_j^c(k)$ is j^{th} variable of mass center in k^{th} iteration, $X_j(k,i)$ is j^{th} variable of ith population solution in k^{th} iteration, f^i is the fitness function value of ith point, and D and N_p are the number of control variable and the population size in the Big Bang phase, respectively.

After calculating the mass center in the kth iteration and Big Bang stage, the new position of each particle is introduced using a normal distribution around the mass center. This method takes the population members as a whole in the Big-Crunch phase that acts as a squeezing or contraction operator and the algorithm generates new candidate solutions in the next iteration of Big Bang phase using normal distribution around the previous center of mass as follows:

$$x_j^{(k+1,i)} = x_j^{c(k)} + \frac{r_i \alpha(x_j^{max} - x_j^{min})}{k+1} \qquad j = 1, 2, \ldots, D \qquad (5)$$

where r_i is a random number that is obtained using a standard normal distribution. This number is repeated for each member of the population in each iteration; α is a constant to limit the search space; x_j^{max} and x_j^{min} are the maximum and minimum acceptable values for j^{th} variable, respectively. After the Big Crunch phase, the algorithm must create new members to be used as the Big Bang of the next iteration step. "Bang" and "Crunch" will be continued until we reach convergence [16].

5. Hybrid Big Bang-Big Crunch algorithm

The BB-BC algorithm has an effective operation in exploitation, but some problems are observed in the exploration stage such as dependency of the algorithm on the initial population and the possibility of being trapped in local optima.

If all candidates are gathered in a small part of search space, the algorithm is more likely to be trapped in a local optimized point, and may not find the optimum solution. One of the solutions is that a great number of random variables are used to prevent the algorithm from getting stuck in the local optimized points but it causes an increase in the function evaluations, calculation time and finally computational cost. In order to solve these weaknesses and modification of exploration capability, this algorithm is combined with the PSO algorithm which is called "Hybrid Big Bang-Big Crunch" (HBB-BC) [17].

The PSO algorithm is inspired by birds swarm pattern, and operates based on the members of population that are called searching particles for food. Each particle moves through a multiple dimension search space with a constant speed. This speed updates constantly by the best experience of each particle (Pbest) or the best experience of all neighbor particles (Gbest).

In HBB-BC algorithm, each parameter updates using three parameters which belong to the previous iteration; these parameters are the center of mass, the best position of each solution, and the best position of all particles. Equation (6) shows the procedure of this updating.

$$x_j^{(k+1,i)} \beta_1 x_j^{c(k)} + \left(1 - \beta_1\right)\left(\beta_2 x_j^{gbest(k)} + \left(1 - \beta_2\right) x_j^{pbest(k,i)}\right) \\ + \frac{r_i \alpha(x_j^{max} - x_j^{min})}{k+1} \qquad j = 1, 2, ..., D, i = 1, 2, ..., Np \tag{6}$$

In this equation, $x_j^{pbest(k,i)}$ is the best experience of ith particle in k^{th} iteration, $x_j^{gbest(k)}$ is the best experience of all particles in k^{th} iteration, and β_1 and β_2 are the adjustable control coefficients related to the penetration of the best collective experience and the best individual experience for the new solution positions, respectively.

Mutation is used to prevent the HBB-BC from trapping into the local optimum as follows:

$$x_j^{(k+1,i)} = x_j^{min} + rand().\left(x_j^{max} - x_j^{min}\right) \tag{7}$$
$$if \ rand(\ ) > P_m$$

where, P_m is the mutation probability and $rand()$ is a random number generated for each particle at each iteration[18].

6. Simulation results and analysis

The surge arrester different models with the rated voltage of 63 kV and 230 kV were simulated using EMTP. The IEEE model has 5 parameters (R_0, R_1, L_0, L_1, C_0), and the pinceti model has 3 parameters (R_0, L_0, L_1).

$$x = [x_1, x_2, x_3, x_4, x_5]^T = [R_0, R_1, L_0, L_1, C]^T \tag{8}$$
(IEEE model)

$$x = [x_1, x_2, x_3]^T = [R_0, L_0, L_1]^T \tag{9}$$
(Pinceti model)

Application of an optimization algorithms determines the optimal values for x_i. The BB-BC and HBB-BC optimization methods are applied to minimize the relative error. The initial parameter values for each model are computed by the procedures described in the references [4, 5].

The applied algorithms change the values for the parameters and calculate the objective function value according to the new residual voltage obtained.

The surge arrester parameters are determined using the BB-BC and HBB-BC algorithms. An impulse current of 10 kA, $8/20 \, \mu s$ are applied to the models. The residual voltage obtained by the simulation are compared with the measured one obtained by the manufacturer [12]. The initial computed parameters and the optimum parameters for each model obtained using the BB-BC and HBB-BC algorithms are listed in tables 6-9.

The optimized peak value for the residual voltage and the relative errors for each model are given in tables 4 and 5. The relative error was calculated using the following equation as follows;

$$Error \% = \frac{X_{sim} - X_{meas}}{X_{meas}} \times 100 \tag{10}$$

In the above equation, X_{sim} and X_{meas} are the peak residual voltage obtained by the simulation and experimental data reported by the manufacturers, respectively. As it can be seen, these algorithms are capable of estimating different parameters, and can effectively model the dynamic characteristic of surge arresters.

Table 4. Residual voltages and relative errors for 63 kV.

Algorithms	10 kA 8/20 µs Models	Peak of Residual voltage (kV)	Error (%)	Standard deviation
BB-BC	IEEE	138.485	1.084	
	Pinceti	137.028	0.02	0.51708
HBB-BC	IEEE	137.849	0.62	
	Pinceti	137.023	0.0173	

Table 5. Residual voltages and relative errors for 230 kV.

Algorithms	10 kA 8/20 µs Models	Peak of Residual voltage (kV)	Error (%)	Standard deviation
BB-BC	IEEE	444.579	-1.42	
	Pinceti	451.035	0.0077	0.6813
HBB-BC	IEEE	447.862	-0.69	
	Pinceti	451.02	0.0046	

The relative error of the residual voltage peak values for the initial and optimized parameter values compared with the values given by manufacturer are presented in figure 4 and 5.

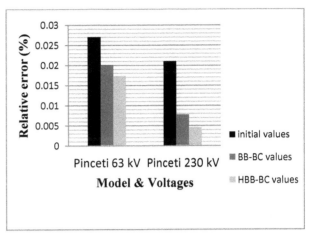

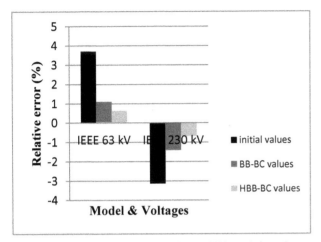

Figure 4. Relative error for a 10 kA (8/20 μs) injected impulse current using the values in tables 4 and 5.

Tables 6-9 show the initial computed parameters for each model, according to the computation described in section 2, as well as the optimum parameter values obtained using the BB-BC and HBB-BC algorithms described in sections 4 and 5. In tables 4 and 5 the peak value of the simulated residual voltage for each one model and relative errors are given, comparing them with the manufacturer's datasheet. As it can be seen, the pinceti model gives a lower error due to its simplicity in comparison to the IEEE model.

Figure 5. Relative error for a 10 kA (8/20 μs) injected impulse current using the values in tables 4 and 5.

Residual voltage peak values with optimized parameter value using BB-BC was compared to those obtained using HBB-BC; they are higher, and more accurate. It is obvious that the use of the HBB-BC algorithm gives more optimum parameters values for the equivalent circuit models.

The results obtained show that the use of the proposed algorithms cause high accuracy and low error between the manufacturer's and the simulated residual voltage. The methods are capable of estimating different parameters, and can effectively model dynamic characteristic of MOV surge arresters.

Table 6. Initial and estimated parameters using BB-BC algorithm for 63 kV.

	IEEE Model		Pinceti Model	
	Initial parameters	Optimized parameters	Initial parameters	Optimized parameters
R_0	99.6 Ω	120.5782 Ω	1 MΩ	1.1473 MΩ
R_1	64.744 Ω	66.7165 Ω	-	-
L_0	0.1992 μH	0.2103 μH	0.365 μH	0.3299 μH
L_1	14.94 μH	11.1919 μH	1.095 μH	1.0847 μH
C	0.1004 nF	0.0673 nF	-	-

Table 7. Initial and estimated parameters using BB-BC algorithm for 230 kV.

	IEEE Model		Pinceti Model	
	Initial parameters	Optimized parameters	Initial parameters	Optimized parameters
R_0	162.5 Ω	173.4655 Ω	1 MΩ	1.1546 MΩ
R_1	105.625 Ω	116.8947 Ω	-	-
L_0	0.325 μH	0.3524 μH	1.17 μH	1.2427 μH
L_1	24.375 μH	28.8533 μH	3.51 μH	3.1519 μH
C	0.0615 nF	0.0839 nF	-	-

Table 8. Initial and estimated parameters using HBB-BC algorithm for 63 kV.

	IEEE Model		Pinceti Model	
	Initial parameters	Optimized parameters	Initial parameters	Optimized parameters
R_0	99.6 Ω	119.5121 Ω	1 MΩ	0.7690 MΩ
R_1	64.744 Ω	68.9275 Ω	-	-
L_0	0.1992 μH	0.1329 μH	0.365 μH	0.3228 μH
L_1	14.94 μH	10.7021 μH	1.095 μH	1.0726 μH
C	0.1004 nF	0.3616 nF	-	-

Table 9. Initial and estimated parameters using HBB-BC algorithm for 230 kV.

	IEEE Model		Pinceti Model	
	Initial parameters	Optimized parameters	Initial parameters	Optimized parameters
R_0	162.5 Ω	158.3645 Ω	1 MΩ	0.8364 MΩ
R_1	105.625 Ω	112.4447 Ω	-	-
L_0	0.325 μH	0.3348 μH	1.17 μH	1.0453 μH
L_1	24.375 μH	31.0672 μH	3.51 μH	3.2849 μH
C	0.0615 nF	0.0374 nF	-	-

7. Conclusion

Metal-oxide surge arresters (MOSAs) are extensively used in power systems due to good performance in over-voltage protection. The correct and adequate modeling of MOSAs characteristics is very important for insulation coordination studies and system reliability. In this work, the mostly used equivalent circuit IEEE and Pinceti models were simulated in EMTP, and then their parameters were optimized using the BB-BC and HBB-BC optimization algorithms. In these methods, the MOSA parameters were estimated based on the comparison between the residual voltage obtained by simulating it with the manufacturer´s results. One of the most advantages of the proposed methods is required only manufacturer data for estimating the initial parameters of MOSA models.

The two models used in this study, simulate and reproduce adequately the ferequency-dependent behavior of MOSAs, giving a very small error after the application of the optimization procedures. The simulation results obtained showed that after an application of the optimization procedures, the error between the simulated and manufacturer´s residual voltage for a given 10 kA, 8/20 μs input impulse current was less than 1.5 percent.

Considering the accuracy of these two optimization algorithms, the results showed that the HBB-BC algorithm is more accurate. Therefore, in order to optimize the parameters of the MOSA models, it is proposed to use the HBB-BC algorithm.

References

[1] Li, H. J., Birlasekaran, S. & Choi, S. S. (2002). A parameter identification technique for metal oxide surge arrester models. IEEE Transactions on Power Delivery, vol. 17, no. 3, pp. 736-741.

[2] Nafar, M., Gharehpetian, G. B. & Niknam, T. (2011). Improvement of estimation of surge arrester parameters by using Modified Particle Swarm Optimization, Energy, vol. 36, no. 8, pp. 4848-4854.

[3] Bayadi, A., (2008). Parameter Identification of ZnO surge arrester models based on genetic algorithms. Electric Power Systems Research, vol. 78, no. 7, pp. 1204-1209.

[4] IEEE Guide for the Application of Metal-Oxide Surge Arrester for Alternating Current Systems, (1997). IEEE Standard C62.22.

[5] Magro, M. C., Giannettoni, M. & Pinceti, P. (2004). Validation of ZnO surge arresters model for overvoltage studies. IEEE Transactions on Power Delivery, vol. 19, no. 4, pp. 1692-1695.

[6] Zinik, B., Babuder, M., Muhr, M., Zitnik M. & Thottappillil, R. (2005). Numerical modeling of metal oxide varistor. Proceedings of the XIVth International symposium on high voltage engineering. Beijing, China, Tsinghua University, pp. 25-29.

[7] Nafar, M., Solookinejad, G., & Jabbari, M. (2014). Comparison of IEEE and Pinceti models of surge arresters. Research Journal of Engineering Sciences, vol. 3, no.5, pp. 32-34.

[8] Nafar, M., Gharehpetian, G. B. & Niknam, T. (2011). A New parameter estimation algorithm for metal oxide surge arrester. Electric Power Components and Systems, vol. 39, no. 7, pp. 696-712.

[9] Christodoulou, C. A., Vita, V., Ekonomou, L., Chatzarakis, G. E. & Stathopulos, I. A. (2010). Application of Powell's optimization method to surge arrester circuit models parameters, Energy, vol. 35, no. 8, pp. 3375-3380.

[10] Christodoulou C. A., Ekonomou L., Fotis G. P., Karampelas P. & Stathopulos I. A., (2010) Parameters' optimisation for surge arrester circuit models, IET Science, Measurement and Technology, vol. 4, no. 2, pp. 86-92.

[11] ABB Switchgear, (1995). "HV Surge Arresters" Technical Information, Ed.3.

[12] ABB, EXLIM-P Metal Oxide Gapless Surge Arresters (2011). DN: GNM110009.

[13] Modrusan, M., (1983), Tests on high-voltage metal oxide surge arresters with impulse currents, Proceedings of the Fourth International Symposium on High Voltage Engineering.

[14] Canadian/American EMTP User Group. (1987). Alternative transients program rule book. Belgium, Leuven.

[15] Abdelhafid, B. (2008), Parameter identification of ZnO surge arrester models based on genetic algorithms, Electric Power Systems Research, vol. 78, pp. 1204-1209.

[16] Osman, K. Erol. & Ibrahim, Eksin. (2006). A new optimization method: Big Bang–Big Crunch. Advances in Engineering Software 37, pp. 106 –111.

[17] Kaveh, A & Talatahari, S. (2009) Size optimization of space trusses using Big Bang-Big Crunch algorithm. Comput Struct, vol. 87, no. (17-18), pp.1129-1140.

[18] Sedighizadeh, M., Esmaili, M., Esmaeili, M., (2014). Application of the hybrid Big Bang-Big Crunch algorithm to optimal reconfiguration and distributed generation power allocation in distribution systems, Energy, vol. 76, no. C, pp. 920-930.

12

Method integration: An approach to develop agent oriented methodologies

E.Ghandehari[1], F.Saadatjoo[1*] and M. A. Z. Chahooki[2]

1. Computer Engineering Department, Science and Art University, Yazd, Yazd, Iran
2. Electrical & Computer Engineering Department, Yazd University, Yazd, Yazd, Iran

*Corresponding saadatjou@sau.ac.ir (F. Saadatjou).

Abstract
Agent oriented software engineering (AOSE) is an emerging field in computer science and proposes some systematic ideas for multi agent systems analysis, implementation and maintenance. Despite the various methodologies introduced in the agent-oriented software engineering, the main challenges are defects in different aspects of methodologies. According to the defects resulted from weaknesses in agent oriented methodologies in different aspects, a combinatory solution named ARA using, ASPECS, ROADMAP and AOR has been proposed. The three methodologies were analyzed in a comprehensive analytical framework according to concepts and Perceptions, modeling language, process and pragmatism. According to time and resource limitations, sample methodologies for evaluation and in titration were selected. This selection was based on the use of methodologies' and their combination ability. The evaluation show that, the ROADMAP methodology supports stages of agent-oriented systems' analysis and the design stage is not complete because it doesn't model all semi agents. On the other hand, since AOR and ASPECS methodologies support the design stage and inter agent interactions, a mixed methodology has been proposed and is a combination of analysis stage of ROADMAP methodology and design stage of AOR and ASPECS methodologies. Furthermore, to increase the performance of proposed methodology of actor models, service model, capability and programming were also added to this proposed methodology. To describe its difference phases, it was used in a case study too. Results of this project can pave the way to introduce future agent-oriented methodologies.

Keywords: *Agent-oriented Software Engineering, Agent-based System, ASPECS, ROADMAP, AOR.*

1. Introduction

Agent-oriented software engineering is a type of engineering with agents as its main abstraction. In other words, agents are the main components of such software. The agent-oriented approach toward software engineering means dividing the problem into several autonomous and interacting agents which interact with each other to achieve the goal they have been designed for [1].

AOSE was developed to respond to the essential needs of software engineering and agent-based computations [2]. Its main goal is to create the methodologies, tools and facilities required for the simple preparation and maintenance of agent-oriented software [3]. As object-oriented software engineering (OOSE) was not able to respond to the needs of agent-oriented software, the emergent need for a new engineering compatible with agent perspectives led to the development of AOSE from OOSE [4]. One of the main challenges ahead of AOSE is that it lacks a complete software development methodology. Although a large number of agent-oriented methodologies have already been proposed, a few of them fully cover software engineering activities and none of them fully supports the development needs of agent-based systems. Therefore, it currently seems necessary to work on developing an integrated and comprehensive methodology [5-8]. In the following Paragraphs studies aimed at developing agent-based methodologies were examined.

Zambonelli et al. added the internet implementable systems modeling to the GAIA methodology. In this study, according to the openness and goals conflict in agents, the ability to model the inter agent relations was added to the model [9]. Jaunet et al. also in 2002 added a hierarchical structure for roles and developing a formal model for the system environment and developing the ability to manage dynamic changes to GAIA methodology and proposed a new one named ROADMAP [8]. Another development in this methodology was performed by Garcia et al. enhanced the interaction, agent and protocol stages and the UML developed model by a combination of this methodology and the AUML [10]. Gonzalez et al. also tried to enhance this method logy by adding agent design stage and a repeatable approach [11]. Agent oriented methodologies enhancement is not limited to GAIA and is continuing on Methodologies like MASE and TROPOS yet. In one of MASE enhancements the ontology stage was added to the analysis stage of the methodology by Dieloet et al. [5]. Another extension named organizational relations modeling was added to the MASE methodology [12]. In TROPOS methodology, a formal goal analysis model was added [13]. A method to associate goals with roles was also added to this methodology [14].

According to these deficits, we first tried to extract some positive and negative properties of ASPECS [15], ROADMAP [8] and AOR [16] methodologies and then a combinational methodology using these properties were proposed. We also tried to achieve a good convergence by segregating models in different analysis and design phases and propose some models (agent, capability and programmer model). This convergence enhances the proposed methodology's abilities and paves the way toward future generation of agent oriented methodologies. To do so, we should continue our research to develop and enhance agent oriented methodologies.

In order to segregate object oriented and agent methodologies we will examine the differences between objects and agents. Then in section three, we pointed out some evaluation indices. In section four, we will introduce selected method in this article. In section five we identify the proposed methodology and analyze its different phases and finally in section six. We propose conclusion and future works in this area.

2. Comparison between object-oriented and agent-oriented approaches

AOSE has evolved from OOSE. In other words, agents have been derived from objects [17]. LIND compared object-oriented systems with agent-oriented ones in terms of hardware, theory,

implementation time, programming language, and designing language [18], producing the following results: a)Objects have a central structure but agents perform distributed computations. b) Objects are more homogenous than agents in a system. c) Agents cannot initiate or destroyed as easily as objects. d) the object's behavior and structure doesn't change but agents learn from their experiments and change their behavior e) objects' interactions are usually a result of the other object demand but agents have their own reactions in front of the environmental or other motivators or the other agents' demand f) objects' interactions are usually synchronous but in agents it is vice versa. g) Encapsulation in agents is stronger than objects.

Since agents are derived from objects, there are also similarities between them. Parameter from both approaches though these similarities and differences could be mapped together. Table 1 presents a typical mapping of object-oriented and agent-oriented approaches.

Table1. Mapping of object-oriented and agent oriented approaches [18].

Object-Oriented Approach	Agent-Oriented Approach
Abstract Class	Generic Role
Class	Domain-Specific Role
Class Variables	Knowledge, Belief
Method	Capability
Inheritance	Role Binding
Prototyping	Specific Role + Personal Knowledge
Compound	Holon Agents
Method Invocation	Message Exchange
Cooperation	Interaction

Table 1 shows that the agent-oriented method has a solution for all object oriented methodology abilities. These solutions are suitable for agent - oriented systems analysis and design.

3. Criteria and evaluation methods

The first and the most important step in every analysis is) to determine its goals [19]. In this study, two purposes for evaluations were proposed. The first objective is to determine the strengths and weaknesses and similarities and differences of the studied methodology to enhance a developed agent-oriented software system. The second objective is to equalize agent oriented methodologies by a combination of their strengths and also proposition of a way to enhance their limitations.

Then, the evaluation framework, which is built, which consists of properties, attributes and measures. Measures used here to evaluate OOSE methodologies are based on current works and other works performed on agent-oriented methodologies [19-22]. The evaluation was focused on the technical properties of the methodologies. Determination of models and common projects were compared with three

methodologies and their significant aspects were evaluated. This subject plays an important role in the next generation of agent-oriented methodologies development.

Next, a methodology evaluation framework is proposed according to properties comparison. It consists of some measures and rules that cover AOSE exclusive features too. Figure 1 shows the agent-oriented methodologies evaluation framework. Figure 1 illustrates the 4 aspects of the evaluation named concepts, modeling language, processes and operation orientation.

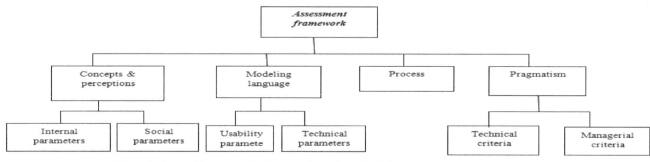

Figure1. General framework of agent oriented methodologies assessment.

Each proposed index is divided into some measures. These indices are discussed comprehensively in table 2 with full details and measures. To evaluate the proposed methodologies according to these 4 indexes, we proposed some questionnaires to experts and analyzed the corresponding answers according to fuzzy Delphi method [23]. We will discuss the results of these evaluations and the answers of the questionnaires next.

3.1. Validity, reliability and measure of questionnaire

To determine the study justifiability, we first performed the basic test for the questionnaire. So, the initial questionnaire was distributed between 11 expert teachers in agent-oriented software engineering field. After collecting the answers, some obscure and unrelated questions were determined, edited, reformed and placed in the final questionnaire and those questions totally unrelated were removed. To determine the questionnaire sustainability, we used the cronbach alpha coefficient. The calculated value for this variable in this study was 0.832 that is acceptable according to the research principles. The measurement scale in this study was the Likert 5 Points measure.

Methodologies investigated by provided parameters in evaluation framework, were analyzed by fuzzy Delphi method. This section investigates similarities and differences of these

three methodologies. So similarities areas of these methodologies are Goal models Co-execution, plans, static & dynamic structure and record model. Table 3 will show similarities of 3 models. Region of differences among three methods according to the assessment of results includes basic needs and the environmental model in ROADMAP methodology and sustain model of the methodology in ASPECS. Table 4 presents the differences in methodology.

Then, according to the results of the assessment, we will have a case study and introduce ARA combined methodology. In order to assess the ability of the proposed methodology, a case study will be used.

3.2. Findings and evaluation results

In the previous section, methods and frames used to assess was described. The principles used in the assessment, indicators were defined in four parts. In this section, using the criteria of evaluation results is presented. The results of the analysis are based on fuzzy Delphi method. Due to the nature of some of the benchmarks, only the presence or absence of the methodology is reviewed.

- The first indicator: Concepts and perceptions
   Property type 1: internal properties

1- Autonomy: autonomy is a key feature for agents. It differentiates them from other entities. According to evaluations, all the three methodologies here have this feature.

Table 2. Concepts and properties covered with evaluation framework indexes.

Index definition of the concepts and features	Index definition	Index

☐ Internal features
Autonomy, mental attitude, goal oriented, response, the Co-executive, located in the environment.
    (The methodology supports the mechanism of self-control, and a range of features, models, objectives, changes in the environment, parallel processing and features an internal model of the environment is checked)
    ☐ Social features
Means of cooperation, teamwork, protocols, communication languages
    (The methodology supports the model of cooperation, teamwork agents display methods and forms of expression and communication protocol between agents of social features to be checked).
	Agents and agent oriented systems concepts	Concepts and Perceptions

☐Usability features
Intelligibility and clarity, distinctness, ease of use
    ☐ Technical features
Compatibility, the ability to track, refining, reusable
    (The methodology supports the modeling techniques to examine the compatibility of the path analysis modeling activities to implement, develop processes and mechanisms for reusing existing components in the form of technical features to be checked).
Software life cycle stages and activities
    ☐ cover the full life cycle
Including the development of methods designed to duplicate the top-down and bottom-up grant.
	Modeling language for model illustration	Modeling language

☐ coating process with sufficient detail Including definitions, initiatives, decision management, quality assurance guidelines and estimates ☐ Support the development of concepts Includes reusable and Prototyping	Software life cycle	Process

☐ management features
Cost
    (Property management fee examined the methodology adopted).
    ☐ Technical features
Applicable range of scalable, flexible distribution
    (The support of the use of different methodologies, different size and design of systems-management and distribution of technical specifications will be reviewed).
	Methodology development aspects	Pragmatism

Table3. Methodologies similarities structure analysis.

Model goal	Model covering methodology	Comparative model
Goal model	ASPECS ، ROADMAP ،AOR	Goal achievement
Co execution model	ASPECS ، ROADMAP	Agent modeling independently
Role model	ASPECS ، ROADMAP ،AOR	Agent role definition
Static and dynamic model	ASPECS ، ROADMAP	Agent internal architecture design
Pre model	ROADMAP ،AOR	Agent relationship model

Table 4. Analysis of differences between methodologies.

Model / Difference model	Model covering methodology	Model objective
Basic needs/ environment model	ROADMAP	requirements /domain demand
Allocation model	ASPECS	Structure definition and relationships

The support level for this parameter is acceptable in all of them. All of them support this property and have some functions and enhancements in agents for that. In addition, the co-execution plot in ASPECS and ROADMAP makes it possible to model agents free from their environment and other entities.

2- Mental orientations: ROADMAP methodology supports these parameters fully with its internal functions and illustrates the agents' knowledge from their environment. The agents' goals are also modeled in this way. On the other hand, ASPECS and AOR have a weaker support for this parameter. ASPECS has the goal plot but cannot illustrate the agents' knowledge.

3- Goal orientation and intractability: The evaluation of the measurements results for these two parameters are difficult. It is well supported by some methodologies. Like previous parameter, these two methodologies get the goals and then perform some operations to achieve them.

4- Co-execution: Support from this parameter varies between methodologies. It varies from bad to good. From experts' point of view, ASPECS has the best support for this model. In this methodology, a single role can be co-executed.

5- Be in environment: Support for this parameter varies from average to good among different methodologies. Experts believe that ROADMAP outperforms others in this respect. They believe that AOR is the worst in this respect. They believe that this is because the AOR doesn't support the environment model.

Property type 2: Social properties

1- Cooperation and team work methods: for this parameter we evaluated the multi agent programming and the team work. In ROADMAP and ASPECS the creators argued [8][15] that these methodologies support general agent oriented cooperation and any other kind of cooperation can be driven from them. But, in experts' point of view, none of these parameters are covered with these methodologies explicitly.

2- Protocol: ASPECS methodology with its analyzer protocol outperforms the two other methodologies. AOR doesn't provide a special model to show protocols, but shows interactions among agents in high levels. ROADMAP doesn't have any explicit definition for protocol except in AUML [24].

3- Communicational Language: Experts believe that, this feature is in all three methodologies. Since the interaction among the agents has some levels of knowledge. (All three agent-oriented methodologies as the communicational language have the aim of speech act).

- The second index: Modeling language
Feature type 1: Usability features

1- Intelligibility and clarity: The measure of how brightly the symbol definition specifies the syntax and symbols models. Symbol provided by the three methods are well understood.

2- Distinctness: The number of static and dynamic models and the different views that show the destination system are good test for these measures. ASPECS methodology of aspects of system dynamics model and protocols, deal with ROADMAP methodology for system dynamics modeling protocols with the exception of some support in the detailed design level, which does not provide strong support. However symbols in the ASPECS methodology look meaningful. However, this methodology does not provide different views of the destination. AOR methodology has models for static and dynamic aspects of the target system and sees the system from a different angle. Experts believe that, modeling language of AOR methodology is not suitable because it does not give you the detailed structure. AOR-oriented methodology is not actually a perspective- oriented methodology.

3- Easy to use: According to experts, and connoisseurs', opinion, all three methodologies are a symbol and using them is simple.

Feature type 2: Technical features

1- Compatibility: for controlling the terms of compatibility, the methodology is tested at different levels. ASPECS methodology supports it well; While ROADMAP and AOR methodologies don't support it. From the perspective of qualified professionals, reason of this weak support is accessibility to supportive tools.

2- Ability to track: Similar to compatibility criteria, ASPECS methodology supports this feature. This methodology provides a clear link between their models. For example, goals, roles, and operating practices will bond together. These connections allow the developer to obtain a model of the design (e.g. interior architecture of agents).

3- Refinement: three methodologies don't have a proper support from this standard. From the perspective of professionals and experts, this issue reflects the fact that the language of modeling three methodologies isn't integrated. In fact, the developers can move through the phases and add details to the model.

4- Reusability: None of the three tested methodologies use techniques explicitly to support the design and use of reusable components. Also, the reuse of existing components in each methodology is not seen.

- The third indicator: The process

1- Development Principles: when looking for the life cycle of software development, it is clear that all three studied methods have architectural design and detailed design. Except for AOR methodology, implementation is supported in two other methodologies. Test and debug are only special for ASPECS methodology. ASPECS is the only methodology which describes the development of the operating system and it is part of the design phase. In view of the development, the methodology ASPECS supports top-down and bottom-up method. While ROADMAP methodology and AOR are appropriate for top-down approaches.

2- The process stages: These processes are described well in analysis and design phase of methodology ASPECS and ROADMAP. While descriptive design in AOR methodology isn't documented well. So from views of experts, this issue is resources' constraints in the AOR methodology.

3- Developmental Support concept: There are several key concepts such as prototyping and reuse of components there. From experts' point of view, none of these three methodologies have subject related to sampling in process or creating a reusable component.

4- Quality assurance guidelines and estimates: Due to lack of agent-oriented methodologies development and from the experts' perspective, a detailed statement can't be done for this parameter.

- The fourth indicator: Pragmatism
Feature type 1: managerial features

Cost: The cost of achieving methodologies and supportive tools is free for all methodologies and its documentations are accessible.

Feature type 2: Technical features

1- Domain applicability: From experts' point of view, there is no limitation for domain of applications of these three methodologies. These domains for an agent-oriented system with autonomic software are reliable and powerful.

2- Scalability: None of these methodologies cover this parameter. From experts view, none of them has proposed anything about this aspect and how it is defined.

3- Distribution: From experts' point of view, ROADMAP and AOR support this parameter implicitly. In their opinion, ASPECS is an exception and the design stage of this methodology, makes it possible to design and allocate agents in the network. That is because of the allocation model.

4. Case study: Housing sales system
In this article, the system of buying and selling house is defined in an online frame and will provide different sections necessary for buying and selling. In this system, people can see information about done trades by searching on site and then decide about buying or selling house. When buying, you should have one third of the amount specified by the Department of Housing and Urban Development and when giving selling request, providing valid document to experts is required (all the stages are done electronically). Buying and selling requirements involve determining what the size, location, year of construction are and how to do deal in terms of with the price; it means that the maximum or the minimum purchase price (buyers and sellers) will be defined. Buyers and sellers can also put provisions in their requirements. For example, according to variable price of house market, seller can choose a special month to show house information in order to have more profit (since in some months house has better price) and this can be a strategy from seller. On the other hand, if the buyer wants to pay money in installments, he can say it. After buyers and sellers requirements, a department's expert will check the trueness of their requirements and the information will be recorded in system if they are true and precise, and after entering the requirements in system, the system will organize housing transactions according to priorities, and according to the restrictions imposed by the parties, buyers and vendors can provide a list of the items in the next 48 hours (minimum and maximum price and other conditions) according to which a deal can be done. After viewing the list, buyers and sellers can

choose and cases on the base of priorities. In requirement, the priority of a deal is on first requirements (both among buyers and sellers). After doing the deal, a housing system will issue deal documents which are certification of department's expert, buying certification, selling certification and temporary certification of deal. After preparing the documents, the relevant certifications will be delivered to the parties. In this system, fees for each transaction will be divided between the parties based on the Ministry of Housing and Urban Development Act.

5. Introduction the methodology of ARA

ARA is an agent-oriented software development methodology that is made of a combination of three ASPECS, ROADMAP and AOR methodologies and actor, planning and capability proposed models. In determining the phase of ARA methodology, three ideas were used are: a) perception and understanding of the agents and mental imagery (objectives and program-planning) during the analysis phase of software development, from basic analysis to used design. b) in order to have a complete understanding from system and environment, the actor model is added to phase analysis of ARA methodology.c) to clarify agents' capabilities in detail and to deter the way of performing these capabilities by agents, two capability and programmer models are proposed in ARA methodology.

Analysis and design of actor consists of a big set of concepts, so understanding all aspects of analysis and design model from a special view is difficult. For this reason, in an ARA methodology, several models that focus on various aspects are defined. These models have various aspects, but are not complete alone, so by putting them together, a complete and understandable view of the system will be achieved.

In choosing models of ARA methodology, noted earlier, a complete evaluation frame is used and covers four main areas of agent-oriented software engineering such as [19-22] concepts, modeling language, process and activism. According to this frame and its parameters, the support of each methodology is evaluated and experts investigated the actor, capacity and programmer proposed models. Thus models used in the ARA methodology of agent-oriented concepts are largely covered and these models do not overlap with each other. Table 5 shows the differences between an ARA methodology and the three invested methodologies.

Table 5. Structural analysis of the difference between the ARA methodology and studied method.

Models/ Difference models	Model goal
Actor model	Fully understanding the environment
Capability model	Determine the Agent capabilities
Programming model	Implication of capabilities by each agent

In order to assess the ability of the proposed methodology, it is used in a case study that is described in Section IV.

5.1. Housing sales system analysis using phases of the proposed methodology

In this part, a method is provided to homogenize three methodologies of ASPECS, ROADMAP and AOR by combining the strengths and avoiding its limitation. In fact, to create a new methodology, some parts of this methodology are used according to the framework presented in the previous step. Using combined method can affect the proposed methodology in order to covers most of the Agent-oriented software engineering and it will be effective in developing next Agent-oriented Methodologies This article used developmental process to combine methods and according to importance of analysis and designing phases in creating qualified and reliable software products, it will focus on these two phase.

5.1.1 Phases of the proposed methodology
1. Analysis phase

The proposed methodology in analysis phase consists of actor model, goal model, knowledge model, environment model and role model and these five models will provide a strong support for defining relationship among system actors, targets, duty and knowledge of system, obtaining environment and defining key roles in system. These models will increase knowledge of developers about system requirements and will provide inputs for next steps (The analysis and design of a system is done by using AUML diagrams).

-Actor model

Organizing and defining the actors of the system under study is one of the important steps in the analysis phase. In this model, the physical attributes of the system are identified. Figure 2 shows the actor system of buying and selling real estate. As you see in figure 2, buying and selling system of house has three actors of seller and buyer / department expert and the Department of Housing and Urban Development.

Each of identified actors in the system has goals.

Figure2. Graph for the system of buying and selling real estate agent.

The aim of the seller and buyer agent / department specialist, is access to basic information about housing (purchase and sale) and / the actor objective of expert is to investigate the trueness of buyers and sellers' information. The actor purpose of the Ministry housing boom, is to go out of recession and prevents a rise in housing prices. Using the graph of the relationship between the active agents can be clearly displayed by the system.

- Goal model

Organizing and identifying goals, are an important step in extraction of requirements. In this model, the overall objectives of the system are determined in different levels.

Figure 3 shows the purpose model and functions of the system of buying and selling property.

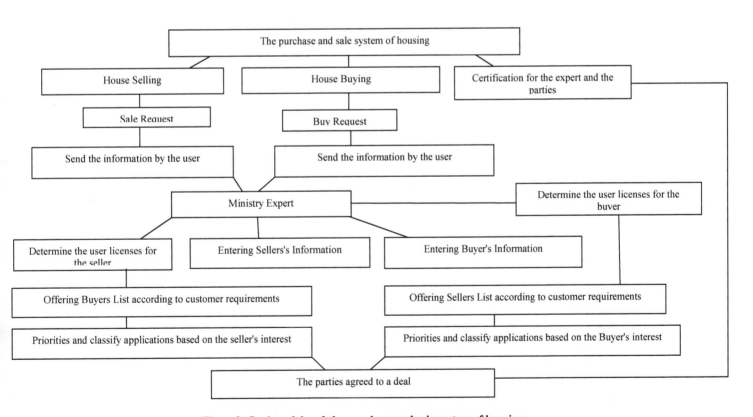

Figure3. Goal model and the purchase and sale system of housing.

As figure 3 shows, house selling and buying system include three parts of buying home, selling home and issuing a license. In this system each of buyers and sellers should first send requirements in order to buy or sell a house. After the requirement is met, all information should be sent completely and truly and after that the expert will confirm the trueness of this information. If there is no problem with information, user license will be issued and related information will be put on it. After this stage, a list will be given to them (list of buyers for sellers and vice versa) that they can use it by the users license and according to this list, the priorities and interests of buyers and sellers will be categorized and if they agree, system will issue the license.

- Knowledge model

A model of system has rules, procedures and limitations. Rules relate to principles that system will make decisions on their basis. Procedures will clarify the performance of system and limitations are necessary for using a system. Table 6 shows the knowledge model for the system of buying and selling a house.

- Environment model

An environment Modeling is used to clarify the scope of the system and functions are specified the recognition of systems. In that respect, the environmental agents and their relationship with

Table 6. Knowledge model of the buying and selling housing system.

Rules	-If the purchase price is equal to or greater than the price the seller, relevant housing information will be displayed to the buyer
	-Provide evidence of Salable Property by seller
	-If the seller price is equal to or greater than the price the buyer, information relevant to buyer will be displayed to the seller
Steps	-The purchase of housing step: Having a third floor price set by the Department of Housing and Urban Development, Offering buy request, taking User license for listed and classified according to priority
	-Offering bank account by the buyer met the third floor of an amount determined by the Department of Housing and Urban Development
Limitations	-Offering valid proof of ownership by the seller
	-Intervals to provide a list of buyers and sellers, are 48 hours after entering information by the ministry's expert

each other will be determined by the system. Also, in this stage the components of system. Show the environment model in the system of buying and selling house (see Figure 4).

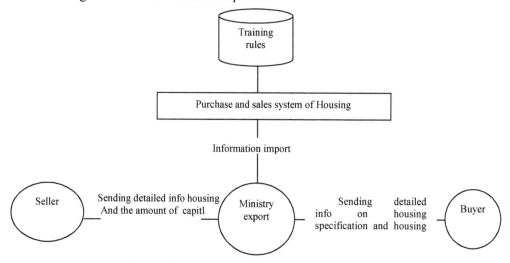

Figure 4. Model for the environment of purchase and sale of housing.

- Role model

In the agent-oriented approach, the agent is considered as a key entity. Thus it can be said that one of the basic needs of the agent-oriented methodology is helping developers to specify the agents of system. In the proposed methodology, a role model technique is used to specify agents, so the roles in systems are extracted precisely and then according to specified roles they are defined. In fact, the role model is the main part to determine the agent, because the agents should be used in the system to carry out their roles. This

model includes the objectives, the sub-roles and responsibilities of the role in the system. The system of buying and selling house includes search, storage and retrieval of information, and user licenses, classifying information and updating information will be provided in depth.

• Role of searching information

This role is defined to enable users to have a search about lists. Thus users can search detailed information by clarifying basic information (national code). Since users have to define some details about the house like its size, year of its construction, and other similar things, so buyers and sellers can see needed information by searching the national code of person from the list. Also users can search their own or other information about priorities. Table 7 shows the role model for searching information.

Table 7. The role model for the searching information.

Role name: Search of information

The Purpose of the role: Providing information on the national code entered by the user

Details of role: Read limitation information (entered national code) that Search operations must be performed based it

Responsibilities: Offering list based on respective national code

• Role of storing and recovery of information

This role is in the frame of storing information according to priorities of users' interests, storing background information that includes all operations that user has done on system till now and storing user information. Table 8 shows role model for storing and recovery information.

Table 8. Role model for the storage and retrieval of information.

Role name: Information storage and retrieval

The Purpose of the role: Store information of preferences, history and user

Details of role: Read the information entered by the user

Responsibilities: Create a list of information for user

• Role of user license

This role is for experts, buyers and sellers that want to enter the system. In fact, the role of user license is to confirm the user information. Table 9 shows the role model for user license.

Table 9. Role model for the role of use licenses.

Role name: User License

The Purpose of the role: User authentication, create the permissions

Details of role: Read the information entered by the user and query the database to test of the validity

Responsibilities: Protection of system Security

• Information classification

Information Classification is defined based on priorities of user's interests. This role has two lists of level 1 and level 2 that user interest are in level1 and other cases are in level 2. Table 10 shows role model for classification role.

Table 10. Role model for the classification role.

Role name: Information Classification

The Purpose of the role: Information Classification based on priorities of user interest in both one and two level

Details of role: Read user preferences

Responsibilities: Create classification in user Priorities at two levels one and two

• Role of updating information

This role provides a list of new added materials to sell and buy house and deals with information and updating list of users' priorities and interests. This role will fetch selling and buying information from database of buying system and fetch desired information from database of urbanization and housing department and provides it for users in some lists. Table 11 shows role model for updating information.

Table 11. Role model for the update information role.

Role name: Update information

The Purpose of the role: Update information and display the status of transactions, update interests and priorities

Details of role: Reading the information from database of buying and selling system of housing and ministry of Housing and Urban Development and User Interests

Responsibilities: Rendering the list of housing added for buying and selling and transactions, Changes in Wish list

In analysis stage, according to target and duty, knowledge, role and environment models, system requirements and its rules and limitations were extracted.

2. Design phase

The proposed methodology in designing a phase includes: agent model, interaction model, capacity model, programmer model and service model. In the agent model, roles are played in any agent. An interaction model will clarify relations between agents to do play roles. Capacity and programmer models are used to modeling the capabilities of agents and to program the way of making these capabilities. The service model point out capabilities that each role should have.

- Agent model

This model is the supplement of the role model in the analysis phase. In this model according to defined roles in role model, an agent will be defined and then each role will be written in an agent. Buying a house and selling system consists of five agents that in table 12, the roles are played written in this agent.

Table 12. Allocation of roles to agent.

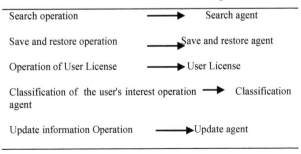

- Interaction model

This model clarifies relations between agents to play roles. In other words, an interaction model will model the way of doing playing roles. In role model 5 roles will be defined for system. The first role is information searching whose interaction model is shown in figure 5.

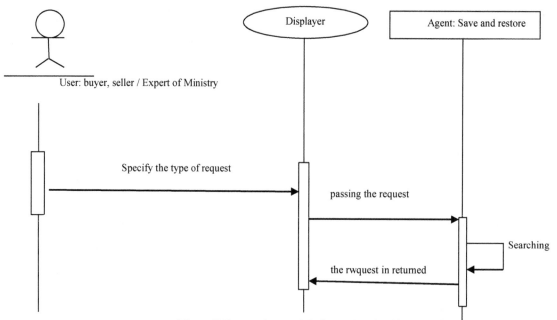

Figure 5. Interaction model of search role of information.

According to figure 5, a user (buyer/seller/expert) will first define the kind of his requirement. Then this request will be given to search agents and this agent search the kind of request from system database and show the result.

Another roles that will be clarified in the role model, is the role of storage and recovery. Figure 6 shows the interaction diagram of this role.

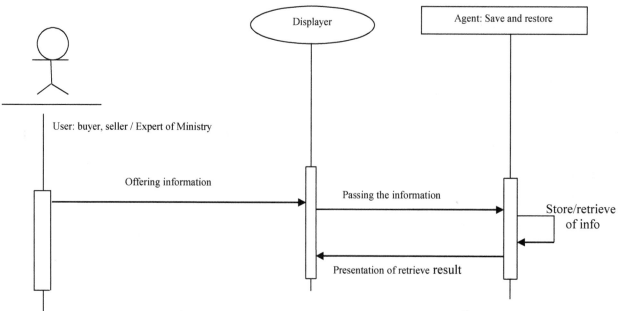

Figure 6. Interaction model for the storage and retrieval roles.

According to figure 6, a user (buyer/seller/expert) should first provide information that need to be stored and recovered, then this information will be given to storage and recovery agent and this agent will make the storage and recovery based on the information and shows the results.

Next, we will discuss interactions models of user license role. Interaction models of user license role are under investigating from two aspects of storing user information and confirm the validity of user's information.

In storing user information, a user has to enter his account information and this information will be given to a user's license agent. This agent will evaluate the information (that passing code and word is correct or not) and if the code is incorrect,

an error alarm will be made and information will be back.

If there isn't any problem, information will be sent to storage and recovery agent and this agent will store the information. Figure 7 shows the interaction model for a user license role in the scope of storage.

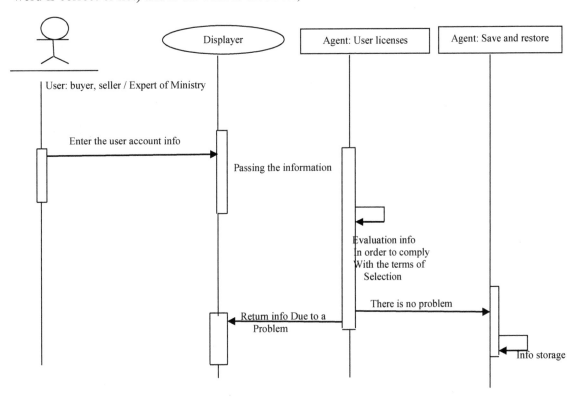

Figure 7. The interaction model of user licenses role within the scope of store.

It should be mentioned that a user (buyer or seller) should register in system just when he/she wants to send a buy/sell request. After requirement is met and if there wasn't any problem in it, experts will give a special password and code to them and last password and code are not needed any more.

For confirming a validity of user information, a user enters his user's information to system and this information will be given to a searching agent and this agent will do searches in system database. Figure 8 shows the interaction model of user license role in the scope of confirming validity.

Another that is clarified in role model is the role of classifying information. In the interaction model of this role, first of all the users will specify

what is in his mind in the list of houses, then this information is given to classification agent who will classify information in level 1 (user interests) and level 2 (other cases). Figure 9 shows the interaction model of information classification.

About updating the role, a user has to clarify the kind of updating (updating information of houses, updating interests of user).
After the kind of updating is clarified, the request is given to searching agent who will search the information based on the updating kindly and results are given to update agent and this agent will update on the list and send information to users. Figure 10 shows the updating role of the interaction model.

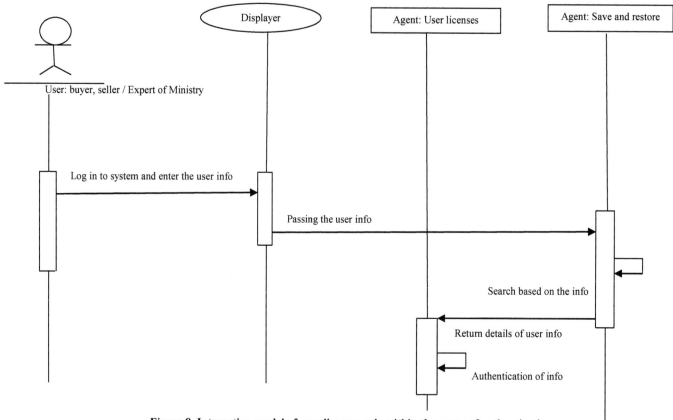

Figure 8. Interaction model of user licenses role within the scope of authentication.

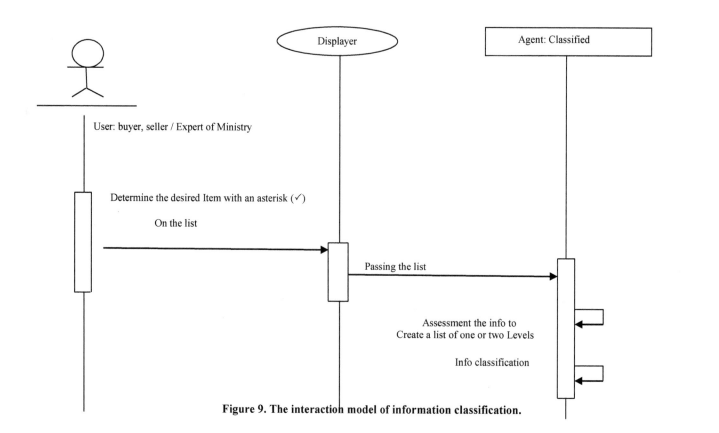

Figure 9. The interaction model of information classification.

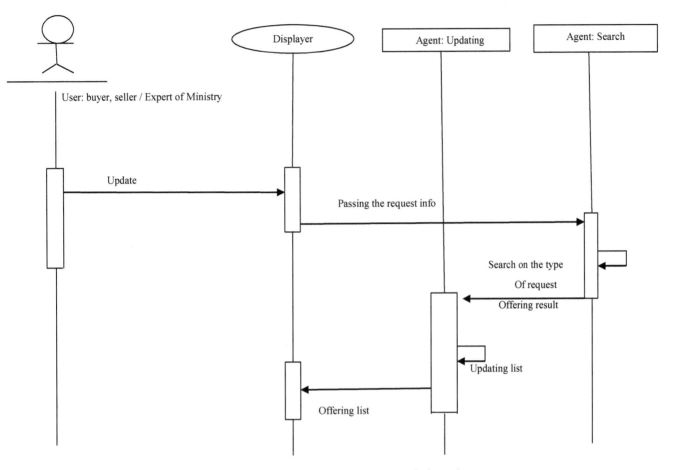

Figure 10. Interaction model on the updating role.

-Capacity and programmer model
This provides model capabilities for agents. Also models will program the stages of performing capabilities. In other words, in this model, the range of agents' duties and the way of doing them are modeled. In the agent model part, five agents were selected that first of them is information searching agent that capability model of this agent is shown in figure 11. Also the programmer model of this agent is shown in figure 12.

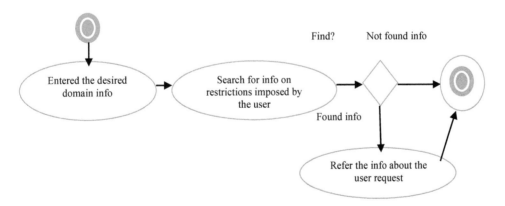

Figure 11. Search capability model.

According to figure 11, the capability of searching agent is modeled according to information provided by users while figure 12 will model this capability by using searching agent.

Another agent recognized in the agent model was storage and recovery agent that didn't need to be modeled through capability and programmer models, since it doesn't have any exception and is modeled in the interaction model in a good way.

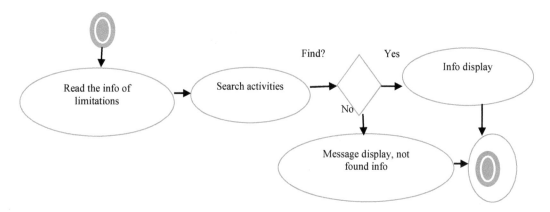

Figure 12. Planner model of search agent.

Next, we will discuss capability and programming model of user license agent. As it was said before, a user license agent plays the role of confirming validity of password and code. So if theses password and code are correct, you can access to system, otherwise, you are not permitted and an error message will be shown. Figure 13 shows the capability model of user license agent.

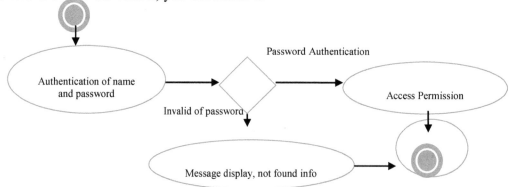

Figure 13. Capability model of user License agent.

In programming the model, the user license agent will read password and code first and then will search for it. If the entered password is correct, entered password will be compare with database password after finding information. Figure 14 shows the programmer model of user license agent. Another agent specified in agent model was information classification agent. In capability model of this agent, first, the user will show his interests according to provided list and classification agent will classify these interests on the base of their priorities

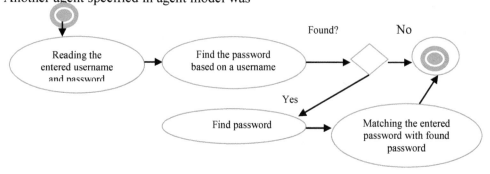

Figure 14. Planner model of user licenses agent.

Figure 15 shows capability model of classification agent. In programming the model, first, the classification agent will receive interest information of user and create two level of 1 and 2, then it will separate information according to liked and disliked priorities, as information about interests are in level 1 and information about dislikes are in level 2. Figure 16 shows the programming model of classification agent.

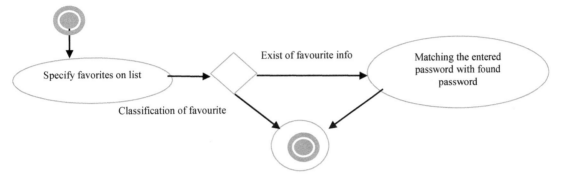

Figure 15. Capability model of the classification agent.

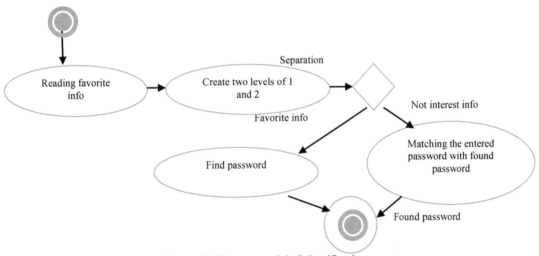

Figure 16. Planner model of classification agent.

Since capability of updating agent is modeled as storage and recovery agent by interaction model, there is no need to use capability and programming models for this agent.

- Service model
The service model is determined using the rules and constraints section of the knowledge model in the analysis phase. In this model every role is associated with at least one service. For every service, inputs, outputs, preconditions and post conditions should be determined. Inputs and outputs are easily extracted from the interaction model. Table 13 shows the service model for the real estate trade system.

Table13. Service model of house buying & selling system.

Service name	Input	Output	Preconditions	Post conditions
Listing real estate information	Seller or buyer ID no	The estate information display	Inserting the usage license	The history time the register.
Information update	New information insertion	Information reforms	Information insert for edition	Event time register for history and saving editions in data bank.
Information ordering	Favorite / un favor information	Illustration of information saved in list 1/2	Information type determination	Time registration for events in the history of the list 1/2 in the information bank.

The proposed methodology is based on the results from the real estate trade system in experts view point with respect to these three methodologies and performed a good support for parameters like autonomy, objective orientation interaction ability, and domain usability. In expert's point of view, models added to the combinational proposed model leads to an increase in convergence between the analysis and design phases. According to the view of the experts due to this modals ARA methodology is suitable for analysis and designing of business and industrial systems. Determination of agent capabilities and presentation of capabilities with these modals is important because of these systems. Analyzing team from the beginning of the project was able to determine the details accurately and the failure of this project has been minimized. Taking in consideration that the procedure of capabilities modal presentation and program is a new procedure, these two models can be used in other engineering software agent oriented methodologies and increase the quality of these methodologies.

6. Conclusion and future work

In this study a developed combinational methodology was used for analysis and design of agent- oriented systems. In this methodology, by combining strengths of ASPECS, ROADMAP and AOR methodologies and adding actor, capability and programmer models, it is possible to use high-level techniques to manage the problem complexity. Using the combinatory method in the proposed methodology led the achievement of two main goals of working standards and redefinition of the main blocks. The proposed methodology in the expert viewpoints and in the form of evaluation parameters in agent-oriented engineering has a good support for parameters like autonomy, goal orientation, react ability and domain usability compared to other methodologies.

Although three methodologies were selected for evaluation and formalization, they aren't a complete to show of all agents' methodologies. There are many important AOSE methodologies that each of them has special different features to support different aspects of operational dominion goals. Therefore future works can focus on expanding selected methodologies and using current evaluation framework to evaluate them. By doing this, uniform stated by models and techniques can be increased. Also by considering potential risks related to quality evaluation used in this article, other studies can be done on quantity experiences

References

[1] Zambonelli, F., Jennings, N. R., & Wooldridge, M. (2005). Multi-agent systems as computational organizations: the Gaia methodology. Journal of Autonomous Agents and Multi-Agent Systems, vol. 9, no. 3, pp. 136-171.

[2] Weiß, G. (2001). Agent orientation in software engineering. The knowledge engineering review, vol. 16, no.4, pp.349-373.

[3] Tveit, A. (2001). A survey of Agent-Oriented Software Engineering, In Norwegian University of Science and Technology, (pp.104-125), 2001.

[4] Garcia-Ojeda, J. C. & DeLoach Robby, S. A. (2009). AgentTool Process Editor: Supporting the Design of Tailored Agent-based Processes, In Procedings of the ACM Symposium on Applied Compting, (pp. 707-714). ACM, 2009.

[5] DiLeo, J., Jacobs, T., & DeLoach, S. A. (2002). Integrating Ontologies into Multiagent Systems Engineering. 4th international bi-conference workshop on agent- oriented Information systems, (pp.23-34), 2002.

[6] DeLoach, S. A. (2014). O-MaSE: An Extensible Methodology for Multi-agent Systems. In Agent-Oriented Software Engineering, vol. 4, no. 3, pp. 173-191.

[7] DeLoach, S. A., & Garcia-Ojeda, J. C. (2014). The O-MaSE Methodology. In Handbook on Agent-Oriented Design Processes, (pp. 253-285), 2014.

[8] Juan, T., Pearce, A., & Sterling, L. (2002). ROADMAP: Extending the Gaia Methodology for Complex Open Systems. The First International Joint Conference on Autonomous Agents & Multi-Agent Systems, pp. 3-10, 2002.

[9] Zambonelli, F., Jennings, N. R., Omicini, A., & Wooldridge, M. J. (2001). Agent-oriented software engineering for internet applications. In Coordination of Internet Agents, pp. 326-346, 2001.

[10] García-Ojeda, J. C., Arenas, A. E., & Alcázar, J. P. (2005). Paving the Way for Implementing Multiagent Systems: Integrating Gaia with Agent-UML. 6th International Workshop Agent-Oriented Software Engineering. Lecture Notes in Computer Science 3950, pp. 179-189, Springer-Verlag, 2005.

[11] Gonzalez-Palacios, J., & Luck, M. (2007). Extending Gaia with Agent Design and Iterative Development. 8th International Workshop Agent-Oriented Software Engineering, LNCS 4951, pp 16-30, 2007. Springer-Verlag, 2007.

[12] DeLoach, S. A. (2002) Modeling Organizational Rules in the Multiagent Systems Engineering Methodology, Proceedings of the 15th Canadian Conference on Artificial Intelligence, pp.54-62.

[13] Giorgini, P., Mylopoulous, J., & Sebastiani, R. (2005). Goal- Oriented Requirements Analysis and Reasoning in the Tropos Methodology. J. of Engineering Applications of Artificial Intelligence, Elsevier, vol. 8, no.2, pp. 159-171.

[14] Jureta, J., Faulkner, S., & Schobbens, P. (2006). Allocating Goals to Agent Roles During MAS Requirements Engineering. 7th Int. Workshop Agent-Oriented Software Engineering, LNCS 4405, pp. 19-34, Springer-Verlag, 2007.

[15] Cossentino, M., Gaud, N., Hilaire, V., Galland, S., & Koukam, A. (2009). ASPECS: an agent-oriented software process for engineering complex systems. J. of Autonomous Agents and Multiagent Systems Systems, vol. 20, no. 2, pp. 260–304.

[16] Wagner, G. (2003). The Agent-Object-Relationship Metamodel: Towards a Unified View of State and Behavior. J. of Information Systems. vol. 28, no. 5, pp. 475-504.

[17] Odell, J. (2002). Objects and agents compared. Joural of object technology, vol. 1, no. 1, pp. 41-53.

[18] Lind, J. (2001). Issues in agent-oriented software engineering. In Agent Oriented Software Engineering (pp. 45-58). Springer Berlin Heidelberg, 2001.

[19] Dam, K. H., & Winikoff, M. (2004). Comparing agent-oriented methodologies. In Agent-Oriented Information Systems, pp. 78-93, Springer Berlin Heidelberg, 2004.

[20] Sturm, A., & Shehory, O. (2004). A framework for evaluating agent-oriented methodologies. In Agent-Oriented Information Systems, pp. 94-109, Springer Berlin Heidelberg,2004.

[21] Ghandehari, E., Saadatjoo, F., & Chahooki, M. A. Z. (2014). AMA: a compound methodology for designing and implementing agent-based systems. J. of Advances in Computer Science, vol. 3, no. 11, pp. 107-114.

[22] Sudeikat, J., Braubach, L., Pokahr, A., & Lamersdorf, W. (2005). Evaluation of agent–oriented software methodologies–examination of the gap between modeling and platform. In Agent-Oriented Software Engineering, pp. 126-141, Springer Berlin Heidelberg,2005.

[23] Hsu, Y. L., Lee, C. H., & Kreng, V. B. (2010). The application of Fuzzy Delphi Method and Fuzzy AHP in lubricant regenerative technology selection. Expert Systems with Applications, vol. 37, no. 1, pp. 419-425.

[24] Bauer, B., Müller, J. P., & Odell, J. (2001). Agent UML: A formalism for specifying multiagent software systems. International Journal of Software Engineering and Knowledge Engineering, vol. 11, no. 3, pp. 207-230.

13

Dynamic characterization and predictability analysis of wind speed and wind power time series in Spain wind farm

N. Bigdeli[*] and H. Sadegh Lafmejani

EE Department, Imam Khomeini International University, Qazvin, Iran.

Corresponding author:nooshin_bigdeli@yahoo.com (N. Bigdeli).

Abstract

The renewable energy resources such as wind power have recently attracted more researchers' attention. It is mainly due to the aggressive energy consumption, high pollution and cost of fossil fuels. In this era, the future fluctuations of these time series should be predicted to increase the reliability of the power network. In this paper, the dynamic characteristics and short-term predictability of hourly wind speed and power time series are investigated via nonlinear time series analysis methods such as power spectral density analysis, time series histogram, phase space reconstruction, the slope of integral sums, the $\delta - \varepsilon$ method, the recurrence plot and the recurrence quantification analysis. Moreover, the interactive behavior of the wind speed and wind power time series is studied via the cross correlation, the cross and joint recurrence plots as well as the cross and joint recurrence quantification analyses. The results imply stochastic nature of these time series. Besides, a measure of the short-term mimic predictability of the wind speed and the underlying wind power has been derived for the experimental data of Spain's wind farm.

Keywords: *Stochastic Behavior, Recurrence Plot, Recurrence Quantification Analysis, Time Series Analysis, Wind Speed, Wind Power.*

1. Introduction

Wind energy is a free, renewable resource of clean energy. Compared with the conventional power plants, wind plants emit no air pollution or greenhouse gases. In fact, wind-based generation is the fastest growing source of renewable energy [1]. However, despite significant environmental benefits, wind power could be highly fluctuating because of the earth's natural atmospheric variability [1]. This variability can put at risk the power system reliability, which in turn requires more backup than the conventional generation in the form of reserve and regulation services. It also poses economical risks for wind farm owners, especially in competitive electricity markets [1]. To fully benefit from a large fraction of wind energy in an electrical grid, it is therefore necessary to predict the electrical energy generated by the wind [2]. The wind production depends on wind speed of the station. Therefore, forecasting the wind speed is an important issue that has increasingly received attentions of many researchers as well [2-7]. In order to forecast the

wind power production, two major questions should be answered. Those are: what is the nature of the wind speed/power time series dynamics and how predictable these time series are? The developed models for wind speed and power dynamics are derived inevitably form these time series. Therefore, one should characterize the nature and predictability of the recorded time series of the wind speed and the related wind power to find the proper model structure as well as the model inputs and to be able to claim the validity of its model.

Based on the above discussions in this paper, we are looking for the nature of the fluctuations of the recorded wind speed and power data to find out whether the fluctuations are from stochastic systems or not. If not, it maybe from a highly nonlinear deterministic or a chaotic systems. Chaotic behavior has been reported in a broad range of scientific disciplines including astronomy, biology, chemistry, ecology, engineering, and physics [8-9] as well as power market indices [10-12]. On the other hand, stochastic time series contains a collection of random variables and is the probabilistic counterpart to a deterministic system. Some examples of stochastic time series are stock market and exchange rate fluctuations, speech, audio and video signals and medical data such as patient's EEG [12]. Time series analysis] is commonly used for responding to the first mentioned question. Different time series approaches have been widely used in the literature for characterizing the properties of natural phenomena [13-15]. In [16], the chaotic behavior of wind time series for averaged weekly wind time series of wind speed has been shown by means of time series analysis tools. Next, in [17], the fractional of this time series has been derived. In [18], a comparative study of different hybrid prediction models has been performed by the authors to forecast the wind power time series from Alberta, Canada. In this study, the time series has been analyzed, briefly based on recurrence plots and correlation analysis to select the proper input sets for the forecasting models. The results of this paper is accordance with the observations in [18] and justifies them, but is more compromising. However, up to authors' knowledge, further study has been done on the characterization and predictability analysis of neither the wind speed nor the wind power. Besides, a question has been remained unanswered for prediction of wind power, that is, how predictable is the wind power in terms of its own time series and in terms of wind speed time series, or both?

In order to answer the above questions, in this paper, at first the experimental wind speed and wind power data from Spain's wind farm has been investigated via different time series analysis methods. The examined methods are power spectral density (PSD) analysis, phase space reconstruction and test of surrogates, test of the fractional dimension and the slope of integral sums, the δ-ε method, and the recurrence plots [19]. The results of these analyses not only emphasize the stochastic nature of these time series with a mimic predictability but also show that there exists some type of the seasonality and non-stationarity in the system dynamics. This result implies that a fixed model cannot perform properly, even in case of de-trended input data, and so, multiple or adaptive models should be developed to forecast such time series.

Further, the individual, cross and joint recurrence quantification analyses have been applied to the wind speed and wind power time series' to investigate the individual and interactive predictability of them. In this context, the degree of synchronization between wind speed and wind power time series dynamics, and the mean and maximum range of validity for the prediction models built based on individual/joint inputs of these time series' will be discussed thoroughly.

The remainder of the paper is organized as follows: In section 2, the experimental data and its time series analysis is provided. In section 3, the interaction analysis of wind speed and wind power time series is performed. The paper is concluded in section 4.

2. The experimental data and time series analysis

Seeking for the nature of the wind time series, in this section, the experimental wind data of Spain's wind farm on May 2005 [5] will be closely studied. The available data that are the hourly wind speed and its related wind power time series for 5 weeks (1200 hours) as shown in figure 1; where figure 1(a) shows the wind speed time series and figure 1(b) shows the related wind power of the interested period versus time in hours. According to figures 1 (a and b), no obvious hallmark of periodicity (such as daily or weekly periodicity) can be observed either in the wind speed or in the wind power time series. These time series behavior may come from both chaotic and stochastic dynamics. Besides, the stationarity of it is under question which should be investigated. From one point of view, wind speed and wind power can be considered as system parameter and system operating point, respectively. Based on this interpretation, the wind power values versus wind speed have been plotted in figure 2. From this figure, with increasing the wind speed, some type of bifurcation occurs in the corresponding wind power values. This bifurcation diagram may, however, be due to a chaotic or stochastic nature of a nonlinear process [20-21]. To distinguish between these two types of processes, several methods such as power spectrum analysis, phase space reconstruction, surrogate testing, test of the fractional dimension and the slope of integral sums, the δ-ε method, and recurrence plots will be performed using the TISEAN package [22] and CRP toolbox of MATLAB [23] as our tools. Besides, the stationarity of the dynamics will be analyzed via recurrence plots.

2.1. The power spectral density

Regarding the behavior of wind speed and wind power in figures 1 and 2, what is important for us,

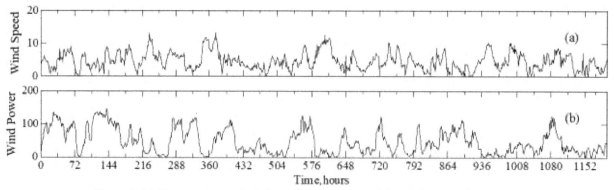

Figure 1. (a) The experimental wind speed time series, and (b) wind power time series.

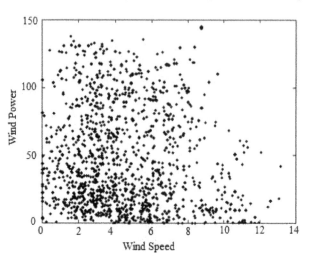

Figure 2. Bifurcation diagram of wind speed versus windpower.

is the answer to this question: "what is the nature of such complex behavior of wind, deterministic chaos or stochastic nature?" To answer this question, first of all, we analyze the power spectral density (PSD) of the data as shown in figure 3. The power spectral density (PSD) of wind speed and power provides information on the character of fluctuations in the time series data. The (PSD) describes how the power of a time series is distributed with frequency. The graph has been derived based on periodogram PSD estimation method. As expected, in figures 3 (a) and (b), there are no regular sharp peaks which is the representative of aperiodic nature of wind speed and wind power time series. Lack of periodic components in these time series implies low predictability of these time series as it would be examined in the next sections. To analyze the results of figure 3 more closely, one should note that existence of the higher harmonics in the spectra indicates that the processes underlying the time series are not linear processes, but there is some kind of nonlinearity [21, 24]. As another point, consider the frequency content of the plots. A broadband dense spectrum which also preserves these properties in small frequency ranges is often

considered as hallmark of chaos. Spectrum of a chaotic system is not solely comprised of discrete frequencies, but has a continuous broadband nature [25]. In case of our data, such a broadband spectrum preserving its properties in small frequency ranges is not observed (See Figures 3 (c) and (d)). These observations imply the stochastic nature of wind speed and wind power. However, since such a type of broadband spectrum may be due to either chaotic or stochastic nature of a time series, some stronger tests should be carried out to distinguish strictly between these two types of dynamics.

2.2. The histogram analysis

Histogram is a graphical representation that shows the distribution of data. It consists of tabular frequencies shown with discrete intervals by adjacent rectangles. The total area of the histogram is equal to the number of data. Next, the experimental probability density function (PDF) of a data can be derived when the y-axis values of the histogram (or number of data in each histogram bin) is normalized by the total number of data. The experimental PDF graphs of the wind speed and wind power data have been illustrated in figure 4. In order to investigate the nature of the wind speed and wind power dynamics, it has been tried to fit a proper random distribution to the experimental PDF via the statistics toolbox of MATLAB [23]. Also, it is observed that the Weibull distribution described by (1) is well fitted to the histogram of the data. That is:

$$f\left(x \mid a,b\right) = \frac{b}{a}\left(\frac{x}{a}\right)^{b-1} e^{-\left(x/a\right)^{b}} \qquad (1)$$

where, $f\left(.\right)$ is the Weibull PDF and a, b are its corresponding parameters. Trying to fit the Weibull PDF to the wind speed and wind power time series', the following parameter are found: For wind speed: $a_1 = 5.1040$, $b_1 = 1.7057$; for wind power $a_2 = 48.9156$, $b_2 = 1.1341$. The well matching of the found PDF's with the experimental PDF of the wind speed and wind power time series may be seen in figures 4(a) and (b), respectively.

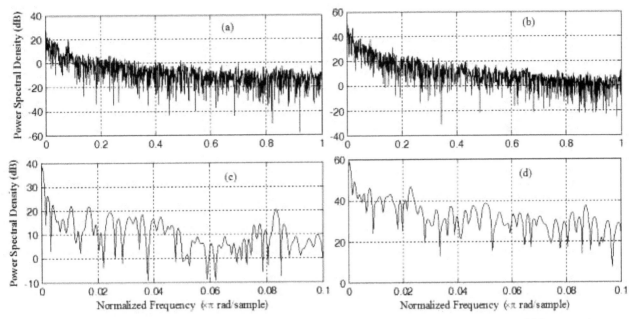

Figure 3. Power spectral density for (a) The wind speed, (b) The wind power, (c) and (d) Figs. 3(a) and 3(b) zoomed out.

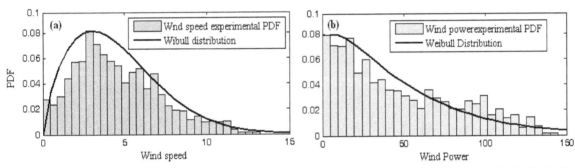

Figure 4. Experimental PDF graphs of (a) wind speed, (b) wind power in comparison with the fitted Weibull distributions.

This observation is another hallmark of stochastic behavior of the wind speed and wind power time series.

2.3. Embedding delay determination

The first step in analyzing a time series is to reconstruct its embedded phase space via methods of delays [22]. In this method, vectors in a new space, *the embedding space*, are formed from time delayed values of the scalar measurements [22]. For implementing this method, two important parameters should be determined firstly: the embedding delay and embedding dimension. In order to find out the embedding delay, two methods may be employed. In the first approach, the first zero cross or first cutoff (corresponding to 95%confidence level) of the autocorrelation function (ACF) is the embedding delay [26]. In the second approach, the first minimum of the average mutual information (MI) is the embedding delay [26]. In this paper, both approaches have been employed to the data and the results are illustrated in figure 5. For these time series, the first approach is inconclusive

because the first zero cross of ACF plot doesn't reveal an integer embedding delay as shown in figures 5 (a) and (c). According to figure 5(b), the first minimum is occurred at 6, so the embedding delay for the wind speed is $\tau = 8$ hours and from figure 5(d), the first minimum is occurred at 8, so for the wind power, the embedding delay is $\tau = 12$ hours. These embedded delays will be used in recurrence plots and recurrence quantification analysis.

2.4. Embedding dimension determination

As mentioned before, embedding dimension determination is the other parameter to be determined for phase space reconstruction. The dimension, where a time delay reconstruction of the system phase space provides a necessary number of coordinates to unfold the dynamics from overlaps on itself caused by projection, is called the embedding dimension [27].A common method to determine the minimal sufficient embedding dimension m is the false nearest neighbor (FNN) method proposed by Kennel et al. [27].

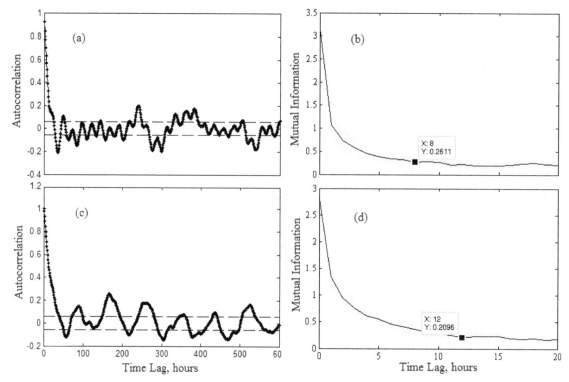

Figure 5. (a) and (b) Wind speed autocorrelation and average mutual information, (c) and (d) Wind power autocorrelation and average mutual information.

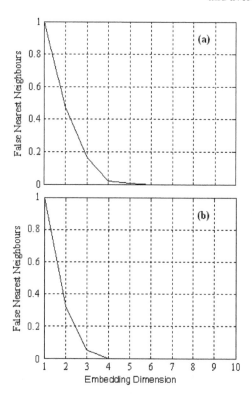

Figure 6. The fraction of false nearest neighbors versus the embedding dimension for (a) Wind speed, (b) Wind power time series.

The detailed description of this algorithm is at [17]. Figure 6 shows the fraction of false nearest neighbors for the considered wind speed and wind power time series. As we see in figure 6, the fraction falls down to zero at $m = 6$ for wind speed

and $m = 4$ for wind power. Therefore, the embedding dimension is 6 and 4 for the wind speed and wind power time series, respectively.

2.5. The phase space reconstruction and test of Surrogates

Mapping time series data into a phase space allows one to view the temporal series in a spatial manner. The distinguishing feature of chaotic processes is their sensitive dependence on initial conditions and highly irregular behavior that makes prediction difficult except in short term. This feature is the so-called "strange attractors" associated with chaotic processes which often have a complex, fractal structure [27]. Based on these properties, one of the most interesting procedures for checking the presence of chaos is based on the ability of recovering the strange attractor of a system in the phase space and especially observation of the so-called butterfly effect [27].The three-dimensional phase spaces of the wind speed data (*WS*) with a delay time of $\tau = 8$ hours, and that of wind power (*WP*) with a delay time of $\tau = 12$ have been shown in figures 7(a) and (b), respectively. As seen, the strange attractor and the butterfly effect are not observed in the reconstructed phase space. Instead, a random like trajectory is demonstrated in the graphs. To develop a better appreciation whether the data set is chaotic or stochastic, one can comparatively assess the phase space maps of the original data with their corresponding surrogated data sets. Surrogate data sets have Fourier decompositions with the same amplitude of the original data set but with random phase components. The method of surrogate data serves as a null hypothesis whose objective is to examine the hypothesis that the original data have come from a random process [8, 28-30]. The method may be used as a reference for visual comparison between the original and random data sets' phase space. These two phase spaces would not look like if the data is a randomly spreading out cloud [8]. The phase space map of the surrogated wind speed and wind power data are shown in figure 8. As it is observed, the surrogated phase space maps do not looks like the original ones. Besides, not strange attractor or butterfly effect is observed in figures 8 (a) and (b). This observation emphasizes the stochastic nature of our data once again.

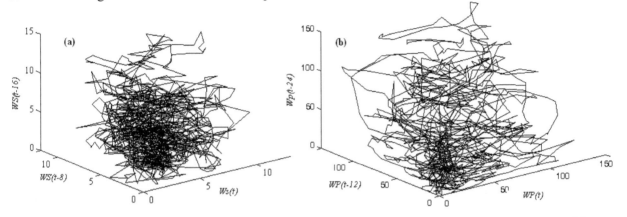

Figure 7. The phase space plot of (a) the wind speed time series ($\tau = 8$), (b) the wind power time series ($\tau = 12$).

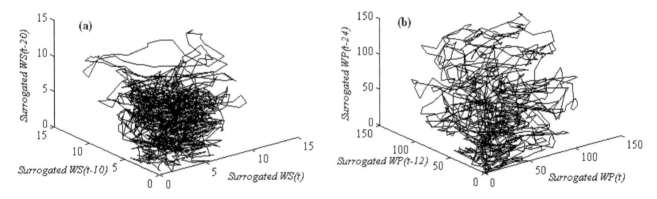

Figure 8. (a) The phase space plot of the surrogated the wind speed ($\tau = 10$); and (b) that of the wind power ($\tau = 12$).

2.6. The slopes of local integral sums

One of the fascinating features of chaotic systems is the fractal dimension of the attractor. Correlation dimension D_2 [8] is a measure for fractal dimension, which is formulated bellow:

$$D_2 = \lim_{r \to 0} \frac{d \log C (m,r)}{d \log(r)} \quad (2)$$

where, $C(m,r)$ is defined by:

$$C(m,r) = constant \times \sum_{i=1}^{N} \sum_{j=i+\mu}^{N} \Theta\left(r - |\vec{x}(i) - \vec{x}(j)|\right) \quad (3)$$

where, $\vec{x}(i), \vec{x}(j)$ denote states embedded in reconstructed phase space with embedding dimension m [31].

$\Theta(.)$ is the Heaviside step function (which is 1 for a positive argument and 0 elsewhere) applied to count the number of pair of points within radius

r and μ is the Theiler correction employed to exclude temporally correlated points [28].

Seeking for fractal attractors, the plots of local slopes of the logarithm of the correlation integrals with respect to the logarithm of r can be investigated. Evidence for a fractal attractor is given if the local slopes are constant for a large enough range of small radii but does not change for embedding dimension higher than a minimal value [20]. In the local slopes plot, if the system has the chaotic behavior, by increasing the embedding dimension, the curve will be saturated and the level at which most of the curves settle down defines the fractal dimension [22]. Figures 9(a) and (b) show the local slopes of the correlation integral versus r for wind speed and wind power time series data, respectively. The embedding delay used for these plots is $\tau = 8$ and

$\tau = 12$ for wind speed and wind power data, respectively. Embedding dimension varies from 1 to 10 from bottom to top of the graphs. As seen in figure 9, there is no indication of a low-dimensional fractal attractor in the graphs. This is another hallmark of stochastic behavior of the wind speed and wind power dynamics.

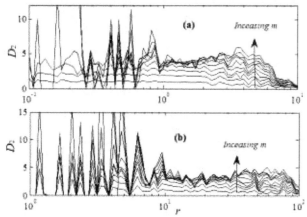

Figure 9. Local slopes of the correlation integrals, for m = 1,..., 10, for (a) Wind speed and (b) Wind power versus *r*.

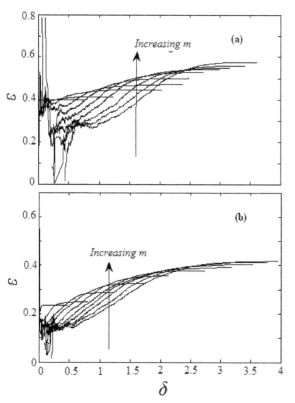

Figure 10. Results for the δ-ε method for (a) wind speed and (b) wind power.

2.7. The $\delta - \varepsilon$ method

The $\delta - \varepsilon$ method was first introduced in [32], where a detailed discussion of the method is given. According to this method, a deterministic dynamics embedded in a sufficiently high-dimensional state space should induce a continuous mapping from past to present states

and the size of the neighborhoods is increased to investigate the continuity. For deterministic processes,ε is expected to decrease to zero for decreasingδ for sufficiently high embedding dimensions [26], but for stochastic processes and processes which are covered by a significant amount of additive observational noise, a non-zero intercept for ε is expected. Figures 10 (a) and (b) show the results of this method for the wind speed and the wind power time series. This method has been employed in the wind speed and power time series by $\tau = 8$ and $\tau = 12$ respectively. The embedding dimensions vary from 1 to 10 from top to bottom of the graphs. As seen in figures 10 (a) and (b), for small δ, ε does not tend to zero. These results emphasize the stochastic nature of the both wind speed and wind power dynamics.

2.8. Recurrence Plots (RP)

Since its introduction by Eckman and Ruelle the recurrence plot has emerged as a useful tool in the analysis of nonlinear, non-stationary time series and useful for finding hidden correlations in highly complicated data [19].With RP, one can graphically detect hidden patterns and structural changes in data or see similarities in patterns across the time series under study [12]. The RPs exhibits characteristic large scale and small scale patterns. Large scale patterns can be characterized as homogeneous, periodic, drift and disrupted, that obtain the global behavior of the system (noisy, periodic, auto-correlated, etc.) [19]. The RP is derived directly from the distance matrix $D = D_{i,j}, i, j = 1, ..., N$ (N is the length of the data series or trajectory):

$$D_{i,j} = \vec{x}_i - \vec{x}_j \qquad (4)$$

By applying a threshold ε:

$$R_{i,j} = \Theta\left(\varepsilon - D_{i,j}\right) \qquad (5)$$

where,Θ is the Heaviside function. And,

$$\Theta(x) = \begin{cases} 0 \, if \, x < 0 \\ 1 \, if \, x \geq 0 \end{cases} \qquad (6)$$

And if $\vec{x}_i \approx \vec{x}_j$ then $R_{i,j} = 1$ if not, then $R_{i,j} = 0$. One assigns a "black" dot to the value one and a "white" dot to the value zero. The two-dimensional graphical representation of $R_{i,j}$and then it is called RP [19].The visual inspection of RPs reveals (among other things) the following typical small scale structures: single dots, diagonal lines as well as vertical and horizontal lines [19, 33]; in addition, even bowed lines may occur [19]. Single, isolated recurrence points can occur if states are rare, if they do not persist for any time, or if they fluctuate heavily [33]. A diagonal line occurs when the trajectory visits the same region of the phase space at different times [33]. RP gives the reader a first impression of the patterns of recurrences which will allow studying dynamical systems and their trajectories like periodic systems, stochastic random systems, and chaotic ones [19]. Long and non-interrupted diagonals are related to periodic motion and the period of oscillation is equal to the vertical distance between these lines. If the diagonals are shorter, it seems that the RP is related to the chaotic systems. The RP with so many single black points with erratic distribution is related to the uncorrelated stochastic signal. All together, we find that the shorter the diagonals are in the RP, the less predictability the system has [12].

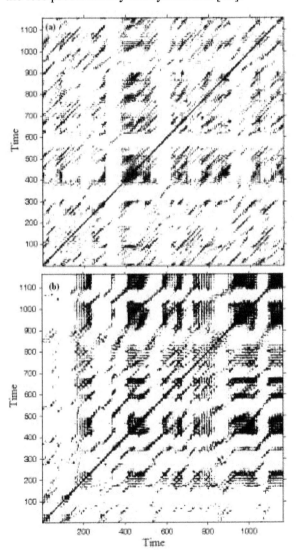

Figure 11. (a) RP of wind speed time series, (b) RP of wind power time series.

The RP of the wind speed and wind power time series has been shown in figures 11 (a) and (b), respectively. The figure has been generated via

the CRP toolbox of MATLAB [34]. In order to plot the RP, the parameter m has been considered 6, 4 for wind speed and wind power, respectively, and the parameter τ has been assumed 8 for wind speed and 12 for wind power. Besides, the Euclidean norm and the threshold of 1.5 have been assumed for plotting the recurrence plots. According to figure 11(a), very short diagonals in wind speed RP imply stochastic nature of wind speed. Moreover, the presence of distributed dark regions as well as white ribbons is indicative of seasonality and unstationarity in the hourly wind speed time series. Altogether, very short-term predictability is concluded from the RP of wind speed. According to figure 11(b), the same properties is observed in the RP of wind power unless the density of dark points is more in some regions with respect to that of the wind speed. Via the RP, the stochastic nature, seasonality and unstationarity is emphasized for wind power as well, but it seems due to its correlated dynamics, the predictability is enhanced here.

2.9. Recurrence quantification analysis (RQA)

In order to go beyond the visual impression yielded by RPs, several measures of complexity which quantify the small scale structures in RPs have been proposed known as recurrence quantification analysis (RQA) [19]. These measures are based on the recurrence point density and the diagonal and vertical line structures of the RP [12]. The simplest RP measure is the recurrence rate (RR) and it is defined as the percentage of dark pixels in recurrence plots by:

$$RR\left(\varepsilon\right)=\frac{1}{N^2}\sum_{i,j=1}^{N}R_{i,j}\left(\varepsilon\right)\times100 \qquad (7)$$

where, N is the length of the time series. The more periodic the dynamic is, the larger the recurrence rate will be [19]. The next measure is DET (% determinism) which is defined as the percentage of recurrence points that form diagonal structures (of at least length l_{min}) as:

$$DET=\frac{\sum_{l=l_{min}}^{N}lp\left(l\right)}{\sum_{l=1}^{N}lp\left(l\right)} \qquad (8)$$

where, $p(l) = p(l,\varepsilon)$ is the histogram of diagonal lines of length l with the recurrence threshold of l_{min}. The threshold l_{min} excludes the diagonal lines which are formed by the tangential motion of the phase space trajectory. A diagonal line of length l means that a segment of the trajectory is rather close during l time segment of the trajectory at a different time. DET plots may be interpreted as a signature of determinism and so predictability in the time series data. The average diagonal line length:

$$L = \frac{\sum_{l=l_{min}}^{N} lp(l)}{\sum_{l=l_{min}}^{N} p(l)} \qquad (9)$$

is the average time that two segments of the trajectory are close to each other, and can be interpreted as the mean prediction time [19]. Another RQA measure considers the length L_{max} of the longest diagonal line found in the RP [19]:

$$L_{max} = \max\left(\{l_i\}_{i=1}^{N_l}\right) \qquad (10)$$

where, $N_l = \sum_{l \geq l_{min}} p(l)$ is the total number of diagonal lines. This measure is related to the exponential divergence of the phase space trajectory. The faster the trajectory segments diverge, the shorter are the diagonal lines and the lower is the measure L_{max}. L_{max} is also an estimator of lower limit of the sum of the positive Lyapunov exponents [24]. Positive Lyapunov exponents gauge the rate at which trajectories diverge, and are the hallmark for dynamic chaos. Altogether, the shorter is the L_{max}, the less predictable is the signal. The Shannon entropy of the probability distribution of the diagonal line lengths $p(l)$ is defined as:

$$ENTR = -\sum_{l=l_{min}}^{N} p(l) \ln p(l) \qquad (11)$$

ENTR reflects the complexity of the RP in respect of the diagonal lines, e.g. for uncorrelated noise the value of ENTR is rather small, indicating its low complexity [19].

The percentage of the recurrence points forming vertical structures is another RQA measure and is known as LAM (% Laminarity) and is defined as [19]:

$$LAM = \frac{\sum_{v=v_{min}}^{N} vp(v)}{\sum_{v=1}^{N} vp(v)} \qquad (12)$$

where, $p(v) = p(v, \varepsilon)$ is the histogram of vertical lines of length v that exceeds a minimal length v_{min} and with recurrence threshold of ε. Laminarity (LAM) represents the occurrence of laminar states in the system without describing the length of these laminar phases. LAM will decrease if the RP consists of more single recurrence points than vertical structures. The average length of vertical structures is called trapping time (TT), which estimates the mean time that the system will stay at a specific state or how long the state will be trapped [19]. It is given by:

$$TT = \frac{\sum_{v=v_{min}}^{N} vp(v)}{\sum_{v=v_{min}}^{N} p(v)} \qquad (13)$$

Finally, the maximal length of the vertical lines in the RP:

$$v_{max} = \max(\{v_l\}_{l=1}^{N_v}) \qquad (14)$$

can be regarded, analogously to the standard measure V_{max}(N_v is the absolute number of vertical lines). In contrast to the RQA measures based on diagonal lines, these measures are able to find chaos-chaos transitions [19]. Hence, they allow for the investigation of intermittency, even for rather short and non-stationary data series. Furthermore, since for periodic dynamics the measures quantifying vertical structures are zero, chaos-order transitions can also be identified [19]. Furthermore, since for periodic dynamics the measures quantifying vertical structures are zero, chaos-order transitions can also be identified [19].The RQA measures of the wind speed and wind power time series with $v_{min} = l_{min} = 6$ and $\varepsilon = 1.5$ have been brought in figures 12 and 13, respectively. According to figure 12(a), the RR plot shows that the wind speed data has weak periodical dynamic as we find out from RP. Predictability for wind speed time series is noticeably small regarding DET measure in figure 12 (b), but figure 12(c) shows that the mean value of the L measure of this data is about 8 which is rather low. Thus, the mimic predictability of the wind speed time series can be concluded. As seen in figure 12(d), L_{max} falls to the low value of 3 in some regular periods. This behavior in conjunction with those observed in figures 12(f) and (h) emphasizes the seasonality and unstationarity of the wind speed. Figure 12 (e)shows the ENTR of wind speed. From this figure, noticeable ENTR is representative of highly complex dynamics of wind speed. Referring to figure 12(g), an almost flat TT plot locating at about 6, is representative of the predictability about 8×6=48 hours ($\tau = 8$) for wind speed.Investigation of figure 11 shows similar results for the RQA measures of the wind power time series. According to this figure, as RR, DET, L and L_{max} have been increased, it is concluded that the wind power is more predictable than wind speed. However, a flat plot of L_{max} as well as lower variations in LAM and v_{max} are representative of lower degrees of dynamic transitions or equivalently more stationarity in the wind speed dynamics. The plot of TT is less flat but its mean value is larger than that of wind speed (it is about 12).In this case, the mean prediction time is about 12×12=148 hours ($\tau = 12$).

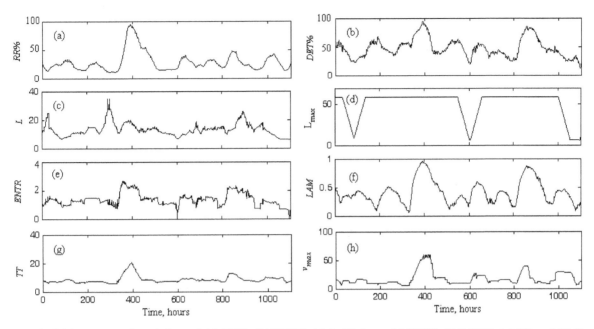

Figure 12. RQA measures for wind speed (a) *RR%*, (b) *DET%*, (c) *L*, (d) *Lmax*, (e) *ENTR*, (f) *LAM%*, (g) *TT*, and (h) *Vmax*.

3. Interaction analysis of wind speed and wind power

3.1. The correlation analysis

One of the most common tools for determination of effective inputs for a forecasting model is the correlation analysis between the underlying time series. The cross correlation between two time series $X = \{x_i, i = 1, ..., N\}$ and $Y = \{y_i, i = 1, ..., N\}$ can be defined as:

$$C_{XY}(m) =$$
$$E\{x_n y^*_{n+m}\} - E(X)E(Y^*), m = 1, ..., N \qquad (15)$$

where, in (15), $E(.)$ and * stand for mathematical expectation and complex conjugate, respectively. Indeed, the cross correlation is employed to examine the linear correlation of two time series. The more slower decays the correlation plot, the more linearly predictable is the Y in terms of X. Figure 13 shows the cross correlation of wind power versus the lagged wind speed time series. From this figure, one may conclude there exists an almost noticeable but decreasing correlation among the wind power time series and almost up to one weak lagged wind speed time series, which may be employed for forecasting this time series.

3.2. The cross recurrence plots (CRP)

As stated earlier, the correlation analysis is a linear tool which reflects the linear dependency of two time series. In the literature, there are some nonlinear tools which investigate the bi-variate dependencies of the time series as well. The CRP is a bi-variate extension of the RP and was introduced to analyze the dependencies between two different systems by comparing their states [19] which can be considered as a generalization of the linear cross-correlation function. Suppose we have two dynamical systems, each one is represented by the embedded state trajectories $\vec{x}_i$ and $\vec{y}_i$ in a m-dimensional phase space. Analogous to the RP (Equations (4) and (5)), the corresponding cross recurrence matrix is defined by [19]:

$$CR^{x,y}_{i,j} = \Theta\left(\varepsilon - \|\vec{x}_i - \vec{y}_j\|\right),$$
$$i = 1, ..., N \ , j = 1, ... M \qquad (16)$$

where, N and M are the lengths of the trajectories of $\vec{x}_i$ and $\vec{y}_i$ which are not required to be identical. However, the both systems are required to be represented in the same m-dimensional phase space, because a CRP looks for those times when a state of the first system recurs to one of the other system [12]. The graphical representation of the matrix CR is called CRP. In this graph, long diagonals are representative of similarity or correlation of the two dynamics. A measure based on the lengths of such lines can be used to find nonlinear interrelations between two systems, which cannot be detected by the common cross-correlation function. The more similar/correlated the two time series are the longer the diagonals and the higher density of dark dots around the main diagonal of the graph [12].Figure 15(a) shows the CRP of the wind speed and wind power. According to that figure, the diagonals are short and the density of the dark dots is low. Therefore, the correlation between two time series is weak as implied before. The transitions as well as white ribbons in this graph are representative of existence a non-stationary nonlinear correlation between these two dynamics.

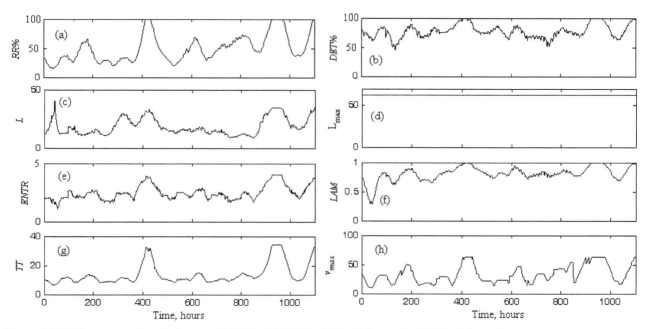

Figure 13. RQA measures for wind power (a) *RR%*, (b) *DET%*, (c) *L*, (d) *Lmax*, (e) *ENTR*, (f) *LAM%*, (g) *TT*, and (h) *Vmax*.

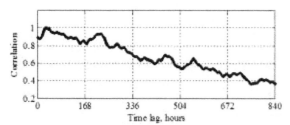

Figure 14. The cross correlation of wind speed and wind power time series.

Therefore, it is concluded that in constructing a forecasting model for wind power prediction, the seasonality and unstationarity should be accounted for by adaptive tuning of the model or constructing seasonal models.

3.3. Cross recurrence quantification analysis (CRQA)

Similar to RQA measures, cross RQA measures (CRQA) are defined. For example, the *RR* of CRPs is known as $CC_2(\varepsilon)$ and is defined as [19]:

$$CC_2(\varepsilon) = \frac{1}{N^2} \sum_{i,j=1}^{N} CR_{i,j}(\varepsilon) \times 100 \qquad (17)$$

Other CRQA measures are defined similar to RQA measures as in Section 2.9 (Equations (8) to (13)). Figure 16 shows the CRQA measures of wind speed and wind power. The results admit the last conclusions and yield very short term cross predictability of the wind power in terms of wind speed time series.

3.4. The joint recurrence plot (JRP)

In order to compare different systems' dynamics, another extension of RP has been developed named joint recurrence plot (JRP). In this method,

the recurrences of each time series to its trajectoryin its respective phase spaces is considered separately to find out times when both of them recur simultaneously, i.e. when a joint recurrence occurs. In this way, the individual phase spaces of both systems are preserved. This type of comparison, especially when we have two physically different systems, makes more sense. JRP of two time series $\vec{x}_i$ and $\vec{y}_i$ embedded in m_x and m_y dimensional phase spaces is defined as [19]:

$$JR_{i,j}^{x,y} =$$
$$\Theta\left(\varepsilon_x - \left\|\vec{x}_i - \vec{x}_j\right\|\right)\Theta\left(\varepsilon_y - \left\|\vec{y}_i - \vec{y}_j\right\|\right), \qquad (18)$$
$$i,j = 1,\ldots,N$$

where, ε_x and ε_y are the corresponding thresholds for time series $\vec{x}_i$ and $\vec{y}_i$. Figure 15(b) shows the JRP of the wind speed and wind power time series. As seen in this figure, the same pattern as Figure 15(a) is observed, but the longer diagonals are formed in the JRP plot.

3.5. Joint recurrence quantification analysis (JRQA)

Similar to RQA measures, joint RQA measures (JRQA) are defined and the *RR* of JRPs of *n* systems with thresholds $(\varepsilon^1, \ldots, \varepsilon^n)$ known as $JC_2(\varepsilon)$ is defined as [25]:

$$JC_2\left(\varepsilon^1,\ldots,\varepsilon^n\right) = \frac{1}{N^2} \sum_{i,j=1}^{N} \prod_{k=1}^{n} R_{i,j}^{\vec{x}(k)}\left(\varepsilon^k\right) \qquad (19)$$

Other JRQA measures are defined similar to RQA measures as in Section 2.9 (Equations (8) to (13)). Figure 17shows the JRQA measures of wind speed and wind power time series. From this figure, it is observed that joint recurrence of the two time series performs more degree of predictability with respect to that of CRP. As seen in this figure, the JRQA measures perform almost flat which is representative of stationarity in the recurrence of the two time series, which corresponds to similarity in recurrence dynamics of the two time series. That is, it is concluded that in constructing the prediction model for wind power, finding the recurrence dynamic model of the wind speed may be so effective.

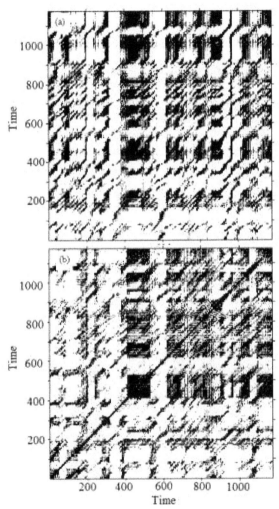

Figure 15. (a) CRP and (b) JRP of wind speed and wind power time series'.

4. Conclusion

The characterization and predictability analysis of wind speed and wind power time series has been considered in this paper. The employed data was the experimental data from Spain's wind farm on May 2005 [5]. The data analysis procedure includes histogram plots, power spectral density (PSD) analysis, the phase space reconstruction and test of surrogates, the slope of integral sum, the $\delta - \varepsilon$ method, recurrence plots (RPs) and recurrence quantification analysis. The analyses are representative of seasonal unstationary stochastic behavior and short term predictability

of wind speed and power time series. In order to investigate the interactive behavior, the mentioned wind speed and wind power, the bi-variate linear and nonlinear analysis methods such as cross correlation analysis, cross recurrence plots, joint recurrence plots, CRQA as well as JRQA were performed as well. The analysis results show that a noticeable similarity exists in the recurrence dynamics of these two time series, which is almost stationary. Nevertheless, the correlation of these two time series is mimic, seasonal and unstationary.

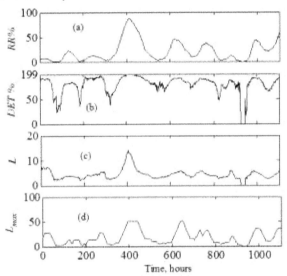

Figure 16. CRQA measures for wind speed and wind power time series (a) *RR%*, (b) *DET%*, (c) *L*, (d) *Lmax*.

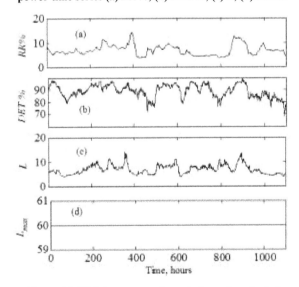

Figure 17. JRQA measures for wind speed and wind power time series (a) *RR%*, (b) *DET%*, (c) *L*, (d) *Lmax*.

References

[1] Amjady, N., Keynia, F. & Zareipour, H. (2011). Short-term wind power forecasting using ridgelet neural network. Elect PowSystRes, vol. 81, no. 12, pp. 2099-2107.

[2] Foley, AM., et al. (2012). Current methods and advances in forecasting of wind power generation. Renewable Energy, vol. 37, no. 1, pp. 1-8.

[3] Fan, S., et al. (2009). Forecasting the wind generation using a two-stage network based on meteorological information. IEEE Trans Energy Conv, vol. 24, no. 2, pp. 474-482.

[4] Jiang, Y., Song, Z. & Kusiak, A. (2013). Very short-term wind speed forecasting with Bayesian structural break model. Renewable Energy, vol. 50, pp. 637-647.

[5] Amjady, N., Keynia. F. & Zareipour, HR. (2011). A new hybrid iterative method for short-term wind speed forecasting. Europ Trans Elect Pow, vol. 21, no. 1, pp. 581-595.

[6] Hong, YY., Chang, HL. & Chiu, CS. (2010).Hour-ahead wind power and speed forecasting using simultaneous perturbation stochastic approximation (SPSA) algorithm and neural network with fuzzy inputs Original. Energy; vol. 35, no. 9, pp. 3870-3876.

[7] Amjady, N., Keynia, F. & Zareipour, HR. (2011). Wind Power Prediction by a New Forecast Engine Composed of Modified Hybrid Neural Network and Enhanced Particle Swarm Optimization, IEEE Trans Sustain Energy, vol.2, no.3, pp. 265-276.

[8] Ng, WW., Panu, US. & Lennox, WC. (2007). Chaos based analytical techniques for daily extreme hydrological observations. J Hydro, vol. 342, no. 1-2, pp. 17-41.

[9] Bigdeli, N. & Haeri, M. (2009). Time-series analysis of TCP/RED computer networks, an empirical study. Chaos, SolitFract, vol. 39, no. 2, pp. 784-800.

[10] Bigdeli, N., Afshar, K. & Amjady, N. (2009). Market data analysis and short-term price forecasting in the Iran electricity market with pay-as-bid payment mechanism. Elect PowSystRes, vol. 79, no. 6, pp. 888-898.

[11] Bigdeli, N. & Afshar, K. (2009). Chaotic behavior of price in the power markets with pay-as-bid payment mechanism. Chaos SolitFract, vol. 42, no. 4,pp. 2560-2569.

[12] Bigdeli, N. & Afshar K. (2009). Characterization of Iran electricity market indices with pay-as-bid payment mechanism. Physica A, vol. 388, no. 8, pp. 1577-1592.

[13] Khoa, TQD., Yuichi, N. & Masahiro, N. (2009). Recognizing brain motor imagery activities by identifying chaos properties of oxy-hemoglobin dynamics time series. Chaos SolitFract, vol. 42, no. 1, pp. 422-429.

[14] Sakai, K., Noguchi, Y. & Asada, S. (2008). Detecting chaos in a citrus orchard; reconstruction of nonlinear dynamics from very short ecological time series. Chaos SolitFract, vol. 38, no. 5, pp. 1274-1282.

[15] Andrade, KC., et al. (2012). Statistical evaluation of recurrence quantification analysis applied on single trial evoked potential studies. Clinical Neurophysiology, vol. 123, no. 8, pp. 1523-1535.

[16] Karakasidis, TE. & Charakopoulos, A. (2009).Detection of low-dimensional chaos in wind time series. Chaos SolitFract, vol. 41, no. 4, pp. 1723-1732.

[17] Chang, TP., et al. (2012). Fractal dimension of wind speed time series. Applied Energy, vol. 93, pp. 742-749.

[18] Bigdeli, N., et al. (2013). A comparative study of optimal hybrid methods for wind power prediction in wind farm of Alberta, Canada. Journal of Renewable and Sustainable Energy Reviews, vol. 27, pp. 20-29.

[19] Marwan, MC., et al. (2007). Recurrence plots for the analysis of complex systems. Physics Reports, vol. 438, no. 5-6, pp. 237-329.

[20] Bigdeli, N., et al. (2007). Characterization of complex behaviors of TCP/RED computer networks based on nonlinear time series analysis methods. Physica D: Nonlin Phenomena, vol. 233, no. 2,pp. 138-150.

[21] Timmer, J., et al. (2000). Pathological tremors: deterministic chaos or nonlinear stochastic oscillators?. Chaos, vol. 10, no. 1, pp. 278-288.

[22] Hegger, R., Kantz, H. & Schreiber, T. (1999). Practical implementation of nonlinear time series methods: the TISEAN package. Chaos, vol. 9, no. 2, pp. 413-38.

[23] The MathWorks, MATLAB [Online]. Available: http://www.mathworks.com.

[24] Grassberger, P. & Procaccia, I. (1983). Measuring the strangeness of strange attractors. Physica D: nonlinear phenomena, vol. 9, pp. 189-208.

[25] Tung, W-w., et al. (2005). Direct characterization of chaotic and stochastic dynamics in a population model with strong periodicity. Chaos SolitFract, vol. 24, no. 2, pp. 645-652.

[26] Strozzi, F., Zaldivar, JM. & Zabilut, JP.(2002). Application of non-linear time series analysis techniques to high frequency currency exchange data. Physica A, vol.312, no. 3-4, pp. 520-538.

[27] Kennel, MB., Brown, R. & Abarbanel, HDI. (1992). Determining embedding dimension for phase-space reconstruction using a geometrical reconstruction. Phys Rev A, vol. 45, no. 2, pp. 3403-3411.

[28] Theiler, J., et al. (1992). Testing for nonlinearity in time series: the method of surrogate data. Physica D, vol. 58, no. 1-4, pp. 77-94.

[29] Schreiber, T. (1998). Constrained randomization of time series data. Phys Rev Lett, vol. 80, no. 10, pp. 2105-2108.

[30] Engbert, R. (2002). Testing for nonlinearity: the role of surrogate data. Chaos SolitFract, vol. 13, no. 1, pp. 79-84.

[31] Takens, F. (1981). Detecting strange attractors in turbulence. Lect Note Math, Springer, New York, vol. 898, pp. 366-381.

[32] Kaplan, D. & Glass, L. (1995). Understanding nonlinear dynamics. Springer.

[33] Marwan, N. & Kurths, J. (2005). Line structures in recurrence plots. PhysLett A, vol. 336, no. 4-5. pp. 349-357.

[34] CRP toolbox for Matlab provided by TOCSY:http://tocsy.agnld.uni-potsdam.de.

14

Optimal adaptive leader-follower consensus of linear multi-agent systems: Known and unknown dynamics

F. Tatari and M. B. Naghibi-Sistani*

Electrical Engineering Department, Ferdowsi university of Mashhad, Azadi square, Mashhad, Iran.

*Corresponding author: mb-naghibi@um.ac.ir (M. B. Naghibi).

Abstract

In this paper, the optimal adaptive leader-follower consensus of linear continuous time multi-agent systems is considered. The error dynamics of each player depends on its neighbors' information. Detailed analysis of online optimal leader-follower consensus under known and unknown dynamics is presented. The introduced reinforcement learning-based algorithms learn online the approximate solution to algebraic Riccati equations. An optimal adaptive control technique is employed to iteratively solve the algebraic Riccati equation based on the online measured error state and input information for each agent without requiring the priori knowledge of the system matrices. The decoupling of the multi-agent system global error dynamics facilitates the employment of policy iteration and optimal adaptive control techniques to solve the leader-follower consensus problem under known and unknown dynamics. Simulation results verify the effectiveness of the proposed methods.

Keywords: *Graph Theory, Leader-follower Consensus, Multi-agent Systems, Policy Iterations.*

1. Introduction

In recent decades multi-agent systems (MASs) are applied as new methods for solving problems which cannot be solved by a single agent. MASs contain agents forming a network which exchange information through the network to satisfy a predefined objective. Information exchanging among agents can be divided to centralized and distributed approaches. Centralized approaches are mainly concentrated and discussed where all agents have to continuously communicate with a central agent. This kind of communication results in a heavy traffic, information loss and delay. Also, the central agent must be equipped with huge computational capabilities to receive all the agents' information and provide them with a command in response. Recently these challenges deviates the stream of studies toward distributed techniques where agents only need to communicate with their local neighbors.

A main problem in cooperative control of MASs is Consensus or synchronization. In consensus problems, it is desired to design simple control law for each agent, using local information, such that the system can achieve prescribed collective behaviors. In the field of control, consensus of MAS is categorized to cooperative regulation and cooperative tracking. In cooperative regulator problems, known as leaderless consensus, distributed controllers are designed for each agent, such that all agents are eventually driven to an unprescribed common value [1]. This value may be a constant, or may be time varying, but is generally a function of the initial states of the agents in the communication network [2]. Alternatively in a cooperative tracking problem, which is considered in this paper, there exists a leader agent. The leader agent acts as a command generator, which generates the desired reference trajectory. The leader ignores information from the follower agents and all other agents are required to follow the leader agent [3,4]. This problem is known as the leader-follower consensus [5], model reference consensus [6], or pinning control [7].

In MASs, the network structure and agents communications can be shown by graph theory tools.

Multi player linear differential games rely on solving the coupled algebraic Riccati equations (AREs). The solution of each player coupled equations requires knowledge of the player's neighbors strategies. Since AREs are nonlinear, it is difficult to solve them directly. To solve ARE, the following approaches have been proposed and extended: backwards integration of the Differential Riccati Equation, or Chandrasekhar equations [8]; eigenvector-based algorithms [9,10] and the numerically advantageous Schur-vector-based modification [11]; matrix-sign-based algorithms [12-14]; Newton's method [15-18]. These methods are mostly offline procedures and are proven to converge to the desired solution of the ARE. They either operate on the Hamiltonian matrix associated with the ARE (eigenvector and matrix-sign-based algorithms) or require solving Lyapunov equations (Newton's method). In all methods, the system dynamics must be known and a preceding identification procedure is always necessary.

Adaptive control [19,20] allows the design of online stabilizing controllers for uncertain dynamic systems. A conventional way to design an adaptive optimal control law is to identify the system parameters first and then solve the related algebraic Riccati equation. However, such adaptive systems are known to respond slowly to parameter variations from the plant. Optimal adaptive controllers can be obtained by designing adaptive controllers with the ability of learning online the solutions to optimal control problems.

Reinforcement learning (RL) is a sub-area of machine learning involved with how to methodically modify the actions of an agent (player) based on observed responses from its environment [21]. RL is a class of methods, which provides online solution for optimal control problems by means of a reinforcement scalar signal measured from the environment, which indicates the level of control performance. This is because a number of RL algorithms [22-24] do not require knowledge or identification/learning of the system dynamics, and RL is strongly connected with direct and indirect optimal adaptive control methods.

In this paper, the optimal adaptive control means the algorithms based on RL that provide online synthesis of optimal control policies. Also, the scalar value associated with the online adaptive controller acts as a reinforcement signal to optimally modify the adaptive controller in an online fashion.

RL algorithms can be employed to solve optimal control problems, by means of function approximation structures that can learn the solution of ARE. Since function approximation structures are used to implement these online iterative learning algorithms, the employed methods can also be addressed as approximate dynamic programming (ADP) [24].

Policy Iteration (PI), a computational RL technique [25], provides an effective means of online learning solutions to AREs. PI contains a class of algorithms with two steps, policy evaluation and policy improvement. In control theory, PI algorithm amounts to learning the solution to a nonlinear Lyapunov equation, and then updating the policy through minimizing a Hamiltonian function. Using PI technique, a nonlinear ARE is solved successively by breaking it into a sequence of linear equations that are easier to handle. However, PI has primarily been developed for discrete-time systems [24,25], recent research findings present Policy Iteration techniques for continuous-time systems [26].

ADP and RL methods have been used to solve multi player games for finite-state systems [27,28]. In [29-32], RL methods have been employed to learn online in real-time the solutions of optimal control problems for dynamic systems and differential games.

The leader-follower consensus has been an active area of research. Jadbabaie et al. considered a leader-follower consensus problem and proved that if all the agents were jointly connected with their leader, their states would converge to that of the leader over the course of time [33]. To solve the leader-follower problem, Hong et al. proposed a distributed control law using local information [34] and Cheng et al. provided a rigorous proof for the consensus using an extension of LaSalle's invariance principle [35]. Cooperative leader follower attitude control of multiple rigid bodies was considered in [36]. Leader-follower formation control of nonholonomic mobile robots was studied in [37]. Peng et al. studied the leader-follower consensus for an MAS with a varying-velocity leader and time-varying delays [38]. The consensus problem in networks of dynamic agents with switching topology and time-delays was proposed in [39].

In the progress of the research on leader-follower consensus of MASs, the mentioned methods were mostly offline and non-optimal and required the complete knowledge of the system dynamics.

The optimal adaptive control contains the algorithms that provide online synthesis of optimal control policies [40]. For a single system, [26] introduced an online iterative PI method which does not require the knowledge of internal system dynamics but does require the knowledge of input dynamics to solve the linear quadratic regulator (LQR) problem. Vrabie et al. showed that after each time the control policy is updated, and the information of state and input must be recollected for the next iteration [26]. Jiang et al. introduced a computational adaptive optimal control method for the LQR problem, which does not require either the internal or the input dynamics [41]. For MASs, [42] introduced an online synchronous PI for optimal leader-follower consensus of linear MASs with the known dynamics. Based on the previous studies, the online optimal leader-follower consensus of MASs under the unknown linear dynamics has remained an open problem.

This paper presents an online optimal adaptive algorithm for continuous time leader-follower consensus of MASs under known and unknown dynamics. The main contribution of the paper is the introduction of a direct optimal adaptive algorithm (data-based approach) which converges to optimal control solution without using an explicit, a priori obtained, model of the matrices (drift and input matrices) of the linear system. We implement the decoupling of multi-agent global error dynamics which facilitates the employment of policy iteration and optimal adaptive control techniques to solve the leader-follower consensus problem under known and unknown dynamics. The introduced method employs PI technique to iteratively solve the ARE of each agent using the online information of error state and input without requiring a primary knowledge of system matrices. For each agent, all iterations are implemented using repeatedly the same error state and input information on some fixed time intervals. In this paper, the employed online optimal adaptive computational tool is motivated with [41], where the method is generalized for leader-follower consensus in MASs.

The paper is organized as follows. Section 2 contains the results from Graph theory, also the problem formulation, node error dynamics and leader-follower error dynamics decoupling are clarified in this section. Section 3 introduces Policy iteration algorithm for leader-follower consensus under known dynamics. Optimal adaptive control design for leader-follower consensus under unknown dynamics is presented in section 4. Simulation results are discussed in Section 5. Finally the conclusions are drawn in section 6.

2. Problem formulation and preliminaries
2.1. Graphs

Graph theory is a useful mathematical tool in multi-agent systems research where information exchange between agents and the leader is shown through a graph. The topology of a communication network can be expressed by either a directed or undirected graph, according to whether the information flow is unidirectional or bidirectional. The topology of information exchange between N agents is described by a graph $Gr = (V, E)$, where $V = \{1, 2, ..., N\}$ is the set of vertices representing N agents and $E \subset V \times V$ is the set of edges of the graph. $(i, j) \in E$ means there is an edge from node i to node j. We assume the graph is simple, e.g., no repeated edges and no self-loops. The topology of a graph is often represented by an adjacency matrix $A_G = [a_{ij}] \in R^{N \times N}$ with $a_{ij} = 1$ if $(j, i) \in E$ and $a_{ij} = 0$ otherwise. Note $(i, i) \notin E, \forall i$, $a_{ii} = 0$. The set of neighbors of a node i is $N_i = \{j : (j, i) \in E\}$, i.e. the set of nodes with arcs incoming to i. If node j is a neighbor of node i, the node i can get information from node j not necessarily vice versa for directed graphs. In undirected graphs, neighbor is a mutual relation. Define the in-degree matrix as a diagonal matrix $D = diag(d_i) \in R^{N \times N}$ with $d_i = \sum_{j \in N_i} a_{ij}$ the weighted in-degree of node i (i.e. i^{th} row sum of A_G). Define the graph Laplacian matrix as $L = D - A_G$, which has all row sums equal to zero. Apparently in bidirectional (undirected) graphs, L is a symmetric matrix. A path is a sequence of connected edges in a graph. A graph is connected if there is a path between every pair of vertices.

The leader is represented by vertex 0. Information is exchanged between the leader and the agents which are in the neighbors of the leader (See Figure 1.).

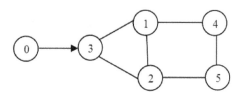

Figure 1. Communication graph.

2.2. Synchronization and node error dynamics

In cooperative tracking control of networked linear systems, we wish to achieve synchronization in the multi-agent system simultaneously optimizing some performance specifications on the agents. Consider an MAS consisting of N agents and a leader, which are in communication through an undirected graph. The dynamics of each agent is

$$\dot{x}_i = Ax_i + B_iu_i \qquad (1)$$

where $x_i \in R^n$ is the measurable state of agent i, and $u_i \in R^m$ is the input of player i. In this section, we assume that A and B_i are accurately known. The matrix B_i is full column rank. The leader labeled, as $i = 0$ has linear dynamics as

$$\dot{x}_0 = Ax_0 \qquad (2)$$

where $x_0 \in R^n$ is the measurable state of the leader. Obviously, the leader's dynamics is independent of others. We take the same internal dynamic matrix (A) for all the agents and the leader to be identical because this case has practical background such as group of birds, school of fishes etc. The following assumption is used throughout the paper.

Assumption 1. The pair $(A, B_i), i = 1, 2, ..., N$ is stabilizable.

The dynamics of each agent (node) can describe the motion of a robot, unmanned autonomous vehicle, or missile that satisfies a performance objective.

Definition 1. The leader-follower consensus of system (1)-(2) is said to be achieved if, for each agent $i \in \{1, 2, ..., N\}$, there is a local state feedback u_i of $\{x_j : j \in N_i\}$ such that the closed-loop system satisfies $\lim_{t \to \infty} \|x_i(t) - x_0(t)\| = 0$, $i = 1, ..., N$ for any initial condition $x_i(0)$, $i = 0, 1, ..., N$.

The design objective is to employ the following distributed control law for agent $i, i = 1, ..., N$

$$u_i = K_i(\sum_{j \in N_i}(x_j - x_i) + g_i(x_0 - x_i)) \qquad (3)$$

where $K_i \in R^{m \times n}$, $i = 1, 2, ..., N$ is a feedback matrix to be designed and g_i is defined to be 1 when the leader is a neighbor of the agent i, and 0 otherwise. Since the proposed feedback controller u_i, depends on both the states of its neighbors and the leader agent states, u_i is a distributed controller. In order to analyze the leader-follower

consensus problem, we denote the error state between the agent i and the leader as $\varepsilon_i = x_i - x_0$. The dynamics of ε_i, $i = 1, ..., N$ is

$$\dot{\varepsilon}_i = A\varepsilon_i + B_iK_i\sum_{j \in N_i}(\varepsilon_j - \varepsilon_i) - B_ig_i\varepsilon_i. \qquad (4)$$

Considering $\varepsilon = (\varepsilon_1^T, \varepsilon_2^T, ..., \varepsilon_N^T)^T$, $G = diag(g_1, ..., g_N)$ and by using the Lapalcian L of Graph Gr, we have

$$\dot{\varepsilon} = [I_N \otimes A - diag(B_iK_i)(H \otimes I_n)]\varepsilon \qquad (5)$$

where $H = L + G$ and $\otimes$ is the Kronecker product. $diag(B_iK_i)$ is an $N \times N$ block diagonal matrix. The matrix H corresponding to Graph topology has the following properties, which are proved in [43]:

1. The matrix H has nonnegative eigenvalues.
2. The matrix H is positive definite if and only if the graph Gr is connected.

Assumption 2. The graph Gr is connected.

The design objective for each agent i is to find the feedback matrix K_i which minimizes the following performance index for linear system (4),

$$J_i = \int_0^\infty (\varepsilon_i^T Q\varepsilon_i + u_i^T Ru_i)dt, \qquad (6)$$

$$i = 1, 2, ..., N$$

where $Q \in R^{n \times n}$, $R \in R^{m \times m}$, $Q = Q^T > 0$, $R = R^T > 0$, with $(A, Q^{1/2})$ observable.

Before we proceed to the design of online controllers, we need to decouple the global error dynamics (5), as discussed in the following.

2.3. Decoupling of Leader-follower error dynamic

Since H is symmetric, there exists an orthogonal matrix $T \in R^{N \times N}$ such that $THT^T = \Lambda = diag\{\lambda_1, \lambda_2, ..., \lambda_N\}$ where $\{\lambda_1, \lambda_2, ..., \lambda_N\}$ are the eigenvalues of matrix H. Based on Assumption 2, Gr is connected therefore H is a positive definite matrix and $\lambda_i > 0, i = 1, 2, ..., N$. Now let $\delta = (T \otimes I_n)\varepsilon$ then (5) becomes

$$\dot{\delta} = (I_N \otimes A)\delta - diag(B_iK_i)(\Lambda \otimes I_n)\delta \qquad (7)$$

Since the obtained global error dynamics (7) is block diagonal, it can be easily decoupled for each agent i, where for each agent we have

$$\dot{\delta}_i = (A - \lambda_iB_iK_i)\delta_i, \quad i = 1, 2, ..., N \qquad (8)$$

$$J_i = \int_0^\infty (\delta_i^T Q \delta_i + u_i^T R u_i) dt \ ,$$

$$i = 1, 2, ..., N \tag{9}$$

In order to find the optimal K_i which guarantees the leader-follower consensus for every agent i, we can minimize (9) with respect to (8), which is easier in comparison with minimizing (6) with respect to (4).

Based on linear optimal control theory, minimizing (9) with respect to (8) to find the feedback matrix K_i can be done by solving the following algebraic Riccati equation for each agent:

$$A^T P_i + P_i A -$$
$$P_i (\lambda_i B_i) R^{-1} (\lambda_i B_i)^T P_i + Q = 0 \tag{10}$$

Based on the mentioned assumptions, (10) has a unique symmetrical positive definite solution P_i^*. Therefore, the optimal feedback gain matrix can be determined by $K_i^* = R^{-1} \lambda_i B_i^T P_i^*$, due to the dependence of K_i to λ_i, each feedback gain depends on the graph topology. Since ARE is nonlinear in P_i, it is usually difficult to directly solve P_i^* from (10), especially for large size matrices. Furthermore, solving (10) and obtaining K_i^* requires the knowledge of A and B_i matrices.

3. Policy iteration algorithm for leader-follower consensus of continuous time linear systems under known dynamic

One of the efficient algorithms to numerically approximate the solution of ARE is the Kleinman algorithm [17]. Here we employ the Kleinman algorithm to numerically solve the corresponding ARE for each agent. The Kleinman method performs as a PI algorithm as discussed in the following.

Algorithm 1. (Policy iteration Kleinman Algorithm)

Step 0: Let $K_i^0 \in R^{m \times n}$ be any initial stabilizing feedback gain.

Step 1: Let P_i^k be the symmetric positive definite solution of Lyapunov equation (11) for the agent i, $i = 1, 2, ..., N$

$$(A - \lambda_i B_i K_i^k)^T P_i^k + P_i^k (A - \lambda_i B_i K_i^k)$$
$$+ Q + K_i^{kT} R K_i^k = 0 \tag{11}$$

Step 2: K_i^{k+1} with $k = 1, 2, ...$ is defined recursively by

$$K_i^{k+1} = R^{-1} \lambda_i B_i^T P_i^k \tag{12}$$

Step 3: $k = k + 1$ and go to step 1.
On convergence. End.

$A - \lambda_i B_i K_i^k$ is Hurwitz and by iteratively solving the Lyapunov equation (11) which is linear in P_i^k and updating K_i^{k+1} by (12) the solution to the nonlinear equation (10) is approximated as $P_i^* \le P_i^{k+1} \le P_i^k$ and $\lim_{k \to \infty} K_i^k = K_i^*$.

Theorem 1. Consider the MAS (1)-(2). Suppose Assumptions 1 and 2 are satisfied. Let $P_i > 0$ and K_i be the final solutions of the Kleinman's algorithm for agent i, $i = 1, 2, ..., N$. Then under control law (3) all the agents follow the leader from any initial conditions.

Proof: Consider the Lyapunov function candidate $V_i = \delta_i^T P_i \delta_i$. The time derivative of this Lyapunov candidate along the trajectory of system (8) is

$$\dot{V}_i = \delta_i^T [(A^T - \lambda_i K_i^T B_i^T) P_i] \delta_i +$$
$$\delta_i^T [P_i (A - \lambda_i B_i K_i)] \delta_i =$$
$$\delta_i^T [A^T P_i + P_i A - 2\lambda_i^2 P_i B_i R^{-1} B_i^T P_i] \delta_i$$
$$= -\delta_i^T [Q + \lambda_i^2 P_i B_i R^{-1} B_i^T P_i] \delta_i \le 0 \tag{13}$$

Thus for any $\delta_i \ne 0$, $\dot{V}_i < 0$, $i = 1, 2, ..., N$. Therefore, system (8) is globally asymptotically stable which implies that all the agents follow the leader.

4. Optimal adaptive control for leader-follower consensus under unknown dynamics

To solve (11) without the knowledge of A, we have [40]

$$\int_t^{t+\Delta t} (\delta_i^T Q \delta_i + u_i^{kT} R u_i^k) d\tau =$$
$$\delta_i^T(t) P_i^k \delta_i(t) - \delta_i^T(t + \Delta t) P_i^k \delta_i(t + \Delta t), \tag{14}$$

By online measurement of both δ_i and u_i^k, P_i^k is uniquely determined under some persistence excitation (PE) condition though matrix B_i is still needed to calculate K_i^{k+1} in (12).

To freely solve (11) and (12) without the knowledge of A and B_i, here the result of [41] is generalized for MAS leader-follower consensus. An online learning algorithm for the leader-follower consensus problem is developed but does not rely on either A or B_i.

For each agent i, we assume a stabilizing K_i^0 is known. Then we seek to find symmetric positive definite matrix P_i^k and feedback gain matrix $K_i^{k+1} \in R^{m \times n}$ without requiring A and B_i matrices to be known.

System (8) is rewritten as

$$\dot{\delta}_i = A_k \delta_i + \lambda_i B_i (K_i^k \delta_i + u_i) \qquad (15)$$

where $A_k = A - \lambda_i B_i K_i^k$. Then using (14), along the solutions of (15), by (11) and (12) we have

$$\delta_i^T(t+\Delta t) P_i^k \delta_i(t+\Delta t) - \delta_i^T(t) P_i^k \delta_i(t) =$$
$$-\int_t^{t+\Delta t} \delta_i^T Q_i^k \delta_i \, d\tau + \qquad (16)$$
$$2\int_t^{t+\Delta t} (u_i + K_i^k \delta_i)^T R K_i^{k+1} \delta_i \, d\tau$$

where $Q_i^k = Q + K_i^{kT} R K_i^k$. Note that in (16), the term $\delta_i^T (A_k^T P^k + P^k A_k) \delta_i$ depending on unknown matrices A and B_i is replaced by $-\delta_i^T Q_i^k \delta_i$, which can be obtained by measuring δ_i online. Also, the term $\lambda_i B_i^T P_i^k$ containing B_i is replaced by $R K_i^{k+1}$, in which K_i^{k+1} is treated as another unknown matrix to be solved together with P_i^k [41].

Therefore, (16) plays an important role in separating the system dynamics from the iterative process. As a result, the requirement of the system matrices in (11) and (12) can be replaced by the δ_i and input information u_i measured online. In other words, the information regarding the system dynamics (A and B_i matrices) is embedded in the error states and input which are measured online.

We employ $u_i = -K_i^0 \delta_i + e$, with e the exploration noise (for satisfying PE condition), as the input signal for learning in (15), without affecting the convergence of the learning process. Given a stabilizing K_i^k, a pair of matrices (P_i^k, K_i^{k+1}), with $P_i^k = P_i^{kT} > 0$, satisfying (11) and (12) can be uniquely determined without knowing A or B_i, under certain condition (Equation (27)).

We employ $\hat{P}_i \in R^{\frac{n \times (n+1)}{2}}$ and $\bar{\delta}_i \in R^{\frac{n \times (n+1)}{2}}$ instead of $P_i \in R^{n \times n}$ and $\delta_i \in R^n$ respectively where

$$\hat{P}_i = [p_{11}, 2p_{12}, ..., 2p_{1n},$$
$$p_{22}, 2p_{23}, ..., 2p_{n-1,n}, p_{nn}]^T_{\frac{n \times (n+1)}{2}} \qquad (17)$$

$$\bar{\delta}_i = [\delta_1^2, \delta_1 \delta_2, ..., \delta_1 \delta_n,$$
$$\delta_2^2, \delta_2 \delta_3, ..., \delta_{n-1} \delta_n, \delta_n^2]^T_{\frac{n \times (n+1)}{2}} \qquad (18)$$

Furthermore, by using Kronecker product representation we have:

$$\delta_i^T Q_i^k \delta_i = (\delta_i^T \otimes \delta_i^T) vec(Q_i^k) \qquad (19)$$

$$(u_i + K_i^k \delta_i)^T R K_i^{k+1} \delta_i =$$
$$u_i^T R K_i^{k+1} \delta_i + \delta_i^T K_i^{kT} R K_i^{k+1} \delta_i =$$
$$[(\delta_i^T \otimes \delta_i^T)(I_n \otimes K_i^{kT} R) + \qquad (20)$$
$$(\delta_i^T \otimes u_i^T)(I_n \otimes R)] vec(K_i^{k+1})$$

Also, for positive integer l, we define matrices $\Delta_{\delta_i \delta_i} \in R^{l \times \frac{n \times (n+1)}{2}}, I_{\delta_i \delta_i} \in R^{l \times n^2}, I_{\delta_i u_i} \in R^{l \times mn}$ such that

$$\Delta_{\delta_i \delta_i} = [\bar{\delta}_i(t_1) - \bar{\delta}_i(t_0), \bar{\delta}_i(t_2) - \bar{\delta}_i(t_1),$$
$$..., \bar{\delta}_i(t_l) - \bar{\delta}_i(t_{l-1})]^T_{l \times \frac{n \times (n+1)}{2}}, \qquad (21)$$

$$I_{\delta_i \delta_i} = [\int_{t_0}^{t_1} \delta_i \otimes \delta_i \, d\tau, \int_{t_1}^{t_2} \delta_i \otimes \delta_i \, d\tau,$$
$$..., \int_{t_{l-1}}^{t_l} \delta_i \otimes \delta_i \, d\tau]^T_{l \times n^2}, \qquad (22)$$

$$I_{\delta_i u_i} = [\int_{t_0}^{t_1} \delta_i \otimes u_i \, d\tau, \int_{t_1}^{t_2} \delta_i \otimes u_i \, d\tau,$$
$$..., \int_{t_{l-1}}^{t_l} \delta_i \otimes u_i \, d\tau]^T_{l \times (mn)} \qquad (23)$$

where, $0 \le t_0 < t_1 < ... < t_l$.

Inspired by [41], (16) implies the following matrix form of linear equations for any given stabilizing gain matrix K_i^k

$$\Theta_i^k \begin{bmatrix} \hat{P}_i^k \\ vec(K_i^{k+1}) \end{bmatrix} = \Xi_i^k \qquad (24)$$

where, $\Theta_i^k \in R^{l \times [\frac{n(n+1)}{2} + mn]}$ and $\Xi_i^k \in R^l$ are defined as:

$$\Theta_i^k = [\Delta_{\delta_i \delta_i},$$
$$-2I_{\delta_i \delta_i}(I_n \otimes K_i^{kT} R) - 2I_{\delta_i u_i}(I_n \otimes R)], \qquad (25)$$

$$\Xi_i^k = -I_{\delta_i \delta_i} vec(Q_i^k)$$

Notice that if Θ_i^k has full column rank, (24) can be directly solved as follows:

$$\begin{bmatrix} \hat{P}_k \\ vec(K_{k+1}) \end{bmatrix} = (\Theta_i^{k^T}\Theta_i^k)^{-1}\Theta_i^{k^T}\Xi_i^k \qquad (26)$$

The steps of the proposed optimal adaptive control algorithm for practical online implementation are presented as follows:

Algorithm 2 (Optimal adaptive learning algorithm):

Step 1: For the agent i employ $u_i = -K_i^0\delta_i + e$ as the input on the time interval $[t_0, t_l]$, where K_i^0 is stabilizing and e is the exploration noise (to satisfy PE condition). Compute $\Delta_{\delta_i\delta_i}, I_{\delta_i\delta_i}$ and $I_{\delta_i u_i}$ until the rank condition in (27) below is satisfied.

Let $k = 0$.

Step 2: Solve $\hat{P}_i^k$ and K_i^{k+1} from (26).

Step 3: Let $k+1 \rightarrow k$, and repeat Step 2 until $\|P_i^k - P_i^{k-1}\| \le \beta$ for $k \ge 1$, where the constant $\beta > 0$ is a predefined small threshold.

Step 4: Use $u_i = -K_i^k\delta_i = -R^{-1}B_i^T P_i^{k*}\delta_i$ as the approximated optimal control policy for each agent i.

It must be noted that in the cases where the solution of (24) does not exist due to the numerical error in $I_{\delta_i\delta_i}$ and $I_{\delta_i u_i}$ computations, the solution of (26) can be obtained by employing the least square solution of (24).

Lemma 1. As proved in [41], the convergence is guaranteed, if Θ_i^k, $i = 1, 2, ..., N$ has full column rank for all k, $k = 0, 1, 2, ...$; therefore, there exists an integer $l_0 > 0$, such that, for all $l > l_0$,

$$rank([I_{\delta_i\delta_i}, I_{\delta_i u_i}]) = \frac{n(n+1)}{2} + mn \qquad (27)$$

Theorem 2. Using an initial stabilizing control policy K_i^0 with exploration noise, once the online information of $\Delta_{\delta_i\delta_i}, I_{\delta_i\delta_i}$ and $I_{\delta_i u_i}$ matrices (satisfying the rank condition (27)) is computed, the iterative process of Algorithm 2 results in a sequence of $\{P_i^k\}_{k=0}^{\infty}$ and $\{K_i^k\}_{k=1}^{\infty}$ which respectively converges to the optimal values P_i^* and K_i^*.

Proof: See [41] for the similar proof.

Several types of exploration noise, such as random noise [44,45], exponentially decreasing probing noise [32] and sum of sinusoids noise [41] are added to the input in reinforcement learning problems. The input signal should be persistently exciting; therefore, the generated signals from the system, which contains the information of the unknown system dynamics, are rich enough to lead us to the exact solution. Here is a sum of sinusoids noise applied in the simulations to satisfy PE condition.

Remark 1. In comparison with the previous research on MASs leader-follower consensus, which is mostly offline and requires the complete knowledge of the system dynamics, this paper has presented an online optimal adaptive controller for the leader-follower consensus, which does not require the knowledge of drift and input matrices of the linear agents.

Remark 2. The main advantage of the proposed method is that the introduced optimal adaptive learning method is an online model-free ADP algorithm.

Moreover, this technique iteratively solves the algebraic Riccati equation using the online information of state and input, without requiring the priori knowledge of the system matrices and all iterations can be conducted by using repeatedly the same state and input information ($I_{\delta_i\delta_i}, I_{\delta_i u_i}, \Delta_{\delta_i\delta_i}$) on some fixed time intervals. However, the main burden in implementing the introduced optimal adaptive method (Algorithm 2) is the computation of $I_{\delta_i\delta_i} \in R^{l \times n^2}$ and $I_{\delta_i u_i} \in R^{l \times mn}$ matrices. The two matrices can be implemented using $n^2 + mn$ integrators in the learning system to collect information of the error state and the input.

5. Simulation results

In this section, we give an example to illustrate the validity of the proposed methods. Consider the graph structure shown in figure 1, similar to [42] focusing on the dynamic of each agent, which is as follows

$$\dot{x}_1 = \begin{bmatrix} -2 & 1 \\ -4 & -1 \end{bmatrix}x_1 + \begin{bmatrix} 2 \\ 1 \end{bmatrix}u_1, \; \dot{x}_2 = \begin{bmatrix} -2 & 1 \\ -4 & -1 \end{bmatrix}x_2 + \begin{bmatrix} 2 \\ 3 \end{bmatrix}u_2,$$

$$\dot{x}_3 = \begin{bmatrix} -2 & 1 \\ -4 & -1 \end{bmatrix}x_3 + \begin{bmatrix} 2 \\ 2 \end{bmatrix}u_3, \; \dot{x}_4 = \begin{bmatrix} -2 & 1 \\ -4 & -1 \end{bmatrix}x_4 + \begin{bmatrix} 1 \\ 1 \end{bmatrix}u_4,$$

$$\dot{x}_5 = \begin{bmatrix} -2 & 1 \\ -4 & -1 \end{bmatrix}x_5 + \begin{bmatrix} 3 \\ 2 \end{bmatrix}u_5$$

with target generator (leader) $\dot{x}_0 = \begin{bmatrix} -2 & 1 \\ -4 & -1 \end{bmatrix}x_0$.

The Laplacian L and matrix G are as follows:

$$L = \begin{bmatrix} 3 & -1 & -1 & -1 & 0 \\ -1 & 3 & -1 & 0 & -1 \\ -1 & -1 & 2 & 0 & 0 \\ -1 & 0 & 0 & 2 & -1 \\ 0 & -1 & 0 & -1 & 2 \end{bmatrix}, \quad G = \begin{bmatrix} 0 & 0 & 0 & 0 & 0 \\ 0 & 0 & 0 & 0 & 0 \\ 0 & 0 & 1 & 0 & 0 \\ 0 & 0 & 0 & 0 & 0 \\ 0 & 0 & 0 & 0 & 0 \end{bmatrix}$$

The cost function of parameters for each agent, namely the Q and R matrices, is chosen to be identity matrices of appropriate dimensions. Since agents dynamics are already stable, the initial stabilizing feedback gains are considered as $K_i^0 = [0 \quad 0], i = 1,2,...,5$.

First we assume that A and B_i matrices are precisely known and we employ the Kleinman policy iteration (Algorithm 1) to reach leader-follower consensus. Figure 2 shows the convergence of $\delta_1, \delta_2, \delta_3, \delta_4, \delta_5$ components trajectories to zero by time in 6 iterations, which confirm the synchronization of all agents to the leader.

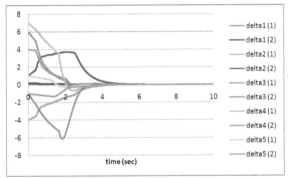

Figure 2. Agents $\delta_i, i = 1,...,5$ trajectories under known dynamics.

The error difference between the parameters of the solution $P_i^k, i = 1,2,3,4,5$ obtained iteratively and the optimal solution P_i^*, obtained by directly solving the ARE, is in the range of 10^{-4}.

Now we assume that A and B_i matrices are unknown and we employ the optimal adaptive learning method (Algorithm 2).

It must be mentioned that the precise knowledge of A and B_i is not used in the design of optimal adaptive controllers. The initial values for the state variables of each agent are randomly selected near the origin. From $t = 0 \, s$ to $t = 2 \, s$ the following exploration noise is added to the agents' inputs to meet the PE requirement, where $w_i, i = 1,2,...,100$ is randomly selected from $[-500,500]$.

$$e = 0.01 \sum_{i=1}^{100} \sin(w_i t) \tag{28}$$

δ_i and u_i information of each agent is collected over each interval of 0.1 s. The policy iteration started at $t = 2 \, s$, and convergence is attained after 10 iterations, when the stopping criteria $\left\| P_i^k - P_i^{k-1} \right\| \leq 0.001$ are satisfied for each $i = 1,2,3,4,5$. Figures 3 and 4 illustrate the convergence of P_i^k to P_i^* and K_i^k to K_i^* for $i = 1,2,3,4,5$ respectively during 10 iterations.

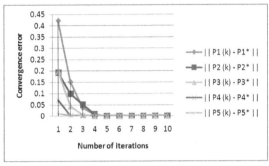

Figure 3. Convergence of P_i^k to P_i^* during learning iterations.

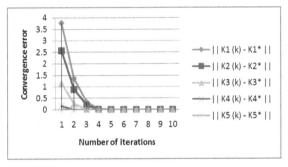

Figure 4. Convergence of K_i^k to K_i^* during learning iterations.

The controller $u_i = -K_i^* \delta_i = -R^{-1} B_i^T P_i^* \delta_i$ is used as the actual control input for each agent $i, i = 1,2,...,5$ starting from $t = 2 \, s$ to the end of the simulation. The convergence of $\delta_1, \delta_2, \delta_3, \delta_4, \delta_5$ components to zero is depicted in figure 5 where the synchronization of all agents to the leader is guaranteed.

As mentioned in table 1, the Kleinman PI method after 6 iterations results in leader-follower consensus in 6 seconds under known dynamics. The introduced optimal adaptive PI learns the optimal policy and guarantees the leader-follower consensus in 12 seconds after 10 iterations under unknown dynamics. Clearly, the introduced optimal adaptive method for unknown dynamics requires more time and iterations in comparison with the method for known dynamics to converge to the optimal control policies.

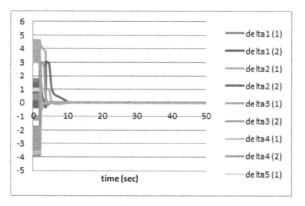

Figure 5. Agents $\delta_i, i = 1,...,5$ **trajectories under unknown dynamics.**

Table 1. Online PI methods comparison under known and unknown dynamics.

Online method	δ_i Convergence time to zero	A and B_i matrices	Number of iterations
Kleinman PI	6 seconds	Known	6
Optimal Adaptive PI	12 seconds	Unknown	10

As illustrated in the simulation results by employing PI technique and optimal adaptive learning algorithm, all agents synchronize to the leader.

6. Conclusions

In this paper, the online optimal leader-follower consensus problem for linear continuous time systems under known and unknown dynamics is considered. The multi-agent global error dynamic is decoupled to simplify the employment of policy iteration and optimal adaptive control techniques for leader-follower consensus under known and unknown dynamics respectively. The online optimal adaptive control solves the algebraic Riccati equation iteratively using system error state and input information collected online for each agent, without knowing the system matrices. Graph theory is employed to show the network topology of the multi-agent system, where the connectivity of the network graph is assumed as a key condition to ensure leader-follower consensus. Simulation results indicate the capabilities of the introduced algorithms.

References

[1] Zhang, H., Lewis, F. & Qu, Z. (2012). Lyapunov, Adaptive, and Optimal Design Techniques for Cooperative Systems on Directed Communication Graphs. IEEE transactions on industrial electronics, vol. 59, pp. 3026 – 3041.

[2] Ren, W., Beard, R. & Atkins, E. (2007). Information consensus in multi vehicle cooperative control. IEEE Control Syst. Mag, vol. 27. No. 2, pp. 71–82.

[3] Hong, Y., Hu, J. & Gao, L. (2006). Tracking control for multi-agent consensus with an active leader and variable topology. Automatica, vol. 42, no. 7, pp. 1177–1182.

[4] Li, X., Wang, X. & Chen, G. (2004). Pinning a complex dynamical network to its equilibrium. IEEE Transactions on Circuits and Systems. I. Regular Papers, vol. 51, no. 10, pp. 2074–2087.

[5] Zhang, H. & Lewis, F. (2012). Adaptive cooperative tracking control of higher-order nonlinear systems with unknown dynamics. Automatica, vol. 48, pp. 1432–1439.

[6] Ren, W., Moore, K. & Chen, Y. (2007). High-order and model reference consensus algorithms in cooperative control of multi vehicle systems. Journal of Dynamic Systems, Measurement, and Control, vol. 129, no. 5, pp. 678–688.

[7] Wang, X. and Chen, G. (2002). Pinning control of scale-free dynamical net-works. PhysicaA, vol. 310(3-4), pp. 521–531.

[8] Kailath, T. (1973). Some new algorithms for recursive estimation in constant linear systems. IEEE Transactions on Information Theory, vol. 19, no. 6, pp. 750-760.

[9] MacFarlane, A. G. J. (1963). An eigenvector solution of the optimal linear regulator problem. Journal of Electronics and Control, vol. 14, pp. 643-654.

[10] Potter, J. E. (1966). Matrix quadratic solutions. SIAM Journal on Applied Mathematics, vol. 14, pp. 496-501.

[11] Laub, A. J. (1979). A Schur method for solving algebraic Riccati equations. IEEE Transactions on Automatic Control, vol. 24, no. 6, pp. 913-921.

[12] Balzer, L. A. (1980). Accelerated convergence of the matrix sign function method of solving Lyapunov, Riccati and other equations. International Journal of Control, vol. 32, no. 6, pp. 1076-1078.

[13] Byers, R. (1987). Solving the algebraic Riccati equation with the matrix sign. Linear Algebra and its Applications, vol. 85, pp. 267-279.

[14] Hasan, M. A., Yang, J. S. & Hasan, A. (1999). A method for solving the algebraic Riccati and Lyapunov equations using higher order matrix sign function algorithms. In: Proc. Of ACC, pp. 2345-2349.

[15] Banks, H. T. & Ito, K. (1991). A numerical algorithm for optimal feedback gains in high dimensional linear quadratic regulator problems. SIAM

Journal on Control and Optimization, vol. 29, no. 3, pp. 499-515.

[16] Guo, C. H. & Lancaster, P. (1998). Analysis and modification of Newton's method for algebraic Riccati equations. Mathematics of Computation, vol. 67, no. 223, pp. 1089-1105.

[17] Kleinman, D. (1968). On an iterative technique for Riccati equation computations. IEEE Transactions on Automatic Control, vol. 13, no. 1, pp. 114–115.

[18] Moris, K. & Navasca, C. (2006). Iterative solution of algebraic Riccati equations for damped systems. In: Proc. of CDC, pp. 2436-2440.

[19] Sastry, S. & Bodson, M. (1989). Adaptive Control: Stability, Convergence, and Robustness. Englewood Cliffs, NJ: Prentice-Hall.

[20] Slotine, J. E. & Li W. (1991). Applied Nonlinear Control. Englewood Cliffs, NJ: Prentice-Hall.

[21] Sutton, R. S. & Barto, A. G. (1998). Reinforcement learning-an introduction. Cambridge, Massachusetts: MIT Press.

[22] Watkins C . J. C. H. (1989). Learning from delayed rewards, PhD Thesis, University of Cambridge, England.

[23] Werbos P. (1989), Neural networks for control and system identification, Proc. Of CDC'89, pp. 260–265.

[24] Werbos, P. J. (1992). Approximate dynamic programming for real-time control and neural modeling. In [24] D. A. White, and D. A. Sofge (Eds.), Hand book of intelligent control. New York: Van Nostrand Reinhold.

[25] Bertsekas, D. P. & Tsitsiklis, J. N. (1996). Neuro-dynamic programming. MA: Athena Scientific.

[26] Vrabie, D., Pastravanu, O., Lewis, F. L. & Abu-Khalaf, M. (2009). Adaptive optimal control for continuous-time linear systems based on policy iteration. Automatica, vol. 45, no. 2, pp. 477–484.

[27] Busoniu, L., Babuska, R. & DeSchutter, B. (2008). A comprehensive survey of multi-agent reinforcement learning. IEEE Transactions on Systems, Man, and Cybernetics Part C: Applications and Reviews, vol. 38, no. 2, pp. 156–172.

[28] Littman, M. L. (2001). Value-function reinforcement learning in Markov games. Journal of Cognitive Systems Research, vol. 2, pp. 55-66.

[29] Dierks, T. & Jagannathan, S. (2010). Optimal control of affine nonlinear continuous- time systems using an online Hamilton–Jacobi–Isaacs formulation. In Proc. IEEE conf. decision and control, pp. 3048–3053.

[30] Johnson, M., Hiramatsu, T., Fitz-Coy, N. & Dixon, W. E. (2010). Asymptotic stackelberg optimal control design for an uncertain Euler lagrange system. In IEEE conference on decision and control, pp. 6686–6691.

[31] Vamvoudakis, K. G. & Lewis, F. L. (2010). On line actor-critic algorithm to solve the continuous-time infinite horizon optimal control problem. Automatica, vol. 46, no. 5, pp. 878–888.

[32] Vamvoudakis, K. G. & Lewis, F. L. (2011). Multi-player non-zero sum games:online adaptive learning solution of coupled Hamilton–Jacobi equations. Automatica, vol. 47, no. 8, pp.1556–1569.

[33] Jadbabaie, A., Lin, J. & Morse, A. S. (2007). Coordination of groups of mobile autonomous agents using nearest neighbor rules. IEEE Transactions on Automatic Control, vol. 48, no. 6, pp. 943-948.

[34] Hong, Y., Gao, L., Cheng, D. & Hu, J. (2007). Lyapunov-based approach to multi agent systems with switching jointly connected interconnection. IEEE Transactions on Automatic Control, vol. 52, no. 5, pp. 943-948.

[35] Cheng, D., Wang, J. & Hu, X., (2008). An extension of Lasall's invariance principle and its application to multi-agent consensus. IEEE Transactions on Automatic Control, vol. 53, no. 7, pp. 1765-1770.

[36] Dimarogonasa, D. V., Tsiotras, P. & Kyriakopoulos, K. J. (2009). Leader-follower cooperative attitude control of multiple rigid bodies. Systems and Control Letters, vol. 58, no. 6, pp. 429-435.

[37] Consolini, L., Morbidi, F., Prattichizzo, D. & Tosques, M. (2008). Leader-follower formation control of nonholonomic mobile robots with input constraints. Automatica, vol. 44, no. 5, pp. 1343-1349.

[38] Peng, K. & Yanga, Y. (2009). Leader-follower consensus problem with a varying-velocity leader and time-varying delays. PhysicaA, vol. 388, no. 2-3, pp., 193-208.

[39] Olfati-Saber, R. & Murray, R. M. (2003). Consensus protocols for networks of dynamic agents. in: Proceedings of 2003 American Control Conference.

[40] Vrabie, D.(2009). Online adaptive optimal control for continue time systems, Ph. D. thesis, The University of Texas at Arlington.

[41] Jiang, Y. & Jiang, Z. P. (2012). Computational adaptive optimal control for continuous time linear systems with completely unknown dynamics. Automatica, vol. 48, pp. 2699-2704.

[42] Vamvoudakis, K. G., Lewis, F. L. & Hudas, G. R. (2012). Multi-agent differential graphical games: Online adaptive learning solution for synchronization with optimality. Automatica, vol. 48, pp. 1598–1611.

[43] Ni, W. & Cheng, D. (2010). Leader-follower consensus of multi-agent systems under fixed and switching topologies. Systems and Control Letters, vol. pp. 59, 209-217.

[44] Al-Tamimi, A., Lewis, F. L. & Abu-Khalaf, M. (2007). Model-free Q-learning designs for linear discrete-time zero-sum games with application to H-infinity control. Automatica, vol. 43, no. 3, pp. 473–481.

[45] Xu, H., Jagannathan, S. & Lewis, F. L. (2012). Stochastic optimal control of unknown linear networked control system in the presence of random delays and packet losses. Automatica, vol. 48, no. 6, pp. 1017–1030.

15

Non-zero probability of nearest neighbor searching

A. Mesrikhani [1*] and M. Davoodi [2]

Department of Computer Science & Information Technology, Institute for Advanced Studies in Basic Sciences (IASBS), Zanjan, Iran.

Corresponding author: mesrikhani@gmail.com (A. Mesrikhani).

Abstract

Nearest neighbor (NN) searching is a challenging problem in data management, and has been widely studied in data mining, pattern recognition, and computational geometry. The goal of NN searching is an efficient report of the data nearest to a given object as a query. In most studies, both the data and the query are assumed to be precise. However, due to the real applications of NN searching such as the tracking and locating services, GIS, and data mining, it is possible for both the data and the query to be imprecise. In such situations, a natural way to handle the issue is to report the data that has a non-zero probability (called the *non-zero NN*) as the NN of a given query. Formally, let P be a set of n uncertain points modeled by some regions. We first consider the following variation in an NN searching problem under uncertainty. If the data is certain and the query is an uncertain point modeled by an axis-aligned parallel segment, we propose an efficient algorithm in $O(n \log n)$ pre-processing and $O(\log n + k)$ query time, where k is the number of non-zero NNs. If both the query and the data are uncertain points modeled by distinct unit segments parallel to the x-axis, we propose an efficient algorithm that reports the non-zero NNs under Manhattan metric in $O(n^2 \alpha(n^2))$ pre-processing and $O(\log n + k)$ query time, where $\alpha(.)$ is the extremely slow growing functional inverse of the Ackermann function. Finally, for the arbitrarily length segments parallel to the x-axis, we propose an approximation algorithm that reports a non-zero NN with a maximum error L in $O(n^2 \alpha(n^2))$ pre-processing and $O(\log n + k)$ query time, where L is the query length.

Keywords: *Nearest Neighbor Searching, Uncertainty, Imprecision, Non-zero Probability.*

1. Introduction

Nearest Neighbor (NN) searching, which is a classic problem in computational geometry, has many applications in robot path planning, facility location, data mining, target tracking, and geographic information systems. In this problem, the goal is the proper pre-processing of a set of n data points in order to report efficiently the data nearest to a given query point. Due to several reasons such as noise, security issues, limited computations, and limited precision of measuring devices, gathering and analyzing real data come with some inevitable errors. Thus the algorithms that work based on the assumption that the data (and also computations) are completely precise fail in face with such a real input [1, 2]. For example, in facial recognition systems, we need to identify a person using some features in a database containing original face images. Due to

the nature of such problems, extracting the features from the original faces (in different positions or video frames), and also the query features are uncertain, and, therefore, the query does not match exactly to one of the original ones, and consequently, it should be handled under uncertainty circumstances [3]. One geometric approach implemented to smooth such uncertainty issues is to consider a tolerance for data, e.g. considering a region —called the *uncertainty region*— like a segment, a rectangle or a disk instead of an uncertain point [4, 5]. Thus an uncertain region is a region containing all the *instances* of an imprecise point. Therefore, since the distance between two imprecise points is not defined precisely, different cases may happen. In fact, the distance between two imprecise points can be defined as the distance between any selected instances from their uncertainty region, especially, the instances resulting in minimum and maximum distances. Such instances can be useful in applications for obtaining the worst and best cases of a solution under imperfect information or uncertain circumstances.

1.1. Problem definition

One way to consider NN searching under uncertainty is to report the data that has a non-zero probability to be an NN of a given query [8]. It means that there is at least one *placement* of instances of uncertain regions such that the reported data is NN of the query. Let $P = \{p_1, ..., p_n\}$ be a set of n uncertain points in a plane whose uncertainty regions are modeled by n regions, e.g. segments. (In this case, we assume that the data has some error only in one direction.) The uncertainty region of $p_i \in P$ is the set of all possible points (*instances*) in which p_i is located. For a query point q, we aim to report all points in P that have a *non-zero probability* to be the NN of q —called *non-zero NN*, denoted by *NzNN*. That means that when an uncertain point p is reported, there is a choice of points (called a *placement*) exactly one instance from each uncertainty region such that the instance of p is the nearest instance to q among all instances. Note that it is possible that q is also an uncertain point. Thus in this case, there is a placement of p and an instance of q like q' such that the instance of p is the nearest instance to q' among all instances (see Figure 1).

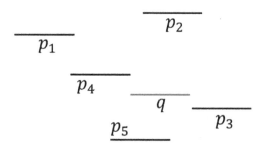

Figure 1. $\{p_3, p_4, p_5\}$ are non-zero NN of uncertain query q.

1.2. Previous work

Under the assumption that the data is precise, a simple and efficient method can be used to find that NN is a decomposing workspace using the Voronoi diagram of the data points in the $O(n \log n)$ time. Thus in the query phase for a given query point q, it is sufficient to report NN in the $O(\log n)$ time by locating q in the Voronoi regions and reporting the corresponding data [6]. For uncertain points and certain query, the original Voronoi diagram has been extended to

the *non-zero probabilistic Voronoi diagram* (*PVD*) [7, 8]. Each cell in PVD contains the points that have non-zero probability to be the NN of the corresponding data. Sember et al. [7] have shown the worst case complexity of PVD for uncertain points modeled by disks is $O(n^4)$ but they did not compute any lower bound for its complexity. Agarwal et al. [8] have shown that if the query is certain and the points are uncertain regions modeled by disks, PVD can be built in the $\theta(n^3)$ time. Hence, it is possible to report NzNN in the $O(\log n + k)$ time, where k is the number of possible non-zero probability points. Also by applying the expected distance between the uncertain points, the problem can be solved in the $O(\log n)$ time using the $O(n)$ space and the $O(n \log n + nm)$ preprocessing time, where m is the number of possible values in the data [9]. Cheng et al. [10] have introduced a method based on branch and prune on the R-tree. Further, Zhang et al. [11] have shown that in d-dimensional, there is no polynomial algorithm to compute PVD, and they combined PVD and R-tree to propose a heuristic method to report NzNN. However, the method did not guarantee a proper performance. Emrich et al. [12,13] have presented an effective criterion for detecting NzNN, and proposed a heuristic method to report NzNN but their method did not guarantee any performance in the worst case.

Beside the region-based models used for modelling uncertainty, other models have been proposed as well. Davoodi et al. [14] have introduced a generalization of the region-based models —called the *λ-geometry* model— for handling a dynamic form of imprecision that allows the precision changes in the input data of the geometric problems. They have also studied the problems of proximity, bounding box, and orthogonal range searching under this model [14, 15]. Meyers et al. [16] have introduced a new model called the linear parametric geometric uncertainty model (LPGUM), and have proposed algorithms to find the closest and farthest pairs and range searching under LPGUM [17].

In some real applications, it is useful to report NN with the highest probability. Yuen et al. [18] have studied the superseding NN search on uncertain spatial databases, i.e. finding the data with the highest probability to be NN of the query. They have shown that sometimes no object is able to supersede NN, and proposed an $O(n^2)$ time algorithm to find the superseding set. Beskales [19] has considered finding the top k probable

NN, and has presented I/O efficient algorithms to retrieve them and extended algorithms to support the threshold queries. Cheema [20] has formalized the *probabilistic reverse NN*, and has proposed an efficient branch and prune algorithm, and retrieved uncertain data that has a probability more than a given threshold. In the reverse NN problem, the goal is to find all the data points whose NNs are a given query point. Xiang [21] has focused on another important query-based problem, namely, *probabilistic group nearest neighbor* (PGNN) query. The goal is specifically given a set Q of query points; a PGNN query retrieves data objects that minimize the aggregate distance (e.g. sum, min, and max) to Q. He has proposed effective pruning methods to reduce the PGNN search space, and has considered extensive experiments to demonstrate the efficiency of the method.

In this work, we studied NN searching for uncertain query and uncertain data, and proposed efficient algorithms to find NzNNs. In section two, we propose an algorithm for certain data and uncertain query when they are modeled by distinct parallel unit segments. Our algorithm works under Manhattan metric in the $O(\log n + k)$ query time with the $O(n \log n)$ pre-processing time and space, where k is the output size. Wang et al. [13] have shown that if the data is certain and the query has m possible locations, the k-NNs can be reported in the $O(m \log m + (k + m)\log^2 n)$ time using the $O(n \log n \log \log n)$ space. For $m = 1$, our algorithm outperforms in both the pre-processing space and the query time. In section three, we propose an $O(\log n + k)$ query time algorithm with $O(n^2 \alpha(n^2))$ pre-possessing time and space for uncertain data and uncertain query, where $\alpha(.)$ is the inverse of the Ackermann's function. Our algorithm guarantees the performance in the worst case, and if the query is exact, it uses less space than the PVD method that uses a $\theta(n^3)$ space. In section four, for uncertain data and uncertain query, we propose an approximation algorithm with the maximum error of the query length. Finally, we draw conclusions, and suggest future works in this area.

2. NN searching for certain data and uncertain query

Let $p = \{p_1, ..., p_n\}$ be a set of n points in the plane. For a given uncertain query point q modeled by an axis-aligned parallel segment, the goal is to report NzNN under Manhattan metric.

This means that if point p is reported, there exists an instance of the query like q' whose NN is p. A popular method —called the *Minmax method* [18]— reports such a nearest data by computing the minimum distance among all the farthest instances of any data. In other words, p_i is NzNN of a certain query point q if:

$$\forall p_j \in P : d_{min}(p_i, q) \leq d_{max}(p_j, q), \quad (1)$$

where, $d_{min}(.,.)$ and $d_{max}(.,.)$ denote, respectively, the minimum and maximum possible distances between two objects. If q is an uncertain query point (e.g. modeled by a segment), the *Minmax method* may report incorrect nearest data because different instances of q can be selected. Figure 2 shows an example of two data points a and b and an uncertain query point q. The bisector of a and b is shown by B_{ab}. It is easy to see that all points above B_{ab} (including all instances of q, especially its end-points q' and q'') are closer to a than to b. Thus b does not have any chance to be NN of q. However, if we use the *Minmax method*, b will be reported as an NzNN. Hence, we define the following definition for reporting NzNN. Point p_i is NzNN of q if and only if $\exists$ an instance q' of q such that

$$\forall p_j \in P : d(p_i, q') \leq d(p_j, q') \quad (2)$$

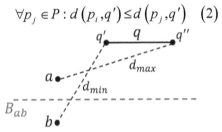

Figure 2. b is not NzNN of q, although it is reported in case that *Minmax* method is applied.

Therefore, to handle the problem, we construct the Manhattan Voronoi diagram in the pre-processing phase. It consists of four different line slopes (horizontal, vertical, and the lines with slopes $\frac{\pi}{4}$ and $\frac{3\pi}{4}$). A set of lines or segments are said to be *c-oriented* if all of them are parallel to at most c possible orientations. The edges of the Manhattan Voronoi diagram are 4-oriented. We use the following theorem to detect NzNN.

Theorem 1 Point $p_i \in P$ is NzNN of a given query point q if and only if q intersects the Voronoi cell of p_i.

Proof. Suppose that point p_i is NzNN of q. Thus there exists an instance of q like q' such that it is nearest to p_i among all points of P. This includes q' lies in the Voronoi cell of p_i, and consequently, q intersects the Voronoi cell of p_i. Conversely, let q' be an instance of q located in the Voronoi cell of p_i. By the definition of the Voronoi cell, we have:

$d(p_i, q') \le d(p_j, q')$, for $j = 1, \ldots, n., i \neq j$.

Thus based on Eq. (2), point p_i is NzNN of q.
∎

Therefore, we can conclude this section by the following theorem.

Theorem 2 Let $P = \{p_1, \ldots, p_n\}$ be a set of n points in the plane, and the query is an uncertain point modeled by an axis-aligned parallel segment. Then NzNN of q can be reported in $O(\log n + k)$ time using the $O(n \log n)$ pre-processing time, where k is the size of the output.

Proof. Based on theorem 1, for finding NzNNs, it is sufficient to find the Voronoi cell(s) containing q. Therefore, using the two end-points of q, we can perform two standard point locations over the Voronoi cells in the $O(\log n)$ time, and report the two cells containing the endpoints —called vc_1 and vc_2. (In the case where both end-points of q lie on the same cell, the problem is easily solved because the Voronoi cells are convex.) In addition, since q is a segment, it intersects the cells between vc_1 and vc_2, and should report all of them. To this end, we have 4-oriented segment intersection searching because edges of the Manhattan Voronoi diagram are 4-oriented, and we can report NzNN in the $O(\log n + k)$ time using the $O(n \log n)$ pre-processing time [22, 23].

3. NN searching for uncertain data and uncertain query

In this section, we consider the case where both the query and the data are uncertain, and we propose an efficient algorithm to find NzNNs. Let $P = \{p_1, \ldots, p_n\}$ be a set of n uncertain points modeled by unit segments parallel to the x-axis (called x-parallel) whose projections onto the x-axis do not intersect each other. Using Eq. (2) for an uncertain query point q modeled by a unit x-parallel segment, we first present a method to detect NzNNs.

3.1. Detecting non-zero NNs

Let $\{q_1, q_2\}$ be the end-points of a given uncertain query point q, and $\{e_i, e_i'\}$ be the end-points of $p_i \in P$ for $i = 1, 2, \ldots, n$. The maximum distance

between p_i and a point $p \in R^2$ occurs on the end-points, and can be computed using the following equation (see Figure 3).

$$d_{max}(p_i, p) = \max(d(e_i, p), d(e_i', p)). \quad (3)$$

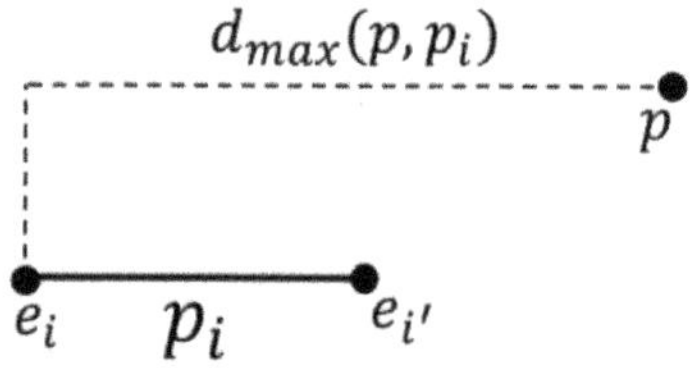

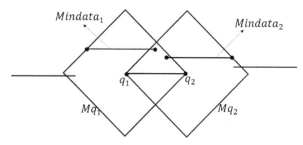

Figure 3. Maximum distance between point p and uncertain point p_i.

In order to detect NzNNs, we use the following method. Consider q_1 as a certain query point, and apply the *Minmax method* [18]. Let $M_1 = \{d_1, \ldots, d_n\}$ be a set of maximum distances between q_1 and $p_i \in P$ for $i = 1, \ldots, n$ (e.g. $d_{max}(q_1, p_i)$). Set $m_1 = min_{1 \le i \le n} d_i$, and let $mindata_1$ be some uncertain point in which $d_{max}(mindata_1, q_1) = m_1$.

We assume a diamond (a disk under Manhattan metric) centered at q_1 with radius m_1. We denote such a diamond by Mq_1. Similarly, we assume Mq_2 using $mindata_2$ and q_2 (see Figure 4). From the geometric viewpoint, these diamonds correspond to the *Minmax* method when the query lies on q_1 or q_2 [8].

Figure 4. Diamonds Mq_1 and Mq_2.

Observation 1 There is no uncertain point that lies completely in Mq_1 (Mq_2), except $Mindata_1$ ($Mindata_2$).

Indeed, existing of an uncertain point that lies completely in Mq_1 (Mq_2) contradicts with the definition for Mq_1 (Mq_2). The following lemma states that any uncertain point intersecting Mq_1 (Mq_2) should be reported as NNzN.

Lemma 1 For an uncertain query point q with end-points $\{q_1, q_2\}$, every uncertain point $p \in P$ that intersects Mq_1 (Mq_2) is a NzNN of q.

Proof. Let e_s be the end-point of p that lies in Mq_1. We show that there is an instance q' of q where $d_{min}(p,q') \leq d_{max}(p_i,q)$ for all $p_i \in P, i = 1,\ldots,n$ and $p_i \neq p$. To this end, we construct a placement such that p is a NzNN of q. For any segment (an uncertain point) that intersects Mq_1, we choose the end-point that lies outside Mq_1 for $mindata_1$, we choose the end-point that lies on the boundary of Mq_1 and finally, for p and q, we choose e_s and q_1 as the instances (see Figure 5). By the definition for Mq_1, we have the following equation:

$$d(e_s,q_1) \leq d_{max}(p_i,q_1) \quad \text{for } i = 1,\ldots,n \quad (4)$$

Thus based on *Eq. (2)*, it can be concluded that p is a NzNN of q.

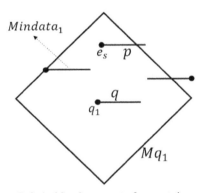

Figure 5. Suitable placement of uncertain points mentioned in proof of lemma 1.

In order to obtain all NNzNs, we should consider all instances of the query that lie between q_1 and q_2. By lemma 1, it is clear that the uncertain points intersecting Mq_1 or Mq_2 are NzNN of q. Furthermore, we need to take into account the points that do not have any intersection with Mq_1 (and Mq_2).

We say that $p_i \in P$ *prunes* $p_j \in P$ with respect to an uncertain query q, if $d_{max}(p_i,q') \leq d_{min}(p_j,q')$ for all instances q' of q. We consider all uncertain points that lie outside Mq_1 and Mq_1 that $mindata_1$ and $mindata_2$ cannot prune them, and define the critical regions C to remove such uncertain points (see Figure 6).

$$C = \{p \in R^2 | d_{min}(p,q')$$
$$\leq d_{max}(mindata_1,q') \ \& \ d_{min}(p,q')$$
$$\leq d_{max}(mindata_2,q') : \forall q' \text{of } q\} \quad (5)$$

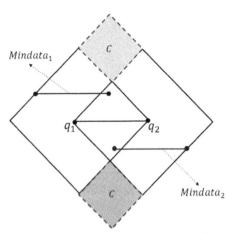

Figure 5. Critical regions with respect to $mindata_1$ and $mindata_2$.

In order to compute the critical regions C, we consider four lines passing through the edges of the diamonds Mq_1 and Mq_2 (see Figure 7). We can construct C by extending the edges for Mq_1 and Mq_2 and finding the intersection points. For example, as shown in figure 7, the critical region that lies above q can be computed by the intersection of lines Lu and Ru of Mq_1 and Mq_2.

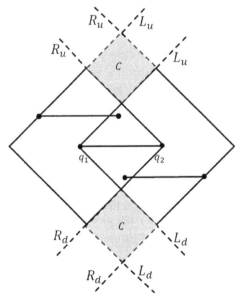

Figure 6. Definition of critical regions C by lines passing through edges of a diamond.

Since, in this section, we assume that the segments are unit, Mq_1 and Mq_2 overlap, thus we have two similar critical regions above and below q. Considering the above one, let v_u be the top-most point of the critical region, and v_d be the intersection point of Mq_1 and Mq_2. Assume two horizontal lines h_u and h_d passing through

v_u and v_d, respectively. Figure 8 shows these notations.

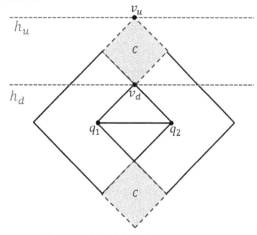

Figure 7. Definitions for h_u and h_d.

Lemma 2 The distance between h_u and h_d (introduced above) is at most L, where L is the query length.

Proof. Without a loss of generality, we assume that Mq_1 is smaller than Mq_2. Let δ be the maximum distance of $mindata_1$ from q_2. We construct a diamond centered at q_2 with radius δ, and denote it by $Maxq_1$. The distance between Mq_1 and $Maxq_1$ is L, which is the sum of the two segments a and b ($a+b=L$) (see Figure 9). The two gray triangles are similar because their angles are equal. It is clear that $e_2 \leq e_1$, and by similarity of the triangles, it can be concluded that $c \leq a$. Therefore, $b+c \leq L$, and the proof is complete.

Corollary 2 If Mq_1 and Mq_2 are disjoint, the distance between h_u and the line passing through q is at most L, where L is the length of q.

Considering figure 10, the proof of the corollary is similar to the proof of lemma 2.

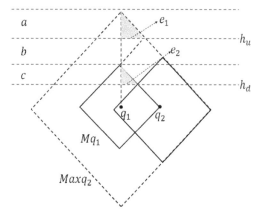

Figure 8. Definition of $Maxq_1$, a, b, and c used in proof of lemma 2.

Theorem 6 Let P be a set of disjoint unit segments as uncertain data. For a given uncertain query point q modeled by an x-parallel segment with length L, the segments intersecting the critical regions (see Eq. (5)) are NzNN of q.

Proof. Suppose that the critical regions above and below q are denoted by c_1 and c_2, and $p_i, p_j \in P$ intersect c_1 and c_2, respectively. Since all the segments are unit, there is no uncertain point that lies completely on c_1 or c_2. Thus we need to show that p_j does not prune p_i. Suppose that both p_i and p_j intersect c_1. We choose the end-point of p_i that lies in c_1 as its instance. Let p be the intersection of the segment perpendicular to q from the instance. We have the following equations under Manhattan metric (see Figure 11).

$$d_{max}(p_j, p) = h_j + v_j,$$

$$d_{min}(p_i, p) = v_i.$$

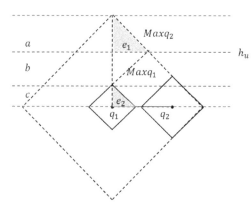

Figure 9. Distance between h_u and query.

Assume, to the contrary, that p_j prunes p_i. Since p_i lies above p_j, $v_j \leq v_i$ and $v_i = v_j + v$ for some $v \geq 0$. According to lemma 2, we know that $v \leq L$ and $h_j \geq L$ (note that members of p do not overlap). Thus we have:

$$h_j = L + h, \text{ for some } h > 0.$$

If p_i is pruned by p_j, we have the following equation:

$$h_j + v_j < v_i \rightarrow L + h < v,$$

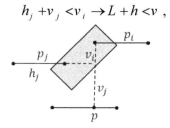

Figure 10 Minimum and maximum distances of p_i and p_j from p.

which is a contradiction to $v \leq L$. If p_i intersects c_1, and p_j intersects c_2, we can get symmetry of p_i with respect to q, and similarly, prove that p_j cannot prune p_i (see Figure 12).

3.2. Reporting non-zero NNs

By the argument in Section 3.1 we must report all the uncertain points that intersect Mq_1, Mq_2 or the critical regions as NzNN, so we need to compute diamonds Mq_1 and Mq_2 to find the critical regions.

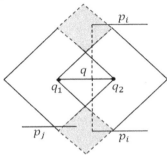

Figure 11. Symmetry of p_i with respect to query point q.

It is clear that $m_1 = min_{1 \leq i \leq n} d_i$ is a lower envelope of $M_1 = \{d_1, ..., d_n\}$, where d_i is the maximum distance between q_1 and $p_i \in P$. The projection of d_i onto the xy-plane is the farthest point Voronoi diagram of p_i. Therefore, the xy-projection of the graph of the function m_1 is a planar sub-division with $O(n^2 \alpha(n^2))$ vertices, and it can be computed in the $O(n^2 \log n)$ pre-processing time, where $\alpha(.)$ is the extremely slow growing functional inverse of the Ackermann's function [8,24]. Thus by pre-processing the projection of m_1 (m_2) onto the point location queries, we can perform two standard point locations for q_1 and q_2, and compute Mq_1 and Mq_2 in the $O(\log n)$ time [6]. By theorem 6 and lemma 1, we need to report all the segments that intersect Mq_1, Mq_2 or the critical regions. Since Mq_1, Mq_2, and the critical regions construct a *4-oriented set*, we can report such segments in the $O(\log n + k)$ time using the $O(n \log n)$ space, where k is the output size [22,23]. Therefore, we can conclude this section by the following theorem.

Theorem 3. Let $P = \{p_1, ..., p_n\}$ be a set of n uncertain points modeled by unit x-parallel segments that do not intersect each other. Then for any uncertain query modeled by an x-parallel segment, we can report NzNNs in the $O(\log n + k)$ time using the $O(n^2 \alpha(n^2))$ space, where k is the output size.

4. Approximation algorithm for NN searching for uncertain data and uncertain query

Let $P = \{p_1, ..., p_n\}$ be a set of n uncertain points modeled by arbitrary x-parallel segments. Then the segments that intersect the defined critical region C in *Eq.* (5) may prune each other. In this case, we report all the segments intersecting Mq_1, Mq_2, and C. For such NN reporting, we claim that the maximum error is L, where L is the query length. This error means that if p_j prunes p_i and we move p_i towards q at most L (under Manhattan metric), there is no segment that prunes p_i any more.

Lemma 3. An uncertain point $p_i \in P$ intersecting the critical region C is a NzNN of query q with maximum error L, where L is the length of q.

Proof. Assume that p_i is pruned by some points in C. The goal is to show that if we move p_i towards q at most L (under Manhattan metric), there is no segment that prunes p_i. If Mq_1 and Mq_2 overlap, according to lemma 2, the maximum distance between p_i and Mq_1 (or Mq_2) is L, and by moving p_i towards q at most L, it intersects Mq_1 (or Mq_2), and the goal is achieved. If Mq_1 and Mq_2 are disjoint, by corollary 2, the maximum distance between p_i and q is L, and by moving p_i towards q at most L, p_i intersects with q, and the proof is complete. The approximation factor L for the mentioned approach is tight. When sizes of Mq_1 and Mq_2 are equal, the amount of error is exactly L. See figure 12 as such a tight example.

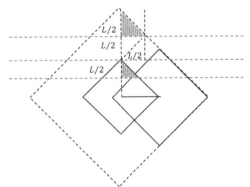

Figure 12. Maximum length for approximation factor.

5. Conclusions and future work

In this paper, we considered the nearest neighbor (NN) searching problem under uncertainty, and proposed algorithms for its variations under Manhattan metric. For the uncertain query and certain data points, we proposed an efficient algorithm that reported non-zero NNs in the $O(n \log n)$ space and $O(\log n + k)$ time, where k is the output size. For the uncertain query and uncertain points modeled by unit segments, we proposed an efficient algorithm that reported non-zero NNs in the $O(n^2 \alpha(n^2))$ space and the $O(\log n + k)$ time. For the uncertain query and uncertain points modeled by segments with arbitrarily length, we proposed an approximation algorithm that reported non-zero NNs with the maximum error L in the $O(n^2 \alpha(n^2))$ space and the $O(\log n + k)$ time, where L is the query length. As a future work, if the data and query are uncertain and the goal is to report non-zero NNs under Euclidean metric, instead of the constructed diamonds explained in section three, we should compute disks and the critical regions whose boundaries are defined by some algebraic equations. Thus we need to design an efficient algorithm for detecting intersection of geometric objects with algebraic equations.

References

[1] Löffler, M. & Snoeyink, J. (2010). Delaunay triangulation of imprecise points in linear time after preprocessing. Computional. Geometry Theory and Application, vol. 43, no. 3, pp. 234–242.

[2] Ostrovsky-Berman, Y. & Joskowicz, L. (2005). Tolerance envelopes of planar mechanical parts with parametric tolerances. Computer Aided Design, vol. 37, no 5: pp. 531–544.

[3] Khoshdel, V. & Akbarzadeh, A. R (2016). Application of statistical techniques and artificial neural network to estimate force from sEMG signals. Journal of Artificial Intelligence & Data Mining. vol. 4, no. 2, pp. 135-141.

[4] Löffler, M. (2009). Data imprecision in computational geometry, PhD Thesis. Department of computer science. University Utrecht.

[5] Khanban, A. A. (2005). Basic algorithms of computational geometry with imprecise input. PhD Thesis. Department of computing imperial college, University of London.

[6] de Berg, M., Cheong, O., Van Kreveld, M. & Overmars, M. (2008). Computational geometry algorithms and applications, third edition, Berlin Heidelberg: Springer-Verlag.

[7] Sember, J. & Evans, W. (2008). Guaranteed voronoi diagrams of uncertain sites. 20th Canadian Conference on Computational Geometry, Montreal, Canada, 2008.

[8] P.K. Agarwal, et al. (2013). Nearest neighbor searching under uncertainty II. 32th symposium on Principles of database systems. New York, USA, 2013.

[9] Zhang, W. (2012). Nearest neighbor searching under uncertainty, PhD Thesis. Duke University.

[10] Cheng, R., Kalashnikov, D. & Prabhakar, S. (2004). Querying imprecise data in moving object environments. IEEE Transactions on Knowledge and Data Engineering, vol. 16, pp.1112 – 1127.

[11] Zhang, P., Cheng, R., Mamoulis, N., Renz, M., Zufile, A., Tang, Y. & Emrich, T. (2013). Voronoi-based nearest neighbor search for multi-dimensional uncertain databases. 29th International Conference on Data Engineering , Brisbane, Australia, 2013.

[12] Emrich, T., et al. (2010). Boosting spatial pruning: on optimal pruning of MBRs. 40th International Conference on Management of data, Indiana, USA ,2010.

[13] Wang, H. & Zhang, W. (2014). L1 Top-k Nearest Neighbor Searching with Uncertain Queries. Proceedings of the VLDB Endowment, vol. 8, no. 1, pp. 13-24.

[14] Davoodi, M., Modades, A., Sheikhi, F. & Khanteimouri, P. (2015). Data imprecision under λ-geometry model. Information Sciences, vol. 295, pp. 126–144.

[15] Davoodi, M. & Mohades, A. (2013). Data Imprecision under λ-geometry: range searching problem. Scientia Iranica, vol. 20 , no.3, pp. 663–669.

[16] Myers, Y. & Joskowicz, L. (2010). Point distance and orthogonal range problems with dependent geometric uncertainties. 14th Symposium on Solid and Physical Modeling, New York, USA, 2010.

[17] Joskowicz, L., Ostrovsky-Berman, Y. & Myers, Y. (2010). Efficient representation and computation of geometric uncertainty: the linear parametric model. Precision Engineering, vol. 34, no. 1, pp. 2–6.

[18] Yuen, S., et al. (2010). Superseding nearest neighbor search on uncertain spatial databases. IEEE Transactions on Knowledge and Data Engineering, vol. 22, no. 7, pp.1041-1055.

[19] Beskales, G., Soliman, M. & Ilyas, I. (2008).Efficient search for the top-k probable nearest neighbors in uncertain databases. Proceedings of the VLDB Endowment, vol. 1, no. 1, pp. 326-339.

[20] Cheema, M., et al. (2010). Probabilistic reverse nearest neighbor queries on uncertain data. IEEE Transactions on Knowledge and Data Engineering, vol. 22, no. 4, pp. 550-564.

[21] Xiang, L. & Chen, L. (2008). Probabilistic group nearest neighbor queries in uncertain databases. IEEE Transactions on Knowledge and Data Engineering, vol. 20, no. 6, pp. 809-824.

[22] Tan, X., Hirata, T. & Inagaki, Y. (1991). The intersection searching problem for c-oriented polygons. Information Processing Letters, vol. 37, no.4, pp. 201–204.

[23] Güting, R. H. (1984). Dynamic c-oriented polygonal intersection searching. Information and control, vol. 63, no. 3, pp.143–163.

[24] Huttenlocher, D. P., Kedem, K., & Sharir, M. (1993). Discrete & Computational Geometry, vol. 9, no.3, pp. 267-291.

16

Optimizing cost function in imperialist competitive algorithm for path coverage problem in software testing

M. A. Saadatjoo and S. M. Babamir[*]

Department of Computer Engineering, University of Kashan, Kashan, Iran

*Corresponding author: babamir@kashanu.ac.ir (S. M. Babamir).

Abstract

The search-based optimization methods have been used for the software engineering activities such as software testing. In the field of software testing, search-based test data generation refers to the application of meta-heuristic optimization methods to generate the test data that cover the code space of a program. Automatic test data generation that can cover all the software paths is known as a major challenge.

This paper establishes a new cost function for automatic test data generation, which can traverse the non-iterative paths of the software control flow graphs (CFGs). This function is later compared with similar cost functions proposed in the other articles. The results obtained indicate the superior performance of the proposed function. Another innovation proposed in this paper is the application of the Imperialist Competitive Algorithm (ICA) in automatic test data generation along with the proposed cost function. Automatic test data generation is implemented through ICA as well as the genetic algorithm and particle swarm optimization algorithm for three software programs with different search space sizes. These algorithms are compared with each other in terms of the convergence speed, computational time, and local search. The test data generated by the proposed method achieved better results than the other algorithms in finding the number of non-iterative paths, convergence speed, and computational time with growing the searching space of the software CFG.

Keywords: *Software Testing, Imperialist Competitive Algorithm, Test Data Generation, Control Flow Graph, Program Complexity, Path Coverage.*

1. Introduction

One of the most important tasks in the process of software quality assurance is software testing, which is too expensive. According to the literature, nearly one-third of the software errors can be avoided by relying on the software testing methods [1]. Different methods are used for software testing. Among others, search-based testing is an effective method for testing a program if it is possible to cover the execution space of the program. It refers to the use of a meta-heuristic optimizing search method to automate test case generation [2]. In the search-based testing methods, a test dataset is provided as a vector of the required values to traverse different execution paths of a program so as to demonstrate the maximum software fault. A test dataset includes a vector with sufficient values to implement the corresponding software. A test data vector is ideal if 1) each of its elements is necessary (i.e. not redundant) and 2) its elements are sufficient (i.e. no other elements are required). These two conditions state that the vector should include the same number of elements as the program execution paths so that inputting each of its elements can lead to the execution of a different program path. If the fist condition is not met, the test will not be complete but if the second one is not met, unnecessary cost will be incurred.

The execution paths of a program, known as the search space, are demonstrated by a Control Flow Graph (CFG). This is a graph that is built according to the program code. The more branches the graph has, the more complex search space it has. Such a complexity has a direct relationship with program testability (see Section 3).

In this article, a new cost function is introduced. This cost function is composed of the cost function introduced in [3] and the recommended parameter. The value of the cost function in the recommended method is obtained by the maximum path coverage, not by choosing the repeated paths of the Control Flow Graph (CFG). To evaluate the new function, the problem of search-based testing in [3] is solved by the recommended cost function. The results obtained show that the traverse of non-iterative paths is more than the one in [3].

Choosing the test data from a software search space is very complex. To overcome this problem, the automatic test data generation techniques can be of help using complete algorithms [4 and 5].

One of the recent evolutionary algorithms that has drawn the attention of researchers in search-based issues is the Imperialist Competitive Algorithm (ICA) [6]. This algorithm has led to better results in different applications in comparison with the Genetic Algorithm (GA) and the Particle Swarm Optimization (PSO) algorithm [7-9]. In [10], these three are compared with one another according to the local search parameters, convergence speed, and computational time. The results obtained showed that ICA is more efficient than the other algorithms. In [11], a hybrid meta-heuristic algorithm based on imperialist competition algorithm is introduced. Their method showed that ICA method has better results in finding global optimum and search speed. In [12], it was tried to solve a discrete Traveling Salesman problem using ICA. The results showed the high capability of this algorithm in solving discrete problems. Since the problem of automatic software test data generation by CFG is of a discrete nature and due to the priorities of ICA in [10], ICA was used in the present work. The aim of this work was to show the efficiency of ICA as an approach recommended versus GA and PSO algorithm in solving the problem of maximum path coverage of search-based testing.

Although ICA has been applied for software cost estimation aimed at software project management [13-15], it has not yet been used for the automatic test data generation software.

Using ICA, we generated the test data that covered more program paths than GA and PSO algorithm, and the generated data was closer to ideal. This work is the first attempt to use ICA through the recommended cost function so as to generate the automatic test data whose efficiency is determined against other related approaches

such as GA and PSO algorithm. According to this experience, the efficiency and capability of the approach was determined based upon its nearness to the ideal data, local research, convergence speed, and computational time. In this work, the recommended algorithm was used to generate the test data for four programs with low, medium, and high degrees of complexity, and the results obtained were evaluated to determine the efficiency of the algorithm.

This paper is organized as what follows. The program CFG is introduced in Section 2. Section 3 deals with the related works. Section 4 addresses ICA (i.e. the proposed algorithm) for the automatic test data generation. The proposed cost function and its evaluation are discussed in Section 5. The use of ICA in software search-based testing is explained in Section 6. Section 7 draws conclusions and proposes directions for future research works.

2. Control flow graph (CFG)

A CFG is a graph in which each node contains one or more successive program statements. It has a start and an end node, and its edges denote the control flow between the program statements. In this graph, the branch points indicate conditional statements [16]. A path starts from a start node and ends with an end node. Figure 2 shows CFG for the program in figure 1 (the number of nodes in figure 2 indicates the number of statements in figure 1.

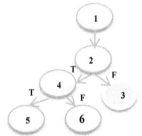

Figure 1. CFG of MAX program.

This graph has six nodes, each of which includes one or more program statements in figure 2, and seven edges each of which denotes the control between the statements. The basic paths are as what follow. The rest of the paths are constructed out of the basic paths, which are three. It should be noted that path 1 will not be evaluated by any test data. Paths such as this are called the infeasible software paths.

    a) 1- 2- 3
    b) 1-2-4-5-6-2-3
    c) 1-2-4-6-4-3

Generation of an adequate test data for maximum CFG path coverage is our main concern in this paper. As the CFG branches increase, the CFG structure becomes more complicated for searching because the number of paths increases too, and thus finding adequate test data that can traverse all the paths becomes difficult. In fact, the number of elements in the search space of source code paths is determined by the number of conditions. This is called program complexity or the McCabe number [17].

In order to automatically generate the test data, the search space for the program must be specified. This space, which shows the structure of the program, is obtained from CFG. The search in this space is carried out in the following three ways: 1) Searching the space for graph nodes in which each node represents an instruction for the program 2) Searching the space for graph edges in which each edge represents a branch in the program 3) Searching the graph paths in which each path is a set of nodes and edges and entails the beginning to the end of the graph. The test data selected as the answers are only those that are able to successfully traverse the maximum part of the search space or the paths of the program CFG.

```
1. void MAX (int x[],int n) {
2.     int max,i=1;
3.     max=x[0];
4. `   while(i<n){
5.     if(x[i]>max)
6.         max=x[i];
7.     i++;
8.     }
#9.   cout<<max;
#10.  }
```

Figure 2. MAX program.

For a software in which the whole program is run in one module, a CFG can be easily depicted so as to determine the number of software paths. However, in a software whose running process includes several intricate modules, depiction of CFG of the whole software is not an easy task. In such structures, first, a CFG is created for each module separately, and the number of paths is determined. Next, based upon the number of paths in each module, the paths in the whole software are estimated. This method was used in the present study to approximate the number of paths.

3. Related works

About 59% of the literature on software engineering is about software testing [2]. The main idea to use methods of evolutionary algorithms for search-based testing is to generate a set of test data that are partly ideal.

3.1. Application of PSO

The PSO algorithm was first introduced in [18] and inspired by a swarm of birds looking for food. In [19], the authors have tried to generate the test data for a program that merges two arrays using PSO. To do so, they generated six methods for traversing paths. However, their experience was of use for simple problems with low complexity, and no evaluation was provided for programs with medium and high degrees of complexity. In this paper, the studied issues were not so complex, and the results obtained were not compared with other approaches. However, the efficiency of the recommended approach was compared with that of the PSO algorithm approach.

3.2. Application of GA

GA can be applied to resolve the optimization issues [20]. The algorithm is also applied to software automatic test data generation for the purpose of path coverage. In generating the test data using this algorithm, a chromosome plays the role of the input vector of the test data, each of which functions as a gene.

In [21-24] have proposed principles and rules for using this algorithm to automatically generate the test data. They generated the test data according to the proposed algorithm for a couple of programs. This algorithm has been used in [22] to generate the test data based on a dynamic method. The proposed method was compared with GA for program branch coverage as the search space. Finding the ideal test data that is able to cover more space is one of the properties of this dynamic method.

Keyvanpour and Homayouni [3] have tried to use a combination of evolutionary and local search methods to generate the test data. Using the Memetic algorithm and a local search method called 'hill climbing', at each stage of test data generation, they tried to reduce the time spent for finding the suitable tests. The cost function that they used was a combination of three parameters including neighborhood, closeness to the border, and branch coverage. At each stage of their proposed algorithm, the generated data was inputted to a neural network for evaluation. They applied their method to a triangle program, and using the local search algorithm, they were able to reduce the number of algorithm iterations to an acceptable level, which made the convergence faster. However, this method was not implemented to solve problems with medium and high degrees of complexity.

Many researchers have used GA to generate the test data for different types of coverage including branch coverage [22], condition-decision coverage [23], path coverage [24-26], and multiple-path coverage [27-29].

As for the present article, its focus has only been placed on path space coverage. In each of the above-mentioned evolutionary methods, a program with low complexity is initially introduced for generating the test data. In the second step, the evolutionary algorithm parameters are set according to the desired program. In the third step, the test data that can cover the search spaces of condition, path, branch, and instructions are generated.

Ahmed and Hermadi [27] have investigated their test data generation method to cover the path space in a program of low complexity. Their desired criterion was the amount of the generated data for traversing one path and then traversing all the paths of the program. Their proposed method failed to generate the least test data with the ability to traverse the most possible paths.

Using GA, Li and Yeh [29] have generated the test data to cover the path space through relational algebra. They examined the CFG paths when coverage of only one path was desired. However, they did not discuss the effectiveness of this method when it was aimed at traversing all the paths. In their method, the focus of each stage of implementing the proposed algorithm was only on traversing one path, and this prevented the generalization of their method to solve the whole problem space. Another drawback of this method is that they used a criterion for comparing the time regardless of the fitness value showing the extent of path coverage.

Zhang and Gong [31 and 32] have compared the speed of implementing their proposed algorithm in generating the test data on two programs (array search and bubble sort) with low complexity. In the current work, this parameter was used to display and evaluate the implementation speed of the proposed method together with the quality of the generated test data (which is dependent upon a fitness function).

Harman and McMinn [33] have evaluated some (local and general) search methods in program tests, and concluded that a method that combines the local and general search can greatly contribute to the optimal generation of the test data, which can properly cover the search space. Their evaluation was based upon the complexity of sample programs, all of which were simple or with low complexity. It was not determined in their work whether their method could account for the time when the problem space expands.

Mansour and Salame [34] have used GA for automatic generation of the test data in problems that work with accurate and real data. Their method was limited to certain data types, and no comparison was made for the amount of path coverage. However, the test data type had no effect on our proposed method since it was determined with respect to the desired problem.

In addition to GA and PSO algorithm, the Artificial Bee Colony (ABC) algorithm is a search-based method used for automatic generation of the test data in order to cover the path space [35]. However, its effectiveness has not been proved for path coverage of programs with high complexity and large search space.

4. Imperialist competitive algorithm (ICA)

In ICA, countries are introduced as problem results (i.e. test data). The characteristics of each country are the desired test data to cover the search space. In this algorithm, in terms of ideal test data selection, powerful countries are opted through a cost function as used in this algorithm. Some countries are selected as imperialists and some others as colonies. Like many other evolutionary algorithms, at the beginning of the algorithm implementation, countries (test data) are randomly selected in the whole problem space. Based upon the power of each country, some are randomly selected as imperialists (i.e. test data that traverses new and more paths compared with the other data in the search space) and some others as colonies. The imperialists and colonies are selected independently. An imperialist and its colonies are called an *empire*. Imperialist competition means the attempt of an imperialist to attract maximum colonies from other empires.

There are two conditions for this algorithm including 1) the algorithm continues based on the described cases until one or more empires remain with regard to the problem (2) the algorithm runs to a certain number of rounds. One may shortly refer to these two as the final condition and convergence. In the case of automatic generation of the test data in this work, each empire will be considered as a test data vector. Each vector represents the test data that traverse at least one new path. The ultimate solution will be the most powerful imperialist, indicating the best set of test data vectors that traverse a maximal number of program paths.

The first step in forming an empire is to establish countries that are randomly placed throughout the space. The structures of the countries vary according to the software under test. In general, a problem with a test vector having n elements is shown as (1):

$$Country = [num_0, num_1, ..., num_n] \qquad (1)$$

Another parameter that plays a crucial role in attracting the countries and developing an empire is the power of each imperialist within the empire or simply the power of each empire. Using the power of an empire, it can be specified which country is shared at the time of competition. To calculate the power of each empire, as mentioned in [3], the ultimate power of that empire is taken into account.

The following section outlines the proposed cost function and its application in ICA for automatic test data generation.

5. Proposed cost function

The first challenge in solving problems by evolutionary algorithms is to design a proper cost function. This aims at generating a minimum test data to traverse maximum paths of a software CFG. Thus a proper cost function should be designed.

The recommended cost function in this paper is composed of the cost function introduced in [3] and a new parameter. For a better understanding of the recommended cost function, all parameters will be discussed.

5. 1. Path traverse probability

A test vector consists of some test data, each of which traverses a path of the graph. The possibility of traversing this path by test data t_i from vector T is:

$$L(Path(t_i)) = \prod_{j=1}^{k} P_j \ (for \ all \ conditions \ in \ path(t_i)) \qquad (2)$$

In (2), k is equal to the conditions in which test data t_i is traversed through its path.

Generally, by taking the following steps, it is possible to obtain the probable parameter of traversing a path by a test vector.

- Obtaining a path that traverses the test vector.
- Using CFG of the software to determine the set of conditions that the test data traverse through and writing an algebraic expression among its conditions.
- Normalizing the algebraic equation by moving one side of this equation to the other side, for example, changing a < b to a-b < 0.
- Calculating the probability of generating a normal algebra.

- Calculating the probable parameter of the path by the data of a T test vector, as follows:

$$P(T) = 1 - \left((1 - L(Path(t_1))) * (1 - L(Path(t_2))) * ... \right) \qquad (3)$$

$L(P(t_1))$ is the probability of selecting a path that is traversed by the test data t_i. If each path has more than one condition, the probability of the test data not to select that path is equal to 1-$L(P(t_1))$. In addition, a test vector is composed of a combination of several test data. Thus this amount is calculated for each test data of one test vector.

5.2. Closeness to boundary values

Experience has shown that test cases close to boundary values are more likely to find program error 4 [4]. The closeness to the boundary is shown by $N(T)$.

Close to the boundary values for a test vector T. This parameter for a test vector is calculated by Eq. 4:

$$N(T) = N(t_1) \times N(t_2) \times ... \qquad (4)$$

where, t_i is the ith test data of test vector T, and $N(t_i)$ is close to the boundary value for t_i that is calculated as follows:

- Obtaining a path that traverses the test vector.
- Using CFG of the software to determine the set of conditions that the test data traverse through and writing an algebraic expression among its conditions.
- In each algebraic expression, all comparison operations $\{<, >, \le, \ge, =\}$ change to $\{=\}$.
- Moving the right side of each algebraic expression to the left side to find the boundary value of that expression.
- Calculating the parameter of closeness to the boundary values for each input test data, as follows:

$$N(t_i) = 1 - |(t_i)/(Max\_Value\_Size)| \qquad (5)$$

where, t_i is the test data input, and Max_Value_Size is the domain of the test data. The closeness to the boundary values is calculated for each existing data on the test vector, and then each value is multiplied by the others to obtain the probability of closeness to the boundary borders of the test vector.

5.3. Edge coverage

Edge coverage means the percentage of edges in CFG covered by the test data vector. Edge coverage is computed using (6), where e is the number of edges traversed by the test vector T, and E is the total number of CFG edges:

$$D(T) = e / E \qquad (6)$$

The aim of this paper was to generate an ideal test data that could cover the maximum paths of a graph. To gain this goal, the parameter of non-iterative path coverage was selected.

5.4. Non-iterative path coverage

To compute the number of paths traversed by a test vector, it is required to determine whether the traversed paths are non-iterative since the test data that do not generate a new path are practically useless. For this purpose, we introduced the concept of Evaluator, and, using this, we generated vectors that created non-iterative paths.

5.4.1. Evaluator

Obtaining the non-iterative traversed paths in CFG by a test data vector was an important part of the present study. An evaluation matrix is used to determine the non-iteratively traversed paths by the test data. Assume that the conditions of a CFG are C_p. Therefore, there are $2C_p$ corresponding algebraic expressions (one corresponding algebraic expression based upon a true condition and one corresponding algebraic expression based upon a false condition). Each Evaluator is an array of paths at the length of $2C_p$ in which each element is a corresponding algebra expression. For every test data, there is an Evaluator. From the beginning, this array is initialized with a zero, i.e. the test data does not traverse any path. When an edge is traversed by the test data, an algebraic expression is selected from $2C_p$ of them, whose corresponding value in the Evaluation array has the value of 1.

After running the program by a test vector, all the Evaluators are calculated based on decimals. If the decimal numbers generated by the Evaluators are unique, non-iterative paths will be traversed. In other words, iteration of each number indicates the traverse of an iterative path. Thus the Evaluator obtained is unique in every path of CFG.

If the number of existing test data is equal to that of vector V_p, then we will have the matrix $Eval_{V_p \times 2C_p}$ in which every row is an array corresponding to the test data.

In graphs with loops, it is possible to make the following equation after generating an Evaluation matrix:

$$Eval[k] = Eval[i] \vee Eval[j] \qquad (7)$$

where, $Eval[i]$ is the ith row of the Evaluation matrix. Here, the kth row of the Evaluation matrix is obtained from the OR logical actions

between the ith and j^{th} rows of the matrix. It should be noted that the test data that generate these Evaluators can traverse a given path more than one time.

The number of lines in the Evaluator obtained from other lines through the Union logical operation is displayed by cnt_Eval. This variable indicates the number of non-iterative paths traversed by the test data. The non-iterative path coverage parameter is computed by cnt_Eval, here referred to as $W(T)$ (Equation 8). The parameter is presented in this paper for the first time:

$$W(T) = \frac{cnt\_Eval}{N_p} \qquad (8)$$

where, N_p represents the number of total estimated paths in the graph.

Simply, the computational steps of $W(T)$ are as follow:

- Using CFG to determine the set of conditions that the test data can traverse.
- Generating the $Eval_{V_p \times 2C_p}$ Evaluation matrix in which V_p is the number of test data of a test vector, and C_p is the number of conditions in CFG.
- Setting the Evaluation matrix according to the input test vector.
- Calculating the decimal number of each row.
- Determining the number of non-iterative paths using cnt_Eval.

According to the above criteria, the proposed cost function is:

$$F(T) = (P(T) + N(T) + D(T) + W(T))/4 \qquad (9)$$

5.5. Evaluating proposed cost function

To generate a test data with high quality, the three parameters path traverse probability, closeness to boundary values, and edge coverage were linearly integrated. As in [3], a cost function was used with the non-iterative path coverage parameter for the purpose of high-quality test data generation. To determine the effect of the non-iterative path coverage parameter, a triangle program was used as the base example to show the automatic test data generation.

Two empirical tests were carried out to evaluate the proposed cost function. In the first one, according to [3], 25 test vectors, each with five test data and three elements (all integer numbers between -32678 and 32677), were involved in the test. The maximum path coverage of CFG depends on the number of test data in a test vector.

In the second test, 90 test vectors, each with 18 test data and three elements, were selected. Since the triangle program had 18 paths and the aim of the article was to traverse the maximum paths of CFG of a program, every test vector had 18 test data. These two tests were carried out with the cost function in [3], the cost function proposed in the present work, and using GA in equal situations. The results of averaging 30 independent tests are shown in table 2.

As shown in this table, using the non-iterative path parameter in the proposed cost function, GA can find all the paths with five test data. This is while, by using the cost function [3], only three paths are traversed. In addition, when the test data increase, the proposed cost function is more successful in finding more paths than the cost function is in [3]. Using the proposed parameter in the cost function prevents generating iterative test data and leads to finding the data that traverses new paths. This is in contrast to the cost function of [3], where only ideal data are important, and iterative or non-iterative data is not important. Finding more paths leads to finding more errors in the software. The aim of this work was to find an ideal test data to traverse the CFG paths through introducing a parameter as explained above.

Owing to its efficacy, the proposed cost function was used to solve a search-based path-coverage problem with ICA.

6. Using ICA in search-based testing

This section addresses the automatic test data generation for path coverage in three software programs with moderate and high degrees of complexity. Figure 3 shows the pseudo-code of generating the test vectors to cover the search space of the software paths using ICA. According to figure 3, after executing the proposed method, countries will compete with each other to gain ideal test data. After the power of each test vector is calculated, ICA comes to be of use.

To test the software comprehensively, a test vector including all the aspects is required. The number of test data in a test vector is proportional to the paths of the software under test.

6.1. Setting-up parameters of ICA

In this section, the parameters required for running ICA are discussed.

6.1.1. Empire formation

As stated in Section 5, an Empire is a set of test vectors. Empire formation means to generate a set of test vectors in all the spaces of a CFG. In the automatic test data generation of a software program and after obtaining the space of the software CFG and determining the structure of each vector as a member of an Empire, we have to determine the role of the test vectors as an empire or a colony. Vectors with a higher cost function are an Empire, and the other vectors (countries) are selected as colonies.

1- Define Fitness	3- Tune ICA parameters
- Identify condition nodes	- Define test-data pattern
- Calculate edge coverage probability	- Define assimilation policy
- Calculate closeness to boundary	4- Generate test data
	- Run program (p) for each test data
- Calculate branch coverage	- Calculate Empire's power
- Calculate path coverage	- Colony absorption
- Calculate finesse value	- Eliminate powerless Empire
2- Define IP according to paths	
	- Check stop conditions

Figure 3. Pseudo-code of generating test data using ICA.

Table 2. Evaluation of proposed cost function in Triangle program using GA.

Cost function	Test number	Test data number	Traversed paths
Cost function introduced in [3]	First	5	3
	Second	18	6
Proposed cost function	First	5	5
	Second	18	14

6.1.2. Assimilation policy

In order to achieve a powerful empire, an imperialist tries to assimilate colonies using a specific assimilation policy. To understand the process, this policy has to be explained first. According to the presented cost function, after calculating the power of each empire and before entering the competition, each imperialist tries to assimilate more colonies. At each step of the algorithm, the imperialist, quite randomly, substitutes 10% of its arrayed elements, as part of the test vector, with identical colony elements. Through this method, the speed and power to reach an optimal answer significantly increases.

What follows is an example of replacing the first element of an imperialist with that of its colony in a triangle problem. In this example, the first epoch of assimilation policy is illustrated. The first element of the empire is replaced with the first element of the colony. This replacement continues to the last element. It means that after n epochs of ICA, all the remaining colonies in the empire look completely like the imperialists. The selected assimilation policy for all the tested programs is as (10):

Before assimilation :

$Country = num_1 \ num_2 \ num_3 ... num_n$

$Imperialist = C_1 \quad C_4 \quad C_2 \ ... \ C_5$

After assimilation :

$Country = num_1 \ num_2 \ num_3 ... num_n$

$Colony = C_2 \quad C_3 \quad C_4 \ ... \ C_1$ \quad (10)

$\Downarrow$

$Colony = C_1 \quad C_3 \quad C_4 \ ... \ C_1$

6.1.3. Final conditions and answers

Like other evolutionary approaches, termination conditions should be defined. In ICA, the goal is to have a single empire as the final condition. In this situation, the test data in the imperialist vector is the final answer. The convergence condition means that the algorithm repeats for a pre-determined number of times, and the cost function value does not change in any iteration; therefore, ICA will end. If the algorithm is not terminated after specific iterations, the Empire that has a higher cost function than the others is the answer. Before showing the efficiency of ICA in search-based testing, it is necessary to introduce the set of tested software and define the structure of the tested vectors (i.e. countries) that are required for traversing the paths.

6.2. Case studies

Four programs (Table 3) were used to evaluate the effectiveness of the proposed method. Each program was selected according to the complexity of the condition structure and the search. Triangle program, as one of the common software programs of generating automatic test data, proved to be proper with which to introduce the proposed method. Two programs from the Siemens database were selected to evaluate the proposed method in big industrial spaces. In order to automatically generate the test data for these applications using the proposed method, the structure of the test vector was initially identified for each of these programs, and CFG was created

for each program. Then based on that, the corresponding Evaluation matrix was created. Finally, a brief description was provided for each software program and for the structure of the test vectors.

6.2.1. Triangle program

Triangle program is one of the common programs that researches use a basic benchmark program.

Table 3. Properties of selected programs.

Program	Task	#paths	Type of complexity	Line of Code (LOC)
Triangle	Determining triangle type	18	moderate	30
Schedule	Scheduling tokens by users	173	high	410
Print-token	Get and print a token out of queue	158	high	563

The code of the triangle software used is in [3], and its CFG is generated. This program has six conditions and 12 algebraic expressions. If a test vector is assumed to consist of four tests, i.e. T={(1,2,5),(5,5,5),(5,4,5),(25,2,7)},the Evaluation matrix will be:

$$Eval = \begin{bmatrix} 0\ 1\ 0\ 1\ 0\ 1\ 1\ 0\ 0\ 0\ 0\ 0 \\ 0\ 1\ 0\ 1\ 0\ 1\ 0\ 1\ 1\ 0\ 0\ 0 \\ 1\ 0\ 0\ 1\ 0\ 1\ 0\ 1\ 0\ 1\ 1\ 0 \\ 1\ 0\ 0\ 1\ 1\ 0\ 1\ 0\ 0\ 0\ 0\ 0 \end{bmatrix}$$

According to the evaluation matrix:
- The 1st test data will not evaluate the condition related to lines 2, 3, and 4 but it can evaluate the condition of line 5 that is in the scalene triangle group.
- The 2nd test data will not evaluate the condition related to lines 2, 3, 4, and 5 but it can evaluate the condition of line 9 that is in the equilateral triangle group.
- The 3rd test data will not evaluate the condition related to lines 3, 4, 5, and 9 but it can evaluate the condition of lines 2 and 12 that are in the isosceles triangle group.
- The 4th test data will not evaluate the condition related to line 3 but it can evaluate the condition of lines 2, 4, and 5 that are in the non-triangle group.

In ICA, each test vector is considered as a country, and defined as (11).

$Country = \{(num_{11}, num_{12}, num_{13}),$

$(num_{21}, num_{22}, num_{23}),...,$

$(num_{K1}, num_{K2}, num_{K3})\}$ \quad (11)

In this equation, each country has some test data that are the inputs of the problem. In the triangle software, each test data has three integers that are the lengths of the triangle lines. According to the triangle software paths, the maximum path that a vector can traverse is 18. Thus $K = 18$, where K is the number of test data used in the test vector.

6.2.2. Schedule program

This program can be taken from the Siemens database as an industrial program with the aim of scheduling the sent items in a network. Moreover, the switch-case control condition makes this software different from the other software programs. The features of this software are presented in table 3, and the program code is available in [36]. CFG is designed for each module of this software, and its paths are extracted. The maximum number of the paths of this software is 173 with respect to CFG of its modules. A country (i.e. test vector) is defined as in (12), where the number of elements in the test data is 23, and the number of paths equals $K = 173$.

$$Country = \{(num_{1,1},...,num_{1,23}),$$
$$(num_{2,1},...,num_{2,23}),..., \qquad (12)$$
$$(num_{K,1},...,num_{K,23})\}$$

6.2.3. Print-token program

This program is extracted from the Siemens database. CFG is made for this software, and its paths are extracted. With respect to CFG of each module, the maximum number of paths in this software is 158. In this work, selection of this software is due to its having more functions and nested call nodes. For this software, a country (or a test vector) is defined as (13). This software has 32 inputs, so the number of elements in each test data is 32, and the paths are calculated as $k = 158$.

$$Country = \{(num_{1,1},...,num_{1,32}),$$
$$(num_{2,1},...,num_{2,32}),..., \qquad (13)$$
$$(num_{K,1},...,num_{K,32})\}$$

6.3. Evaluating efficiency of ICA for path coverage in search-based testing

To evaluate the efficiency of ICA over GA and PSO Algorithm, the cost function proposed in Section (5) and the parameter introduced in [10] are used. The corresponding criteria are presented in the following:

a. Convergence speed: this criterion is the number of repetitions of algorithms to get a final condition and find a final answer. In this paper, the final

answer is a test vector that has a higher cost function.

b. Computational time: this criterion is the time of executing an algorithm at specified intervals.

c. Local search: the maximum non-iterative path in a search space is introduced using this criterion. The different nature of the softwares introduced in part (7) can be of use to investigate the ability of the selected algorithms in meeting the above criteria. For GA and PSO Algorithm, each gene and particle is a country introduced in part (7). The selected generations and the final conditions are the same in the three evolutionary algorithms. Table 4 shows the general settings of algorithms for running each of the programs introduced in table 3. To have a fair comparison between the evolutionary algorithms, a standard implementation should be ensured.

Table 4. General settings of algorithms.

Program	Triangle	Schedule	Print-token
Test data length	3	23	32
Path number	18	173	158
Population	2000	5000	5000
Maximum repetition	200	500	500

The parameters ICA, GA, and PSO are presented in table 5 based on [10], [37], and [38], respectively. Random initializations are selected in generations. The proposed cost function is used in the implementation of evolutionary algorithms shown in table 6. This means that the results of ICA are obtained using the proposed cost function.

The average results of 30 sequential executions for four programs are shown in table 6. In this table, the second column shows the paths traversed by the ideal test vector. The third column shows the steps of executing the algorithm to reach the final conditions.

The fourth column shows the execution time of the algorithm to reach the optimal answer. Among all the available paths in CFG, the fifth column shows the traverse percentage of the algorithm. The quality of the generated test data through the cost function in each algorithm is shown in the last column of the table. The following results are obtained from table 6:

a. In problems with bigger search spaces, ICA is repeated less than in the other two methods in the search space of CFG.

b. Computational time of the PSO algorithm is shorter than that of GA and ICA due to fewer operators.

c. In bigger search spaces, the searching power of ICA is more. The higher rate of path coverage in big problems is a good proof.

d. Although cost function structures are similar, it is obvious that the test data selected by ICA has a higher quality than those selected by the other two methods (i.e. when the cost function value is higher, selection chances are better).

Table 5. Basic algorithm parameters.

Algorithms	ICA			GA				PSO	
Parameters	Coefficient power	Imperialist number	Revolution rate	Mutation	Cross-over	Probability	Selection method	Inertia weight	Acceleration
Values	0.05	10% of total countries	0.2	0.01	Two Point	1	Binary tournament	0.09	2

Table 6. Average results of simulation for 30 runs.

Algorithm	Program	Local search (No. of paths)	Convergence speed (No. of algorithm operations)	Computational time (minute) (runtime of algorithm)	Path coverage percentage	Cost function value
Imperialist Competitive Algorithm	Triangle	15.5	23.4	0.21	0.86	0.75
	Schedule	148.3	132.6	30.55	0.85	0.85
	Print-token	137.4	178.4	35.53	0.86	0.88
GA	Triangle	15.5	49.3	0.94	0.86	0.71
	Schedule	101.4	177.88	140.13	0.58	0.63
	Print-token	92.2	470.37	186.99	0.58	0.68
PSO Algorithm	Triangle	16.5	86.6	0.19	0.91	0.77
	Schedule	61.1	66.2	4.93	0.35	0.41
	Print -token	53.6	46.23	5.15	0.34	0.38

7. Conclusions and perspective for future research works

In the present work, we applied ICA for the optimal generation of the test data. In order to enhance the optimization process in this regard, the cost function algorithm was re-designed and a new parameter, namely non-iterative path coverage, was added to it. For automatic test data generation by evolutionary algorithms, a new cost function was proposed. This cost function serves to compute the parameter of "non-iterative path coverage". In this situation, only the set of test data that have traversed the non-iterative paths of CFG are selected by this cost function. To this end, an Evaluation matrix was used for detecting these paths.

The cost function was used to detect the non-iterative paths of three software programs in a search-based testing problem. In this work, we used ICA, for the first time, for the automatic test

data generation, which could have maximum path coverage of CFG. Three criteria including local search, computation time, and convergence speed were involved in the evaluation of ICA, as compared to GA and PSO algorithm.

The evaluation results showed that:

- As the search space for the problem increased, ICA gained a higher convergence speed.
- It was also found that a higher path coverage speed in bigger problems signified the ICA power in a local search.
- As another finding, a higher cost function rate in ICA served as an indication of the value of ideal data, as compared with the other algorithms.
- Finally, the computing time in PSO turned out to be shorter than that in the other algorithms, which could be

- attributed to the smaller number of computational operators in the structure of PSO.

To evaluate the capability of the proposed method in detecting faults, mutation testing will be used in our future research work.

Acknowledgment

The authors wish to thank University of Kashan for supporting this research work with grant No. 577242.

References

[1] Aggarwal, K. & Singh, Y. (2007). Software Engineering (3rd Ed.). New Age International Publishers

[2] Peeze, M. & Young, M. (2007). Software Testing and Analysis: Process, Principles and Techniques, John Wiley, Sons

[3] Keyvanpour, M. R., Homayouni, H. & Shirazee, H. (2011). Automatic Software Test Case Generation. Software Engineering, vol. 5, pp. 91-101.

[4] Singh, H. (2004). Automatic generation of software test cases using genetic algorithms. A thesis in Thapar University Patiala may.

[5] Shimin, L. & Zhangang, W. (2011). Genetic Algorithm and its Application in the path-oriented test data automatic generation. Procedia Engineering, vol. 15, PP. 1186 – 1190.

[6] Atashpaz-Gargari, E. & Lucas, C. (2007). Imperialist Competitive Algorithm: An Algorithm for Optimization Inspired by Imperialistic Competition. IEEE Congress on Evolutionary Computation, Singapore, pp. 4661-4667.

[7] Lucas, C., Nasiri-Gheidari, Z. & Tootoonchian, F. (2010). Application of an imperialist competitive algorithm to the design of a linear induction motor. Energy Conversion and Management, vol. 51, pp. 1407-141.

[8] Bahrami, H., Faez. K. & Abdechiri, M. (2010). Imperialist competitive algorithm using chaos theory for optimization. Computer Modelling and Simulation (UKSim), 12th International Conference on IEEE, pp. 98-103.

[9] Wang, G., Zhang, J. B. & Chen, J. W. (2011). A novel algorithm to solve the vehicle routing problem with time windows: Imperialist competitive algorithm. Advances in Information Sciences and Service Sciences, vol. 3, no. 5, pp. 108-116.

[10] Hosseini, S., Al Khaled, A. (2014). A survey on the Imperialist Competitive Algorithm metaheuristic: Implementation in engineering domain and directions for future research. Applied Soft Computing, vol. 24, pp. 1078-1094.

[11] Roustaei, R. & Yousefi Fakhr, F. (2016). A hybrid meta-heuristic algorithm based on imperialist competition algorithm. Journal of AI & Data Mining, In Press.

[12] Yousefikhoshbakht, M. & Sedighpour, M. (2013). New Imperialist Competitive Algorithm to solve the travelling salesman problem. Computer Mathematics, vol. 90, pp. 1495-1505.

[13] Gharehchopogh, F. S. & Maroufi, A. (2014). Approach of software cost estimation with hybrid of imperialist competitive and artificial neural network algorithms, Journal of Scientific Research and Development, vol. 1, pp. 50-57.

[14] Pourali, A. & Sangar, A. B. (2015). A new approach in software cost estimation with hybrid of imperialist competitive algorithm and ant colony algorithm. Academiea Royale Des Sciences D Outre-Mer Bulletin Des Seances, vol. 4, pp. 106-113.

[15] Sadeghi, B., Khatibi, V., Esfandiari, M. & Hosseinzadeh, F. (2015). A Novel ICA-based Estimator for Software Cost Estimation, Advances in Computer Engineering and Technology, vol. 1, pp.15-24.

[16] Hutcheson, M. L. (2003). Software Testing Fundamentals: Methods and Metrics. John Wiley, Sons.

[17] Qingfeng, D. & Xiao, D. (2011). An improved algorithm for basis path testing. Management and Electronic Information (BMEI), International Conference on, vol. 3, pp. 175-178.

[18] Kennedy, J. & Eberhart, R. (1995). Particle swarm optimization. Proceedings of IEEE international conference on neural networks, vol. 4, no. 2, pp. 1942-1948.

[19] Andalib, A. & Babamir, S. M. (2014). A New Approach for Test Case Generation by Discrete Particle Swarm Optimization Algorithm. 22nd Iranian Conference on Electrical Engineering, pp. 1180–1185.

[20] Sivanandam, S. N & Deepa. S. N. (2008). Genetic Algorithm Optimization Problems. Springer Berlin Heidelberg.

[21] Papadakis, M. & Malevris, N. (2012). Mutation based test case generation via a path selection strategy. J.Information and Software Technology, vol. 54, pp. 915-932.

[22] Pachauri, A. & Srivastava, G. (2013). Automated test data generation for branch testing using genetic algorithm: An improved approach using branch ordering, memory and elitism. Systems and Software, vol. 86, pp. 1191-1208.

[23] Miller, J., Reformat, M. & Zhangm, H. (2006). Automatic test data generation using genetic algorithm and program dependence graphs. Information and Software Technology, vol. 48, pp. 586-605.

[24] Babamir, S. M. & Babamir, F. S. (2009). Test-Data Generation for Program Path Coverage Using Genetic Algorithm. 4th annual International CSI Computer Conference.

[25] Sthamer, H. (1995). The Automatic Generation of Software Test data using genetic algorithms. Ph.D. Thesis, University of Glamorgan, UK.

[26] Michael, C., McGraw, G. & Schatz, M. (2001). Generating Software Test Data by Evolution. IEEE Transactions. Software Engineering, vol. 27, pp. 1085-1110.

[27] Ahmed, M. A. & hermadi, I. (2008). GA-based multiple paths test data generator. Computers & Operations Research, vol. 35, pp. 3107-3124.

[28] Bueno, P. M. S. & Jino, M. (2002). Automatic test data generation for program paths using genetic algorithms. Software Engineering. Knowledge Engineering, vol. 12, pp. 691-709.

[29] Lin, J. C. & Yeh, P. L. (2001). Automatic test data generation for path testing using GAs. Information Sciences, pp. 47-64.

[30] Watkins, A. & Hufnagel, E. M. (2006). Evolutionary test data generation: A comparison of fitness functions. Software: Practice and Experience, vol. 36, pp. 95-116.

[31] Gong, D., Zhang, W. & Zhang, Y. (2011). Evolutionary generation of test data for multiple paths coverage. Chinese Journal of Electronics, vol. 19, pp. 233-237.

[32] Zhang, W., Gong, D., Yao, X. & Zhang, Y. (2010). Evolutionary generation of test data for many paths coverage. Control and Decision Conference (CCDC), Chinese, pp. 230-235. IEEE.

[33] Harman, M. & McMinn, P. (2010). A Theoretical and Empirical Study of Search-Based Testing: Local, Global, and Hybrid Search. IEEE Transactions on Software Engineering, vol. 36, pp. 226-247.

[34] Mansour, N. & Salame, M. (2004). Data generation for path testing. Software Quality Control, vol. 12, pp. 121–136.

[35] Suri, B. & Snehlata, B. (2011). Review of Artificial Bee Colony Algorithm to Software Testing. Research and Reviews in Computer Science (IJRRCS), vol. 2, pp. 706-711.

[36] Rothermel, G., Elbaum, S., Kinneer, A & Do, H. Software artifact infrastructure repository. Available: http://www.cse.unl.edu/~galileo/sir.

[37] Boyabatli, O. & Sabuncuoglu, I. (2004). Parameter selection in genetic algorithms. Systemics, Cybernetics and Informatics, vol. 4, pp. 78.

[38] Rezaee, J. A. & Jasni, J. (2013). Parameter selection in particle swarm optimization: a survey. Experimental & Theoretical Artificial Intelligence, pp. 527-542.

17

A geometry preserving kernel over riemannian manifolds

Kh. Sadatnejad, S. Shiry Ghidary[*] and M. rahmati

Computer Engineering & Information Technology, Amirkabir University of Technology, Tehran, Iran.

Corresponding author: Shiry@aut.ac.ir (S. Shiry).

Abstract

Kernel trick and projection to tangent spaces are two choices for linearizing the data points lying on Riemannian manifolds. These approaches are used to provide the pre-requisites for applying the standard machine learning methods on Riemannian manifolds. Classical kernels implicitly project data to a high-dimensional feature space without considering the intrinsic geometry of the data points. Projection to tangent spaces truly preserves topology along radial geodesics. In this paper, we propose a method for extrinsic inference on Riemannian manifold based on the kernel approach. We show that computing the Gramian matrix using geodesic distances, on a complete Riemannian manifold with unique minimizing geodesic between each pair of points, provides a feature mapping that is proportional with the topology of data points in the input space. The proposed approach is evaluated on real datasets composed of EEG signals of patients with two different mental disorders, texture, and visual object classes. To assess the effectiveness of our scheme, the extracted features are examined by other state-of-the-art techniques for extrinsic inference over symmetric positive definite (SPD) Riemannian manifold. The experimental results obtained show the superior accuracy of the proposed approach over approaches that use the kernel trick to compute similarity on SPD manifolds without considering the topology of dataset or partially preserving the topology.

Keywords: *Kernel Trick, Riemannian Manifold, Geometry Preservation, Gramian Matrix.*

1. Introduction

Many problems in computer vision and signal processing lead to handling non-linear manifolds. Two different approaches in analysis over manifolds are reported in the literature. In one approach, the data points lie on a non-linear manifold that is embedded in R^n. The other approach corresponds to the cases where the data points do not form a vector space but lie on a non-linear manifold with a known structure. In the former approach, the structure of manifolds is unknown; therefore, the manifolds are modeled by graph, and the geodesic distances are approximated by the shortest path on the graph. The manifold learning techniques such as locally linear embedding (LLE) [45], Hessian LLE (HLLE) [43], local tangent space alignment (LTSA) [44], Laplacian eigenmap (LE) [46], non-negative patch alignment framework (NPAF) [47], and Isomap [49] are some methods of this approach that try to extract low-dimensional manifold from high-dimensional data while the topological structure of the manifold is preserved. The difference between these methods is in the geometrical property that they try to preserve. The latter approach that appears in many problems of computer vision consists of analysis over manifolds with well-studied geometries. The exact geometry of these manifolds can be achieved by closed-form formulae for the Riemannian operations [36]. Orthogonal matrices that form Grassmann manifold, 3D rotation matrices that form a special orthogonal group (SO(3)), and normalized histograms that form unit n-sphere (S^n) are some instances of the latter approach. The symmetric positive definite (SPD) matrices are another example that form a Riemannian manifold. Covariance region descriptors [1, 3, 5, 6, 9, 23, 25, 26, 28, 30], diffusion tensors [15], and structure tensors [36] provide SPD matrices in the computer vision and signal processing applications.

Since SPD matrices can be formulated as a Riemannian manifold [5], classical machine-learning methods that assume data points form a vector space have to deal with some challenges to be applicable on this manifold. Projecting manifold data points to tangent spaces using Riemannian *log* map [5] and embedding into Reproducing Kernel Hilbert Space (RKHS) using kernel functions [3, 7, 35] are two existing approaches in the literature to address the above issue. The Riemannian logarithmic map projects points lying over the manifold to the Euclidean space; therefore, the Euclidean-based learning techniques can be applied to the manifold data points. Iterative projections by Riemannian exponential and logarithmic map in this approach impose computational load to the learning process. On the other hand, approximating true geodesic distance between manifold points using associated Euclidean distance in tangent space preserves the manifold structure partially.

To overcome these limitations, using the kernel, the latter approach is applied to implicitly map manifold points into RKHS using the kernel function. The classical kernel functions do not consider the topology of data points on the manifold. Using the Euclidean distance in computing dissimilarities on manifolds may corrupt the intrinsic geometry of manifolds in feature space.

Harandi et al. [7] and Jayasumana et al. [35] considered the geometry of the manifold of SPD matrices by computing the similarities based on the geodesic distances. Using Gaussian kernel based on distances computed using different Riemannian metrics is the proposed approach in these two research works. The drawback of this approach is missing the non-linear structure of the data points in the feature space resulted by Gaussian kernel.

Vemulapalli et al. [52], Wang et al. [53], and Huang et al. [54] addressed the issue of learning over Riemannian manifold as a kernel-learning and metric-learning problem. All the proposed approaches are based on projecting all the data points in a single tangent space using the Riemannian log map. Vemulapalli et al. [52] considered the topology of data points in input space and their discrimination in feature space in the kernel-learning process. The base kernels that they applied in the learning process were based on projecting all the points in a single tangent space. In addition, using LEM_RBF [52] as a base kernel in their proposed approach leads to a non-linear feature space, while the geometry of the feature space is not considered in their proposed approach.

The Wang et al.'s proposed approach [53] for learning over SPD manifold is relied on projecting the data points to a tangent space and using linear discriminant analysis and partial least square in the resulting Euclidean space.

Huang et al. [54] addressed the learning over Riemannian manifold as a metric learning problem. They projected all the data points in a single tangent space, and then projected the data points in another Euclidean space with more discriminability.

All these methods inherit the shortcomings of projection to a tangent space approach.

Due to the smooth changes of labels on the manifolds that were confirmed by the compactness hypothesis, preserving the topology of manifolds in projection to Euclidean space is effective on the efficiency of the classical learning methods. Therefore, in this work, we try to provide the pre-requisites for applying the classical machine-learning methods on SPD manifolds by learning a kernel that preserves the geometry of manifolds. The concept of preserving geometry may incorrectly suggest manifold learning techniques. Since the main challenge of manifold learning techniques is preserving geometry, to clarify the distinction between geometry based kernel on SPD manifold and manifold learning techniques on a non-linear manifold with specified geometry, in this work, some experiments were done on the SPD manifold.

The main contribution of this paper is to introduce an appropriate base kernel over the manifold of SPD matrices with the aim of considering the topology of data points in input space and its geometry in feature space. We use the properties of SPD Riemannian manifolds in the proposed kernel. The exact geodesic distance between any two points is computable using Riemannian metric. We compute Gramian matrix of projections at feature space. This method uses the geodesic distance to preserve the topology of data points in the feature space, the same as topology on the manifold. All kernel-based methods that are formulated based on the inner product of samples are applicable to implicit feature space by applying Gramian matrix instead of explicit coordinate of samples. The proposed kernel over SPD manifold is used for extrinsic inference.

This paper is organized as what follows. The related literature is reviewed in section 2. In section 3, we review the mathematical preliminaries that are required to become familiar with Riemannian geometry. In section 4, we describe our contribution for providing the pre-requisites for learning over the SPD Riemannian manifold including computing the Gramian matrix of training data and its generalization to test samples. The experiments on real datasets are presented in section 5, and are discussed in section 6. Finally, we conclude this paper in section 7.

2. Related works

There is a rich literature regarding kernel learning and also manifold learning. A thorough review on these topics is beyond the scope of this paper. Recently, different useful applications have used covariance matrices for describing objects. These applications lead to applying machine-learning methods on an SPD manifold. In this study, we review some research works that rely on learning on SPD manifold.

As mentioned in section 1, learning on Riemannian manifolds relies on transferring the manifold data points to a vector space [3, 5, 7]. At the approach that linearization is done by mapping tangent spaces using the Riemannian *log* map, the true geodesic distance between the points lying on different radial geodesics would not be preserved. Therefore, the intrinsic geometry is not preserved completely in projection to the tangent space. Porikli et al. [5, 27, 29, 31] applied the ensemble-based techniques to overcome the weakness of projection to tangent space for classifying the data lying on the SPD Riemannian manifold. Computing geometric mean that is the base point of weak learners imposes a computational load to the learner. Barachant et al. [9] projected the data points to the tangent space at global geometric mean, and then used classical classifiers for discrimination. It is obvious that mapping all points to a single tangent space in the case that all the data points do not lie on the same radial geodesic cannot preserve the global topology of the dataset, and may bring poor results. In another research work, Barachant et al. [3] used a combination of two existing approaches for linearizing Riemannian manifolds. They applied a kernel [55] that was based on the geometry of the data, and examined it in BCI application. They applied Riemannian metric to compute the inner product in the tangent space at geometric mean. Unfortunately, in the case that the data points are mapped globally to a single tangent space, the inner product between points on different geodesics are not induced from the true geodesic distance between them and depends on the base point. Therefore, the implicit mapping of their

proposed kernel can change the intrinsic topology of the manifold. Harandi et al. [7] proposed a kernel that applied a true geodesic distance between points to compute the inner product in the Hilbert space. Applying an exponential map with an arbitrary bandwidth was their choice in computing the inner product. Sensitivity to kernel's bandwidth [2] and choosing this kernel without fine tuning of its parameter can change the geometry of the dataset in feature space such that degrade the performance. Since the proposed kernel puts the data points on the surface of a sphere, applying the methods that rely on Euclidean metric can bring poor results in the resulting non-linear feature space. Early research works show that considering the geometry of data points in feature space can improve the accuracy of classification [32]. A traditional example of using kernel for linearization is kernel PCA. Applying kernel PCA as a method for dimensionality and noise reduction on non-linear data points relies on the assumption that the data points are flattened in feature space using the kernel function. The kernel type and its parameters are arbitrary and mainly motivated by the hope that the induced mapping linearizes the underlying manifold [8]. Since the geometrical interpretation of the various kernels is difficult, and strongly depends on its parameters, applying inappropriate kernels may cause unfortunate results [2], [34]. In the case that the local principal components of the feature space is not in the direction of global principal components of full manifold, the kernels do not linearize accurately; therefore, poor results are obtained. For example, Gaussian kernel, as defined in (1), brings a non-linear feature space. It puts the data points on the surface of a sphere and modifies the Euclidean distance in such a way that the samples that are far apart become orthonormal, and the points that are very close to each other tend to lie on the same point.

$$K(X_i, X_j) = \exp(- \| X_i - X_j \|_2^2 / \sigma^2) \qquad (1)$$

By changing the value of the variance parameter of Gaussian kernel, the geometry of the feature space changes accordingly [2]. Since the actual geometry of data points may not be preserved through linearization by this kernel, the learners that are trained at the transformed space may bring poor results [2], [8].

The weakness of projection to tangent space in mapping to Euclidean space, and the drawbacks of classical kernels show the necessity of proposing appropriate techniques for linearizing non-linear manifolds with a known structure. The compactness hypothesis that states similar objects has a close representation, and smooth changes of labels over manifold are our motivations for preserving geometry in projection to feature space.

3. Background

In this section, we review some basic concepts in Riemannian geometry that are necessary for reading the paper. We introduce the metric, which is used on SPD matrix space in this paper and its associated $\log$ and $\exp$ map.

3.1. Mathematical preliminaries

A homeomorphism is a continuous bijective map whose inverse is continuous. A topological manifold is a connected Hausdorff space that for every point of the manifold, there is a neighborhood U, which is homeomorphic to an open subset V of R^d. The homeomorphism between these two sets U and $(\phi : U \to V)$ is called a (coordinate) chart. A family of charts that provides an open-covering of the manifold is called an atlas, $\{U_\alpha, \phi_\alpha\}$. A differentiable manifold is a manifold with an atlas such that all transitions between the coordinate charts are differentiable of class C^∞.

$$\phi_\beta \circ \phi_\alpha^{-1} : \phi_\alpha(U_\alpha \cap U_\beta) \to \phi_\beta(U_\alpha \cap U_\beta) \quad (2)$$

where, ϕ_β and ϕ_α are the coordinate charts corresponding to the U_α and U_β neighborhoods on the manifold. A Riemannian manifold (M, g) is a differentiable manifold M that is endowed with a smooth inner product (Riemannian metric $g(u,v)$) on each tangent space $T_X M$. The inner product (Riemannian metric) in Riemannian manifolds is a metric that allows measuring similarity or dissimilarity of two points on the manifold [11, 12, 17].

A curve $\gamma : I \subset R \to M$ is a geodesic if the rate of change of $\dot{\gamma}$ has no component along the manifold for all $t \in I$ or $\ddot{\gamma}$ is 0 [22]. Given a vector v in the tangent space $T_X M$, there is a geodesic $\gamma(t)$ that is characterized by its length, where geodesic issued from $\gamma(0) = X$, and $\dot{\gamma} = v / \| v \|$. Two points on the manifold may have multiple geodesic between them but the one that minimizes the length is called the minimizing geodesic. In a geodesically complete manifold, each pair of points admits minimizing geodesic. Minimizing geodesic between points may not be unique [22].

The exponential map, $\exp_X(v)$, maps a tangent vector $v \in T_X M$ into a point Y on the manifold. Its inverse is called logarithm map, $\log_X(Y)$, which maps a point on the manifold to a point at tangent space.

The point lying on the geodesic that passes through X with tangent vector v has $dist(X,Y) = \| v \| = <v,v>^{1/2}$.

The radial geodesics are all the geodesics that pass through X. Normal coordinates with center X is the local coordinates defined by the chart $(U, \exp_X^{-1})$. Normal coordinates can preserve the distances on radial geodesics. For example, a sphere that is unfolded onto a plane in normal coordinates can preserve the distances on great circles [13, 19, 22].

3.2. Mappings and distance in SPD matrix space

In this paper, we use the covariance matrices as the descriptors of data points. The Riemannian metric, exponential and logarithm map, and geodesic distance on symmetric positive definite matrix space are defined as what follow.

An invariant Riemannian metric or inner product on the tangent space of the symmetric positive definite matrices is defined as ([14, 15, 24]):

$$<y,z>_X = trace(X^{-1/2} y X^{-1} z X^{-1/2}) \quad (3)$$

where, y and z are two tangent vectors in the tangent space formed at X point over Riemannian manifold. The Riemannian exponential map is defined as:

$$\exp_X(y) = X^{1/2} \exp(X^{-1/2} y X^{-1/2}) X^{1/2} \quad (4)$$

where, y is a tangent vector and X is a base point over the manifold. The Riemannian $\log$ map on a point on the Riemannian manifold is defined as:

$$\log_X(Y) = X^{1/2} \log(X^{-1/2} Y X^{-1/2}) X^{1/2} \quad (5)$$

where, X and Y are two points on the manifold, and matrix exponential and logarithm are calculated as:

$$\exp \Sigma = \sum_{k=0}^{\infty} \Sigma^k / k! = U \exp(D) U^T, \Sigma = U D U^T \quad (6)$$

$$\log \Sigma = \sum_{k=1}^{\infty} (-1)^{k-1} (\Sigma - I)^k / k = U \log(D) U^T, \Sigma = U D U^T$$

In (6), it is assumed that Σ is decomposed into eigenvalues and vectors. Note that the $\exp$

operator on matrices always exists, while the log operator is only defined on symmetric matrix with positive eigenvalues [24].

The distance between two points on SPD manifold associated with the Riemannian metric is computed by:

$$d_G^2(X,Y) = <\log_X(Y), \log_X(Y)>_X \quad (7)$$
$$= trace(\log^2(X^{-1/2}YX^{-1/2}))$$

In the tensor space with the metric (3), there is one and only one minimizing geodesic between any two tensors. The Riemannian log map is defined uniquely at all points on the manifold, and the exponential map is global diffeomorphism [8, 15].

4. Global geometry preserving kernel

In this section, we describe our method for providing the pre-requisites for learning in the space of SPD matrices using the properties of Riemannian manifolds. This mapping implicitly transfers the data points to a vector space, while the intrinsic geometry of the dataset is preserved by preserving the geodesic distances. First, we describe the proposed algorithm, which is used to compute the Gramian matrix of a set of points on the SPD Riemannian manifold at an implicit linearized space, and then investigate its generalization to unseen cases. We call the proposed kernel GGPK, which is the abbreviation of the global geometry preserving kernel.

4.1. Flattening an SPD Riemannian manifold

Let $P = \{X_i\}_{i=1}^N$ be the set of points on a Riemannian manifold. The geodesic distance between two points X_i and X_j on Riemannian manifold is computed by mapping to tangent space at one of these points and computing the length of the tangent vector that joins $\log_{X_i}(X_i)$ to $\log_{X_i}(X_j)$, which is given in (7). Assume that the pairwise squared geodesic distances stored in an N-by-N matrix D_G is given as:

$$D_G = [d_G^2(X_i, X_j)]_{1 \le i,j \le N} \quad (8)$$

where, d_G denotes the geodesic distance between two points on the manifold. The symmetric positive definite matrix space with the associated metric is a geodesically complete manifold, and has the structure of a curved vector space [14]. Satisfaction of the manifold assumption implies that defining geometry based on distance along the manifold and preserving it in feature space can bring appropriate

projection for classification. Therefore, the distance between the two points $\phi(X_i)$ and $\phi(X_j)$ in the feature space is defined as:

$$d_E^2(\phi(X_i), \phi(X_j)) = \| \phi(X_i) - \phi(X_j) \|_2^2 \quad (9)$$
$$= d_G^2(X_i, X_j),$$
$$D_E \leftarrow D_G$$

where, X_i and X_j are the points on the manifold, ϕ is an implicit feature mapping from SPD Riemannian manifold to a Euclidean space for developable manifolds or a pseudo-Euclidean space for non-developable manifolds, d_G denotes the geodesic distance on the manifold, and d_E denotes the Euclidean distance in the feature space, which is L$_2$ norm of dissimilarity. D_G denotes a matrix of geodesic distances on SPD manifold that is assigned to the matrix of Euclidian distances between points in the feature space, D_E. This assignment is done implicitly using the kernel function. We recall that:

$$\| \phi(X_i) - \phi(X_j) \|_2^2 = \quad (10)$$
$$< \phi(X_i) - \phi(X_j), \phi(X_i) - \phi(X_j) > =$$
$$< \phi(X_i), \phi(X_i) > + < \phi(X_j), \phi(X_j) >$$
$$- 2 < \phi(X_i) - \phi(X_j) >$$

Thus:

$$< \phi(X_i) - \phi(X_j) > = -(\| \phi(X_i) - \phi(X_j) \|_2^2 - (11)$$
$$< \phi(X_i), \phi(X_i) > - < \phi(X_j), \phi(X_j) >)/2 =$$
$$- (d_E^2(\phi(X_i), \phi(X_j)) - < \phi(X_i), \phi(X_i) >$$
$$- < \phi(X_j), \phi(X_j) >)/2$$

Since ϕ function, and consequently, the coordinate of points in the feature space are unknown, computing the inner product between any two points in the projected space is done implicitly using double centering [8], [49], [51] on D_E. The double centering is performed by subtracting the means of the elements of each row and column, and adding the mean of all of the entries of D_E to the corresponding element of D_E [8]. $\phi(X_i)$ is assumed to be centered. This assumption has no effect on the distances:

$$d_E^2(\phi(X_i), \phi(X_j)) = \| \phi(X_i) - \phi(X_j) \|_2^2 \quad (12)$$
$$= \| (\phi(X_i) - c) - (\phi(X_j) - c) \|_2^2$$

where, c is a constant translation vector. Thus we have:

$$\mu_r(i) = \sum_{j=1}^{N} d_E^2(\phi(X_i), \phi(X_j)) / N = \tag{13}$$

$$\sum_{j=1}^{N} \|\phi(X_i) - \phi(X_j)\|_2^2 / N =$$

$$\sum_{j=1}^{N} < \phi(X_i) - \phi(X_j), \phi(X_i) - \phi(X_j) > / N =$$

$$< \phi(X_i), \phi(X_i) > -2 < \phi(X_i), \sum_{j=1}^{N} \phi(X_j) / N >$$

$$+ \sum_{j=1}^{N} < \phi(X_j), \phi(X_j) > / N =$$

$$< \phi(X_i), \phi(X_i) > + \sum_{j=1}^{N} < \phi(X_j), \phi(X_j) > / N$$

where, N denotes the number of data points, and $\mu_r(i)$ denotes the mean of the ith row of D_E. Since D_E is a symmetric matrix, the mean of the jth column, $\mu_c(j)$, can be computed as:

$$\mu_c(j) = < \phi(X_j), \phi(X_j) >$$
$$+ \sum_{i=1}^{N} < \phi(X_i), \phi(X_i) > / N \tag{14}$$

and the mean of all of the entries of D_E, μ is:

$$\mu = \sum_{i=1}^{N} \sum_{j=1}^{N} d_E^2(\phi(X_i), \phi(X_j)) / N^2 \tag{15}$$

$$= \sum_{i=1}^{N} \sum_{j=1}^{N} \|\phi(X_i) - \phi(X_j)\|_2^2 / N^2$$

$$= \sum_{i=1}^{N} < \phi(X_i), \phi(X_i) > / N + \sum_{j=1}^{N} < \phi(X_j), \phi(X_j) > / N$$

Thus:

$$\mu_r(i) + \mu_c(j) - \mu = < \phi(X_i), \phi(X_i) >$$
$$+ < \phi(X_j), \phi(X_j) > \tag{16}$$

$$= \sum_{i=1}^{N} \sum_{j=1}^{N} < \phi(X_i) - \phi(X_j), \phi(X_i) - \phi(X_j) > / N^2$$

$$= \sum_{i=1}^{N} < \phi(X_i), \phi(X_i) > / N - 2 \sum_{j=1}^{N} < \phi(X_i), 0 > / N$$

$$+ \sum_{j=1}^{N} < \phi(X_j), \phi(X_j) > / N$$

Using (11) and (16), we have:

$$< \phi(X_i), \phi(X_j) > = -1/2(d_E^2(\phi(X_i), \phi(X_j))$$
$$- \mu_r(i) - \mu_c(j) + \mu) \tag{17}$$

Since D_E and the average of each row, column, and all the elements of D_E are computable, therefore, an N-by-N Gramian matrix can be defined as:

$$G = [< \phi(X_i), \phi(X_j) >]_{1 \le i, j \le N}$$
$$\tag{18}$$

Gramian matrix, G, which can be computed based on the computable terms, is a similarity measure on feature space, induced from intrinsic dissimilarity in input space, and can be used as a non-parametric kernel in kernel-based methods.

4.2. Generalization to test points

To generalize the proposed non-parametric kernel to unseen data, we need to update the components that are used in computing the kernel in learning process. To improve the computational complexity of generalization to test samples, the mean values of rows, columns, and all the entries of the D_E matrix for the training dataset are saved.

The inner product between a test sample X and the previous training samples is computed by updating the geodesic and Euclidean distance matrices:

$$D_G \leftarrow \begin{bmatrix} [D_G] & d^2{}_G(X_i, X) \\ d^2{}_G(X, X_j) & 0 \end{bmatrix}_{1 \le i, j \le N}, \tag{19}$$

$$D_E \leftarrow D_G$$

Thus the mean values of each row (μ_r), column (μ_c), and the mean of all the entries of D_E (μ) are updated as follow:

$$\mu_r(i) \leftarrow N * \mu_r(i) + d_E^2(\phi(X_i), \phi(X)) / (N+1) \tag{20}$$

$$\mu_c(j) \leftarrow N * \mu_c(j) + d_E^2(\phi(X), \phi(X_j)) / (N+1)$$

$$\mu \leftarrow N^2 * \mu + 2 \sum_{i=1}^{N} d_E^2(\phi(X_i), \phi(X)) / (N+1)^2$$

where, $\mu_r(i)$ denotes the mean of the ith row and j^{th} column. The mean values of row and column, which corresponds to the new sample, are computed as:

$$\mu_r(N+1) = \sum_{j=1}^{N} d_E^2(\phi(X), \phi(X_j)) / (N+1) \tag{21}$$

$$\mu_c(N+1) \leftarrow \mu_r(N+1)$$

and the inner product corresponding to the new sample and the other observations is computed as follows:

$$\forall j = 1..N, G(X, X_j) = < \phi(X), \phi(X_j) > =$$
$$-1/2(d_E^2(\phi(X), \phi(X_j))) - \mu_r(N+1) - \mu_c(j) + \mu) \tag{22}$$

In the case of developable manifolds, since manifolds have isometry with Euclidean space, double centering brings inner product in a Euclidean space. Assuming $V = [v_1 \ldots v_N]^T$, where $v_i \in R$, $1 \le i \le N$, so:

$$V^T G V = [v_1 \ldots v_N][< \phi(X_i), \phi(X_j) >]_{1 \le i, j \le N}[v_1 \ldots v_N]^T$$
$$\tag{23}$$

$$= \sum_{i=1}^{N} \sum_{j=1}^{N} v_i < \phi(X_i), \phi(X_j) > v_j$$

$$= \sum_{i=1}^{N} v_i < \phi(X_i), \sum_{j=1}^{N} v_j \phi(X_j) >$$

$$= < \sum_{i=1}^{N} v_i \phi(X_i), \sum_{j=1}^{N} v_j \phi(X_j) > = \| \sum_{i=1}^{N} v_i \phi(X_i) \|_2^2 \ge 0$$

As $V^T G V \ge 0$ thus G matrix satisfies the Mercer's

condition, and can be used as a kernel for mapping to RKHS. In the case of non-developable manifolds, due to the intrinsic curvature of the manifold, the Gramian matrix does not satisfy the Mercer's condition.

Using the proposed topology preserving kernel that induces similarities from the distance along the manifold, every kernel-based method that is formulated using the inner product of samples can be used for inference (i.e. clustering, classification, …) on the proposed implicit feature space. For example, the kernel support vector machine (SVM) [10], [18], [21], which is a suitable choice for complex datasets due to its robustness, was used in our experiments. Applying other kernels without considering their type and parameters that determine the topology of data points in feature space may bring undesirable overlapping of points, and may produce weak results.

5. Results

We applied the linear discriminant analysis (LDA) [50] and SVM as the discriminative methods using different kernels on several real datasets; the characteristics of datasets and also the experimental results are reported in this section. To clarify the difference between the proposed kernel over SPD manifold and the classical manifold-learning techniques, a comparison between them is made.

5.1. EEG datasets and pre-processing

Two-class EEG datasets are used in this work. The participants of this study were 43 children and adolescents (21 cases of ADHD, 22 patients with BMD) ranged from 10 to 22 years old. The diagnosis is based on the DSM_IV criterion [4], [20]. For each patient, within three minutes, the EEG signals were recorded in eyes-open and eyes-closed resting conditions. These signals were recorded using 22 electrodes according to the 10-20 international recording system. Impedances of electrodes were lower than $10\,K\Omega$ through the recording, and the sampling rate was 250 Hz. In the pre-processing phase, the signals were filtered by a Butterworth low-pass filter (order 7) with 40 Hz cut-off frequency to remove the additive high-frequency noises [20].

The feature vectors were generated by estimating the empirical covariance matrix between channels [9].

In the cases that covariance matrices had eigenvalues less than or equal to zero, we changed the eigenvalues such that all of them became positive, and scaled them such that the distance between eigenvalues was preserved. For this purpose, we added the absolute value of the minimum of eigenvalues to all the eigenvalues, increased them with a small positive value, and reconstructed the matrix with this new eigenvalues and previous eigenvectors.

$$C_{new} = Udiag(\lambda_1 + \mid \min(\lambda_{\min}(C),0) \mid +\varepsilon \quad (24)$$
$$,....\lambda_{n+} \mid \min(\lambda_{\min}(C),0) \mid +\varepsilon)U^T$$

where, $C = U\Lambda U^T$, Λ is a diagonal matrix whose diagonal entries are the eigenvalues of C (denoted as λ_i) and U is the matrix of eigenvectors of C. ε is a small positive value.

With this modification, the distance between different eigenvalues are preserved, and the matrix becomes positive definite.

To remove the dependency between the train and test samples, the leave-one-out cross-validation method was performed. In each round, one patient was dedicated as test set and the others were considered as a validation and train set [20].

Ensemble-based techniques, as a promising approach for improving analysis on EEG datasets, are applied in different applications such as BCI, and mental disorder recognition [39- 41]. These techniques improve the accuracy and stability of the algorithms. Avoiding over-fitting and reducing variance are some other advantages that have been reported for ensemble-based techniques. In experiments on the EEG datasets, different classifiers were aggregated using an ensemble-based technique. These classifiers were trained on different subsets of EEG channels. Since the high dimensionality of the covariance matrix of all channels leads to the problem of curse of dimensionality, we generated multiple views on the EEG datasets. The covariance matrices of multiple subsets of channels, composed of 2 or 3 channels, were estimated separately, and then the learning procedure in each of these views was performed. Finally, the results of different views were combined using the majority voting technique. F7-FZ, F3-F7, FP2-F7, T3-F7, and FZ-CZ-F7 indicate the selected channel name in international 10-20 systems. In this work, the channel selection was performed experimentally. The subsets corresponding to different positions on the scalp were selected randomly and used for training the classifiers. These classifiers were tested on the validation set. Some of the selected subsets that on average led to a higher accuracy on the validation set were selected for our experiments.

5.2. Texture classification

In this experiment, we applied the Brodatz texture

dataset [33]. 12 different types of textures were used in the learning process. All textures were gray-scale images that were resized to 512 × 512 pixels. Each image was divided into four equal parts. For each image, two parts that were 256 × 256 pixels were devoted as the training set, and the remaining made the test set. To describe each part of the image, covariance matrices in windows with random height, width, and center were computed.

In these experiments, 10 random subsets were selected for describing each part of the image. Each pixel was described using $[I(x,y), |\partial I/\partial x|, |\partial I/\partial y|, |\partial^2 I/\partial x^2|, |\partial^2 I/\partial y^2|]$. Thus the experimental covariance matrix in each window that was computed by 24 would be a 5 × 5 matrix [7]:

$$C_w = \sum_{i=1}^{N} (F_i - \mu_w)(F_i - \mu_w)^T /(N-1) \tag{25}$$

where, N denotes the number of pixels in each window, F_i is a feature vector that describes the ith pixel of the window w and μ_w shows the mean value in that window.

5.3. Visual object classes
The main goal of this experiment is to recognize the objects from a number of visual object classes in realistic scenes without pre-segmenting the objects. PASCAL VOC 2012 that includes person, animal, vehicle, and indoor categories with twenty

object classes are used in this work [42]. For each class, the presence/absence of an example of that class in the test images is determined by a binary classifier. To describe each image, the covariance matrices of pixels, which are described using $[I_R(x,y), I_G(x,y), I_B(x,y), |\partial I_R/\partial y|, |\partial I_G/\partial x|, |\partial I_G/\partial y|, |\partial I_B/\partial x|, |\partial I_B/\partial y|]$, are computed by (25). Descriptors would be a 9 × 9 matrix. Parameters are tuned on the validation set and evaluated in a subset with 1200 instances of the test set.

5.4. Experimental results
In this work, the extracted features from different classes are classified by kNN, SVM, LDA, and kernel LDA and kernel SVM with different kernels. For fine tuning the penalty term of SVM and Lagrange multiplier in KLDA, a wide range of values is assessed. The optimal performance on the validation set determines the suitable values for these terms. In the case that the kernel methods have parameters such as the variance parameter in RBF and GGK kernels, these parameters are tuned by assessing the performance on the validation set.

Accuracy of different classifiers on different subsets of channels on eyes-open and eyes-closed datasets and accuracy of an ensemble of these learners are reported in tables 1 and 2.

Table 1. Accuracy of different classifiers (1-NN, 3-NN, linear SVM, SVM with RBF, TSK, GGPK, and GGK kernels) on different subsets of EEG signals of ADHD and BMD patients at eyes-open resting condition.

Classifiers	Channel subsets					
	F7-FZ	F3-F7	FP2-F7	T3-F7	FZ-CZ-F7	MajorityVote
1-NN	72.09%	60.47%	65.12%	67.44%	62.79%	72.09%
3-NN	55.81%	76.74%	67.44%	74.42%	67.44%	76.74%
Linear SVM	72.09%	86.05%	62.79%	55.81%	81.40%	86.05%
SVM-RBF	79.07%	86.05%	72.09%	76.74%	79.07%	86.05%
SVM-TSK [3]	74.42%	81.40%	69.77%	72.09%	79.07%	81.45%
SVM-GGK[7]	81.40%	86.05%	**81.40%**	88.37%	81.40%	86.05%
SVM-GGPK	**93.02%**	**95.35%**	79.07%	**93.02%**	**86.05%**	**95.35%**
LDA	67.44%	76.74%	62.79%	55.81%	74.42%	83.72%
LDA_TSK	72.09%	62.79%	**74.42%**	65.12%	72.09%	81.40%
LDA_GGK	79.07%	81.40%	69.77%	76.74%	79.07%	81.40%
LDA-GGPK	**81.40%**	**81.40%**	67.44%	**83.72%**	81.40%	**86.05%**

Table 2. Accuracy of different classifiers (1-NN, 3-NN, linear SVM, SVM with RBF, TSK, GGPK, and GGK kernels) on different subsets of EEG signals of ADHD and BMD patients at eyes-closed resting condition.

Classifiers	Channel subsets					
	F7-FZ	F3-F7	FP2-F7	T3-F7	FZ-CZ-F7	Majority Vote
1-NN	67.44%	58.14%	79.07%	72.09%	79.07%	79.07%
3-NN	67.44%	67.44%	76.74%	67.44%	74.42%	74.42%
Linear SVM	62.79%	69.77%	65.12%	67.44%	72.09%	67.44%
SVM-RBF	72.09%	72.09%	79.07%	76.74%	69.77%	72.09%
SVM-TSK [3]	69.77%	69.77%	76.74%	65.12%	74.42%	74.42%
SVM-GGK[7]	79.07%	69.77%	88.37%	**83.72%**	81.40%	83.72%
SVM-GGPK	**86.05%**	**76.74%**	**88.37%**	79.07%	**86.05%**	**88.37%**
LDA	46.51%	69.77%	65.12%	65.12%	72.09%	72.09%
LDA_TSK	69.77%	60.47%	72.09%	69.77%	81.40%	74.42%
LDA_GGK	81.40%	69.77%	83.72%	76.74%	81.40%	81.40%
LDA-GGPK	72.09%	72.09%	81.40%	76.74%	83.72%	86.05%

Tables 3 and 7 contain accuracy of classification on Brodatz texture and PASCAL VOC2012 dataset, respectively. Comparison between the proposed and some other topology preserving kernels on Riemannian manifolds are reported in these tables.

The TSK kernel, which partially preserves the topology [3] and Gaussian kernel using geodesic distance (GGK) [7], are geometric kernels that are used for comparison with GGPK.

The effectiveness of linearization and preserving the global topology of the dataset by GGPK is compared with RBF and Linear SVM that does not consider the intrinsic geometry of the dataset.

The manifold learning methods such as LLE, HLLE, LE, Isomap, NPAF, and LTSA are used as a feature extractor on covariance matrices. Intrinsic dimensionality of the target is determined by maximum likelihood intrinsic dimensionality estimator (MLE) [37]. SVM with RBF kernel is used for classification. Comparison between the proposed approach and the results evolved on a reduced dataset by the manifold learning techniques are mentioned in tables 4, 5, 6, and 8. These experiments run over random subsets of Brodatz texture dataset, subsets of EEG dataset, and VOC 20012 dataset.

Table 3. Accuracy of linear SVM, SVM with RBF, TSK [3], and GGPK kernels on 12 different types of textures of Brodatz texture dataset.

Classifiers	Accuracy
Linear SVM	74.58%
SVM-RBF	80.83%
SVM-TSK	86.67%
SVM-GGPK	90.00%

Table 4. Accuracy of SVM with RBF kernel trained on features extracted using LLE, HLLE, LE, LTSA, Isomap, and NPAF from different textures from Brodatz dataset.

Classifiers	Texture No.					
	1-2	11-12	5-6	1-2-3	1-2-3-4-5-6	1-2-3-4-5-6-7-8-9-10-11-12
SVM-GGPK	98.33%	99.17%	100.0%	92.22%	90.83%	90.00%
LLE+SVM-RBF	75.83%	77.50%	61.67%	73.33%	30.55%	29.17%
HLLE+SVM-RBF	59.17%	50.83%	51.67%	55.57%	34.44%	27.22%
LE+SVM-RBF	80.00%	84.17%	65.83%	80.83%	44.72%	35.41%
LTSA+SVM-RBF	50.00%	55.83%	61.67%	54.81%	34.72%	27.08%
Isomap + SVM-RBF	75.00%	51.67%	55.00%	70.56%	37.22%	18.47%
NPAF + SVM-RBF	87.50%	61.67%	70.83%	75.56%	41.94%	33.33%

Table 5. Accuracy of SVM with RBF kernel trained on features extracted using LLE, HLLE, LE, LTSA, Isomap, and NPAF on different subsets of EEG signal of ADHD and BMD patients at eye-open resting condition.

Learning Techniques	Channel Subsets		
	All channels	Fp1, Fp2, Fpz, F3, F4, F7, F8, FZ, C3, C4, CZ, T3	T4, T5, T6, P3, P4, PZ, O1, O2
SVM-GGPK	**83.72%**	**74.42%**	**83.72%**
LLE+SVM-RBF	35.00%	55.00%	58.14%
HLLE+SVM-RBF	25.58%	46.51%	46.51%
LE+SVM-RBF	69. 77%	67.44%	79.07%
LTSA+SVM-RBF	72.09%	30.23%	72.42%
Isomap + SVM-RBF	67.44%	44.19%	62.79 %
NPAF + SVM-RBF	74.42%	62.79%	48.84%

Table 6. Accuracy of SVM with RBF kernel trained on features extracted using LLE, HLLE, LE, LTSA, Isomap, and NPAF on different subsets of EEG signal of ADHD and BMD patients at eye-closed resting condition.

Learning Techniques	Channel subsets		
	All channels	Fp1, Fp2, Fpz, F3, F4, F7, F8, FZ, C3, C4, CZ, T3	T4, T5, T6, P3, P4, PZ, O1, O2
SVM-GGPK	**83.72%**	**83.72%**	**81.40%**
LLE+SVM-RBF	48.84%	44.19%	51.16%
HLLE+SVM-RBF	46.51%	46.51%	41.86%
LE+SVM-RBF	48.84%	67.44%	48.84%
LTSA+SVM-RBF	39.53%	37.21%	44.19%
Isomap + SVM-RBF	32.56%	58.14%	30.23%
NPAF + SVM-RBF	46.51%	62.79%	51.16%

6. Discussion

In our experiments, several real-world datasets and classifiers were used to evaluate several kernel functions and manifold learning techniques. From these experiments, the following results were achieved:

The superiority of SVM-GGPK and LDA-GGPK over Linear SVM and LDA (Tables 1, 2, 3, and 7) shows the effectiveness of the proposed approach, and implies that measuring dissimilarities using the Euclidean distance in non-linear feature space does not reflect dissimilarities truly. The superiority of SVM-GGPK and LDA-GGPK over kNN (Tables 1, 2) and SVM-RBF (Tables 1, 2, 3,

7), which use Euclidean distance for measuring dissimilarities, approves this finding. The geometry-based kernels such as TSK, GGK, and GGPK gain higher discrimination rates in comparison with the RBF and linear kernels. This means that considering the geometry of data points in input space can be effective at learning kernel and outperforms generalization of the classifiers.

The proposed kernel has no parameter, which is one of its superiorities over the RBF and GGK kernels whose performances strongly depend on the bandwidth of the kernel.

Table 7. Accuracy of SVM with linear, RBF, GGK, and GGPK kernels trained on PASCALVOC2012 dataset.

Learning Techniques	Class name			
	Aeroplane	Bird	Bottle	Car
SVM-Linear	80.75%	40.00%	14.33%	61.17%
SVM-RBF	78.25%	91.25%	19.75%	60.42%
SVM-GGK	84.76%	94.60%	21.33%	**67.33%**
SVM-GGPK	**87.75%**	**94.83%**	**24.00%**	66.83%

Table 8. Accuracy of SVM with RBF kernel trained on features extracted using LLE, HLLE, LE, LTSA, Isomap, and NPAF on subsets of PASCALVOC2012 dataset.

Learning Techniques	Class name			
	Aeroplane	Bird	Bottle	Car
SVM-GGPK	**87.75%**	**94.83%**	24.00%	**66.83%**
LLE+SVM-RBF	50.67%	49.83%	49.50%	50.67%
HLLE+SVM-RBF	48.75%	53.08%	49.75%	50.08%
LE+SVM-RBF	50.67%	50.33%	48.75%	49.67%
LTSA+SVM-RBF	54.50%	51.83%	48.00%	44.42%
Isomap + SVM-RBF	64.08%	49.67%	37.83%	50.25%
NPAF + SVM-RBF	70.67%	52.92%	**55.00%**	43.67%

Table 9. p-value resulted by applying paired t-Test for comparison between SVM-GGPK and other compatitors on ADHD/BMD dataset in classification problem.

	SVM-GGPK/ SVM-GGK	SVM-GGPK/ SVM-TSK	SVM-GGPK/ SVM-RBF	SVM-GGPK/ Linear SVM	SVM-GGPK/ 3-NN	SVM-GGPK/ 1-NN
Eyes-open	0.0293	0.0013	0.0011	0.0195	0.0021	3.6875e-04
Eyes-closed	0.1576	2.1248e-04	0.0080	0.0019	1.9118e-04	0.0035

Table 10. p-value resulted by applying paired t-Test for comparison between SVM-GGPK and other compatitors on Brodatz texture dataset in dimensionality reduction problem.

	SVM-GGPK/ LLE+SVM-RBF	SVM-GGPK/ HLLE+SVM-RBF	SVM-GGPK/ LE+SVM-RBF	SVM-GGPK/ LTSA+SVM-RBF	SVM-GGPK/ Isomap+SVM-RBF	SVM-GGPK/ NPAF+SVM-RBF
Brodatz	0.0054	7.1445e-05	0.0092	8.6519e-05	0.0024	0.0061

Experiments show the superiority of the proposed approach over the techniques that rely on manifold learning. Conventional manifold learning techniques are applicable only on the cases in which a manifold is embedded in the Euclidean space. In this work, our input space is composed of symmetric positive definite matrices. Since the features can be formulated as a Riemannian manifold and live in a non-Euclidean space, applying the classical manifold learning methods on this manifold is not compatible with the pre-requisites of the conventional manifold learning techniques. Weak generalization of manifold learning-based methods, which are reported in tables 4, 5, 6, and 8, confirm this fact. Therefore, to apply the manifold learning methods over Riemannian manifolds, it is required to modify some parts of these methods that depend on the manifold structure [36]. Some reasons that lead to inconvenience of the manifold learning techniques that are examined in this study over Riemannian manifold are listed what follows.

LE tries to preserve locality in projection to the low-dimensional space and uses the Laplacian matrix for representing manifold. The shortcoming of LE on Riemannian manifolds is the result of approximating true geodesic distance by graph distance.

LLE computes a weight matrix such that a data point can be constructed as a linear combination of its neighbors, and its aim is to preserve local linearity in a low-dimensional space. In the Euclidean case, this aim is achieved by solving a least-squares problem, while in the Riemannian case, it is required to solve an interpolation problem on the manifold. The cost function that should be minimized and the interpolation on the Riemannian manifold are some challenges that make LLE on Riemannian manifold different from the classical one.

A learning process in HLLE consists of computing the mean and a set of principal components from the neighborhood of each point. In the Euclidean case, this can be done using PCA, while on the Riemannian manifolds, computing mean can be done in an iterative procedure, and computing principal components on the manifold has some challenges. For example, the principal geodesic analysis [38] was proposed to compute the principal components on Riemannian manifolds.

In the case of LTSA, in the first stage, a local parameterization of data points should be provided. This stage is computed by the assumption that the data points are embedded in the Euclidean space, and the Taylor series expansion in the Euclidian space around the base point of tangent space lead to finding local coordinates at the corresponding tangent space that is computed using PCA. Since LTSA estimates the tangent space of the Riemannian manifold at a point using available data samples in the neighborhood of the base point, sampling conditions such as the sampling extent and density affect the estimated tangent space. Running PCA on some instances of the Riemannian manifold leads to inaccurate local information, which brings poor results in classification.

Isomap tries to preserve the global geometry in projection to the low-dimensional space and use the geodesic distance for capturing the intrinsic geometry of the manifold. Isomap represents the manifold using a graph on the available data points and approximates the geodesic distance using graph distance. The density of input data and bad sampling may lead to disconnectivity of graph and partial covering over training data. Over-estimation of geodesic distance and linear shortcuts near regions of high surface curvature are two disadvantages of Isomap that are the result of the estimation of geodesic distance by graph distance. These shortcomings can lead to overlapping of data points, and may decrease generalization of learners over SPD manifold.

Manifold learning techniques, which are not compatible with SPD Riemannian manifold, may corrupt the topology of data points. In multi-class cases, by increasing the number of classes, mapping to low-dimensional space cause more overlapping between different classes, and lead to weakness of classifiers.

To show the statistical significance of superiority of the proposed approach, we apply the statistical test on the ADHD/BMD dataset in two eyes-closed and eyes-open resting condition in classification problem (Table 9) and on Brodatz texture dataset in dimensionality reduction problem (Table 10). The resulting p-values in most cases indicate the significant superiority of the methods that relied on using GGPK kernel in both the classification and dimensionality reduction problems.

7. Conclusion

In this paper, we proposed a global projection technique for mapping points lying on the SPD Riemannian manifold to feature space such that the topology of input space is preserved. Learning kernel over SPD manifold by computing the Gramian matrix, based on squared geodesic distance, was our contribution.

Superiority over approaches that partially preserve topology such as approaches that are relied on projection to tangent space or approaches that do not preserve topology such as some Euclidean distance-based kernels shows effectiveness of the preserving topology.

In comparison with methods that are based upon the traditional manifold learning techniques, superiorities are observed in the experiments. The shortcoming of manifold learning methods over SPD manifold can be the result of living SPD manifold in non-Euclidean space, while these methods do computation with the assumption that data points live in the Euclidean space.

References

[1] Pennec, X. (2006). Intrinsic statistics on Riemannian manifolds: Basic tools for geometric measurements. Journal of Mathematical Imaging and Vision, vol. 25, no. 1, pp. 127-154.

[2] Wang, J., Lu, H., Plataniotis, K. N., & Lu, J. (2009). Gaussian kernel optimization for pattern classification. Pattern Recognition, vol. 42, no. 7, pp. 1237-1247.

[3] Barachant, A., Bonnet, S., Congedo, M., & Jutten, C. (2012). BCI Signal Classification using a Riemannian-based kernel. In 20th European Symposium on Artificial Neural Networks, Computational Intelligence and Machine Learning (ESANN), pp. 97-102.

[4] Sadatnezhad, K., Boostani, R., & Ghanizadeh, A. (2011). Classification of BMD and ADHD patients using their EEG signals. Expert Systems with Applications, vol. 38, no. 3, pp. 1956-1963.

[5] Tuzel, O., Porikli, F., & Meer, P. (2008). Pedestrian detection via classification on riemannian manifolds. IEEE Transactions on Pattern Analysis and Machine Intelligence, vol. 30, no.10, pp. 1713-1727.

[6] Subbarao, R., & Meer, P. (2009). Nonlinear mean shift over Riemannian manifolds. International Journal of Computer Vision, vol. 84, no. 1, pp. 1-20.

[7] Harandi, M. T., Sanderson, C., Wiliem, A., & Lovell, B. C. (2012). Kernel analysis over Riemannian manifolds for visual recognition of actions, pedestrians and textures. IEEE Workshop in Applications of Computer Vision (WACV), pp. 433-439, 2012.

[8] Lee, J. A., & Verleysen, M. (2007). Nonlinear dimensionality reduction. Springer Science & Business Media.

[9] Barachant, A., Bonnet, S., Congedo, M., & Jutten, C. (2012). Multiclass brain–computer interface classification by Riemannian geometry. IEEE Transactions on Biomedical Engineering, vol. 59, no. 4, pp. 920-928.

[10] Friedman, J., Hastie, T., & Tibshirani, R. (2001). The elements of statistical learning. Springer, Berlin: Springer series in statistics.

[11] Lee, J. M. (2006). Riemannian manifolds: an introduction to curvature. Springer Science & Business Media.

[12] Jost, J. (2008). Riemannian geometry and geometric analysis. Springer Science & Business Media.

[13] O'neill, B. (1983). Semi-Riemannian Geometry with Applications to Relativity. Academic press.

[14] Rossmann, W. (2002). Lie groups: an introduction through linear groups. Oxford University Press.

[15] Pennec, X., Fillard, P. & Ayache, N. (2006). A Riemannian framework for tensor computing. International Journal of Computer Vision, vol. 66, no. 1, pp. 41-66.

[16] Kim, S. J., Magnani, A., & Boyd, S. (2006). Optimal kernel selection in kernel fisher discriminant analysis. In Proceedings of the 23rd international conference on Machine learning ACM, pp. 465-472.

[17] Lin, T., & Zha, H. (2008). Riemannian manifold learning. IEEE Transactions on Pattern Analysis and Machine Intelligence, vol. 30, no. 5, pp. 796-809.

[18] Bottou, L., & Lin, C. J. (2007). Support vector machine solvers. Large scale kernel machines, pp. 301-320.

[19] Gallier, J. (2011). Geometric methods and applications: for computer science and engineering. Springer Science & Business Media.

[20] Sadatnezhad, K., Boostani, R., & Ghanizadeh, A. (2010). Proposing an adaptive mutation to improve XCSF performance to classify ADHD and BMD patients. Journal of neural engineering, vol. 7, no. 6, pp. 066006.

[21] Cristianini, N., & Shawe-Taylor, J. (2000). An introduction to support vector machines and other kernel-based learning methods. Cambridge university press.

[22] Dey, T. K., & Li, K. (2009). Cut locus and topology from surface point data. In Proceedings of the twenty-fifth annual symposium on Computational geometry ACM, pp. 125-134.

[23] Porikli, F., Tuzel, O., & Meer, P. (2006). Covariance tracking using model update based on lie algebra. In Computer Vision and Pattern Recognition, IEEE Computer Society Conference, vol. 1, pp. 728-735.

[24] Förstner, W., & Moonen, B. (2003). A metric for covariance matrices. Springer Berlin Heidelberg. In Geodesy-The Challenge of the 3rd Millennium.

[25] Tuzel, O., Porikli, F., & Meer, P. (2006). Region covariance: A fast descriptor for detection and

classification. Springer Berlin Heidelberg. In Computer Vision–ECCV, pp. 589-600.

[26] Tuzel, O., Subbarao, R., & Meer, P. (2005). Simultaneous multiple 3D motion estimation via mode finding on Lie groups. Tenth IEEE International Conference in Computer Vision, vol. 1, pp. 18-25.

[27] Tuzel, O., Porikli, F., & Meer, P. (2007). Human detection via classification on riemannian manifolds. In Computer Vision and Pattern Recognition, IEEE Conference on pp. 1-8.

[28] Guo, K., Ishwar, P., & Konrad, J. (2010). Action recognition using sparse representation on covariance manifolds of optical flow. In Advanced Video and Signal Based Surveillance (AVSS), Seventh IEEE International Conference, pp. 188-195.

[29] Tosato, D., Farenzena, M., Spera, M., Murino, V., & Cristani, M. (2010). Multi-class classification on riemannian manifolds for video surveillance. Springer Berlin Heidelberg. In Computer Vision–ECCV, pp. 378-391.

[30] Li, X., Hu, W., Zhang, Z., Zhang, X., Zhu, M., & Cheng, J. (2008). Visual tracking via incremental log-euclidean riemannian subspace learning. In Computer Vision and Pattern Recognition. IEEE Conference, pp. 1-8.

[31] Sanin, A., Sanderson, C., Harandi, M. T., & Lovell, B. C. (2012). K-tangent spaces on Riemannian manifolds for improved pedestrian detection. 19th IEEE International Conference on Image Processing (ICIP), pp. 473-476.

[32] Courty, N., Burger, T., & Marteau, P. F. (2012). Geodesic analysis on the Gaussian RKHS hypersphere. Springer Berlin Heidelberg. In Machine Learning and Knowledge Discovery in Databases, pp. 299-313.

[33] Randen, T., & Husoy, J. H. (1999). Filtering for texture classification: A comparative study. IEEE Transactions on Pattern Analysis and Machine Intelligence, vol. 21, no. 4, pp. 291-310.

[34] Xiong, H., Swamy, M. N. S., & Ahmad, M. O. (2005). Optimizing the kernel in the empirical feature space. IEEE Transactions on Neural Networks, vol. 16, no.2, pp. 460-474.

[35] Jayasumana, S., Hartley, R., Salzmann, M., Li, H., & Harandi, M. (2013). Kernel methods on the riemannian manifold of symmetric positive definite matrices. IEEE Conference in Computer Vision and Pattern Recognition (CVPR), pp. 73-80.

[36] Goh, A., & Vidal, R. (2008). Clustering and dimensionality reduction on Riemannian manifolds. IEEE Conference on Computer Vision and Pattern Recognition, pp. 1-7.

[37] Lim, I. S., de Heras Ciechomski, P., Sarni, S., & Thalmann, D. (2003). Planar arrangement of high-dimensional biomedical data sets by isomap

coordinates. In Computer-Based Medical Systems, 16th IEEE Symposium, pp. 50-55.

[38] Fletcher, P. T., & Joshi, S. (2007). Riemannian geometry for the statistical analysis of diffusion tensor data. Signal Processing, vol. 87, no. 2, pp. 250-262.

[39] Polikar, R. (2006). Ensemble based systems in decision making. Circuits and Systems Magazine, vol. 6, no. 3, pp. 21-45.

[40] Sun, S., Zhang, C., & Zhang, D. (2007). An experimental evaluation of ensemble methods for EEG signal classification. Pattern Recognition Letters, vol. 28, no. 15, pp. 2157-2163.

[41] Polikar, R., Topalis, A., Parikh, D., Green, D., Frymiare, J., Kounios, J., & Clark, C. M. (2008). An ensemble based data fusion approach for early diagnosis of Alzheimer's disease. Information Fusion, vol. 9, no. 1, pp. 83-95.

[42] Everingham, M., Van Gool, L., Williams, C. K., Winn, J., & Zisserman, A. (2012). The PASCAL visual object classes challenge results.

[43] Donoho, D. L., & Grimes, C. (2003). Hessian eigenmaps: Locally linear embedding techniques for high-dimensional data. Proceedings of the National Academy of Sciences, vol. 100, no. 10, pp. 5591-5596.

[44] Zhang, Z. Y., & Zha, H. Y. (2004). Principal manifolds and nonlinear dimensionality reduction via tangent space alignment. Journal of Shanghai University (English Edition), vol. 8, no. 4, pp. 406-424.

[45] Roweis, S. T., & Saul, L. K. (2000). Nonlinear dimensionality reduction by locally linear embedding. Science, vol. 290, no. 5500, pp. 2323-2326.

[46] Belkin, M., & Niyogi, P. (2003). Laplacian eigenmaps for dimensionality reduction and data representation. Neural computation, vol. 15, no.6, pp. 1373-1396.

[47] Guan, N., Tao, D., Luo, Z., & Yuan, B. (2011). Non-negative patch alignment framework. IEEE Transactions on Neural Networks, vol. 22, no. 8, pp. 1218-1230.

[48] Van der Maaten, L. (2013), Affiliation: Delft University of Technology. Matlab Toolbox for Dimensionality Reduction (v0.8.1b).

[49] Yan, S., Xu, D., Zhang, B., Zhang, H. J., Yang, Q., & Lin, S. (2007). Graph embedding and extensions: a general framework for dimensionality reduction. IEEE Transactions on Pattern Analysis and Machine Intelligence, vol. 29, no. 1, pp. 40-51.

[50] Scholkopft, B., & Mullert, K. R. (1999). Fisher discriminant analysis with kernels. Neural networks for signal processing IX.

[51] Kung, S. Y. (2014). Kernel methods and machine learning. Cambridge University Press.

[52] Vemulapalli, R., Pillai, J. K., & Chellappa, R. (2013). Kernel learning for extrinsic classification of

manifold features. In Proceedings of the IEEE Conference on Computer Vision and Pattern Recognition, pp. 1782-1789.

[53] Wang, R., Guo, H., Davis, L. S., & Dai, Q. (2012). Covariance discriminative learning: A natural and efficient approach to image set classification. In Computer Vision and Pattern Recognition, pp. 2496-2503.

[54] Huang, Z., Wang, R., Shan, S., Li, X., & Chen, X. (2015). Log-Euclidean Metric Learning on Symmetric Positive Definite Manifold with Application to Image Set Classification, pp. 720-729.

[55] Zare, T., Sadeghi, M. T., Abutalebi, H. R., & Kittler, J. (2017). Composite Kernel Optimization in Semi-Supervised Metric. Journal of AI and Data Mining, vol. 5, no. 2, pp. 259-273.

18

Bridging the semantic gap for software effort estimation by hierarchical feature selection techniques

S. Beiranvand* and M. A. Z. Chahooki

Electrical & Computer Engineering Department, Yazd University, Yazd, Iran.

*Corresponding author: saba.beiranvand@stu.yazd.ac.ir (S.Beiranvand).

Abstract

Software project management is one of the significant activates in the software development process. Software development effort estimation (SDEE) is a challenging task in the software project management. SDEE has been an old activity in computer industry from 1940s, and thus it has been reviewed for several times. A SDEE model is appropriate if it provides the accuracy and confidence simultaneously before a software project contract. Due to the uncertain nature of development estimates, and in order to increase the accuracy, researchers have recently focused on machine learning techniques. Choosing the most effective features to achieve higher accuracy in machine learning is crucial. In this work, for narrowing the semantic gap in SDEE, a hierarchical filter and wrapper feature selection (FS) techniques and fused measurement criteria are developed in a two-phase approach. In the first phase, the two-stage filter FS methods provide start sets for the wrapper FS techniques. In the second phase, a fused criterion is proposed to evaluate the accuracy in wrapper FS techniques. The experimental results show the validity and efficiency of the proposed approach for SDEE over a variety of standard datasets.

Keywords: *Software Development Effort Estimation (SDEE), Software Cost Estimation (SCE), Machine Learning (ML), Hierarchical Feature Selection (FS).*

1. Introduction

Software project management is the most important activity in any software engineering methodology. SCE for development and maintenance processes in software engineering is a challenging activity, on which many researches have focused. Similarly, SDEE is the process of effort prediction for software system development. SDEE includes software development and maintenance efforts. In software engineering researches, cost and effort estimation are used equivalently [1-4].

Accurate estimation of development cost has an important role in the success or failure of a software project. Algorithmic methods, expert judgment, and ML techniques are the general approaches in these area. Algorithmic methods are only based on the old data. Therefore, advances in software engineering are not considered in them. With regard to the rapid advancement in these areas, new effective features are recognized. Also in order to investigate the various feature effects, constant and fixed methods are not sufficient. Since algorithmic methods use a constant proven formula to calculate the software cost, these new feature effects on the system performance cannot be evaluated.

Expert judgment methods are applied by experts in a particular organization. Hence, the same accuracy in other organizations is not provided by them. Due to the uncertainty in estimating software cost, using uncertain and flexible machine learning techniques plays an important role in accuracy improvement in SDEE. The ability to perform intelligent computational methods for modeling complex set of relationships between effort and influencing factors and also their ability to learn from the old project data are the main advantages of the ML methods [5].

SDEE is an old process that began simultaneously with the computer industry in the 1940s [5]. In 1980, many developments were introduced on its models and techniques [6]. In the same year, Boehm et al. modified the COCOMO model previously developed by them. The result obtained was a new model called COCOMOII. From 1990s onwards, extensive researches were carried out for improvement of software industry and information technology [6]. Categorization of cost estimation methods is represented in figure 1.

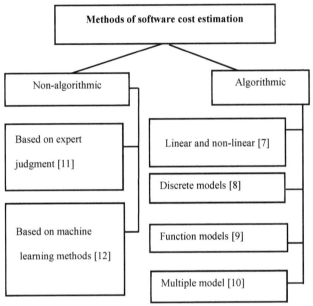

Figure 1. Categorization of cost estimation.

In general, SDEE based on algorithmic models is expressed as (1) [13].

$$EFFORT = F(x_1, x_2, \dots) \qquad (1)$$

In this formula, the order x1, x2, ... expresses the features of each project. Effort estimation based on different algorithmic models is usually different from the other models. In these methods, the estimated model is formulated based on a specific algorithm. A variety of algorithmic models are shown in Fig. 1. Since these models are based on the old data and cannot consider current developments in programming languages, hardware, and software engineering, decision-making is difficult based on the results [1].

In expert judgments, there is usually no need for the old data. Expert judgment is often based on the reuse of determiner previous projects, which may not be documented perfectly. The results obtained show that 62% of the software projects in the organizations are estimated by this method. The advantage of this method is its customization for any specific organization culture, which makes it more accurate than the algorithmic methods. Also in many cases, it has been proven that it has more accuracy than the other preferred models. However, this estimation is subjective, and is based upon each logic expert. Here upon, its advantages can also be considered as its

drawbacks. The estimated costs of each expert is only based on his experiences in a specific organization culture, and is not perfect in other organizations [1].

In the ML techniques, patterns of the old project data are learned, and can be used for effort prediction in new projects [1]. In SDEE, many researches have been performed by the ML approach [12]. In ML, a supervised method learns a model from the labeled training data. In the ML classification methods, labels are discrete, whereas in the regression ones, labels are continuous. Where the costs or efforts are calculated as numeric values in software projects, regression methods are studied as the ML models in SDEE researches. The ML algorithms in SDEE are divided into 6 categories [3] as case base reasoning (CBR) [12], artificial neural networks (ANNs) [14], decision trees (DT) [15], Bayesian networks (BN) [16], support vector regression (SVR) [14], and association rules (AR) [17].

Searching for useful and effective subset of features is known as the approach in the ML area to increase the learning model accuracy. Since all the ML hypotheses are potentially susceptible to the wrong, irrelevant, and redundant features [18], SCE models use a large set of features for estimation that are called cost determination. All of these features are not effective for accurate estimation. Thus in SCE, feature selection (FS) algorithms are used, which have the ability of selecting the subset of most instructive cost determination correctly, and can achieve high accuracy of ML algorithm [19].

In the ML studies, complexity and usability of classifier or regressor are dependent on the number of input features. In this area, two main methods as feature selection (FS) and feature extraction were used for feature reduction. In FS, researchers were concerned to find k features of d original features, which gave the most effective information. In feature extraction, k features were extracted from d initial features in a linear or non-linear manner [35]. Many researchers have focused on the efficiency improvement in SDEE by reducing the sample project features [34].

Different ML algorithms have been compared in [12] to estimate the cost of the software with different datasets. The effect of backward selection on each ML algorithm was studied in this work. Datasets in SDEE were divided into the within-company and cross-company categories [20-22]. In [34], the FS effect has been investigated to SDEE within-company and cross-company datasets, and it has been concluded that cost estimation with less features provides equivalent or better accuracy than estimation with all features. In SDEE, both the filter [34] and wrapper [34] FS techniques have been used. Also in [35], a combination of filter and wrapper techniques have been developed. Studies on SCE have indicated that using the ML algorithms with dimension reduction methods can improve the accuracy.

Some of the researchers have used the isolation and connection analysis to dimension reduction in SCE [27]. Extensive research works have been conducted on finding the best subset of the cost determination, wrapper method, and climbing hills [19]. In [28], using the linear regression and wrapper FS, cost determination has been ranked based on the number of repeat times in different groups and then removing the features with lower ranks. In [29], linear regression and wrapper FSS have been implemented. The results show that a combination of pruning rows (samples) and pruning columns (features) can significantly improve the effort estimation, particularly in the small datasets.

In [30], optimum accuracy has been achieved in this area using the feature weightings and comparative methods based on euclidean distance by using filter FS. In addition, some researchers have developed genetic algorithms to achieve a suitable weight for features [31, 32].

In [19], researchers have examined the balance between the features of the old datasets to reduce cost determination, while maintaining accuracy. They have used nine known FSS methods to select the most effective features. In [33], a combined method has been provided based on the mutual information and clustering features. They have combined the supervised learning and unsupervised learning methods. In unsupervised learning, the features are clustered based on the similarity between them and the clusters using hierarchical clustering. Then in the unsupervised learning stage, the feature that is most similar to the effort feature is selected as the representative of any cluster.

In this work, a hierarchical FS approach was developed. A set of features were arranged in a descending order according to different correlation criteria in the filter methods. The start set for wrapper-based methods can be initiated by different combinations of multiple-ordered feature sets. In this study, due to the importance of the initial feature sets for convergence and accuracy in wrapper methods, a hierarchical approach was developed to achieve the advantages of both the filter and wrapper methods in SDEE. Also the evaluation criterion is an important factor that

influences the effectiveness of the wrapper methods. Literature review on SDEE shows that median magnitude of relative error (MMRE) and prediction accuracy (PRED) are widely used as the evaluation criteria for the wrapper FS methods. In the second phase of the proposed evaluation function (EF) method, a fused MMRE and PRED evaluation criterion is used for improving the total accuracy results. The innovation of this paper is presented in two parts: (1) developing a hierarchical structure of the filter and wrapper methods in effective FS in SDEE, and (2) developing a fused criterion in the evaluation phase of the wrapper methods that improves semantic gap in SDEE and selects the most effective features at the same time in SCE by considering two main error rate criteria.

The remainder of this paper is structured as follows: 'FS techniques' section is provided in section 2. In Section 3, we describe the general framework of the proposed method. The empirical setup of implementation on a variety of datasets is described in section 4. Finally, in section 5, concluding remarks and further works are discussed in detail.

2. FS techniques

''Curse of dimensionality'' was originally discussed by Bellman in 1961. The small sample set and high dimensionality problems are two major challenges in many applications. In general, a large number of features cause the increase of complexity in data analysis and reduce the performance of learning methods such as classification, regression, and clustering. Therefore, dimensional reduction becomes an important issue for improving the efficiency. The most popular approaches in feature reduction are classified into two categories, FS and feature extraction. In FS, sample s with d features is generated from sample x with D features, where d<D. Traditional FS methods attempt to find a global optimal sub-space. It is necessary to mention that in feature extraction, the features of s are transformed into a different feature space, and thus there might be no correspondence between the two feature sets. The mathematical expressions and ideas underlying the feature extraction algorithms have been described in [34]. Heretofore, different FS methods have been proposed. These methods have been divided into three categories based on the filtering, wrapper, and embedded methods. Also these methods can be divided into two categories based on the learning dependent (wrapper, embedded) and learning independent (filter) algorithms [35]. In

the filter methods, the features are selected based on correlation of the specific criteria such as mutual information (MI) and correlation coefficients. In the wrapper methods, learning algorithms are used to determine the correlation between a subset of the features by a prediction model. In the embedded methods, the FS process and training of learning algorithms are integrated. These methods are appropriate when the feature numbers are small. One of the most common approaches in this category is learning by decision tree [35]. Since the filter and wrapper methods are used in the proposed method, these are introduced in the following section.

2.1 Filter methods

In order to check the relationship between the two features, first of all, a suitable similarity or correlation measure is required. This criterion may be considered as the function of the interaction between variables, rather than a function of their values. In this regard, correlation function may be linear or non-linear. In this function, the amount of information shared between the two variables should be considered. However, to develop this idea, quantitative information is needed. Topic of mathematics called information theory is related to correlation measurement [35]. A flowchart of the filter methods is illustrated in figure 2.

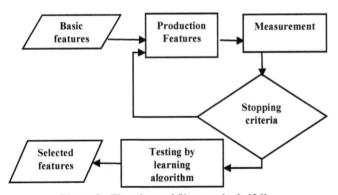

Figure 2 . Flowchart of filter methods [36].

Each filter FS method consists of three main steps: (1) production of features, (2) measurement, and (3) testing by the learning algorithm. A sub-set of features is produced in the production step. Then in the measurement step, the feature information in the current time is measured. The above two steps are performed iteratively until the results are not consistent with the assessment criteria. Afterward, the evaluation process is terminated with a threshold of measurement results. Thus maximum information must be contained in the final feature set. Test step is performed by a supervised learning algorithm.

2.2 Wrapper methods

A workflow of the wrapper method is shown in figure 3. Its process is the same as the filter methods, except that the measurement step has been replaced by a learning algorithm. This is the main reason that the wrapper methods are slow. On the other hand, the wrapper method learning algorithm can lead to better results in most cases. The process is stopped when the results obtained are worsened or the number of features reach a pre-determined threshold.

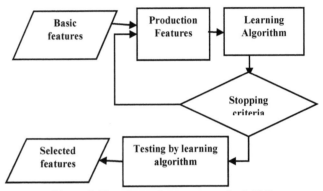

Figure 3. Flowchart of wrapper methods [36].

In regard to the point that the limited scope is most effective in the applicability of the wrapper FSS methods, the hierarchical structure of the filter and wrapper methods are used. In this approach, various combinations of filtering methods are being tested, and the most effective one is combined with the wrapper methods. Also due to the fact that the evaluating criteria in the wrapper methods impact directly on selecting effective features, in this work, hybrid criteria were utilized.

3. Proposed method

In this section, effective FS approach is presented based on utilizing a combination of both wrapper and filter. Filtering methods are faster than wrapper methods. However, the wrapper methods are more accurate than the filtering ones [37]. Thus by combining these methods, the advantages of each method can be used to eliminate the disadvantages of the other one.

In the proposed method, at first, the features are ranked based on the P filtering feature selection methods and selected TP of features that have better rank in every method as the selected features. Using the two operators AND and XOR, two final sets of proposed features are produced from the filtering methods. Then the AND set is considered as the basic one, and by using a regression algorithm, the initial accuracy is evaluated based on the fused criteria.

Furthermore, by using the two wrapper feature selection methods, the most effective features of the AND and XOR sets are selected. The AND set is considered as the input for the backward FFS method (Algorithm 2), and the XOR set is considered as input to the forward the FSS method (Algorithm 3). These two methods are repeated to increase the accuracy, and finally, the most effective features for each dataset are selected. A chart of the proposed method is shown in figure 4.

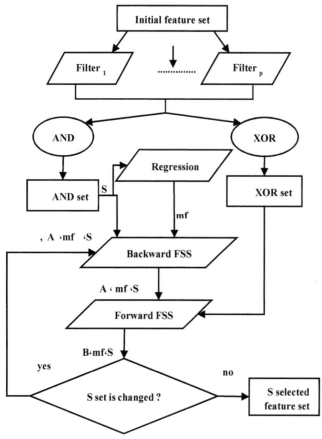

Figure 4. Flowchart of proposed method.

Various filtering methods are used in this article but in the wrapper ones, only the simple greedy forward and backward FS methods are used. Pseudo-code of the proposed method for combination of these methods is represented in Algorithm 1. In this method, using the fused function within the wrapper methods, a combination of criteria are generated for assessing the effectiveness of the selected features. This approach causes a higher reduction in the semantic gap by selecting the effective features. For this purpose, all evaluation criteria are passed to fused function. The result is a combined criterion as m that inherits all criteria measures. Two sets of A and B are constructed from the output of the filter methods. Common features of the filter methods are assigned to A, and consequently, non-common features are assigned

to B. The rest of the proposed method is followed by the two wrapper methods (Algorithms 2, 3) in an iterative manner. This iteration continues until the accuracy is converged to an optimal value. The output of the proposed method is the selected feature set.

ALGORITHM 1.   Hierarchical FS algorithm

Input:
$X=\{x^t, r^t\}_{t=1}^{N}$ *where x^t is a sample, r^t is its associated effort, and N is the number of samples. Also any x^t is represented as [x1, x2... xD], where D is the number of sample features.*
$M=\{m_i\}_{i=1}^{K}$ *where mi is the ith measure criterion in application, and K is the number of measurement criteria.*
$F=\{f_i\}_{i=1}^{P}$ *where f_i is the ith filter method, and P is the number of filtering methods.*

Process:
         for p=1: P
S_p = filter (f_i, X, t_p), *where Sp is a sorted set of top tp selected features by fi on X.*
                  end
m=fusion (M), where fusion returns a fused measurement criterion.
$A=AND_1^P Sp$
$R=XOR_1^P Sp$
$s = A$
mf=regression(X,s,m), where mf is accuracy result evaluated by m.
repeat
[s A mf]= BFS-Function (X,s, A,m,mf)   backward FS
[s R mf]= FFS-Function (X,s, B,m,mf)   forward FS
until (*mf* is not better than previous values)
Output:
s, where s is the optimum subset of original features

ALGORITHM 2. BFS-Function (X,s, A,m,mf)

Input:
$X=\{x^t, r^t\}_{t=1}^{N}$ *where x^t is a sample, r^t is its associated effort, and N is the number of samples. Also any x^t is represented as [x1, x2... xD], where D is the number of sample features.*
S, where S is the initial subset for backward FS.
A, where A is the additive subset for backward FS.
M, where m is the measurement criterion.
Mf, where Mf is the accuracy result of the previous step.
PROCESS:
         n=1
         Max=Size(B)
      while (n≤Max)
      while (f=selected next element of A)
                  S=s−f
                  [accuracy] = regression(X,S,m)
            If accuracy>Best result in this iteration
                        Best=accuracy
                        b=f
      end
      end
      if Best> mf
                  s=s − b
                  A=A − b
                  mf=Best
      else
                  break
      end
                  n=n+1
      end
Output:
s, where s is the optimum subset of features.
mf, where mf is the accuracy of regression form s features.

ALGORITHM 3. FFS-Function (X,s, B,m,mf)
Input:

$X=\{x^t, r^t\}\ _{t=1}^{N}$, *where x^t is a sample, r^t is its associated effort, and N is the number of samples. Also any x^t is represented as [x1, x2... xD], where D is the number of sample features.*
S, where s is the initial subset for forward FS.
B, where B is the additive subset for forward FS.
M, where m is the measurement criterion.
Mf, where Mf is the accuracy result of previous step.
PROCESS: FFS-Function (X,s, B,m,mf)
    n=1
    Max=Size(B)
  while (n≤Max)
  while(f=selected next element of B)
      S=s ∪ f
    [accuracy] = Regression (X, S)
    If accuracy>Best result in this iteration
        Best=accuracy
        b=f
  end
  end
  if Best> previous Best result
      S=S ∪ b
      B=B − b
    mf=Best
  else
      break
  end
    n=n+1
  end
Output:
s, where s is the optimum subset of features.
mf, where mf is the accuracy of regression from s features.

4. Empirical setup

In this section, the implementation and analysis of experimental results in different datasets are represented. First the criteria and datasets used are proposed. Then the results are presented, and finally, the results are compared and verified by the results of other researches. With the purpose of implementing the proposed methods, the FEAST tools are used, taken from [38].

4.1. Performance metrics

In this paper, in order to evaluate the accuracy of this idea in the SDEE, the proposed method implements various datasets in these fields, and the evaluation criteria of these fields are used to analyze the results. In this field, various evaluation criteria are used. The most commonly used criteria are MRE, which represents the difference between the estimated costs and actual costs, MMRE, which represents the average estimation error for the total sample (training samples and test samples), and PRED(X), which represents the percentage of samples whose magnitude of relative error is less than or equal to the value of X. Also in some studies, the median estimation error or MDMRE has been used. The description of the formula used for the criterion defined above will be followed.

$$MRE = \frac{|Actual\ Effort - Estimated\ Effort|}{Actual\ Effort} \tag{2}$$

- *Actual Effort* is the real project's effort.
- *Estimated Effort* is the estimated Effort by the algorithm.

$$MMRE = \frac{1}{n}\sum_{i=1}^{n}\left(\frac{|Estimated(i) - Actual(i)|}{Actual(i)}\right) \tag{3}$$

- *Actual Effort* is the real project's effort.
- *Estimated Effort* is the estimated Effort by the algorithm.

$$MDMRE = Median\ (MRE) \tag{4}$$

$$PRED(x) = \frac{k}{n} \tag{5}$$

- X is the difference in most research works that is equal to 0.25.
- K is the number of samples, and the difference between their estimated cost and their actual cost is equal or less than x.
- N is the total number of tested samples.

Therefore, the higher value for PRED (0.25) results in the less error rate of the evaluated algorithm, and the estimated cost for the number of tested sample error rate is equal to or less than 0.25. Thus by picking up the features that result in lower MMRE and higher PRED, the semantic gap can be reduced in the estimation procedure.

4.2. Datasets

In this study, three popular datasets in SDEE (cocomo81, coconasa93, and Desharnais) were used. They will be briefly introduced, and their usage will be followed. Studies on SDEE with the ML algorithms using the validation methods divides the dataset into two groups, training dataset and test dataset, from which the former is used for learning algorithms. Accuracy of the test dataset is the main goal of the results of evaluating the algorithm accuracy. For this purpose, in this study, two methods titled LOOCV and 10-fold cross validation were used.

Cocomo81

This dataset consists of a variety of 63 commercial, scientific, systematic, proactive, and supportive software projects. There are 16 independent variables that are determined by the product, project computers and personal characteristics by hour per person [19]. The dataset features are listed in table 1.

Coconasa93

This dataset includes 93 examples of projects implemented using different canters of NASA, during 1971 to 1987, with 23 independent features, which consist of 16 common features with cocomo81 and 7 other independent features and one dependent feature of effort. These features are categorical. The first pre-processing was carried out in this study, transforming the categorical data to the numerical data. Other features of coconasa93 that are not present in cocomo81 are listed in table 2.

Table 1. Cocomo81 dataset features.

No	Feature	Full name
X_1	rely	required software reliability
X_2	data	data base size
X_3	cplx	process complexity
X_4	time	time constraint for cpu
X_5	stor	main memory constraint
X_6	virt	machine volatility
X_7	turn	turnaround time
X_8	acap	analysts capability
X_9	aexp	application experience
X_{10}	pcap	programmers capability
X_{11}	vexp	virtual machine experience
X_{12}	lexp	language experience
X_{13}	modp	modern programing practices
X_{14}	tool	use of software tools
X_{15}	sced	schedule constraint
X_{16}	loc	Line of code
X_{17}	Effort	Effort

Table 2. Surplus features than cocomo81 in coconasa93.

No	Feature	Full name
X_{18}	Unique id	record number real
X_{19}	project name	project name
X_{20}	cat2	category of application
X_{21}	frog	Flight or ground system?
X_{22}	center	which nasa center
X_{23}	year real	year of development
X_{24}	mode	development mode

Desharnais

The original version of this dataset contains 81 projects of generated projects by a candidate software house that have been described in 12 features. The second and third features in four samples are miss value. For this reason, this dataset has been used differently in various articles. In some papers, 4 samples have been put aside and the other 77 samples have been used [19]. Other researchers have removed the miss value columns from the set of columns [39]. In this work, both methods in these datasets were used. The features of this dataset are described in table 3.

Table 3. Original Desharnais dataset features.

No	Feature	Full name
X_1	Project	Project id
X_2	TeamExp	Team experience (measured in years)
X_3	ManagerExp	Manager's experience (measured in years).
X_4	Yearend	Year End
X_5	Length	Project's duration (measured in months).
X_6	Effort	Actual development effort (in person-hours)
X_7	Transactions	Count of basic logical transactions in the system
X_8	Entities	Number of entities in the system's data model.
X_9	Points Adjust	Adjusted Function Points count.
X_{10}	Envergure	Scale of the project.
X_{11}	PointsNonAjust	Unadjusted Function Points count
X_{12}	language	Language

4.3. Experimental result

Here are the results of various tests on the test datasets introduced in the previous section. The best results for each dataset were marked bold. Some studies have used a combination of the MMRE and PRED criteria for ranking the algorithms used in this field that are displayed with the EF symbol [40]. This method is produced by fusion function.

$$EF = \frac{PRED(0.25)}{1 + MMRE} \qquad (6)$$

In this study, EF that is a combination of the criteria for FS is used. The selected features provide a higher EF. In the research works carried out in the FS field in SDEE, usually the MMRE criteria and, less often, the PRED criteria are used for FS. As mentioned, we looked for the features that provided a lower MMRE and higher PRED. Thus when the EF criteria are used, the selected features will have these two conditions. In this work, a multi-layer perceptron (MLP) neural network learning algorithm was developed for the wrapper FS. Artificial neural networks (ANNs) contain a lot of highly inter-connected processing elements called neurons. They usually operate in parallel, and are configured with a regular architecture. Each neuron is connected via a communicative link with other neurons. Each communicative link has a weight that represents the information about the input signal. Neuron calculates a sum of input weights, and if the total weight is more than a threshold, produces an output. This process continues until one (or more) output(s) is (are) produced. The estimate models can be trained using the old training data to produce the results by fine-tuning the algorithm parameter values to reduce the difference between the actual and estimated efforts [34]. The MLP neural network in this study consisted of an input layer, a hidden layer, and an output layer. The parameters of the proposed algorithm in this paper were set by the values presented in table 4.

Table 4. Values of method parameters in this work.

Parameter	Value
k	3
p	2
T_p (cocomo81)	10
T_p (coconasa93)	10
T_p (Desharnais with 81 sample)	4
T_p (Desharnais with 77 sample)	5

Based on the results of the implementation of various compounds in the Desharnais dataset with 77 cases and 12 features, it is clear that the method is effective and from different combinations; only 2 cases have reduced accuracy. Among the compounds tested, 9 different combinations achieved the highest possible accuracy. The 10-Fold cross-validation method was used to evaluate the dataset. This data was divided into 10 equal parts, one as the test data and the other 9-folds were considered as the training data. Similar to similar articles, this process were carried out for ten times and the average results were presented. In Desharnais, for the dataset consisting of 81 samples and 9 features, all combinations increased accuracy. In fact, the accuracy of all compounds was greater than that for the conventional MLP. Among the various compounds, by combining the Mifs and Relief filter methods, the highest accuracy can be achieved. From the experimental results of the Cocomo81 dataset, it can be concluded that a combination of different FS methods in the dataset is effective and has a higher accuracy. Based on the comparison of different combinations in the filtering step, except one compound, all the combinations caused a higher accuracy. A combination of two methods, Betagamma and Relief, provided the highest accuracy. In the coconasa93 dataset, we used the LOOCV validation method to evaluate the technique. In this form, the dataset was divided for 93 times, containing 92 training and one testing samples. Finally, the average of the results of 93 times division was presented. The results obtained showed that the method was effective in the coconasa93 dataset. From 37 different

compounds, 31 compounds provided an accuracy higher than the simple MLP algorithm. The best accuracy was the result of a combination of the MRMR and Cief filter methods, and the lowest accuracy was the result of a combination of the Cief and Icap methods. The results of the implementation of these methods in cocomo81 and coconasa93 are shown in table 5, and the results of its implementation in Desharnais with both approaches are presented in table 6.

According to different compounds, **Size** is known as the most effective feature, which is common in all datasets. Also the two features **Cplx** and **Tool** of COCOMO81, two features **VIRT** and **VEXP** of COCONASA93, and the **Transactions** and **Entities** features from Desharnais with 81 samples and **length, entities** and **envergure** features of Desharnais with 77 samples in all compounds were identified as excess features (less important one).

Table 5. Results of implementation on Desharnais dataset.

Dataset	Deshar77				Deshar88			
Method	MMRE	MDMRE	PRED	EF	MMRE	MDMRE	PRED	EF
No method	0.6296	0.4492	31.1688	19.1262	0.9067	0.4574	28.3951	14.8923
Jmi,MRMR	0.6613	0.3485	43.0357	25.9041	0.6211	0.3536	39.5062	24.3702
Jmi, Mifs	0.4952	0.3568	40.3571	26.9909	0.6211	0.3536	39.5062	24.3702
Jmi,Disr	0.6613	0.3485	43.0357	25.9041	0.6082	0.3479	39.5062	24.5654
Jmi,Icap	**0.4742**	**0.3320**	**41.6071**	**28.2240**	0.6082	0.3479	39.5062	24.5654
Jmi,Condred	0.6774	0.3467	42.8571	25.5499	0.6211	0.3536	39.5062	24.3702
Jmi,Betagamma	0.6774	0.3467	42.8571	25.5499	0.6211	0.3536	39.5062	24.3702
MRMR,Mifs	0.4952	0.3568	40.3571	26.9909	0.6211	0.3536	39.5062	24.3702
MRMR,Disr	0.6613	0.3485	43.0357	25.9041	0.6211	0.3536	39.5062	24.3702
MRMR,Icap	**0.4742**	**0.3320**	**41.6071**	**28.2240**	0.6211	0.3536	39.5062	24.3702
MRMR,Condred	0.6774	0.3467	42.8571	25.5499	0.6211	0.3536	39.5062	24.3702
MRMR,Betagamma	0.6774	0.3467	42.8571	25.5499	0.6211	0.3536	39.5062	24.3702
MRMR,Relief	**0.4742**	**0.3320**	**41.6071**	**28.2240**	0.6527	0.3437	40.7407	24.6516
Mifs,Condred	0.6680	0.3651	40.1786	24.0873	0.6211	0.3536	39.5062	24.3702
Mifs,Relief	0.5154	0.3643	36.4286	24.0391	**0.6182**	**0.3245**	**40.7407**	**25.1773**
Disr,Mifs	0.4952	0.3568	40.3571	26.9909	0.6211	0.3536	39.5062	24.3702
Disr,Condred	0.6774	0.3467	42.8571	25.5499	0.6211	0.3536	39.5062	24.3702
Disr,Betagamma	0.6774	0.3467	42.8571	25.5499	0.6211	0.3536	39.5062	24.3702
Cief,Jmi	**0.4742**	**0.3320**	**41.6071**	**28.2240**	0.6082	0.3479	39.5062	24.5654
Cief,MRMR	**0.4742**	**0.3320**	**41.6071**	**28.2240**	0.6211	0.3536	39.5062	24.3702
Cief,Mifs	0.5106	0.3573	36.4286	24.1148	0.6211	0.3536	39.5062	24.3702
Cief,Disr	0.4742	0.3320	41.6071	28.2240	0.6082	0.3479	39.5062	24.5654
Cief,Condred	0.5148	0.3726	42.1429	27.8204	0.6211	0.3536	39.5062	24.3702
Icap,Mifs	0.5106	0.3573	36.4286	24.1148	0.6362	0.3860	37.0370	22.6363
Icap,Disr	**0.4742**	**0.3320**	**41.6071**	**28.2240**	0.6082	0.3479	39.5062	24.5654
Icap,Cief	0.7081	0.4517	29.8214	17.4584	0.6362	0.3860	37.0370	22.6363
Icap,Betagamma	0.5148	0.3726	42.1429	27.8204	0.6211	0.3536	39.5062	24.3702
Condred,Icap	0.5148	0.3726	42.1429	27.8204	0.6211	0.3536	39.5062	24.3702
Condred,Relief	0.5148	0.3726	42.1429	27.8204	0.6211	0.3536	39.5062	24.3702
Betagamma,Mifs	0.6680	0.3651	40.1786	24.0873	0.6211	0.3536	39.5062	24.3702
Betagamma,Cief	0.5148	0.3726	42.1429	27.8204	0.6211	0.3536	39.5062	24.3702
Betagamma,Condred	0.6492	0.3451	41.7857	25.3372	0.6211	0.3536	39.5062	24.3702
Relief,Jmi	**0.4742**	**0.3320**	**41.6071**	**28.2240**	0.6211	0.3536	39.5062	24.3702
Relief,Disr	**0.4742**	**0.3320**	**41.6071**	**28.2240**	0.6082	0.3479	39.5062	24.5654
Relief,Cief	0.7098	0.4351	31.0714	18.1727	0.6527	0.3437	40.7407	24.6516
Relief,Icap	0.7098	0.4351	31.0714	18.1727	0.6527	0.3437	40.7407	24.6516
Relief,Betagamma	0.5148	0.3726	42.1429	27.8204	0.6211	0.3536	39.5062	24.3702

Table 6. Results of implementation on cocomo81 and coconasa93 datasets.

Dataset	Coconasa93				Cocomo81			
Method	MMRE	MDMRE	PRED	EF	MMRE	MDMRE	PRED	EF
No method	1.2484	0.4193	30.1075	13.3908	1.9239	0.6926	20.6349	7.0572
Jmi,MRMR	1.1433	0.3908	39.7849	18.5626	1.7703	0.7331	22.2222	8.0216
Jmi,Mifs	0.9439	0.4226	36.5591	18.8075	2.1427	0.5026	28.5714	9.0913
Jmi,Disr	1.1216	0.3711	38.7097	18.2454	1.9773	0.6803	26.9841	9.0633
Jmi,Icap	1.4547	0.4453	34.4086	14.0172	1.6392	0.5820	23.8095	9.0214
Jmi,Condred	0.9989	0.4103	35.4839	17.7519	1.7009	0.6477	22.2222	8.2277
Jmi,Betagamma	0.9989	0.4103	35.4839	17.7519	1.7703	0.7331	22.2222	8.0216
MRMR,Disr	1.1632	0.3724	38.7097	17.8948	1.9773	0.6803	26.9841	9.0633
MRMR,Cief	**1.1865**	**0.3398**	**44.0860**	**20.1627**	1.6392	0.5820	23.8095	9.0214
MRMR,Condred	1.1632	0.3724	38.7097	17.8948	1.7009	0.6477	22.2222	8.2277
MRMR,Betagamma	1.1632	0.3724	38.7097	17.8948	1.6170	0.7323	20.6349	7.8849
MRMR,Relief	1.0595	0.4062	36.5591	17.7512	1.6760	0.6917	25.3968	9.4905
Mifs,MRMR	1.0591	0.4053	37.6344	18.2768	2.1427	0.5026	28.5714	9.0913
Mifs,Disr	0.9439	0.4226	36.5591	18.8075	2.1427	0.5026	28.5714	9.0913
Mifs Icap	1.2549	0.4766	32.2581	14.3055	2.1427	0.5026	28.5714	9.0913
Mifs,Condred	0.9439	0.4226	36.5591	18.8075	1.7672	0.6637	23.8095	8.6041
Mifs,Betagamma	0.9439	0.4226	36.5591	18.8075	2.1427	0.5026	28.5714	9.0913
Mifs,Relief	0.9238	0.4657	31.1828	16.2093	1.7611	0.6973	22.2222	8.0483
Disr,Cief	1.1808	0.3773	41.9355	19.2298	1.7484	0.6544	26.9841	9.8182
Disr,Icap	0.8894	0.6938	20.4301	10.8128	1.7484	0.6544	26.9841	9.8182
Disr,Condred	1.1444	0.3560	40.8602	19.0547	1.7710	0.7567	23.8095	8.5925
Disr,Betagamma	1.1444	0.3560	40.8602	19.0547	1.9773	0.6803	26.9841	9.0633
Cief,Jmi	1.1821	0.3640	40.8602	18.7252	1.6392	0.5820	23.8095	9.0214
Cief,Disr	1.1808	0.3773	41.9355	19.2298	1.7484	0.6544	26.9841	9.8182
Cief,Icap	3.5438	0.8240	17.2043	3.7864	1.7484	0.6544	26.9841	9.8182
cief,Betagamma	1.2384	0.4104	30.1075	13.4503	2.1774	0.5798	28.5714	8.9920
Cief,Relief	3.1438	0.7860	18.2796	4.4113	1.6271	0.6293	22.2222	8.4589
Icap,MRMR	1.4198	0.4650	35.4839	14.6639	1.6392	0.5820	23.8095	9.0214
Icap,Condred	0.9534	0.6348	25.8065	13.2108	2.3809	0.6853	25.3968	7.5119
Icap,Betagamma	0.9534	0.6348	25.8065	13.2108	1.6392	0.5820	23.8095	9.0214
Icap,Relief	2.5552	0.7525	16.1290	4.5368	1.4194	0.7333	22.2222	9.1852
Condred,Cief	1.2384	0.4104	30.1075	13.4503	1.6753	0.5807	28.5714	10.6797
Condred,Betagamma	1.1691	0.3753	36.5591	16.8546	1.7009	0.6477	22.2222	8.2277
Condred,Relief	1.0188	0.4816	34.4086	17.0440	1.6606	0.6923	22.2222	8.3523
Betagamma,Disr	1.1472	0.3912	36.5591	17.0263	1.9773	0.6803	26.9841	9.0633
Betagamma,Relief	1.0188	0.4816	34.4086	17.0440	**1.6352**	**0.7146**	**28.5714**	**10.8421**
Relief,Jmi	1.1399	0.3698	39.7849	18.5921	1.7681	0.7319	20.6349	7.4545
Relief, Disr	1.1170	0.3377	39.7849	18.7933	2.4197	0.7967	22.2222	6.4983

4.4. Comparing the results with other works

In this section, in order to verify the accuracy of the proposed method in this work, the enhanced experimental results are compared with other studies [12]. Here, we should emphasize that the validation method used in this paper is similar to the method used in comparative literature. As shown in table 7, the results of this work are better than the results of comparative literature in all datasets. In evaluation, the best results of experiments on each dataset were compared with the works done by others. In [12], different learning algorithms have been implemented on different datasets, and due to the MLP usage in this study, the best results of [12] with the MLP algorithm after FS have been considered in comparison. It is necessary to repeat that the original coconasa93 dataset has 93 projects with 24 features. In [12], this dataset with 16 features has been used. In [12], "* 100" has been removed from the MDMRE formula. In other words, in their presented formula, the output has not been multiplied by 100. In order to create the conditions to compare, their results have been multiplied by 100. In table 7, a comparison is presented between the experimental results of this paper and other studies.

5. Conclusion

In this work, a hierarchical FS approach in SCE was developed. In the proposed approach, the accuracy and time complexity were improved. Using the wrapper methods, the learning algorithm must be run in each round for evaluating the effectiveness of each feature. Thus the filter methods were utilized for limiting the scope of the search into the most effective features, which reduce the number of search in the wrapper methods, and consequently, have a lower computational complexity.

The filter methods have higher speeds, while their accuracy is not acceptable. The wrapper methods have lower speeds, and due to the use of ML algorithm, they have higher accuracy. Combination of the filter and wrapper methods resulted in an optimal performance by eliminating the weaknesses of each approach and using the advantages of the other ones. This method was evaluated on the cocomo81, coconasa93, and Desharnais datasets. The results obtained indicated the effectiveness of the method. According to different compounds, the common feature of all datasets, "size" feature, is known as the most effective one.

Table 7. Comparison between experimental results of this work and other studies.

Dataset	Paper		MMRE	MDMRE	PRED	EF
COCOMO81+	This Paper		1.6352	0.7146	28.5714	10.8421
LOOCV	[12]		-	0.79	17.5	-
Coconasa93+	This Paper		1.1865	0.3398	44.0860	20.1627
LOOCV	[12]		-	0.38.5	37.6	-
Desharnais81+	This Paper		0.6182	0.3245	40.7407	25.1773
LOOCV	[39]		0.6480	0.3708	-	-
Desharnais77+	This Paper		0.4742	0.3320	41.6071	28.2240
10-Fold	[19]	BFE	0.592	-	37.7	23.71
		FFS	0.577	-	38.2	24.22
		BSWF	0.618	-	38.6	23.85
		FSWF	0.600	-	37.3	23.31
		LSBFE	0.592	-	37.2	23.36
		LSFFS	0.596	-	36.3	22.74
		GARSON	0.606	-	44.7	27.83
		LSGA	0.607	-	35.5	22.09
		GA	0.570	-	37.6	23.94

In the future, we intend to work on other combinations of the filter and wrapper methods. In this study, we used a combination of the filter methods in the first phase. Composition of more filter methods may provide more accuracy. In this work, we used a multi-layer neural network algorithm as a learning algorithm. In the future works, we intend to implement this approach in the other learning algorithms. In this work, the EF criteria for SF in the SCR were used for the first time. This criterion consists of a combination of two important evaluation criteria used in other articles in this issue. The proposed method has a function to combine the different evaluation criteria used in this field. We are going to provide more powerful combinations of evaluation criteria using techniques such as genetic programming by fused function.

References

[1] Pandey, P. (2013). Analysis of the Techniques for Software Cost Estimation. International Journal of Software Engineering Research & Practices, vol. 3, no. 1, pp. 9-15.

[2] Wal, A. S., Gupta, V., & Kumar, R. (2012). Emerging Estimation Techniques. International Journal of Computer Applications, vol. 59, no. 8, pp. 30-34.

[3] Wen, J., Li, S., Lin, Z., Hu, Y., & Huang, C. (2012). Systematic literature review of machine learning based software development effort estimation models. Information and Software Technology, vol. 54, no. 1, pp. 41-59.

[4] Kumari, S., & Pushkar, S. (2013). Comparison and analysis of different software cost estimation methods. International Journal of Advanced Computer Science and application, vol. 4, no. 1, pp. 153-157.

[5] Keim, Y., Bhardwaj, M., Saroop, S., & Tandon, A. (2014). Software Cost Estimation Models and Techniques: A Survey. In International Journal of Engineering Research and Technology, vol. 3, no. 2, pp. 1763-1768.

[6] Zaid, A., Selamat, M. H., Ghani, A. A. A., Atan, R., & Wei, K. T. (2008). Issues in software cost estimation. International Journal of Computer Science and Network Security, vol. 8, no.11, pp. 350-356.

[7] Bailey, J. W. & Basiii, V. R. (1981). A meta-model for software development resource expenditures. 5th international conference on Software engineering, IEEE press, 1981.

[8] Wolverton, R. W. (1974). The cost of developing large-scale software. Computers. IEEE Transactions on Software Engineering, vol. 100, no. 6, pp. 615-636.

[9] Putnam, L. H. (1978). A general empirical solution to the macro software sizing and estimating problem. IEEE transactions on Software Engineering, vol. 4, no. 4, pp. 345-361.

[10] Venkatachalam, A. R. (1993). Software cost estimation using artificial neural networks. International Joint Conference on Proceedings, IEEE press, 1993.

[11] Helmer, O. (1966). Social technology (vol. 9). New York: Basic Books.

[12] Dejaeger, K., Verbeke, W., Martens, D., & Baesens, B. (2012). Data mining techniques for software effort estimation: a comparative study.

Software Engineering, IEEE Transactions on Software Engineering, vol. 38, no. 2, pp. 375-397.

[13] Bitaraf, A., yakhchi, M., Mahjobi, B. (2012), The optimal method for estimating the cost of using software-based Perceptron Neural Network Data Mining. 2th National Conference on soft Computing and Information Technology, mahshahr, Iran, 2012. (in persian)

[14] Attarzadeh, I., & Ow, S. H. (2010). Proposing a new software cost estimation model based on artificial neural networks. 2th International Conference on Computer Engineering and Technology (ICCET), IEEE press, 2010.

[15] Nassif, A. B., Azzeh, M., Capretz, L. F., & Ho, D. (2013). A comparison between decision trees and decision tree forest models for software development effort estimation. 3th International Conference on Communications and Information Technology (ICCIT), Chennai, India, 2013.

[16] Radlinski, L. (2010). A survey of bayesian net models for software development effort prediction. International Journal of Software Engineering and Computing, vol. 2, no. 2, pp. 95-109.

[17] Bibi, S., Stamelos, I., & Angelis, L. (2008). Combining probabilistic models for explanatory productivity estimation. Information and Software Technology, vol. 50, no. 7, pp. 656-669.

[18] Kirsopp, C., Shepperd, M. J., & Hart, J. (2002). Search heuristics,case-based reasoning and software project effort prediction. The Genetic and volutionary Computation Conference, New York. Morgan Kaufmann Publishers, 2002.

[19] Papatheocharous, Efi, et al. (2012). Feature subset selection for software cost modelling and estimation. arXiv preprint arXiv:1210.1161.

[20] Alpaydin, E. (2014). Introduction to machine learning. MIT press.

[21] Chen, Z., Menzies, T., Port, D., & Boehm, B. (2005). Feature subset selection can improve software cost estimation accuracy. ACM SIGSOFT Software Engineering Notes, vol. 30, no. 4, pp. 1-6.

[22] Mendes, E., Lokan, C., Harrison, R., & Triggs, C. (2005). A replicated comparison of cross-company and within-company effort estimation models using the ISBSG database. 11th IEEE International Symposium, IEEE press, 2005.

[23] Mendes, E., & Lokan, C. (2009). Investigating the use of chronological splitting to compare software cross-company and single-company effort predictions: a replicated study. 13th Conference on Evaluation & Assessment in Software Engineering (EASE), BCS, 2009.

[24] Mendes, E., Kalinowski, M., Martins, D., Ferrucci, F., & Sarro, F. (2014). Cross-vs. Within-company cost estimation studies revisited: An extended systematic review. 18th International Conference on Evaluation and Assessment in Software Engineering, ACM, London, England, 2014.

[25] Liu, H., Wei, R., & Jiang, G. (2013). A hybrid feature selection scheme for mixed attributes data. Computational and Applied Mathematics, vol. 32, no. 1, pp. 145-161.

[26] Li, Y. F., Xie, M., & Goh, T. N. (2009). A study of mutual information based feature selection for case based reasoning in software cost estimation. Expert Systems with Applications, vol. 36, no. 3, pp. 5921-5931.

[27] Menzies, T., Port, D., Chen, Z., & Hihn, J. (2005), Specialization and extrapolation of software cost models. 20th IEEE/ACM international Conference on Automated software engineering, California, USA, 2005.

[28] Chen, Z., Menzies, T., Port, D., & Boehm, B. (2005). Finding the right data for software cost modeling. Transactions on Software Engineering, vol. 22, no. 6, pp. 38–46.

[29] Jalali, O., Menzies, T., Baker, D., and Hihn, J. (2007). Column pruning beats stratification in effort estimation. International Workshop on Predictor Models in Software Engineering, Washington, USA, 2007.

[30] Auer, M., Trendowicz, A., Graser, B., Haunschmid, E., & Biffl, S. (2006). Optimal project feature weights in analogy-based cost estimation: Improvement and limitations. IEEE Transactions on Software Engineering, vol. 32, no. 2, pp. 83–92.

[31] Huang, S. J., & Chiu, N. H. (2006). Optimization of analogy weights by genetic algorithm for software effort estimation. Information and software technology, vol. 48, no. 11, pp. 1034–1045.

[32] Keung, J. W., Kitchenham, B. A., & Jeffery, D. R. (2008). Analogy-X: providing statistical inference to analogy-based software cost estimation. IEEE Transactions on Software Engineering, vol. 34, no. 4, pp. 471–484.

[33] Song, Q., Ni, J., & Wang, G. (2013). A fast clustering-based feature subset selection algorithm for high-dimensional data. IEEE Transactions on Knowledge and Data Engineering, vol. 25, no. 1, pp. 1–14.

[34] Chahooki, M. A. Z., & Charkari, N. M. (2014). Shape classification by manifold learning in multiple observation spaces. Information Sciences, vol. 262, pp. 46-61.

[35] Brown, G., Pocock, A., Zhao, M. J., & Luján, M. (2012). Conditional likelihood maximisation: a unifying framework for information theoretic feature selection. The Journal of Machine Learning Research, vol. 13, no. 1, pp. 27-66.

[36] Hsu, H. H., Hsieh, C. W., & Lu, M. D. (2011). Hybrid feature selection by combining filters and wrappers. Expert Systems with Applications, vol. 38, no. 7, pp. 8144-8150.

[37] Halaku, F., Eftekhari, M., Esmaeeli, A. (2011). The combination of ridge regression and correlation coefficients for select the important features of nucleotide polymorphism database (SNP), 19th ICEE, Tehran, Iran. (in Persian)

[38] Pocock, A. C. (2012). Feature selection via joint likelihood (Doctoral dissertation, University of Manchester).

[39] Kosti, M. V, et al (2010). DD-EbA: An algorithm for determining the number of neighbors in cost estimation by analogy using distance distributions. arXiv preprint arXiv:1012.5755.

[40] Araujo, R. D. A., de Oliveira, A. L. I, & Soares, S. C. B. (2009). A morphological-rank-linear approach for software development cost estimation. 21th International Conference on Tools with Artificial Intelligence, New Jersey, USA, pp. 630-636, 2009.

19

Delay-dependent stability for transparent bilateral teleoperation system: An LMI approach

A. Khosravi[1*], A.R. Alfi[2], A. Roshandel[1]

1. Department of Electrical and Computer Engineering, Babol University of Technology, School of Computer Engineering
2. Faculty of Electrical and Robatic Computer Engineering, Shahrood University of Technology, Iran

*Corresponding author: akhosravi@nit.ac.ir (A. Khosravi)

Abstract

There are two significant goals in teleoperation systems: Stability and performance. This paper introduces an LMI-based robust control method for bilateral transparent teleoperation systems in presence of model mismatch. The uncertainties in time delay in communication channel, task environment and model parameters of master-slave systems are called a model mismatch. The time delay in communication channel is assumed to be large, unknown and asymmetric, but the upper bound of the delay is assumed to be known. The proposed method consists of two local controllers. One local controller namely local slave controller is located on the remote site to control the motion tracking and the other one is located on the local site namely local master controller to preserve the complete transparency by ensuring force tracking and the robust stability of the closed-loop system. To reduce the peak amplitude of output signal respect to the peak amplitude of input signal in slave site, the local slave controller is designed based on a bounded peak-to-peak gain controller. In order to provide a realistic case, an external signal as a noise of force sensor is also considered. Simulation results show the effectiveness of proposed control structure.

Keywords: *Bilateral teleportation system, Complete Transparency, Robust control, Large Time Delay, Linear MatrixInequality.*

1. Introduction

It is common that timedelay is often a source of instability and/or poor performance of many systems. Therefore, stability analysis and control design problems of the time delay systems have drawn an increasing attention during the last two decades. Bilateral teleoperation system is one of the most well-known areas of such systems. In bilateral teleoperation, a human operator applies force to the master in order to produce the desired motion. The motion of master is transmitted to the slave system a communication channel. The slave system tracks the motion of master system and sends back the reflected force from task environment to the master. Bilateral teleoperation system can be generically described by means of the block diagram shown in Figure 1.

Transparency is the major criterion for the performance of teleoperation systems. If the slave accurately reproduces the master's commands and the master correctly feels the slave forces, then the human operator experiences the same interaction as the slave would. This is called transparency in teleoperation systems [1]. In other words, the ideal responses (i.e. the complete transparency) for the teleoperation system with time delay can be defined as follows:

- The force that the human operator applies to the master robot is equal to the force reflected from the task environment. This can help the operator to realize the force sensation.
- The master position/velocity is equal to the slave position/velocity.

Because of the importance of stability and transparency in bilateral teleoperation systems, several control schemes have been proposed in literatures [2]-[18]. Some researchers have analyzed the transparency of teleoperation systems, when there is no time delay in communication channels. Moreover, in some cases, in order to make the system transparent, acceleration of the master and the slave must be sent to the other side. However, acceleration measurement is not an easy task [2]-[7]. In some papers, it has been assumed that the time delay in communication channel is constant [8]-[12]. In addition, some proposed methods in literatures are not stable for large time delays (with or without uncertainties in the time delay) [13]-[16]. Moreover, in some articles, the forward and the backward time delays have been assumed identical [8], [13], [17]-[23]. Some researchers have also proposed different control strategies, such as three and four-channel control methods for teleoperation systems in presence of the time delay with good transparency. Nevertheless, these methods are difficult to realize [24]. In [25] and [26], a simple structure design proposed for bilateral transparent teleoperation systems in presence of time delay uncertainty. In the proposed control method, to achieve complete transparency, direct-force measurement-force reflecting control has been used.

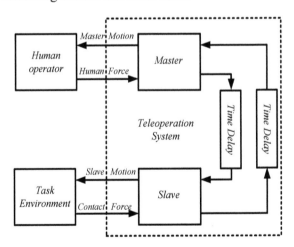

Figure 1. A general framework of bilateral teleoperation system.

Recently, the LMI-based approaches have been employed to deal with stability and stabilization problems [27] such as teleoperation systems. In 2008, an LMI approach to robust H_∞ and L_l controllers design for a bilateral teleoperation system introduced [28]. Although the time delay of communication channel was assumed to be

large, unknown and randomly time varying, but the upper bounds of the time delay interval and the derivative of the delay were assumed to be known. In 2009, the teleoperation system with asymmetric time delays has been also studied in the form of LMI [29]. The stability condition based on LMI has been used to optimize the allowable maximum delay values. In this method, the upper bounds and the derivative of time delay have been assumed to be known. The main drawback of these papers is that the complete transparency has not been achieved.

It is noticeable that there are two different methods to investigate the stability of delay systems: 1) delay-independent stability and 2) delay-dependent stability [30]. The delay-independent stability is defined for any length of nonnegative delay values, while the delay-dependent stability is referred to as the property in which the system is stable for any time delay values as long as $T \leq T_{max}$. So, the delay-dependent stability criterion assumes prior knowledge on the upper bounds of the delay values.

This paper presents a novel LMI-based robust control design for bilateral teleoperation systems in presence of model mismatch. Also, the uncertainties in time delay in communication channel, task environment and model parameters of master-slave systems are called model mismatch. The main goals of the proposed control method are: 1) the closed-loop control system is delay-dependent stable with asymmetric time delays while the whole system is complete transparent; 2) the motion/force scaling can be selected arbitrarily. In other words, it is applicable to micro-micro manipulation. In the proposed method, the time delay in communication channel is assumed to be unknown, but the upper bound of delay is assumed to be known. This assumption is very general for the time delay. Since the time delay of the practical systems are often bounded, it is reasonable to assume the upper bound on the time delay. To achieve these goals, the proposed method consists of two local controllers. One local controller namely local slave controller is located on the remote site to control the motion tracking and the other one is located on the local site namely local master controller to preserve the complete transparency by ensuring force tracking and the robust stability of the closed-loop system. By applying an LMI-based convex optimization method, a time response can be achieved with smaller settling time accompanied by lower control efforts in local and remote sites.

This paper is briefly outlined as follows: the modeling of bilateral teleoperation systems including time delay in communication channel is presented in section II. Section III introduces the standard representation of control system. The main results are represented in section IV. This section is assigned to the design of local controllers. The stability analysis of the proposed control structure is also described. Section V shows the simulation results. Finally, section VI draws conclusions and gives some suggestions for the future works.

2. System description
2.1. Structure of teleoperation system
Figure 2 depicts the structure of bilateral teleportation system. In this figure, G is the transfer function of the system, C shows the local controller, indices m and s denote the master and the slave systems, respectively, f_e is the contact force from task environment, f_r is the reflected force from the remote environment, f_h demonstrates the force applied to the master system by the human operator, T_{ms} and T_{sm} are the forward (from master to slave) and backward (from slave to master) time delays, respectively. Moreover, Z_e is the impedance of the task environment and $v(t)$ represents the sensor noise of the force measurement in the remote site. Finally, K_p and K_f are the arbitrary motion and force scaling factors, respectively.

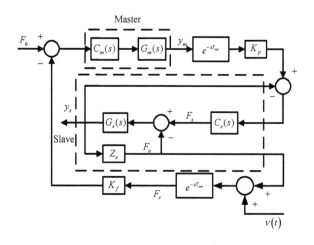

Figure 2. Teleportation system structure.

It is noticeable that because of using direct-force measurement-force reflecting control, the utilization of force sensor is inevitable. Hence, the noise of sensor in the remote site must be considered. This issue has not been investigated in

[25], [26]. The following assumptions have to be stated first:

Assumption 1: The forward and backward time delays are assumed to be bounded and can be non-identical.

Assumption 2: The slave system acts on hard task environment.

Assumption 3: The contact force f_e is measurable.

2.2. Modeling of time delay
In the proposed control methodology, the time delay uncertainty is modeled in multiplicative form. According to assumption 1, a new bounded variable denoted by T can be defined as a summation of the forward and the backward time delays.

$$T = T_{ms} + T_{sm}, \quad 0 \leq T \leq T_{max} \quad (1)$$

Based on fluid flow model [31], the time delay T can be represented as follows:

$$T = \frac{1}{2}\left(T_{max} + T_{min}\right) + \frac{1}{2}\left(T_{max} - T_{min}\right)\beta, \quad -1 \leq \beta \leq 1 \quad (2)$$

Where T_{max} and T_{min} are the upper bound and the lower bound of T, respectively and the parameter β specifies the uncertainty region. Let define a new parameter γ as

$$\gamma = \frac{1}{2T_{max}}\left(T_{max} - T_{min}\right) \quad (3)$$

Substituting (3) into (2) yields

$$T = (1 - \gamma)T_{max} + \gamma T_{max}\beta, \quad 0 \leq \gamma \leq 0.5 \quad (4)$$

The parameters β and γ are real constants to be determined based on application. The first term of (4) shows a constant delay part while the second term represents the uncertain delay time. By using the first-order Pade' approximation, the exponential delay transfer function is written as

$$e^{-sT} = e^{-s(1-\gamma)T_{max}}e^{-s\gamma\delta T_{max}} \cong \frac{1 - sT/2}{1 + sT/2} \quad (5)$$

$$\approx \left(\frac{1 - s(1-\gamma)T_{max}/2}{1 + s(1-\gamma)T_{max}/2}\right)\left(\frac{1 - s\gamma T_{max}\beta/2}{1 + s\gamma T_{max}\beta/2}\right)$$

Hence, the uncertain delay part given in (5) can be expressed as a multiplicative uncertainty.

$$\frac{1-s\,\gamma T_{\max}\,\beta/2}{1+s\,\gamma T_{\max}\,\beta/2} = 1 - \frac{s\,\gamma T_{\max}\beta}{1+s\,\gamma T_{\max}\,\beta/2} \qquad (6)$$

$$= 1 + W_{mT}(s)\Delta$$

Where Δ is the perturbation function with $\|\Delta\|_\infty < 1$ and

$$W_{mT}(s) = \frac{s\,\gamma T_{\max}\beta}{1+s\,\gamma T_{\max}\,\beta/2} \qquad (7.1)$$

is a multiplicative uncertainty weigh. As $W_{mT}(s)$ cannot cover all possible uncertain delay, the following modified weighting function is used [32]:

$$W_{mT}(s) = \frac{s\,\gamma T_{\max}\beta}{1+s\,\gamma T_{\max}\,\beta/3.465} \qquad (7.2)$$

Figure 3 shows the configuration of time delay uncertainty used in this paper. It should be noted that the lower bound of time delay is also frequently equal to zero.

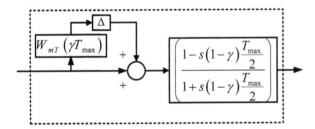

Figure 3. Configuration of time delay uncertainty

3. Standard representation of control system

Figure 4 shows the standard control representation for the local controllers design, i.e. local master controller C_m and local slave controller C_s. In this figure, u is the control input, w is a vector of exogenous signal (reference input signal, disturbance and sensor noise signals) and y is the measurement output signal. Z is also a vector of output signals $(z_1\ z_2\ \dots\ z_i)^T$ related to the performance of the control system. The state space of the structure shown in Figure 4 is defined as follows:

$$\dot{x} = Ax + B_w w + Bu \qquad (8)$$

$$Z = C_z x + D_{zw} w + D_z u$$

$$y = Cx + D_w w$$

Our goal is to find a dynamical output-feedback controller with state space realization given in (9) such that makes desired changes in the outputs' vector.

$$\dot{\zeta} = A_K \zeta + B_K y \qquad (9)$$

$$u = C_K \zeta + D_k y$$

In (9), ζ represents a vector of the controller's states and u and y were introduced before.

Next section presents how we can obtain the structure shown in Figure 4 for local master and slave controllers design.

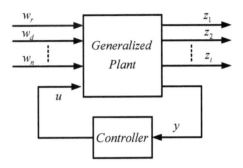

Figure 4. Standard control system representation.

4. Controller design

This section is assigned to the local controllers design. As mentioned before, to achieve robust stability and complete transparency, two local controllers are designed: One controller in the remote site C_s namely local slave controller, and the other in the local site C_m namely local master controller. The local slave controller is responsible for tracking the master commands and the local master controller is in charge of force tracking as well as guaranteeing the robust stability of the closed-loop system. Without loss of generality, the position of master and slave systems are considered. The scaling factors betweenmaster and slave are also set to unity. It should be recalled that the designer can select arbitrary values for motion/force scaling.

4.1. The local slave controller

First, in order to design the local slave controller, the slave control system is reformulated in such a way that it is converted to an equivalent block diagram in a standard control system representation given in Figure 4. Let define the following variable

$$G'_s(s) = \frac{G_s(s)}{1+Z_e G_s(s)} \qquad (10)$$

Hence, referring Figure 2, the standard of slave control system can be shown as Figure 5. Base on control theory, the feedback control system in Figure 5 can be shown as the standard control system representation in Figure 4.

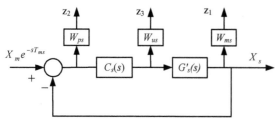

Figure 5. The structure of local slave controller design

In Figure 5, C_s is the local slave controller; W_{ms} is the uncertainty weighting function due to variations in the dynamics of the slave system. W_{ps}, and W_{us} are also the performance and the controller weighting functions, respectively. In addition, motion tracking, to reduce the peak amplitude of output signal respect to the peak amplitude of input signal, a bounded peak-to-peak gain controller for the slave system can be constructed from Theorem 1. The peak-to-peak gain for a transfer function; G_i is defined as [33]:

$$\|G_i\|_{peak} := sup \left\{ \begin{array}{l} \|z_j(T)\| : x_{cl}(0) = 0, T \geq 0, \\ \|w_i(t)\| \leq 1 \, for \, t \geq 0 \end{array} \right\} \quad (11)$$

Where x_{cl} denotes the closed-loop state vector. This relation measures the maximum norm of output signal z_j for inputs w_j whose amplitude does not exceed one. Recall that there is no exact characterization for the peak-to-peak norm in the LMI framework, but it is possible to deduce the upper bounds for $\|G_i\|_{peak}$ [33].

Theorem 1: Consider the closed-loop system in Figure 5. Motion tracking with lower maximum overshoot via local slave controller C_s can be met by solving the following minimization LMI.Based on this, a bounded peak-to-peak gain controller can be constructed for the slave system if there exist X, Y, μ, λ and ζ as follows [33]:

mininmize $\lambda > 0$,

$$\begin{pmatrix} \Pi_{11} + \lambda X & * & * \\ \Pi_{21} + \lambda I & \Pi_{22} + \lambda Y & * \\ \Pi_{31} & \Pi_{32} & -\mu I \end{pmatrix} < 0,$$

$$\begin{pmatrix} \lambda X & \lambda I & 0 & * \\ \lambda I & \lambda Y & 0 & * \\ 0 & 0 & (\zeta - \mu)I & * \\ \Pi_{41} & \Pi_{42} & \Pi_{43} & \zeta I \end{pmatrix} > 0 \quad (12)$$

where Π_{11}, Π_{21}, Π_{31}, Π_{22}, Π_{41}, Π_{32}, Π_{42}, Π_{43} can be obtained from

$$\Pi_{11} := AX + XA^T + B\hat{C}_k + \left(B\hat{C}_k\right)^T \quad \Pi_{21} := \hat{A}_k + \left(A + B\hat{D}_kC\right)^T \quad (13)$$

$$\Pi_{22} := \hat{A}^TY + YA + B\hat{C}_k + \left(B\hat{C}_k\right)^T \quad \Pi_{32} := \left(YB_w + \hat{B}_kD_w\right)^T$$

$$\Pi_{43} := D_{z_1w} + D_{z_1}\hat{D}_kD_w \quad \Pi_{41} := C_{z_1}X + D_{z_1}\hat{C}_k$$

$$\Pi_{31} := \left(B_w + B\hat{D}_kD_w\right)^T \quad \Pi_{42} := C_{z_1} + D_{z_1}\hat{D}_kC$$

*sign is used to show the transpose components while A, B_w, $C_z$and D_{zw} and D_{zw} are related matrices to the desired output channel from the state space realization of the generalized plant, and $\hat{A}_k$, $\hat{B}_k$, $\hat{C}_k$ and $\hat{D}_k$ represent the transformed parameters of the local slave controller which used in order to preserve the linearization of the design problem. If λ is chosen as a positive constant, the minimization of ζ will be a convex optimization. The real parameters of the controller can be constructed from the following relations [33]:

$$D_k := \hat{D}_k \quad (14)$$

$$C_k := \left(\hat{C}_k - D_kCX\right)M^{-T}$$

$$B_k := N^{-1}\left(\hat{B}_k - YBD_k\right)$$

$$A_k := N^{-1}\left(\hat{A}_k - NB_kCX - YBC_kM^T - Y(A + BD_kC)X\right)M^{-T}$$

Where N and M are nonsingular matrices that should satisfy $MN^T = I - XY$.

4.2. The local master controller
Considering the uncertainty in the time delay as well as the measurement noise accompanied by the reflected force, utilization of a multi-objective H_2/H_∞ controller in the master side is inevitable. The roles of local master controller $C_m(s)$ are to provide robust stability to the overall system and ensure the force tracking based on multiobjective H_2/H_∞ approach. The force tracking means that the reflecting force F_e has to follow the human operator force F_h. First, we define the following variable:

$$G_s''(s) = \frac{G_s'(s)}{1 + C_s(s)G_s'(s)} \quad (15)$$

Then, Figure 2 can be simplified as in Figure 6. Now, since sending the contact force through the reflection path of communication channel performs the force tracking, a new output in the block diagram of Fig. 6 can be defined as F_r. Hence, the structure of local master controller design can be redrawn as in Figure 7. In Figure 7, W_{m2} is the uncertainty weighting function related to the time delay introduced in section 2.2 and W_{pm} and W_{um} are the performance and controller weighting functions which are chosen based on objectives of the local master controller design (characteristics of the time response and maximum value of the control signal). Consequently, the local master controller C_m can be constructed from Theorem 2.

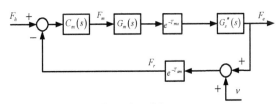

Figure 6. The closed-loop structure

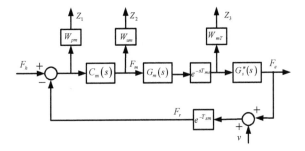

Figure 7. The structure of local master controller design.

Theorem 2: Consider the closed-loop control system in Figure 7. The local master controller with tracking error bound γ would exist if there exist X and Y that can satisfy the minimization of the following convex optimization inequality [33]:

$$mininmize \ \gamma \tag{16}$$

$$Subject \ to \begin{pmatrix} \Lambda_{11} & 0 \\ 0 & \Lambda_{22} \end{pmatrix} < 0, \begin{pmatrix} X & I & * \\ I & Y & * \\ M_{31} & M_{32} & Q \end{pmatrix} > 0$$

$$, Tr(Q) < \nu, \ D_{z_2 w} + D_{z_2} \hat{D}_k D_w = 0$$

where Π_{11}, Π_{21}, Π_{31}, Π_{22}, Π_{41}, Π_{32}, Π_{42}, Π_{43} introduced in (12) and

$$\Lambda_{11} = \begin{pmatrix} \Pi_{11} & * & * & * \\ \Pi_{21} & \Pi_{22} & * & * \\ \Pi_{31} & \Pi_{32} & -\gamma I & * \\ \Pi_{41} & \Pi_{42} & \Pi_{43} & -\gamma I \end{pmatrix} \tag{17}$$

$$\Lambda_{22} = \begin{pmatrix} \Pi_{11} & * & * \\ \Pi_{21} & \Pi_{22} & * \\ \Pi_{31} & \Pi_{32} & -I \end{pmatrix}$$

$$M_{31} := C_{z_2} X + D_{z_2} \hat{C}_k$$

$$M_{32} := C_{z_2} + D_{z_2} \hat{D}_k C$$

where * and the variables A, B_w, C_z, D_{zw}, $A\square_k$, $B\square_k$, $C\square_k$ and $D\square_k$ have been introduced before.

5. Simulation results

The one-degree of freedom manipulator is used for the master and the slave systems similar to many papers in this field [34]. The dynamic equation of the master and the slave systems are considered as

$$\frac{y_m}{u_m} = \frac{1}{M_m s^2 + B_m s} \quad \begin{array}{l} m_{min} \le M \le m_{max} \\ b_{min} \le B \le b_{max} \end{array} \tag{18}$$

$$\frac{y_s}{u_c} = \frac{1}{M_s s^2 + B_s s} \quad z_{e\,min} \le Z_e \le z_{e\,max}$$

Where B is the viscous friction coefficient, M is the mass, u is the input, Z_e is the impedance of the environment and indices m and s are for the master and the slave, respectively. The parameter values are given in Table 1. To evaluate the effectiveness of the proposed method in the presence of model mismatch, simulations are carried out for three cases:

Case 1: The time delay uncertainty.

Case 2: The time delay uncertainty and the parameter uncertainty in the slave system.

Case 3: The time delay uncertainty as well as the parameter uncertainties in the slave system and the task environment.

Table 1. System parameters

Symbol	Amount
M_m	1.5
B_m	11
m_{min}	0.1
m_{max}	3.9
b_{min}	3
b_{max}	27
T_{min}	0
T_{max}	3
Z_e	2
z_{emin}	1
z_{emax}	3
K_p	1
K_f	1

In simulations, two different inputs, which are the most common and generic dynamic test for control scheme, are utilized in simulations; step input and sinusoidal input. As a result, the control performance is evaluated by applying a step and a sinusoidal force exerted by human operator. It is necessary to recall that a large time delay is considered in the simulation. The time delay in bilateral teleoperation systems is defined small for $T \le 0.001\,sec$ [25], [26]. As it mentioned in section 2 in part B, the parameter α is set to 0.5. In all cases, the multiplicative uncertainty weight for time delay given in (7.2).

$$W_{mT}(s) = \frac{1.5s}{0.4329s + 1} \tag{19}$$

As shown in Figure 8, the opted weighting functions can cope with the time delay uncertainties and the variation of parameters in the slave system. The corresponding weighting functions depicted in Figures 5 and 7 are given in Table 2 and 3, respectively. Moreover, Table 4 represents the obtained local controllers in different cases. From Theorem 1, to reduce the effect of uncertainty in the parameters of slave system and task environment in both Case 2 and Case 3, a bounded peak-to-peak gain controller (i.e. local slave controller C_s) in the remote site is employed. In addition, from the generalized structure given in (8) and Theorem 2, the local master controller C_m is obtained. Recall that the reduced order of local master controllers C_m using Normalized Coprime Factorization (NCF) method is given in Table 4.

Simulation results are shown in Figures 9-13. These figures are the human force, the transparency response (position and force tracking), and the controller signals. Recall that force tracking error is a difference between human operator force f_h and reflected force f_r in presence measurement noise, whereas position tracking error is a difference between position of master x_m and slave x_s. From these figures, it can be seen that the designed controllers can meet the objectives i.e. robust stability and complete transparency. Furthermore, the local master controller can reduce the measurement noise accompanied by the reflected force from remote environment. Finally, to show the stability and performance index of the system in presence of model mismatch, μ analysis is used. Figures 13a and 13b

illustrate the μ bound of the closed-loop stability and performance with designed local controllers. Since the values of μ bound related to the stability of system is smaller than one and near one for the performance, the designed controllers preserve the robust stability in presence model mismatch while the performance of system does not change effectively.

6. Conclusion

To achieve robust stability and complete transparency, this paper proposed a novel LMI-based robust control design for bilateral teleoperation systems in presence of uncertainties in time delay in communication channel, task environment and model parameters of master-slave systems, which is called model mismatch. Methodology in this paper focused on the time delay in communication channel assumed to be large and unknown, but the upper bound of the delay was assumed to be known. This assumption is very general for the time delay in communication channel. Two local controllers: One on the master side and the other one on the slave side were designed. The slave controller guarantees the position tracking and the master controller guarantees force tracking as well as the robust stability of the overall closed-loop system. Simulation results show the feasibility of the proposed control method. Future works in this research domain will include considering unbounded time delay in communication channel for proposed structure and some analytical and practical work and conditions for stability robustness of the closed-loop system.

Table 2. Corresponding weighting function for local slave controller design shown in Figure 5

Weighting Function	Case 1	Case 2	Case 3
$W_{ps}(s)$	–	1	1
$W_{us}(s)$	–	$W_{us2} = 0.001$	$W_{us3} = 0.008$
$W_{ms}(s)$	–	$W_{ms2}(s) = \dfrac{18.05(s+1.035)}{s+5.499}$	$W_{ms3}(s) = \dfrac{17.352\ (s+0.07123)}{s+2.759}$

Table 3. Corresponding weighting function for local master controller design shown in Figure 7

Weighting Function	Case 1	Case 2	Case 3
$W_{pm}(s)$	$\dfrac{0.065}{s+0.0001}$	$\dfrac{0.065}{s+0.0001}$	$\dfrac{0.065}{s+0.0001}$
$W_{um}(s)$	0.0001	0.0001	0.0001
$W_{mT}(s)$	$\dfrac{1.5s}{0.4329s+1}$	$\dfrac{1.5s}{0.4329s+1}$	$\dfrac{1.5s}{0.4329s+1}$

Table 4. Local controllers

Cases	Local master controller	Local slave controller
Case 1	$C_{m_1}=\dfrac{5.2221(s+0.7381)(s^2+7.429s+41)}{(s+3.02)(s+1.293)(s^2+4.963s+49.57)}$	$C_{s_1}(t)=\dfrac{82.22s+10.9603}{s}$
Case 2	$C_{m_2}=\dfrac{0.6378(s+15.05)(s+0.5056)(s+0.0002)}{(s+8.587)(s+0.0004)(s^2+1.576s+0.7693)}$	$C_{s_2}=\dfrac{2.97\times10^5(s+9.993)}{(s^2+123.4s+7088)}$
Case 3	$C_{m_3}=\dfrac{0.4805(s+89.52)(s+10.57)(s+0.0004)}{(s+4.608)(s+0.0008)(s^2+7.032s+130.5)}$	$C_{s_3}=\dfrac{6.35\times10^6(s+27.02)}{(s^2+378.1s+5.28\times10^4)}$

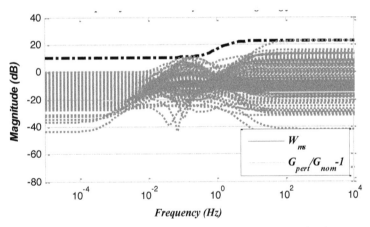

Figure 8a. Bode diagram of the weighting function W_{ms} for the uncertain slave system G/G_0-1

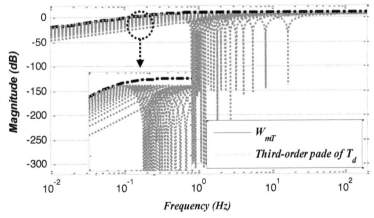

Figure 8b. Bode diagram of the multiplicative weight function W_{mT} for third order Pade' approximation of time delay.

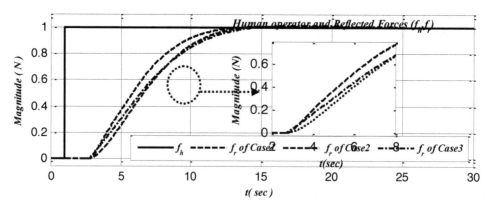

Figure 9a. Force tracking for step input (Human operator F_h and reflected forceF_r)

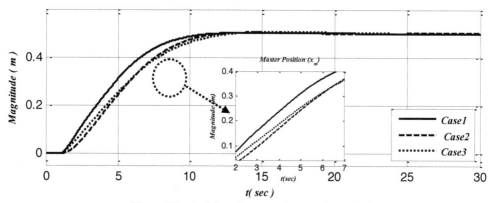

Figure 9b. Force tracking error for step input

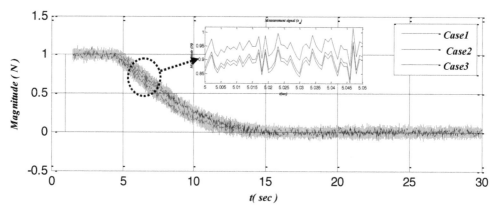

Figure 10a. Position of master for step input (x_m)

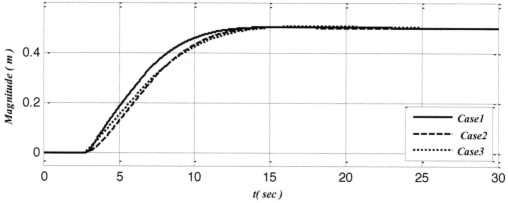

Figure 10b. Position of slave for step input (x_s)

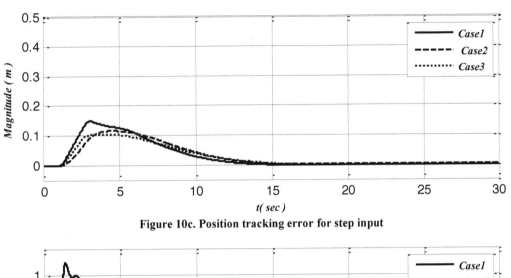

Figure 10c. Position tracking error for step input

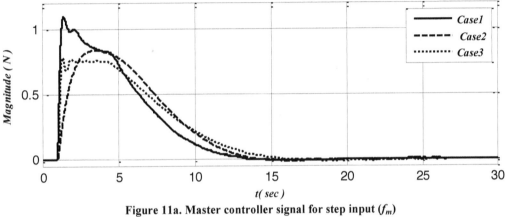

Figure 11a. Master controller signal for step input (f_m)

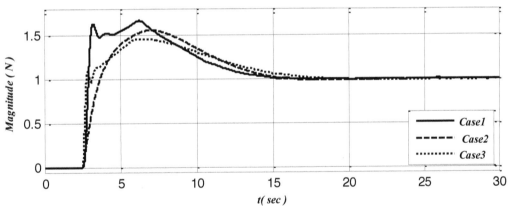

Figure 11b. Slave controller signal for step input (f_s)

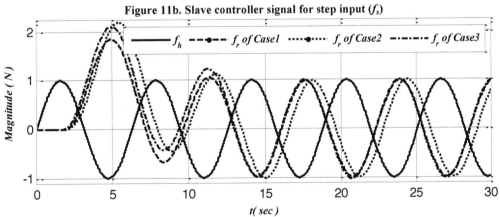

Figure 12a. Force tracking for sinusoidal input (Human operator F_h and reflected force F_r)

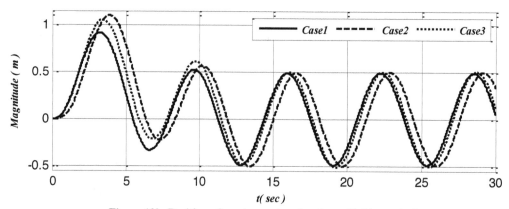

Figure 12b. Position of master system for sinusoidal input (x_m)

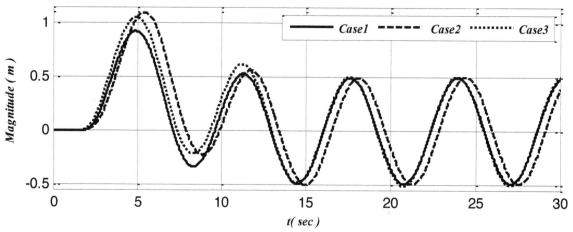

Figure 12c. Position of slave system for sinusoidal input (x_s)

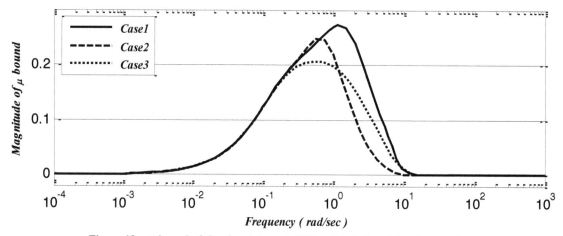

Figure 13a. μ bound of the closed-loop stability with designed local controllers

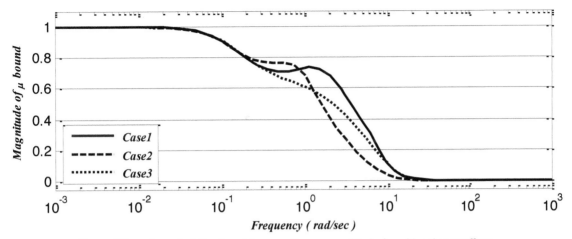

Figure 13b. μ bound of the closed-loop performance with designed local controllers

References

[1] Smith, A., Mobasser, F. and Hashtrudi-Zaad, K. (2006). Neural network based contact force observers for haptic applications. IEEE Transactions on Robotics. 22(6), 1163-1175.

[2] Lawrence, D. A. (1993). Stability and transparency in bilateral teleoperation. IEEE Transactions on Robotics and Automation. 9(5), 625-637.

[3] S. E. Salcudean, M. Zhu, W. H. Zhu, K. Hashtrudi-Zaad. (2000). Transparent bilateral teleoperation under position and rate control. Robotics Research. 19, 1185-1202.

[4] Hannaford. B. (1998). Stability and performance tradeoffs in bilateral telemanipulation. IEEE Conference on Robotics and Automation, 584-589.

[5] Ni, L. and Wang, D. W. L. (2002). A gain-switching control scheme for position-error-based force reflecting teleoperation. 10th IEEE Symposium Haptic Interfaces for Virtual and Teleoperator Systems.

[6] Kim, J., Chang, P. H. and Park, H. S. (2005). Transparent teleoperation using two-channel control architectures. Conference on Robotics and Automation. 2824-2831.

[7] Yokokohji, Y. and Yoshikawa, T. (1994). Bilateral control of master-slave manipulators for ideal kinesthetic coupling-Formulation and experiment. IEEE Transactions on Robotics and Automation. 10(5), 605-620.

[8] Garsia-Valdovinos, L. G., Parra-Vega, V. and Artega, M. A. (2007). Observer-based sliding mode impedance control of bilateral teleoperation under constant unknown time delay [J]. Robotics and Autonomous Systems. 55, 609-617.

[9] Cho, H. C. and Park, J. H. (2005). Stable bilateral teleoperation under a time delay using a robust impedance control. Mechatronics. 15, 611-625.

[10] Zhu, W. H. and Salcudean, S. E. (2000). Stability guaranteed teleoperation: An adaptive motion/force control approach. IEEE Transactions on Automatic Control. 45(11), 1951-1969.

[11] Lee, D. and Spong, M. W. (2006). Passive bilateral teleoperation with constant time-delay. IEEE Transactions on Robotics. 22(2), 269-281.

[12] Slama, T., Aubry, P., Vieyres, P. and F. Kratz. (2005).Delayed generalized predictive control of bilateral teleoperation systems. 6th IFAC World Congress, Prague.

[13] Arcara, P. and Melchiorri, C. (2002). Control schemes for teleoperation with time delay: a comparative study. Robotics and Autonomous Systems. 38, 49-64.

[14] Buttolo, P., Braathen, P. and Hannaford, B. (1994). Sliding control of force reflecting teleoperation: preliminary studies. Presence. 3(2), 158-172.

[15] Anderson, R. and Spong, M. W. (1989). Bilateral control of teleoperators with time delay. IEEE Transactions Robotics and Automation. 34(4). 494-501.

[16] Park, J. H. and Cho, H. C. (1999). Sliding-mode controller for bilateral teleoperation with varying time delay. IEEE Conference on Advanced Intelligent and Mechtronics. 311-316.

[17] García-Valdovinos, L. G., Parra-Vega, V. and Artega, M. A. (2007). Observer-based sliding mode impedance control of bilateral teleoperation under constant unknown time delay. Robotics and Autonomous Systems. 55(8), 609-617.

[18] Namerikawa, T. and Kawada, H. (2006). Symmetric impedance matched teleoperation with position tracking. IEEE Conference on Decision and Control. 4496-4501.

[19] Liu, X., Wilson, W. J. and Fan, X. (2005). Pose reflecting teleoperation using wave variables with

wave prediction. IEEE International Conference on Mechatronic and Automation. 1642-1647.

[20] Azorín, J. M., Reinoso, O., Aracil, R. and Ferre, M. (2004). Control of teleoperators with communication time delay through state convergence. Robotic Systems. 21,167-182.

[21] Ueda, J. and Yoshikawa, T. (2004). Force-reflecting bilateral teleoperation with time delay by signal filtering. IEEE Transactions on Robotics and Automation. 20(3), 613-619.

[22] Eusebi, A. and Melchiorri, C. (1998). Force reflecting telemanipulators with time-delay: stability analysis and control design. IEEE Transactions on Robotics and Automation. 14(4), 635-640.

[23] Oboe, R. and Fiorini, P. (1998). A design and control environment for internet-based telerobotics. Robotic research. 17(4), 433-449.

[24] Hashtrudi-Zaad, K. and Salcudean, S. E. (2002). Transparency in time-delayed systems and the effect of local force feedback for transparent teleoperation. IEEE Trans. Robotics Automation. 18(1), 101-114.

[25] Alfi, A. and Farrokhi, M. (2008). A simple structure for bilateral transparent teleoperation systems with time delay. Dynamic Systems, Measurement, and Control. 130(4), 1-9.

[26] Alfi, A. and Farrokhi, M. (2008). Force reflecting bilateral control of master-slave systems in teleoperation. Intelligent and Robotic systems. 52(2), 209-232.

[27] Gu, K., Kharitonov, V. L. and Chen, J. (2003). Stability of time-delay systems. Springer, Birkhusera.

[28] ShaSadeghi, M., Momeni, H. R. and Amirifar, R. (2008). H_∞ and L_1 control of a teleoperation system via LMIs. Applied Mathematics and Computation. 206, 669-677.

[29] Hua, C. C. and Liu, P. X. (2009). Convergence analysis of teleoperation systems with unsymmetric time-varying delays. IEEE Transactions Circuits System.-II: Express Briefs. 56(33), 240-243.

[30] Xu, B. and Liu, Y. H. (2009). Delay-dependent/delay-independent stability of linear systems with multiple time-varying delays. IEEE Transactions on Automatic Control. 48(4), 697-701.

[31] Filipiak. J. (1988). Modelling and control of dynamic flows in communication networks. Berlin: Springer.

[32] Goktas, F., Smith, J. M. and Bajcsy, R. (1996). μ-Synthesis For Distributed Control Systems with Network-Induced Delays. 35th Conference on Decision and Control. 813-814.

[33] Scherer, C., Gahinet, P. and Chilali, M. (1997). Multiobjective output-feedback control via LMI optimization. IEEE Transactions on Automatic Control. 42(7), 896-911.

[34] Hokayem, P. F. and Spong, M. W. (2006). Bilateral teleoperation: an historical survey. Automatica. 42,2035-2055.

20

Using the modified shuffled frog leaping algorithm for optimal sizing and location of distributed generation resources for reliability improvement

M. Heidari, M. Banejad[*], A. Hajizadeh

Shahrood University of Technology, Shahrood, Iran

Corresponding author: m.banejad@gmail.com (M. Banejad)

Abstract

Restructuring the recent developments in the power system and problems arising from construction as well as the maintenance of large power plants lead to increase in using the Distributed Generation (DG) resources. DG units due to its specifications, technology and location network connectivity can improve system and load point reliability indices. In this paper, the allocation and sizing of distributed generators in distribution electricity networks are determined through using an optimization method. The objective function of the proposed method is based on improving the reliability indices, such as a System Average Interruption Duration Index (SAIDI), and Average Energy Not Supplied (AENS) per customer index at the lowest cost. The optimization is based on the Modified Shuffled Frog Leaping Algorithm (MSFLA) aiming at determining the optimal DG allocation and sizing in the distribution network. The MSFLA is a new mimetic meta-heuristic algorithm with efficient mathematical function and global search capability. To evaluate the proposed algorithm, the 34-bus IEEE test system is used. In addition, the finding of comparative studies indicates the better capability of the proposed method compared with the genetic algorithm in finding the optimal sizing and location of DG's with respect to the used objective function.

Keywords: *Distributed Generation, Reliability, Optimization, Modified Shuffled Frog Leaping Algorithm, Optimization.*

1. Introduction

Due to restructuring and competition in power systems and changes in management and ownership of electricity industry, the role of DGs is expected to increase in future. Also, some factors, such as environmental pollution, problems due to establishment of new transmission lines, increase the use of these DGs. Although, the use of DGs in the distribution electricity networks can lead to have lower loss, higher reliability, etc, it can also apply a high capital cost to the system. This demonstrates the importance of finding the optimal size and placement of DGs. In the recent years, several studies have been carried out to locate optimally the DG units on distribution systems [1]-[9]. The improvement of system characteristics is the focus of most papers and is the main objective of DG placement. Virtually most of the DGs related papers have studied loss minimization and voltage profile improvement

[2], [9] and a few papers have investigated the role DGs for improving the reliability [1, 10] In [1], Wang and Sing applied Ant Colony algorithm to determine the optimal DG allocation and they study the impact of DG placement on the reliability indices. In [2], Wang and Nehrir presented analytical approaches for determining optimal location of DG to minimize the power losses. Celli et al in [3] proposed a multi-objective formulation for the DG placement in distribution feeders for minimization the objective programming and decision theory to find the best plan for distribution system with DG. Hedayati et al in [5] presented a method for optimal DG placement in order to reduce the power losses and improve voltage profile. Their method was based on the analysis of power flow continuation and determination of most sensitive buses to voltage collapse. In [6], Borges and Falcao proposed a

method for optimal DG placement for minimizing the network l and guaranteeing acceptable reliability level and voltage profile. Haghifam et al in [7] presented a method to locate DG units in the distribution networks in an uncertain environment for minimizing monetary cost index, technical risks (including risks of voltage and loading constraints) and an economic risk. They employed fuzzy numbers to model uncertain environment. In [8], Hyoung Lee et al apply Kalman filter algorithm to find an optimal placement of DG in order to minimize the losses of network. Popovic et al in [9] used a sensitivity analysis for DG placement in the network with respect to security constraints.

From the reliability aspect, considering load shedding results in more realistic optimization method. As an example, in [18], it is assumed that if the total DGs rating in an island are less than the total loads located in that island, then no loads can be served and all those loads are shed untill the feeder under fault is repaired.

Because allocation and sizing of distributed generation units have a discrete natures of the…??, it encounters a number of local minima. To overcome this issue, a reliable optimization algorithm should be used. The optimization approaches are mostly divided into analytical and heuristic approaches. In the non-smooth functions, the heuristic methods have higher accuracy compared with the analytical approaches. In the analytical methods, the optimization may be trapped in a local minimum [12]. In the literature, several optimization techniques have been applied to the DG placement issue, such as Ant Colony algorithm [1], genetic algorithm [3], [6], [7], [9], Kalman Filter Algorithm [8] and analytical based methods [2, 4, 5].

The SFLA in this paper is used to achieve an optimal response. To accelerate the algorithm convergence and to prevent the algorithm from converging it to a wrong answer, a new parameter is added to the original formulation to create a Modified Shuffled Frog-Leaping (MSFL) algorithm [26].

This paper focuses on the following sections. The effect of DG on system reliability and reliability assessment is introduced in the next section. In section III, formulation of problem is presented and a composite reliability index is also defined. In section IV, the proposed method for optimal DG placement by shuffled frog leaping algorithm is detailed. Simulation results and conclusion are discussed in sections V and VI, respectively.

2. Distribution system reliability assessment

Reliability evaluation of distribution electricity network has received a great attention of many researchers and the numerous papers have published in this case. However, evaluation methods distribution electricity network need more development [10], [11]. In this paper, the failure impact of each element on load points is considered as well as the average failure rate of the element. Then, the interruption frequency and duration at each load point are calculated to eventually compute the system reliability indices. The important issue focuses on the effect of network structure, switches, supply ability of loads from the main source of power or other resources. Islanding of DGs should be modeled suitably in each error simulation. More explanation is about a distribution system is provided in Figure 1 that is supplied by DG units. For example, if in this figure a fault occurs in first section (ab), with no DG connected to feeder, all load points service must be interrupted during repair operation, but with DG connected (bus c), some load points, due to DG capacity can be restored via DG source. So, DGs can decrease the duration of outage and as a result, system reliability is increased.

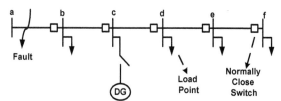

Figure 1. A radial feeder with one DG

The DG has a positive effect on distribution system on blackouts of the supply [11], [13].

In this paper, the difference between reliability of distribution system with and without DG in failure rate and outage time index is calculated. The distributed generation is represented by four-state Markov process as depicted in Figure 2, where λ and μ respectively, are bus/DG failure and repair rates.

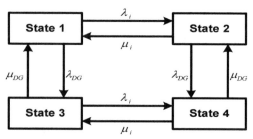

Figure 2. A four state representation for typical distribution system with one DG.

Direction shown in Figure 1 shows the transition between modes. DG and busi is in normal condition.

In the first state, DG and busi are in the normal condition. In the second state, error occurred in the system and bus connection is interrupted The DG interrupted in the third state, but the bus is not connected yet. In fourth state, DG and transmission has been interrupted and bus is isolated. For our four-state system, matrix P is given by:

$$P = \begin{bmatrix} 1-(\lambda_i + \lambda_{DG}) & \lambda_i & \lambda_{DG} & 0 \\ \mu_i & 1-(\mu_i + \lambda_{DG}) & 0 & \lambda_{DG} \\ \mu_{DG} & 0 & 1-(\lambda_i + \mu_{DG}) & \lambda_i \\ 0 & \mu_{DG} & \mu_i & 1-(\mu_i + \mu_{DG}) \end{bmatrix} \quad (1)$$

The matrix P is known as the stochastic transitional matrix [14], [15]. It represents the transitional probabilities between states for one step of the Markov chain. The limiting probabilities pi corresponding to each state can be evaluated from (2) and (3).

$$p_i = \begin{bmatrix} \dfrac{\mu_i \mu_{DG}}{L} & \dfrac{\lambda_i \mu_{DG}}{L} & \dfrac{\mu_i \lambda_{DG}}{L} & \dfrac{\lambda_i \lambda_{DG}}{L} \end{bmatrix} \quad (2)$$

$$L = (\lambda_i + \mu_i)(\lambda_{DG} + \mu_{DG}) \quad (3)$$

Finally, bus failure rate and repair rate, connected to DG can be evaluated from (4) and (5).

$$\lambda_i^{bus} = \frac{p_2 \lambda_{DG} + p_3 \lambda_i}{p_1 + p_2 + p_3} \quad (4)$$

$$U_i^{bus} = p_4 \quad (5)$$

3.Problem formulation

The objective of DGs placement in a radial feeder is to maximize the distribution network reliability under certain constraints at the lowest cost. The standard reliability indices are used in this paper [16]: System Average Interruption Duration Index (SAIDI), System Average Interruption Frequency Index (SAIFI) and Average Energy Not Supplied per customer index (AENS). They are defined as follows:

$$SAIFI = \frac{\sum_i \lambda_i . N_i}{\sum_i N_i} \quad (6)$$

Where N_i is the number of customers of load point i and λ_i is the failure rate.

$$SAIDI = \frac{\sum u_i N_i}{\sum N_i} \quad (7)$$

where u_i is the outage time.

$$AENS = \frac{\sum L_{a(i)} u_i}{\sum N_i} \quad (8)$$

where $L_{a(i)}$ is the average load connected to load point i.

For the purpose of optimization, the proposed objective function is expressed in Equation (9), which includes composite reliability indices and DG cost through the weighted aggregation of these indices.

$$OBF = w_{SAIFI} . \frac{SAIFI}{SAIFI_T} + w_{SAIDI} . \frac{SAIDI}{SAIDI_T} + w_{AENS} . \frac{AENS}{AENS_T} + w_{C_{DG}} . \frac{C_{DG}}{C_{DGT}} \quad (9)$$

where the weighting coefficients represent the relative importance of the objectives and the subscript T indicates the target value.

These reliability indices are the most widely used indices to perform the reliability assessment in the distribution network. In this formulation, we incorporate the desired values and these reliability indices are empirically justified [10].

The DG cost is formulated as:

$$C_{DG} = C_{Install} + \left(\sum_{t=1}^{T_{yr}} C_{O\&M} \frac{(1+IF)^t}{(1+IR)^t} \right) \quad (10)$$

where C_{INSTAL} is the total installation cost for DGs, $C_{O\&M}$ is the total operation and maintenance cost for DGs, IR is the interest rate, IF is the Inflation rate and T_{yr} is the number of years in the study timeframe.

4.Implementation of SFLA

The SFLA originally developed as a population-based meta-heuristic by M. Eusuff and K. Lansey in 2003 performed an informed heuristic search using any mathematical function to find a solution of optimization problem [22]. It combines the benefits of both the genetic-based memetic algorithm and the social behaviour-based PSO algorithm [23].

This algorithm has been inspired by the frog's life as a group when the frogs are in search of food. A shuffling strategy allows for the exchange of information between local groups to move toward a global optimum point [24]. The description and comments of algorithm implementation are presented as follows.

Step 1: Coding

Each possible size and location for DG placement needs to be integrated into each population. In this method, eight bits encode each solution. From the first to fourth bits indicate the locations for DG placement. The rest of the bits show the capacity of the installed unit.

The bits and their corresponding information for one candidate location are shown in Figure 3.

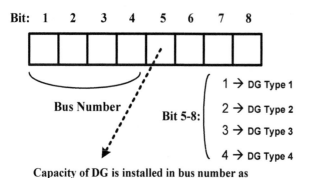

Capacity of DG is installed in bus number as shown in first bit

Figure 3. Bit information for each candidate location of DG.

Step 2: Initializing the population and partition frogs into memeplexes

An initial population of P frogs in the marsh is created randomly. Then, the frogs are arranged in a descending order according to their fitness. Then, the P frogs are partitioned into m memeplexes, each containing n frogs ($P = m \times n$). In this procedure, the first frog moves to the first memeplex, the second frog moves to the second memeplex and the mth frog moves to the mth memeplex, then $(m + 1)$th frog goes back to the first memeplex and so on.

Step 3: Local exploration

In each memeplex, the frogs with the best and the worst fitness are determined and named as X_b and X_w, respectively. Also, the position of frog with the global best fitness among the memeplexes is identified as X_g. Then, in each memeplex, the frogs with the worst fitness (not all frogs) apply a process (move toward to X_w) to improve their memes.

Regarding the selection of the X_w, it is not always desirable to use the best frog, because the frog's tendency would be to concentrate around the frog, which may be local optimum. So, to avoid trapping in local optima, a submemeplex is constructed in each memeplex, which consists of frogs chosen on the basis of their corresponding fitness. Probabilistic roulette wheel is used to select submemeplex in each memeplex. This

selection strategy is to give higher weights to frogs that have higher fitness values and to give less weight to those with lower fitness values.

A triangular probability distribution is used to assign this weight:

$$P_k = \frac{2(n+1-k)}{n(n+1)} \quad k = 1,\dots,n \qquad (11)$$

where P_k is the probability of the k_{th} frog being selected to form a submemeplex, and n is the number of frogs in a memeplex. In each memeplex, the frog with the best performance has the highest probability $p_1 = 2/(n + 1)$ and the frog with the worst performance has the lowest probability $p_n = 2/n (n + 1)$ of being selected for the submemeplex [25].

The best global frog's position is represented by X_{sg}. The best and the worst frog's position are represented by X_{sb} and X_{sw} respectively in each submemeplex. The worst frog's position in the submemeplex is updated as follows (as shown in Figure 4):

$$D_i = round\left(rand \times \left(X_{sb} - X_{sw}\right)\right) \qquad (12)$$

$$X_w(new) = X_w(old) + D_i \qquad (-D_{max} \le D_i \le D_{max}) \qquad (13)$$

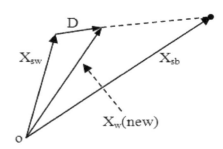

Figure 4. The original of the frog leaping rule.

Where D_{max} is the maximum allowed change in position of frog in each leaping and rand is a random number between 0 and 1. If this process produces a better solution, X_w (new) replaces the worst frog's position (X_w (old)). Otherwise, the calculations in Equations (12) and (13) are repeated with replacement of X_{sb} by X_{sg}. If no improvement is achieved in this case, then a new solution is randomly generated to replace the worst frog (X_{sw}). These calculations continue in a memeplex for a specific number of iterations [23].

Step 4: Check convergence criteria

If the defined convergence criteria are satisfied or the output does not change for a specific number of iterations, the program will be terminated and the results will be printed, and the rest of the program goes to Step 3.

4.1. Modified Shuffled Frog Leaping Algorithm (MSFLA):

As explained in the previous section, in each submemeplex, the worst frog corrects its position towards the best frog's position or the global best position in the same submemeplex. But according to Equations (12) and (13) and Figure 4, the possible new position of the worst frog is limited in the line segment between its current position ($X_{sw}(old)$) and the best frog's position (X_{sb}). Also, the worst frog will never jump around this line or over the best one (see Figure 5). This limitation leads to slow down the speed of optimization convergence. This leads to the issue that the algorithm converges to the wrong answers. In order to solve this limitation, the use of new equations are employed instead of using the Equations (12) and (13) as explained in [26]:

$$D_i = round\ (rand \times C\ (X_b - X_w) + W) \qquad (14)$$

$$W = \left[r_1 w_{1,max}, r_2 w_{2,max}, ..., r_{NF} w_{NF,max} \right]^T \qquad (15)$$

$$X_w\ (new) = \begin{cases} X_w + D & \text{if } |D| \le D_{max} \\ X_w + \dfrac{D}{\sqrt{D^T D}} D & \text{if } |D| \ge D_{max} \end{cases} \qquad (16)$$

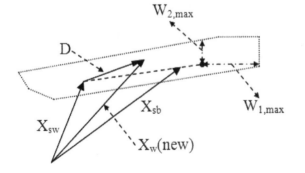

Figure 5. The modification of the frog leaping rule.

Where rand is a random number between 0 and 1, C is a constant chosen in the range between 1 and 2, r_i are random numbers between -1 and 1, $w_{i,\ max}$ are the maximum range that frog sees in the i_{th} dimension of the search space and D_{max} is the maximum allowed change in position of frog in each leaping.

5. Simulations Results

To validate the proposed method, the 34-bus IEEE test system, as shown in Figure 6, is studied. The system is modeled with all of its detailed parameters using MATLAB2009b software. The

system is divided into four zones for reduce number of customer that are affected blackouts.

The reliability index weights are chosen as follows:
WSAIFI = 0.30, WSAIDI = 0.30, WAENS = 0.33 and WPDG = 0.07. The target values of the reliability indices are set as follows: SAIFIT = 10, SAIDIT = 100, AENST = 300 and CDGT = 10000000. They are empirically selected and show the reasonably level of reliability [10]. The interest rate (r), the Inflation rate and the number of years in the study timeframe (Tyr) are chosen 0.1, 0.18 and 20 respectively [7]. The specifications lines and loads of the test system are shown in Table 3, 4 [13], [17].

The MSFLA parameters that are used to tune the performance of the MSFLA allocation, as follows:
Population size: 100 individuals
Number of memeplexe: 20
Number of submemeplex for each memeplex: 3
The variable c: 1.8
The variable wi, max: [0.1 0.1 0.1 0.1 0.1 0.1 0.1 0.1]
The variable Dmax: 10

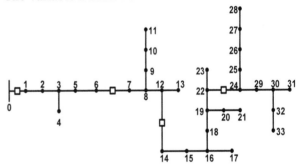

Figure 6. Test system

The DG types available for the tests and the corresponding investment, maintenance, operating cost are shown in Table 1. The cost of DG unit, DG site, construction and survey fees, diagnostic and protection equipment, and fuel delivery equipment are included in the investment cost. The maintenance costs are annual mechanical and electrical inspection and recondition cost. The operating cost includes labor cost for service, taxes and fuel cost. Those cost related data is mainly based on the book of Willis and Scott [19], [20].

Table 2 shows the main system reliability indices prior to DG installation and the reliability indices considering the DG placement are obtained by the method. Three places after the implementation of MSFLA for distributed generation units are proposed (The bus 18, 25 and 28, respectively with capacities of 700, 500 and 1000 kW). It can be observed that the system average interruption duration and system average interruption frequency and energy not supply indices improve the DG installation. Figure 7 shows the convergence process of the MSFLA when used to optimize DGs placement in 34-bus IEEE test system.

Table 1. The cost for dg types

Type	DG Specification	Investment cost ($)	Maintenance cost ($/yr)	Operating cost ($/yr)
1	300 kW mini Gas turbine	182000	11630	78000
2	500 kW mini Gas turbine	330000	21140	142000
3	700 kW mini Gas turbine	410000	27310	178000
4	1000 kW mini Gas turbine	550000	32240	237000

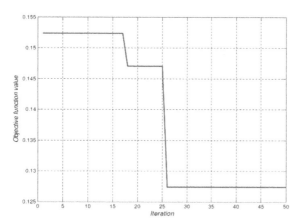

Figure .7. Convergence curves for the objective function with MSFLA

Next, we compare the MSFLA with the GA algorithm. The convergence process and the reliability indices are obtained by GA method shown in Table 2 and Figure 8, respectively. This method purposes four places for distributed generation units. The buses are 16, 19, 25 and 28, with capacities of 700, 500,300, 1000 kW, respectively.

Table 2. Comparison of outputs before and after installation of dgs

		SAIFI	SAIDI	AENS	C_{DG} (M$)	C_{INT} (M$)
Without DGs		8.7	92.4	461.4	-------	361.39
With DGs	GA	1.31	9.91	49.57	9.0166	38.792
	MSFLA	1.36	8.65	43.27	7.9049	33.838

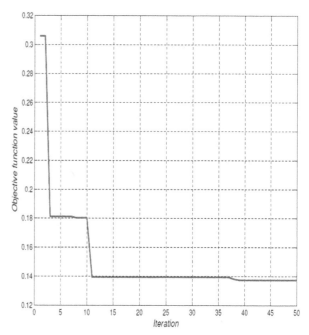

Figure 8. Convergence curves for the objective function with Genetic Algorithm.

The last element in Table 2 can be identified with SAIDI, which is the average interruption duration per year per customer. The interruption cost is obtained by using Equations (12) [12].

$$C_{\text{INTERRUPTION}} = (\sum_{t=1}^{20} NC \times SAIDI \times CI \times \frac{(1+IF)^t \times (1+IG)^t}{(1+IR)^t}) \quad (12)$$

where NC is the number of customers, CI is the cost of interruption per hour for a customer and IG is the Load Growth rate.

The number of customers is 354 in the test system, the cost per 1 minute interruption is assumed 7$ and load growth rate is chosen 0.1 [21]. As observed in Table 2, after installation of DGs, interruption cost decreases. The proposed method is based on MSFLA, and total cost decreases from M$ 361.39 to M$ 33.838. This difference, M$ 327.552, is much more than the total cost of DGs, M$ 7.9049.

As shown in Figure 7, Figure 8 and Table 2, objective function value for the proposed MSFLA method is less than the GA method. It means that better locations are found for achieving higher system reliability through the proposed MSFLA. The proposed method is based on MSFLA will converge in the 26th generation, whereas the method based on GA in 37th is converged. The difference and potential advantage of the MSFLA over genetic algorithms is that information is spread among all individuals in the population, whereas in a GA only parent or their siblings are allowed to interaction. Therefore, Modified

Shuffled Frog Leaping Algorithm in convergence speed and computation time and memory use is superior to the Genetic Algorithm.

Table 3. Loads specification of the test system

BUS No.	No. Customers	Q KVAR	P KW	BUS No.	No. Customers	Q KVAR	P KW
1	0	0	0	18	1	2	4
2	0	0	0	19	0	0	0
3	11	29	55	20	0	0	0
4	0	0	0	21	0	0	0
5	3	8	16	22	90	225	450
6	0	0	0	23	3	7	15
7	0	0	0	24	1	1	2
8	0	0	0	25	6	7	23
9	0	0	0	26	0	0	0
10	0	0	0	27	83	20	414
11	7	17	34	28	9	23	45
12	27	70	135	29	17	393	83
13	1	2	5	30	41	121	206
14	8	20	40	31	16	43	82
15	1	2	4	32	13	41	67
16	10	23	52	33	0	0	0
17	0	0	0	34	6	14	28

Table 4. Loads specification of the test system

Line No.	From Bus	To Bus	λ(f/yr)	Line No.	m Bus	To Bus	λ(f/yr)
1	34	1	0.983	18	16	18	14.035
2	1	2	0.65	19	18	19	0.04
3	2	3	12.282	20	19	20	1.98
4	3	4	2.212	21	20	21	4.024
5	3	5	14.291	22	19	22	1.867
6	5	6	11.33	23	22	23	0.617
7	6	7	0.04	24	22	24	2.221
8	7	8	0.118	25	24	25	0.107
9	8	9	0.651	26	25	26	0.512
10	9	10	18.349	27	26	27	1.387
11	10	11	5.236	28	27	28	0.202
12	8	12	3.891	29	24	29	0.77
13	12	13	1.154	30	29	30	1.021
14	12	14	0.32	31	30	31	0.328
15	14	15	7.789	32	30	32	0.106
16	15	16	0.198	33	32	33	1.85
17	16	17	8.891				

6. Conclusion

In this paper, a new objective function is introduced for the placement and sizing of DGs optimally with respect to the reliability indices improvement. To evaluate the proposed algorithm, the 34-bus IEEE test system, is used. The results are finally compared with the no DG condition and it shows that reliability indices especially ENS has improved remarkably with optimal placement of distributed generation. The test results show that this proposed method is capable to improve service reliability, reduces the customer outage costs and decreases the power cost. In addition, the result demonstrated the better characteristics of the MSFLA in comparison with the GA especially in terms of solution quality and number of iterations.

References

[1] Wang, L. and Singh, C. (2008). Reliability-Constrained Optimum Placement of Reclosers and Distributed Generators in Distribution Networks Using an Ant Colony System Algorithm. IEEE Transactions on Systems, Man, and Cybernetics-Part C: Applications and Reviews. 38(6), 757-764.

[2] Wang, C. and Nehrir, M. H. (2004). Analytical Approaches for Optimal Placement of Distributed Generation Sources in Power Systems. IEEE Transactions on Power Systems. 19(4), 2068-2076.

[3] Celli, G., Ghiani, E., Mocci, S. and Pilo, F. (2005). A Multi Objective Evolutionary Algorithm for the Sizing and Sitting of the Distributed Generation. IEEE Transactions on Power Systems. 20(2), 750-757.

[4] Carpinelli, G., Celli, G., Mocci, S., Pilo, F., and Russo, A. (2005). Optimisation of Embedded Generation Sizing and Sitting by Using a Double Trade-Off Method. IEE Proceedings of Generation, Transmission and Distribution. 152(4), 503-513.

[5] Hedayati, H., Nabaviniaki, S. A. and kbarimajd, A. (2008). A Method for Placement of DG Units in Distribution Networks. IEEE Transactions on Power Delivery. 23(3), 1620-1628.

[6] Borges, C. L. T. and Falcao, D. M. (2006). Optimal distributed generation allocation for reliability, losses, and voltage improvement. International Journal of Power and Energy Systems. 28(6), 413-420.

[7] Haghifam, M. R., Falaghi, H. and Malik, O. P. (2008). Risk-Based Distributed Generation Placement, IET Generation, Transmission and Distribution. 2(2), 252-260.

[8] Lee, S. H. and Park, J. W. (2009). Selection of Optimal Location and Size of Multiple Distributed Generators by Using Kalman Filter Algorithm. IEEE Transactions on Power Systems. 24(3), 1393-1400.

[9] Popovic, D. H. Greatbanks, J. A., Begovic, M. and Pregelj, A. (2005). Placement of distributed generators and reclosers for distribution network security and reliability. International Journal of Power and Energy Systems. 27(5-6), 398-408.

[10] Li, W., Wang, P., Li, Z. and Liu, Y. (2004). Reliability Evaluation of Complex Radial Distribution Systems Considering Restoration Sequence and Network Constraints. IEEE Transaction on Power Delivery. 19(2), 753-758.

[11] Falaghi, H. and Haghifam, M. R. (2005). Distributed Generation Impacts on Electric Distribution Systems Reliability: Sensitivity Analysis. EUROCON.

[12] Ziari, I., Ledwich, G., Ghosh, A., Cornforth, D. and Wishart, M. (2010). Optimal Allocation and Sizing of DGs in Distribution Networks, PES General Meeting, USA.

[13] Daly, P. A. andMorrison, J. (2001). Understanding the Potential Benefits of Distributed Generation on Power Delivery Systems.IEEE Rural Electric Power Conference, Arkansas.1 -13. [14] Billinton, R. and Allan, R. N. (1992). Reliability Evaluation of Engineering Systems, 2nd Edition (Pelenum Press).

[15] Wand, P. and Billinton, R. (2001). Time sequential simulation technique for rural distribution system reliability cost/worth evaluation including wind generation as alternative supply. IEEE proc.Genr.Transm.Distrib.148(4), 355- 360.

[16] Brown, R. E. (2002). Electric Power Distribution Reliability (CRC Press).

[17] Kersting, W. H. and Las Cruces, N. M. (1991). Radial Distribution Test Feeders. IEEE Trans. On Power Systems. (Vol.6, n. 3).

[18] Borges, C. L. T. and Falcao, D. M. (2006). Optimal Distributed Generation Allocation for Reliability, Losses and Voltage Improvement. International Journal of Electrical Power and Energy Systems. 28(6), 413-420.

[19] Willis, H. L. and Scott, W. G. (2000). Distributed power generation-planning and evaluation. (Marcel Dekker Inc, 2000).

[20] Teng, J. H., Liu, Y. H., Chen, C.-Y. and Chen, C. F. (2007). Value-based distributed generator placements for service quality improvements. Electrical Power and Energy Systems. 29, 268–274.

[22] Amiri, B., Fathian, M. and Maroosi, A. (2009). Application of shuffled frog leaping algorithm on clustering. Int. J. Adv. Manuf. Technol. 45, 199–209.

[23] Elbeltagi, E., Hegazy, T. and D. Grierson. (2005). Comparison among five evolutionary-based optimization algorithms. Adv. Eng. Inf. 19,(1), 43–53.

[24] Vakil Baghmisheh, M.T., Madani, K. and Navarbaf, A. (2011). A discrete shuffled frog optimization algorithm,Springer Science.

[25] Eusuff, M., Lansey, K. and Pasha, F. (2006). Shuffled frog-leaping algorithm: a memetic meta-heuristic for discrete optimization. Engineering Optimization. 38, 129–154.

[26] Huynh, T. H. (2008). A modified shuffled frog leaping algorithm for optimal tuning of multivariable PID controllers, In: IEEE International Conference on Industrial Technology, Chengdu. 1-6.

21

QoS-Based web service composition based on genetic algorithm

M. AllamehAmiri, V. Derhami, M. Ghasemzadeh*

Department of Electrical and Computer Engineering, Yazd University, Yazd, Iran.

Corresponding author: m.ghasemzadeh@yazd.ac.ir (M. Ghasemzadeh)

Abstract

Quality of service (QoS) is an important issue in the design and management of web service composition. QoS in web services consists of various non-functional factors, such as execution cost, execution time, availability, successful execution rate, and security. In recent years, the number of available web services has proliferated, and then offered the same services increasingly. The same web services are distinguished based on their quality parameters. Also, clients usually demand more value added services rather than those offered by single, isolated web services. Therefore, selecting a composition plan of web services among numerous plans satisfies client requirements and has become a challenging and time-consuming problem. This paper has proposed a new composition plan optimizer with constraints based on genetic algorithm. The proposed method can find the composition plan that satisfies user constraints efficiently. The performance of the method is evaluated in a simulated environment.

Keywords: *Web Service, Web Service Composition, Quality of Service, QoS, Genetic Algorithm.*

1. Introduction

According to W3C definition "a web service is a software system designed to support interoperable machine-to-machine interaction over a network". It is an XML based, self-described software entity which can be published, located, and used across the internet using a set of standards, such as Simple Object Access Protocol (SOAP), Web Service Description Language (WSDL), and Universal Description, Discover and Integration (UDDI) [1]. Since web services can enable computer-computer communication in a heterogeneous environment, hence they are very suitable for an environment such as the internet. People can use the standardized web service model for rapid design, implement and extended applications. Many enterprises and corporations provide different web services to be more responsive and cost-effective. Google's SOAP

Search API for information inquiry [2] and Amazon web services for doing enormous e-commerce activities [3] are good examples of such systems. A number of standards and protocols have been designed to use and publish web services over the internet. Some of the most commonly used standards are UDDI, SOAP and WSDL. Universal Description Discovery and Integration (UDDI) is an XML-based registry that provides a standard set of specifications for service description and discovery. It defines the information model, the service providers API for registering and publishing services and the API for service requesters to inquire for services. Web service provider registers their web services into UDDI registries. Simple Object Access Protocol (SOAP) is an XML based protocol specification for exchanging information between peers in the decentralized, distributed environment. SOAP provides a simple and lightweight mechanism to communicate with web services. SOAP can form the foundation layer of a web services protocol stack. Web Service Description Language (WSDL) is used to describe the interfaces of all web services regardless of the underlying technology. The WSDL is defined: Services as collections of network endpoints, or ports. When service provider wants to register a web service to UDDI server (web service directory), it describes web service by WSDL and puts it in UDDI registry. As service requester looks for a web service in UDDI server, s/he receives the WSDL file of web services Figure 1 shows the IBM standard architecture of web services. This architecture provides a three level procedure to find an appropriate web service. First, service provider describes its web services in WSDL Format and puts them in a web service directory (registering web service). Then, service requester searches into web service directory to find a suitable web service. Finally, after selecting the web service, service requester can interact with the web service using SOAP protocol. There are some sophisticated applications that cannot be performed using a single, isolated web service. Consequently we need to use a composition of web services to perform complex tasks. An Example of synthesizing web services is a travel planning web service. When the client uses web

service based system to plan a trip, the following steps will be taken into consideration in the service process.

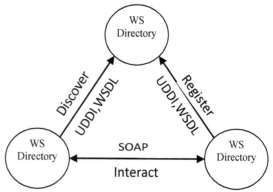

Figure 1. Standard architecture of web services.

At first, the client contacts a travel agency web service to reserve a hotel room and an airplane seat. Then the client selects the best reservation plan among the plans suggested to him/her by considering factors like schedule, financial condition, weather conditions and some other factors. In addition, the client may request services, such as a car rental agency or insurance. After all web services are selected, the client pays the reservation fee to the travel agency. Figure 2 provides an example of travel agency candidate web services and Figure 3 represents all composition plans of the candidate web services.

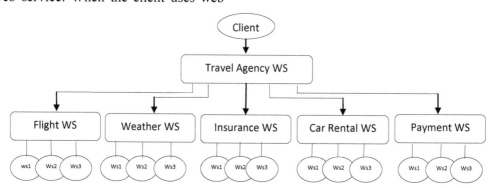

Figure 2. An example of travel Agency web service and candidate web services for each task.

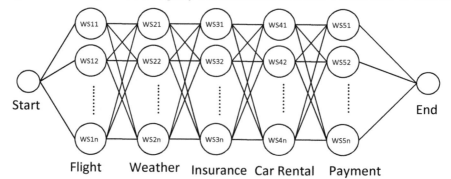

Figure 3. All composition plans for travel agency example.

Web service composition creates new functionalities by aggregating different services based on a specific workflow [4]. When there are more than one candidate web services for a task or process, there will be various combinations of web services having the same functionality with different qualities. For instance, if there are m tasks and n candidate web services, the number of all possible plans is n^m. In general, finding a composition plan that fulfils a client's QoS requirement is a time-consuming optimization problem. Combining web services of high QoS values in a reasonable computation time has been recognized as an important problem of web service composition [6]. We need to find a composition plan satisfying client's constraints without checking all combinations. This will be impractical even if there are a few services and tasks in the workflow. Typical QoS factors associated with a web service are executive cost and time, availability, successful execution rate, reputation, and usage frequency [5]. Also, there are other properties other than the above-mentioned factors, such as reliability, security and so on. To obtain a composition plan, we should first create a QoS model to describe the QoS aspects of web services. To create an appropriate model, service requester and service provider should agree on same definitions to the extent possible. After creating a QoS model, the second step is QoS based on web service discovery and selection. Unfortunately, WSDL only addresses functional aspects of a web service and does not contain any useful description for non-functional requirements [14]. Using the QoS model, service requester can filter inappropriate web services. A number of studies on web service selection have been carried out [7, 8]. One of the most well known techniques is "matchmaking" that is employed in situations where services with semantic descriptions for their functional attributes are available on the Internet search system [7]. It should be noted that the process of filtering web services consists of functional matchmaking and non-functional matchmaking. In functional matchmaking, web services that have different functionalities from the client are filtered out and on the other hand, in non-functional matchmaking, web services that don't have the appropriate quality are eliminated. At this stage, the candidate web services for each task are selected. In [8], a new QoS-based service registration and discovery model to explore the feasibility of QoS involving into UDDI registry

information is suggested. In this model, service providers have to send QoS claims to service QoS certifiers, responding to the third party or forum web services, for certification. The service customer is responsible for verifying QoS claims. Finally, if QoS claims pass QoS certifier verification, the QoS information will be registered in the UDDI registry associated with function description. In the last stage, we should obtain the optimized web service composition plan from all available plans. As mentioned above, trying all combinations of web services is time consuming. A problem of web service composition is usually an NP-hard [9]. Several solutions have been suggested so far to solve this problem that one of them such as [10] is based on Leaner programming and some are based on AI (e.g. [6]). Genetic algorithm is effective approach to solve some kind of hard problem [22, 23, 24, 25, 26]. Our approach uses the genetic algorithm [20, 21] to solve this problem. To escape from local optimums, we present some modifications in crossover, mutation and selection approach. The remaining sections of this paper are organized in order. Next section presents related work. The third section describes the QoS model of web service composition. The fourth section proposes our GA based on composition algorithm. The computational results of the algorithm are given in the fifth section and the sixth section includes conclusion and future work.

2. Related work

Web service discovery and QoS based on the web service composition offer interesting applications of constraint satisfaction methods. In [10] a multiple criteria decision making with weighted sum model (to select a service) and integer programming (IP) approaches with branch and bound (to select an optimal solution) have been proposed. In [6] constraint satisfaction based on solution which combine simulated annealing [17, 18, 19] approach with Tabu search [16] has been proposed. The Tabu search is used for generating neighbour plans and simulated annealing heuristic is applied for accepting or rejecting the neighbour plan. In [11] a QoS-based web service composition algorithm that combines local strategy and global strategy has the following features. Initially, the services that have low QoS value are eliminated by local strategy and then the problem has reduced to a multi-dimension multi-choice 0-1 knapsack problem solved by the heuristic method. In [12] a model that expands traditional UDDI to describe the QoS attributes of web services is presented. Also, a service proxy is added to this model by which all service compositions requested by service requester are found, bound and invoked. In [13] an automated web service composition is performed by hierarchical task network and SHOP2 HTN system is developed. This system takes OWL-S service model as input (client requirement) and executes the plan as a system result. High probability of Getting stuck in local optimum is the main problem of these methods. This is because it is unable to work more than one composition plan at the same time. At the same time, the probability in methods such as genetic algorithms and fish swarm algorithms working on several composition plans are less than above-mentioned method.

3. QoS based web service model
3.1. QoS properties description

The most important QoS properties used in this paper are response time, execution cost, availability, reputation and successful execution rate. The response time can be defined in several ways. For example, it can be defined as the time between sending request and receiving respond. This period involves receiving request massage time, queuing time, execution time and receiving response time by requester. Measuring these time sections is very difficult because they depend on network conditions. Alternatively, it can be measured as the time between receiving request by service provider and sending response to service requester. This time includes queuing time and execution time only affected by the web service workload. This value must be continuously updated for each web service because the work load of web service may change during the work time. Execution cost is a fee received by service provider from service requester for each execution. This fee is determined by service provider and may change according to web service provider's financial policy. Availability is the degree that a web service is accessible and ready for immediate use. This value can be defined as [uptime/ (uptime + downtime)]. Downtime includes the time that web service is inaccessible and time taken to repair it. This value should be updated by service provider. Reputation is the average reputation score of a web service evaluated by the clients. The individual reputation scores are likely to be subjective, but the average score becomes trustable as the total number of the usages increases [6]. The successful Execution Rate is the

percentage of requests that a web service perform successfully when web service is available. It is computed by dividing the number of successful performed requests by the total number of requests. The QoS properties used in this paper is summarized in Table 1.

Table 1. Description of QoS peoperties used in this paper

QoS property	Description
Response Time	Time between receiving request and sending response
Execution cost	Execution cost per request
Availability	$\dfrac{UpTime}{UpTime + DownTime}$
Reputation	$\dfrac{\sum Rep_i}{TotalNumber\ Of\ Usage}$
Successful Execution Rate	$\dfrac{Numer\ of\ Successful\ Request}{TotalNumber\ of\ Request}$

Notations

Descriptions of notations used in this paper are as follow:

m: number of tasks.

n: number of candidate web services for each task.

p_i: i-th atomic process of a composition schema ($1 \leq i \leq m$).

ws_{ij}: j-th candidate web service for the ith atomic process, ($1 \leq i \leq m$, $1 \leq j \leq n$).

d: index of QoS property .

w_d: weight of the d-th QoS constraint defined by a client.

Con_d: permissible value of the d-th QoS property (constraints).

Agg_d: aggregated value of the d-th QoS property of a composition plan.

b_{ij}: binary decision variable (0 or 1). If $b_{ij}=1$ then j-th candidate web service is selected for i-th process.

3.2. QoS-based evaluation of web services

Since each QoS property may be measured in various metrics, they should be normalized for appropriate evaluation. The QoS properties are divided into two categories: First, negative values, such as response time and execution cost, and second, positive values, such as availability and reputation. The higher value in negative properties indicates the lower quality and the higher one in positive properties represent higher quality and vice versa. The following equations are used to normalize positive and negative properties, respectively:

$$q_{nrm} = \begin{cases} \dfrac{q - q_{\min}}{q_{\max} - q_{\min}} & q_{\max} - q_{\min} \neq 0 \\ 1 & q_{\max} - q_{\min} = 0 \end{cases} \quad (1)$$

$$q_{nrm} = \begin{cases} \dfrac{q_{\max} - q}{q_{\max} - q_{\min}} & q_{\max} - q_{\min} \neq 0 \\ 1 & q_{\max} - q_{\min} = 0 \end{cases} \quad (2)$$

After normalization, the local value of each web service that is candidate for a task will be computed from the following formula. Where Q is the number of QoS properties.

$$Local\, Value\, of\, ws_{ij} = \sum_{i=0}^{q} w_i q_i \quad (3)$$

3.3. Aggregation value of QoS property

Generally, composition plans are constituted from serial, cycle, XOR-parallel, and AND-parallel execution patterns. According to the definition of QoS properties in section 3.1, the aggregative value of web service composition is calculated regarding to its workflow pattern. The description and aggregation values of workflow patterns are discussed below.

Serial pattern is an execution pattern in which services are executed one after another and there is no overlap between execution periods of web services. Figure 4 illustrates this pattern and Table 2 represents the aggregation value of this pattern. According to Table 3 to calculate aggregation value of response time and execution cost, each web service value should be added to each other. Besides, in order to calculate aggregation value of availability and successful execution rate, web services values should be multiplied by each other because web services are independent from each other. The aggregative value of reputation is obtained by taking average of reputation values of web services.

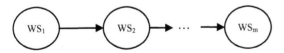

Figure 4. Serial Pattern.

Cycle pattern is a kind of sequential pattern in which the web service executes for limited cycles. According to Table 3, the aggregation values of this pattern are similar to sequential pattern. Figure 5 describes this pattern.

Table 2. Aggregative QoS value for serial pattern

Response Time	$\sum_{i=0}^{m} WS.RT$
Execution Cost	$\sum_{i=0}^{m} WS.EC$
Availability	$\prod_{i=0}^{m} WS.Ava$
Successful Execution rate	$\prod_{i=0}^{m} WS.Suc$
Reputation	$\dfrac{\sum_{i=0}^{m} WS.\mathrm{Re}\,p}{m}$

Figure 5. A cycle pattern.

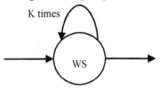

Table 3. Aggrigative QoS value for a cycle pattern

Response Time	$m*(WS.RT)$
Execution Cost	$m*(WS.RT)$
Availability	$WS.Ava$
Successful Execution rate	$WS.Suc$
Reputation	$WS.\mathrm{Re}\,p$

XOR-parallel pattern is an execution pattern in which after the completion of the prior web service, one of the following web services just executes. In this pattern execution of each component is non-deterministic; therefore, to calculate the aggregation QoS effect of this pattern, the worst case should be calculated. We can obtain aggregative QoS values of this pattern as described in Table 4. Figure 6 depicts this pattern.

AND-parallel pattern is an execution pattern in which after the completion of the prior web service, the entire subsequent web services are executed simultaneously. The aggregative QoS values of this pattern are described in Table 5. Notice that to obtain aggregative response time, we use the Max function, because all subsequent components are executed simultaneously. Figure 7 describes this pattern.

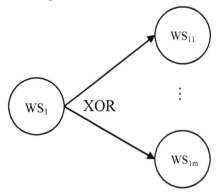

Figure 6. XOR-parallel pattern.

Table 4. Aggregative QoS value for XOR-parallel pattern

Response Time	$Max(WS.RT)$
Execution Cost	$Max(WS.EC)$
Availability	$Min(WS.Ava)$
Successful Execution rate	$Min(WS.Suc)$
Reputation	$Min(WS.\mathrm{Re}\,p)$

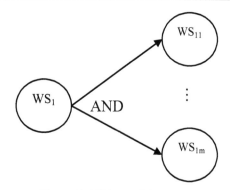

Figure. 7. AND-parallel pattern.

Table 5. Aggrigative QoS value for XOR-parallel pattern

Response Time	$Max(WS.RT)$
Execution Cost	$\sum_{i=0}^{m} WS.EC$
Availability	$\prod_{i=0}^{m} WS.Ava$
Successful Execution rate	$\prod_{i=0}^{m} WS.Suc$
Reputation	$\dfrac{\sum_{i=0}^{m} WS.\mathrm{Re}\,p}{m}$

4. The GA based algorithm

In this section, we present our approach to find an optimal web service composition plan Since the number of all composition plans of this problem is very large (n^m), some ideas to improve GA are presented so that it quickly converges the appropriate composition plan. We introduce some idea for initialization, crossover and mutation of chromosomes. Also the method to escape from local optimum is represented. If the algorithm cannot find the optimal plan in a specific time, without losing best plans of previous step, the algorithm will escape from local optimum.

Constraints

There are two constraints. The first constraint is that only one web service among candidate web services should be chosen for a task. In other words, the equation (4) has to be satisfied. The second constraint is that the service composition must satisfy user constraints. For negative QoS properties, such as execution cost and time the aggregation values must be smaller than user constraints. For positive QoS properties, aggregation values must be greater than user constraints. Equation (5) describes this constraint.

$$\sum_{i=0}^{n} b_{ij} = 1 \quad 1 \le i \le m \tag{4}$$

$$\begin{cases} Agg_d \le Con_d & \text{For negetive constraints} \\ Agg_d \ge Con_d & \text{For posotive constraints} \end{cases} \tag{5}$$

Algorithm construction

To obtain relation between local optimum and global optimum chromosomes, several experiments have been carried out. We design a small example of composition plan with m=10 and n=6 in which the number of plans is 10^6. Initially, all web services should be sorted according to their local values. Then, the best composition plan is found by using enumeration methods. In this method, all composition plans are obtained and evaluated. Table 6 shows the percentage of web services that are selected for global optimum plan. The closer this amount is to 9, the higher its local value will be. About 36.6% of web services in the composition plans have best local values too. It can be inferred that about 70% of web services that are selected for the best composition plan belong to 30% of the best web services that have high local values. Figureure. 8 depicts the values of fitness function of all plans.

In this diagram, each two adjacent points that demonstrate two adjacent plans, differ only in one web service. As depicted in this figure, for this small example, several local optimums exist so the algorithm should be changed so that it can escape from them; to escape from these local optimums, the various forms of randomness is required.

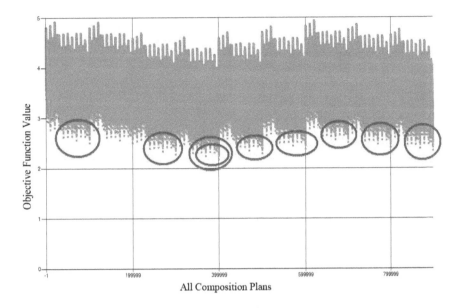

Figure. 8. Value of all plans in example with 6 tasks and 10 web services.

Table 6. Relation between Local and global optimum

WS number	Percentage of repeat in best plan
1	2.2%
2	1.6%
3	4.4%
4	5.5%
5	6.2%
6	9.0%
7	12.2%
8	22.3%
9	36.6%

Construction of chromosome is described in Figure 9. Each chromosome consists of m genes and each gene has a value between 1 to n.

1...n	1...n	...	1...n	1...n
Gene$_1$	Gene$_2$		Gene$_{m-1}$	Gene$_m$

Figure 9. Chromosome structure.

The main body of the algorithm is summarized in Table 7 and specifications of its functions are described in Tables 8, 9, 10, 11 and 12. At first, we should calculate local value of each web service. This is done prior to execution of composition plan optimization. Local value is a criterion of goodness among the candidate web services of a specific task. To obtain the local value, the QoS properties are normalized according to equations (1) and (2), and then the local value is calculated using equation (3). To obtain an optimized composition plan at first, web services candidate for a task are sorted according to their local values. In the next step, chromosomes are generated. 20% of all chromosomes are selected from 20% of best web services that have high local value and the remaining 80% is selected randomly. For each chromosome fitness function is calculated by using equation (9). It is derived from objective functions of [6, 10, 15]. D_1 is used for negative values and D_2 is used for positive values. If the fitness function value is equal or smaller than 0, it will mean that the appropriate composition plan satisfying user constraints is found.

$$D_1 = \sum w_d . (\frac{Agg_d}{Cond_d} - 1) \quad if \ Agg_d \geq Con_d$$

(For negetive values)

$$D_2 = \sum w_d . (\frac{Agg_d}{Cond_d} - 1) \quad if \ Agg_d \leq Con_d$$

(For posotive values)

Fitness Function $= D_1 - D_2$ (9)

Crossover is a function to combine two or more parent chromosomes and obtain one or more child chromosomes. We define two kinds of crossover. In crossover type 1 shown in Figure 10, genes of a child are inherited from parents alternatively. In crossover type 2 shown in Figure 11, a certain percentage of genes are inherited from one parent and the other genes are inherited from the other parent. For crossover operation, 20% of best chromosomes having high fitness are combined with each other by crossover type 1 and for the remaining 80%, each chromosome is combined with a randomly selected chromosome belonging to 20% of chromosomes with high fitness function by crossover type 2.

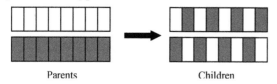

Parents   Children

Figure 10. Crossover type 1.

Parents   Child

Figure 11. Crossover type 2.

To select chromosomes for the next step (selection function), constant number of best chromosomes from the previous step are selected and replaced with worst chromosomes in current step. This results in preservation of best chromosomes but accelerates the convergence of the algorithm to the local optimum. To escape from local optimum we design mutation and partial initialization chromosomes functions. In mutation, some genes of some chromosomes that are selected randomly will change with probability of P_m.

To fix the selection function accelerating the convergence of the algorithm to the local optimum, the Partial initialization chromosomes function is presented. In this function, a constant number of best chromosomes are kept and other chromosomes are generated randomly again.

5. Experiments

We have accomplished several experiments to evaluate our algorithm. The programming language used to do the evaluation is Java and the algorithm is executed on desktop PC with Pentium 2.2 GHz dual core CPU and 3 GB of RAM. We compare the execution time of our algorithm with enumeration method. The first experiment was performed with 30, 50 and 100 tasks. For each task we have 30, 40 and 50 web services. As shown in Figureure. 12, the maximum execution time of the algorithm is 377 milliseconds. In a separate run, another experiment is performed with 100 web services in which the number of tasks is 20, 40 and 50. In this experiment the maximum time is equal to 240 milliseconds. The results are shown in Figureure.

13. Figure 14 shows the result of enumeration method. In enumeration method, the plans are generated until the suitable plan is founded. From this diagram, it can be inferred that the time of execution increases exponentially when number of tasks increase linearly. Furthermore, we compare our work with the work represented in [6]. They provide a solution for composition plan optimization using a combination of Tabu search and simulated annealing approach. The result of this comparison is shown in Figure 15.

Table 7. Main body of algorithm

Function Composition_Plan_Optimizer
Sort all web services according to their local value;
Initialize chromosomes ();
Sort all chromosomes according to their local score;
Counter=0;
While not find appropriate plan do
Crossover ();
Sorts all web services according to their local score;
Selection ();
Sorts all web services according to their local score;
Mutation ();
Sorts all web services according to their local score;
Counter=counter+1;
If (counter % T=0) Do
Partial_initialization_Chromosome();
End if
End While
End Function

Table 8. Initialization chromosomes function

Function Initialization Chromosome
For 20% of population do
Select chromosome genes are selected randomly from 20% of best web services
End For
For 80% of population do
Select chromosome genes are selected randomly.
End For
End Function

Table 9. Crossover function

Function Crossover
20% of best chromosomes are combined with each other by crossover type 1.
80% of remaining chromosomes are combined with 20% of best chromosomes with crossover type 2.
End Function

Table 10. Selection function

Function Selection
Replace N number of best chromosomes from previous step with N worst chromosomes of current step
End Function

Table 11. Mutation function

Function Mutation
With probability of P_m, some genes of some chromosomes are changed randomly
End Function

Table 12. partial_initialization_chromosomes function

Function Partial_initialization_chromosomes
Keep N number of the best chromosomes and other chromosomes are initialized again.
End Function

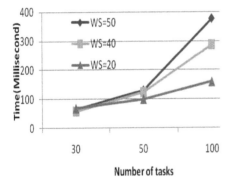

Figure 12. Performance of GA based algorithm

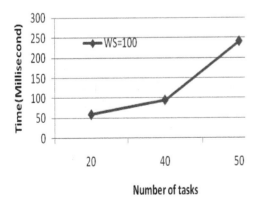

Figure 13. Performance of GA based algorithm with 100 tasks.

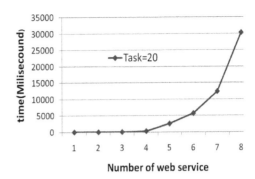

Figureure. 14. Performance of enumeration method

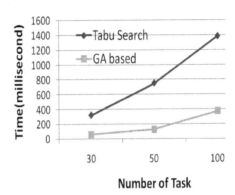

Figureure. 15. Compare with Tabu search approach

Furthermore, one of the important factors having the significant impact on the execution time is the population size. Figureure. 16 shows the impact of the population size on the execution time. In this experiment, the number of web services is 100 and the numbers of tasks are 20, 40 and 50 respectively. As it can be inferred from the diagram, the best population size is in range of 300 to 500.

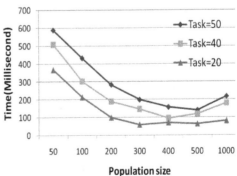

Figure 16. Impact of population number on the performance of algorithm (web service=100).

6. Conclusion

In this paper, we showed how can find the suitable web service composition using genetic algorithms. Some new ideas for generating chromosomes, selection and crossover functions were proposed. The experimental results demonstrated the advantages of the proposed ideas are to overcome local optimums. Experimental results show that since GA is a K beam search, it can find suitable composition plan much faster than other random search approaches. Therefore, it can be concluded that applying genetic algorithms in such problems has a great effect on improving computation time. As a future work, we suggest examining effects of using different formulas for fitness function.

Acknowledgements

This work was partially supported by Iranian Telecommunication Research Center (ITRC).

References

[1] CURBERA, F., M. DUFTLER, R. KHALAF, W. NAGY, N. MUKHI, S. WEERAWARANA, Unraveling the Web Services web, An Introduction to SOAP, WSDL and UDDI, IEEE Internet Computing, Vol. 6, (2002), pp. 86–93.

[2] KOSHMAN, S., Visualization-based Information Retrieval on the Web, Library and Information Science Research Vol. 28, (2006), pp. 192–207.

[3] CHEN, L.S., F.H. HSU, M.C. CHEN, Y.C. HSU, Developing Recommender Systems With the Consideration of Product Profitability for Sellers, Information Sciences, Vol 178, (2008), pp. 1032–1048.

[4] CHEN, Y., L. ZHOU, D. ZHANG, Ontology-Supported Web Service Composition: An Approach to Service-Oriented Knowledge Management in Corporate Services, Database Management Vol 17, (2006), pp. 67–84.

[5] O'SULLIVAN, J., D. EDMOND, A.T. HOFSTEDE, What's in a service? Distributed and Parallel Databases Vol 12, (2002), pp. 117–133.

[6] KO, J.M, C.O. KIM, I. KWON, Quality-of-Service Oriented Web Service Composition Algorithm and Planning Architecture, Systems and Software, Vol. 81, (2008), pp. 2079–2090.

[7] WANG, P., K.M. CHAO, C.C. LO, On Optimal Decision for Qos-Aware Composite Service Selection, Expert Systems with Applications, Vol 37, (2010), pp. 440–449

[8] RAN, S., A Model for Web Services Discovery with QoS, ACM SIGecom Exchanges, Vol 4, 2003, pp. 1 – 10.

[9] CANFORA, G., M.D. PENTA, R. ESPOSITO, M.L. VILLANI. An Approach for Qos-Aware Service Composition Based on Genetic Algorithms. Proc. Int. Conf. on Genetic and evolutionary computation, Washington DC, USA, (2005), pp. 1069–1075.

[10] HUANG, A.F.M., C.W. LAN, S.J.H. YANG, An Optimal Qos-Based Web Service Selection Scheme, Systems and Software, Vol 81, (2008), pp. 2079–2090.

[11] AI, W.H, Y.X. HUANG, H. ZHANG, N. ZHOU, Web Services Composition and Optimizing Algorithm Based on QoS, Proc. Int. Conf. on Wireless Communications, Networking and Mobile Computing, Dalian, (2008), pp. 1-4.

[12] LIU, Z., J. LI, J, LI, A. AN, J. XU, A Model for Web Services Composition Based on Qos and Providers' Benefit, Proc. Int. Conf. on Wireless communications, networking and mobile computing, Beijing, China, (2009), pp. 4562-4565.

[13] SIRIN, E., B. PARSIA, D. WU, J. HENDLER, D. NAU, HTN Planning for Web Service Composition Using SHOP2, Web Semantics Vol 1, (2004), pp. 377–396.

[14] D'AMBROGIO, A, A Model-driven WSDL Extension for Describing the QoS of Web Services, Proc. IEEE Int. Conf. on Web Services, (2006), pp. 789 – 796.

[15] LIANG, W.Y., C.C. HUANG, H.F. CHUANG, The Design With Object (DWO) Approach to Web Services Composition, Computer Standards & Interfaces, Vol 29, (2007), pp. 54-68.

[16] FERCHICHI, S.E., K. LAABIDI, S. ZIDI Genetic Algorithm and Tabu Search for Feature Selection, Studies in Informatics and Control, Vol. 18, No. 2, (2009).

[17] AARTS, E.H.L., P.J.M. VAN LAARHOVEN, Simulated Annealing: Theory and Applications, D. Reidel Publishing Company, (1987).

[18] CHAISEMARTIN, P., G. DREYFUS, M. FONTET, E. KOUKA, P. LOUBIÈRES, SIARRY P., Placement and Channel Routing by Simulated Annealing: Some Recent Developments, Computer Systems Science and engineering, Vol. 41, (1989).

[19] METROPOLIS, N., A.W. ROSENBLUTH, M.N. ROSENBLUTH, A.H. TELLER, E. TELLER, Simulated Annealing, J. Chem. Phys. 21, (1953).

[20] PATNAIK, S., Genetic Algorithms: A Survey, IEEE computer society, Vol. 27, No. 6, pp.17-26, (1994).

[21] ZOMAYA, P.F., Parallel Genetic Algorithms, Parallel & Distributed Computing, Handbook, McGraw Hul, (1996).

[22] RAJKUMAR, R. , P. SHAHABUDEEN, P. NAGARAJ, S. ARUNACHALAM, T. PAGE, A Bi-Criteria Approach to the M-machine Flowshop Scheduling Problem, Studies in Informatics and Control, Vol. 18, No. 2, (2009).

[23] DRIDI, H., R. KAMMARTI, M. KSOURI, PIERRE BORNE, A Genetic Algorithm for the Multi-Pickup and Delivery Problem with Time Windows, Studies in Informatics and Control, Vol. 18, No. 2, (2009).

[24] KAMMARTI, R., I. AYACHI , M. KSOURI, P. BORNE, Evolutionary Approach for the Containers Bin-Packing Problem, Studies in Informatics and Control, Vol. 18, No. 4, (2009).

[25] BOUKEF, H., M. BENREJEB, P. BORNE, A Proposed Genetic Algorithm Coding for Flow-ShopScheduling Problems, International Journal of Computers, Communications & Control, Vol. 2 , No. 3, (2007), pp. 229-240.

[26] CUBILLOS, C., E. URRA, N. RODRÍGUEZ, Application of Genetic Algorithms for the DARPTW Problem, International Journal of Computers, Communications & Control, Vol. 4, No. 2, (2009), pp. 127-136.

22

Image quality enhancement in digital panoramic radiograph

S. Asadi Amiri[1*], E. Moudi[2]

1. Department of Computer Engineering, University of Shahrood Technology, Shahrood, Iran
2. Department of Dental Maxillofacial Radiology, University of Medical Science Babol, Babol, Iran

*Corresponding author: asadi_amiri@yahoo.com (Asadi Amiri)

Abstract

One of the most common positioning errors in panoramic radiography is the palatoglossal air space above the apices of the root of maxillary teeth. It causes a radiolucency obscuring the apices of maxillary teeth. In the case of this positioning error, the imaging should be repeated. This causes the patient to be exposed to radiation again. To avoid the repetition of exposing harmful X-rays to the patient, it is necessary to improve the panoramic images. This paper presents a new automatic panoramic image enhancement method to reduce the effect of this positioning error. Experimental results indicate that the enhanced panoramic images provide with adequate diagnostic information specially in maxilla sinusoid region. Hence, this technique dispenses the need for repetition of X-ray imaging.

Keywords*: Image Enhancement, Gamma Correction, Panoramic Radiography, Gray Level Co-Occurrence Matrix, Homogeneity.*

1. Introduction

Panoramic radiographs are most useful clinical images for diagnostic problems requiring a broad coverage of the jaws. Common example includes evaluation of trauma location of third molars, extensive dental or osseous disease, known or suspected large lesions, temporomandilular joint (TMJ) pain and developmental anomalies [1]. It was reported that above 90% of panoramic radiographs have at least one positioning error. Figure 1 shows the most common positioning error in the radiographs. Once the patient's tongue is not contacted with the palate during the exposure, this error, known as palatoglossal air space, may occur [2].

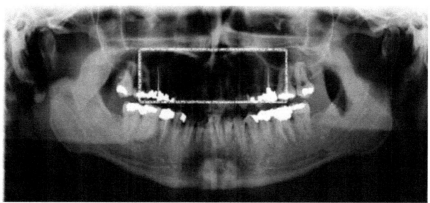

Figure 1. An example of a panoramic radiograph with a positioning error (The area depicted by the rectangle).

There is not any technical solution to solve this problem. Hence, the radiologist should again expose the X-ray to the patient to re-capture the image. This paper proposes a new technique to enhance panoramic images for better diagnostic information. This technique improves the visual appearance of panoramic image by increasing the contrast, adjusting brightness, and enhancing visually important features. This technique uses an adaptive approach to enhance the entire image especially in maxilla sinusoid region.

Due to technical limitations, many imaging devices do not display the actual appearance of objects. This technical limitation known as gamma distortion often disturbs the image. The gamma distortion in an image is not monotonic. It mainly depends on the relative illumination reflection of objects in the image. In other words, image distortion depends on the depth, texture, and relative reflection of objects in the image. Since a panoramic radiograph contains objects with a variety of texture and depth such as tongue and teeth, gamma distortions may not be the same as all objects. Hence, it needs an adaptive approach to enhance the image.

This paper proposes a new technique for estimating the gamma values in the panoramic image. For the local gamma correction the image is divided into overlapping windows. Then the gamma value of each window is estimated by minimizing the homogeneity of gray level co-occurrence matrix (GLCM).This feature indicates how details of objects are visible in the image; the lower the value of this feature represents more visibility of the image details. Using the homogeneity feature of the co-occurrence matrix to measure the visibility of image details, a proper gamma value will be assigned to each window.

Next section focuses on gamma correction for image enhancement. In Section 3, gray level co-occurrence matrix is presented. The proposed algorithm is introduced in Section 4. Sections 5 and 6 described the results, and the conclusions respectively.

2. Gamma correction

Gamma correction for image enhancement has been described in depth in [3,4]. Many devices used for capturing, printing or displaying the images generally apply a transformation, called power-law [5]; the image of each pixel of the image has a nonlinear effect on luminance:

$$g(u) = u^{\gamma} \tag{1}$$

In the above equation, $u \in [0, 1]$ denotes the image

pixel intensity, γ is a positive constant introducing the gamma value. This equation using the value of γ typically can be determined experimentally through passing a calibration target with a full range of known luminance, which values through the imaging device. When the value of γ is known, inverting this process is trivial:

$$g^{-1}(u) = u^{1/\gamma} \tag{2}$$

Often such a calibration is not available or the direct access to the imaging device is not possible [6]. Hence an algorithm is needed to reduce the effects of these nonlinearities without any knowledge about the imaging device.

In addition to this problem, as mentioned before, these nonlinear effects aren't consistent across all regions of the image. In other words, the value of gamma may change from one region to another [6,7]. Hence a local enhancement process adjusts the image quality in different regions, so that the details in dark or bright regions are brought out to the human viewers [8].

It is noted that image enhancement techniques, such as a histogram equalization may not be used to enhance images suffering from gamma distortion. The main objective of histogram equalization is to achieve a uniform distributed histogram by using the cumulative density function of the input image. This may not be a suitable objective, where brightness of some areas (or objects) in the image is satisfactory [9]. In histogram equalization technique, the pixel values are either added or multiped by a value [5]. It mainly cares about histogram of the image not the actual appearance of the image which is the case in the gamma correction.

Hence, conventional image enhancement techniques, such as global brightness, contrast enhancement, and histogram equalization are incapable of providing satisfactory enhancement results for images suffering from gamma distortion.

Imaging devices apply the power-law transformation on each of the pixel image; hence, gamma correction is required to enhance each pixel of the image. Figure 2 shows an example of gamma correction superiority to histogram equalization in the image enhancement. The image enhancement using gamma correction has more subtle diagnostic information. We have used the co-occurrence matrix to find the image details for a better gamma estimation.

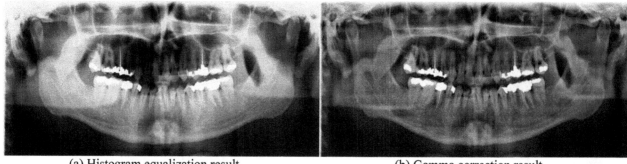

(a) Histogram equalization result   (b) Gamma correction result

Figure 2. Comparison between gamma correction and histogram equalization in enhancing the panoramic radiograph shown in Figure 1.

3. Gray level co-occurrence matrix

The gray level co-occurrence matrix is often used for feature extraction in texture analysis of an image. The co-occurrence matrix of a gray level image is regarded as a two dimensional matrix. Its size is proportional to the number of gray levels in an image. For instance, the images used in this paper have 256 gray levels; thus, their GLCM is a matrix of size 256×256. In contrast to histogram, GLCM describes the relationship between the values of neighbouring pixels. It measures the probability that a pixel of a particular gray level occurs at a specified direction and a distance from its neighbouring pixels. This can be calculated by the function $P(i,j,d,\theta)$, where i is the gray level at location with coordinate (x,y), j is the gray level of its neighbouring pixel at a distance d and a direction θ from a location (x,y) [10]. θ usually ranges from: 0, 45, 90, to 135 [11]. This is mathematically defined by (3):

$$P(i,j,d,\theta) = \# \{(x_1,y_1)(x_2,y_2)|f(x_1,y_1) \quad (3)$$
$$= i, f(x_2,y_2) = j,$$
$$|(x_1,y_1) - (x_2,y_2)| =$$
$$d, \angle((x_1,y_1),(x_2,y_2)) = \theta\}$$

In [12], fourteen different features of GLCM have been defined. These features consist of texture information, but there may be a correlation between them. This paper focuses on the homogeneity feature extracted from co-occurrence matrix P; this feature is illustrated below.

$$P(i,j,d,\theta) = \sum_{i}^{256} \sum_{j}^{256} \frac{P(i,j,d,\theta)}{1 + |i-j|} \quad (4)$$

Homogeneity returns a value that measures the closeness of distribution of GLCM's elements to the GLCM diagonal, and its range is from 0 to 1. In other words, it describes how uniform the texture is. Figure 3 shows three images with different gamma condition along with their co-occurrence matrix. As it can be conceived from the images, when the amount of γ is less than one, the transformed image becomes lighter than the original image (see Figure 3(a)); and when the amount of γ is greater than one, the transformed image becomes darker than the original image (see Figure 3(c)). When the gamma value is one, there is no change on the pixels value (see Figure 3(b)). It needs to be noted that extracted homogeneity feature from associated co-occurrence matrix reveals that, this feature has the minimum value for image with good gamma condition. As discussed above, this feature represents how uniform the texture is. Figures 3(a, c) are two distorted images that their details are not clearly revealed. The details can be clearly seen in Figure 3(b), and the homogeneity value in Figure 3(e) indicates that the image is not uniform similar to the other two images.

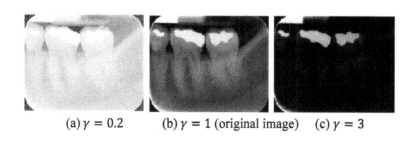

(a) $\gamma = 0.2$ (b) $\gamma = 1$ (original image)   (c) $\gamma = 3$

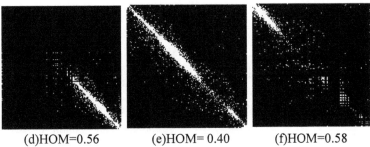

(d)HOM=0.56   (e)HOM= 0.40   (f)HOM=0.58

Figure 3. Three images with different gamma condition and their associated co-occurrence matrix with extracted homogeneity feature.

4. Proposed method

This paper proposed an adaptive gamma correction method to enhance the quality of panoramic images. As noted above in section…, these images often suffer from the root of maxillary teeth area. The basic idea is the fact that the homogeneity value in an image not suffering from gamma distortion has a lower value (near to zero). These homogeneity values can be calculated by co-occurrence matrix. The gamma value is then estimated by minimizing these homogeneities.

The image in the adaptive gamma correction is divided into overlapping windows. A sliding window of size 100×200 is moved across the image from the top-left side to the bottom-right by fifty pixels in each movement. A value of 100×200 pixels was chosen for images with the size 1500×3000 as this window size gives the best trade-off between the rendering of local details and the need for reducing space dimensionality. To find a proper gamma value for each window, we apply a range of inverse gamma values from 0.1 to 3 intervals 0.1 in each window. Different windows may need different gamma value for a proper enhancement. To find the best gamma value for each window, we compute the co-occurrence matrix of the window to extract the homogeneity feature. Then, the gamma value associated with the minimum homogeneity is considered as the best gamma value for enhancement.

Figure 4(a) displays a window of panoramic image. To find a proper gamma value for enhancing this window, different inverse gamma values are applied on the window and the homogeneity value is computed. Then the homogeneity values are plotted as a function of inverse gamma values (see Figure 4(d)). The gamma value associated with the least homogeneity offers the most suitable one for enhancing the window. Figures. 4(b,c) were modified with $\gamma^{-1} = 0.53$ and at $\gamma^{-1} = 1.67$.

In this approach, each window in the image has its own gamma value. Because of overlapping windows, pixels may settle under different windows; hence, different gamma values may apply. We apply only one gamma value on each pixel, which is the average of the gamma values in the covering windows. In other words, a matrix M of gamma values with the same size as the image is achieved. To enhance the image, according to equation (2) the gamma values are applied to each pixel. Figure 5(a) shows the result. As it is shown in this figure, this approach has unpleasure blocking effects on the image.

In this step, to eliminate the blocking effects, first we apply average filter on M containing the gamma values. Then the filtered gamma values are applied to the image for gamma correction. Figure 5(b) shows this result. Clearly, the blocking effects have been removed.

5. Experimental results

As mentioned earlier, one of the most common positioning errors is due to not contacting the tongue with the hard palate during capturing. It causes large airway shadow to be created over the roots of the maxillary teeth due to the gamma distortion. Hence, the goal of the present research is to estimate the gamma value of a panoramic image in a local approach. To evaluate the performance of the proposed approach in the enhancing a panoramic image, we have used thirty different radiograph samples collected at Babol Oral & Maxillofacial Radiology Center, Babol, Iran. This technique improves the quality of all the thirty radiographs, and considerly removes the large airway shadow over the roots of the maxillary teeth. The results of four samples with our proposed method are illustrated in Figure 6. As can be observed, in addition to improving the overall images, roots of maxillary teeth are also clearly visible. In general, it can be concieved that the enhanced images with our proposed method looks much better with more details compared to the original image.

6. Conclusions

The palatoglossal air space shadow appears, as a radiolucent area over the apices of the maxillary teeth is one of the most common errors in panoramic radiography. This effect reduces the diagnostic quality of radiographs. A new gamma correction method for panoramic radiography image enhancement is proposed in this paper. This proposed method improves the overall image especially the roots of maxillary teeth. The finding provides dentists with a sufficient amount of information to improve their diagnosis.

References

[1] Goaz, P.W., White, S.C., Oral radiology: Principles and Interpretation fifth ed. Philadelphia, 2004.

[2] Glass, B. J., Seals, R.R., Williams, E.O., Common errors in panoramic radiography of edentulous patients, J. Prosthodont, 1994, 3, 68-73.

[3] Hassanpour, H., Asadi Amiri, S., Image quality enhancement using pixel wise gamma correction via svm classifier, International Journal of Engineering, 2011, 24, 301-311.

[4] Asadi Amiri, S., Hassanpour, H., Pouyan, A.K., Texture based image enhancement using gamma correction, J. Scientific Research, 2010, 6, 569-574.

[5] Gonzalez, R. C., Woods, R. E., Digital image processing Prentice Hall Upper Saddle River, 2002.

[6] Farid, H., Blind inverse gamma correction, J. IEEE Transactions on Image Processing, 2001, 10, 1428-1433.

[7] Shi, Y., Yang, J., Wu, R., Reducing illumination based on nonlinear gamma correction, In Proc. ICIP San Antonio, 2007, 529-539.

[8] Lee, S., Content-based image enhancement in the compressed domain based on multi-scale α-rooting algorithm, J. Pattern Recognition Letters, 2006, 27, 1054-1066.

[9] Chen, Q., Xu, X., Sun, Q., Xia, D., A solution to the deficiencies of image enhancement, J. Signal Processing, 2010, 90, 44-56.

[10] Gastaldo, P., Zunino, R., Heynderickx, I., Vicario, E., Objective quality assessment of displayed images by using neural networks, J. Signal Processing Image Communication, 2005, 643-661.

[11] Voicu, L.I., Myler, H.R., Weeks, A.R., Practical considerations on color image enhancement using homomorphic filtering, J. Electronic Imaging, 1997, 6, 108-113.

[12] Haralick, R. M., Shanmugan, K., Dinstein, I., Textural features for image classification, J. IEEE Trans. SMC, 1973, 3, 610-621.

(a) Original image

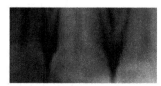
(b) Modified image with $\gamma^{-1} = 0.53$

(c) Modified image with $\gamma^{-1} = 1.67$

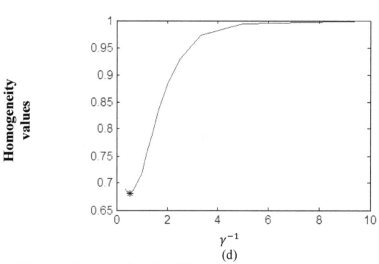
(d)

Figure 4. Diagram of homogeneity values for thirty different inverse gamma images from 0.1 to 3. The deep point represented by the asterisk reaches a unique minimum at $\gamma^{-1} = 0.53$.

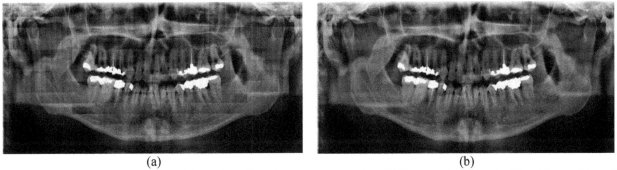

(a)   (b)

Figure 5. (a) Image enhancement with blocking effects in gamma correction, (b) Image enhancement without the problem of blocking effect.

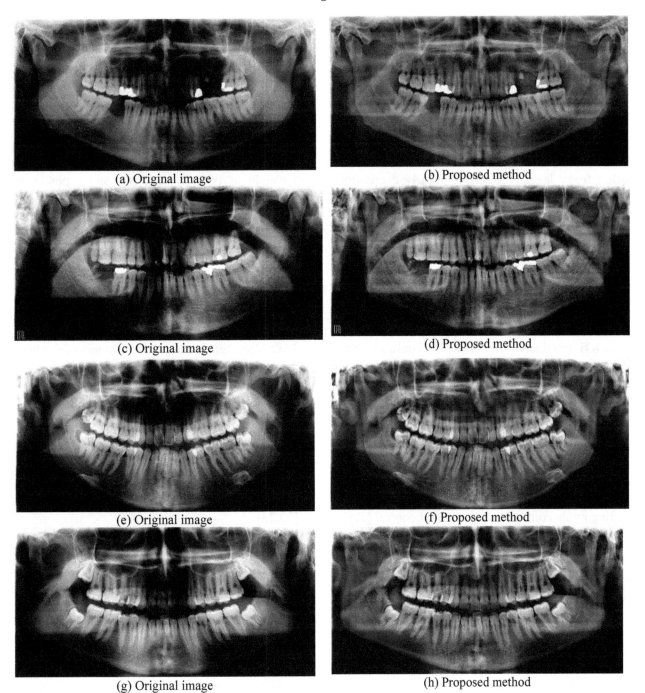

(a) Original image   (b) Proposed method

(c) Original image   (d) Proposed method

(e) Original image   (f) Proposed method

(g) Original image   (h) Proposed method

Figure 6. Image enhancement by our proposed method.

23

Designing an adaptive fuzzy control for robot manipulators using PSO

F. Soleiman Nouri*, M. Haddad Zarif and M. M. Fateh

Department of Electrical Engineering and Robotics, University of Shahrood, Iran.

Corresponding author: solaimannourifatemeh@yahoo.com (F. Soleiman Nouri).

Abstract

This paper presents a designing an optimal adaptive controller for tracking down the control of robot manipulators based on particle swarm optimization (PSO) algorithm. PSO algorithm has been used to optimize parameters of the controller and hence to minimize the integral square of errors (ISE) as a performance criteria. In this paper, an improved PSO using a logic is proposed to increase the convergence speed. In this case, the performance of PSO algorithms such as an improved PSO (IPSO), an improved PSO using fuzzy logic (F-PSO), a linearly decreasing inertia weight of PSO (LWD-PSO) and a nonlinearly decreasing inertia weight of PSO (NDW-PSO) are with parameter accuracy and convergence speed. As a result, the simulation results show that the F-PSO approach presents a better performance in the tracking down the control of robot manipulators than other algorithms.

Keywords: *Particle Swarm Optimization (PSO), Robot Manipulators, Adaptive Controller, Improved PSO Using Fuzzy Logic (F-PSO), Integral Square of Errors (ISE).*

1. Introduction

Robot manipulators are multi-input/multi-output (MIMO) nonlinear system with couplings that have to face many structured and unstructured uncertainties such as payload parameter, un-modeled dynamics, external disturbance and friction. The design robust controller for robot manipulators and their application is one of the considerable topics in a control field; so many control techniques have been proffered to control robot manipulator such as the PID control method [1], adaptive control [2,3], combined adaptive sliding mode controllers [4], optimal control [5,6] and intelligent approaches [7].

The PSO algorithm comprises a simple structure, and it is easy to be implemented, independent from initial guess and does not need any objective function's gradient. Due to the good characteristics of this algorithm, it has been applied in the diversity of investigation field. For instance, in [9-11], PSO is presented to setting the optimal parameter of PID controller. In [12], proposed to use PSO and its application to train weights of artificial neural network. In [13], the author employed the PSO algorithm to optimize

the parameter of tracking a controller. In [14], PSO is proffered to solve the systems of nonlinear equations. In [15], the proposed algorithm has been used to solve nonlinear optimal control. In [16], the PSO algorithm is used to optimize the parameters of controller to position/force control of constrained robot manipulators.

Fuzzy logic is based on fuzzy set theory. A fuzzy logic controller is composed of its rule base and membership function. Fuzzy logic system was used to approximate any nonlinear function [22,23].

In this paper, the particle swarm optimization utilized to drive the optimal parameters of adaptive controller for robot manipulators. The performance of an improved PSO using fuzzy logic (F-PSO) is compared with PSO with linearly decreasing inertia weight (LDW-PSO), nonlinear inertia weight PSO (NDW-PSO) and improved PSO (IPSO). The simulation results confirmed that the F-PSO has better performance than other algorithm mentioned above. The rest of paper is organized as follows: Section 2 presents the mathematical description of robot manipulator.

Section 3 illustrates the particle swarm optimization. Section 4 shows the design of controller parameters based on PSO. Section 5 illustrates the simulation results on a robot manipulator and comparisons between algorithms. Section 6 concludes the paper.

2. Dynamics of robot manipulators

In the absence of friction or other disturbance, the dynamic equation of a multi-input/multi-output robot manipulator system can be written as [2, 4]:

$$M(q)\ddot{q} + C\left(q,\dot{q}\right)\dot{q} + G(q) = \tau \qquad (1)$$

Where q is a $n \times 1$ vector of generalized coordinate, the position vector of a robot manipulator. $\dot{q}$ is a $n \times 1$ vector of first derivative of generalized coordinate, the velocity of a robot manipulator. $\ddot{q}$ is a $n \times 1$ vector of second derivative of generalized coordinate, the acceleration of a robot manipulator. $M(q)$ is a $n \times n$ symmetric positive definite matrix of manipulator inertia. $C\left(q,\dot{q}\right)$ is a $n \times 1$ vector of centrifugal and coriolis torque. $G(q)$ is a $n \times 1$ vector of gravitational torque. τ is a $n \times 1$ vector of generalized control input torque or force. The (1) can be stated as follows [2]:

$$M(q)\ddot{q} + C\left(q,\dot{q}\right)\dot{q} + G(q) = Y\left(q,\dot{q},\ddot{q}\right)\beta = \tau \qquad (2)$$

Where $Y\left(q,\dot{q},\ddot{q}\right)$ is a $n \times p$ matrix called regressor. β is a $p \times 1$ uncertain vector.

A number of useful properties of robot dynamic is expressed as follows [8]:

Property 1. An appropriate definition of coriolis and centrifugal matrix makes that the

$$N\left(q,\dot{q}\right) = \dot{M}(q) - 2C\left(q,\dot{q}\right) \quad \text{is skew}$$

symmetric. This property is very important to stability analysis.

Property 2. The $M(q)$ is a symmetric positive definite matrix, such that:

$$0 < \mu_1 I \le M(q) \le \mu_2 I$$

μ_1, μ_2 are positive constant and I is the identity matrix.

2.1. Adaptive controller design

The control law has been given as follows [2]:

$$\tau = M(q)(\ddot{q}_d - \Lambda(\dot{q} - \dot{q}_d)) + C\left(q,\dot{q}\right)(\dot{q}_d - \Lambda(q - q_d)) + G(q) + K\sigma \qquad (3)$$

Where k is a definite positive matrix, σ is an error of velocity.

$\tilde{q}, \dot{\tilde{q}}, \dot{q}_r, \ddot{q}_r$ are defined as:

$$\tilde{q} = q - q_d, \quad \dot{\tilde{q}} = \dot{q} - \dot{q}_d, \quad \dot{q}_r = \dot{q}_d - \Lambda\tilde{q} \quad , $$
$$\ddot{q}_r = \ddot{q}_d - \Lambda\dot{\tilde{q}} \qquad (4)$$

Where $\tilde{q}$ indicates the position tracking error, $\dot{\tilde{q}}$ represents the velocity, $\dot{q}_r$ is called reference Velocity that is utilized to guarantee the convergence of the tracking error, $\ddot{q}_r$ is the reference acceleration, Λ is a positive definite matrix and σ is obtained as:

$$\sigma = \dot{q}_r - \dot{q} = \dot{\tilde{q}} + \Lambda\tilde{q} \qquad (5)$$

In the presence of uncertainties, a control law is proposed as:

$$\tau = \hat{M}(q)\ddot{q}_r + \hat{C}\left(q,\dot{q}\right)\dot{q}_r + \hat{G}(q) + K\sigma$$
$$= Y\left(q,\dot{q},\dot{q}_r,\ddot{q}_r\right)\hat{\beta} + K\sigma \qquad (6)$$

Where $\hat{M}(q)$ is the estimate of the $M(q)$, $\hat{C}\left(q,\dot{q}\right)$ is the estimate of the $C\left(q,\dot{q}\right)$, $\hat{G}(q)$ presented the estimate of the $G(q)$ and also $\hat{\beta}$ denoted the estimate of the β.

Attention to replace the recent control law in the (2), so modeling errors consists of:

$$\tilde{M} = \hat{M} - M \quad \tilde{C} = \hat{C} - C \quad \tilde{G} = \hat{G} - G \qquad (7)$$

In order to analysis the stability of the system and obtain convergence tracking error, the Lyapunov function candidate is suggested as follows:

$$v(t) = \frac{1}{2}\left[\sigma^T H\sigma + \tilde{\beta}^T \Gamma^{-1}\tilde{\beta}\right] \qquad (8)$$

The adaptation law can be expressed as:

$$\hat{\beta} = -\Gamma Y^{\mathrm{T}} \sigma \qquad (9)$$

Using this upper equation, the derivative of $v(t)$ is given as:

$$\dot{v}(t) = -\sigma^{\mathrm{T}} K_D \sigma \le 0 \qquad (10)$$

3. Particle swarm optimization

Particle swarm optimization algorithm is a stochastic evolutionary computation approach. It is inspired by the social behavior such as a flock of bird or a school of fish. This algorithm introduced by Eberhart and Kennedy in 1995 [17]. PSO contains a group of solutions that called particles.

These particles are moved in and evaluates the cost function of its position that has been placed in space. Particle adjusted its movement based on corresponding experience of particle and associated experiences of particle that led to the particle moves in the direction of better solution [15]. At each iteration, each particle for updating its velocity and position utilized equations in the following order:

$$V_i^{k+1} = wV_i^k + c_1 rand_1 \times (\text{Pbest}_i^k - X_i^k)$$
$$+ c_2 rand_2 \times (\text{Gbest}^k - X_i^k) \qquad (11)$$

$$X_i^{k+1} = X_i^k + \mathrm{T}_s V_i^{k+1} \qquad (12)$$

Where X_i^k is the current position of ith particle at the kth iteration. T_s is the sampling period. V_i^k is the Current velocity of ith particle at the kth iteration. w is the inertia weight which acquires an important task in the PSO convergence behavior since it is used to balance the global and local search ability. c_1, c_2 are positive constants, correspond to cognitive and social parameter respectively, called learning factors. $rand_1, rand_2$ are random numbers with uniform distribution in the range of 0 to 1. Pbest_i^k is the best position of ith particle at the kth iteration called as personal best. Gbest^k is the global best position among all the particles in the swarm at the kth iteration called global best. The algorithm is repeated several times until the pause condition such as number of iteration or sufficiently good fitness [15].

PSO does exhibit some shortages. It may convergence to a local minimum, therefore

researchers try to improve the performance of the PSO with different settings, e.g. w, C_1, C_2 [15].

In this work, we employed the IPSO, NDW-PSO, LDW-PSO and F-PSO, they are approaches that improved the performance of PSO and finally, F-PSO algorithm is compared with the other algorithms.

3.1. Linearly decreasing inertia weight PSO

Linearly decreasing inertia weight PSO was abbreviated to LDW-PSO, the inertia weight decreases linearly from w_{max} to w_{min}, the equation is used for adapting the inertia weight in PSO as follows [19, 20]:

$$w^t = w_{min} + \frac{iter_{max} - t}{iter_{max}} \cdot (w_{max} - w_{min}) \qquad (13)$$

$iter_{max}$ Denotes to maximum number of iteration and t denotes to current of iteration.

3.2. Nonlinear inertia weight PSO

Nonlinear inertia weight PSO was abbreviated to NDW-PSO. In this mechanism, the inertia weight decreases as same pervious approach but nonlinearity [18].

$$w^t = w_{min} + (\frac{iter_{max} - t}{iter_{max}})^n \cdot (w_{max} - w_{min}) \qquad (14)$$

3.3. Improved PSO

The values of w, c_1, c_2 is very important to ensure convergent behavior and to optimally trade-off exploration and exploitation. In [21], Author used an improved PSO as follows:

$$w^t = 1/\left(1 + \exp(-\alpha F(\text{gbest}^t))^n\right) \qquad (15)$$

$$c_i = 1/\left(1 + \exp(-\alpha F(\text{gbest}^t))^n\right) \qquad (16)$$

$$\alpha = 1/\mathrm{F}\left(gbest^t\right) \qquad (17)$$

This adaptation appliance changes in conformity to the rate of the global best fitness improvement.

3.4. Particle swarm optimization with using fuzzy

Fuzzy is used for designing and modeling for system that need to advance mathematics and probabilities. The important part of fuzzy system was a knowledge base that is comprised fuzzy IF-THEN rules. Fuzzy is used to improve the performance of PSO. A fuzzy system will be employed to adjust the learning factors c_1, c_2 with best fitness and iteration. The best fitness measure the performance of the best solution found so far. To design a fuzzy-PSO need to have ranges of best fitness and iteration. Therefore, the best fitness and iteration have to normalize into $[0,1]$ that defined as follows [22, 23]:

$$NCBPE = \frac{CBPE \_ CBPE_{min}}{CBPE_{max} - CBPE_{min}} \qquad (18)$$

Where $CBPE$ is the current fitness value, $CBPE_{min}$ is the best fitness value and $CBPE_{max}$ is the worst fitness value.

$$Iteration = \frac{iteration}{iteration_{max}} \qquad (19)$$

In this mechanism, the best fitness and iteration are inputs and c_1, c_2 are outputs in the fuzzy system. The c_1, c_2 obtained from fuzzy were used to PSO and for adjusting w, we employed the IPSO that mentioned in [15]:

$$w^t = 1/\left(1 + \exp(-\alpha F(\text{gbest}^t))^n\right) \qquad (20)$$

$$\alpha = 1/F\left(\text{gbest}^t\right) \qquad (21)$$

We suggest fuzzy rules:

1. If (iteration is low) and (CPBE is low) then (c1 is low)(c2 is high)
2. If (iteration is low) and (CPBE is medium) then (c1 is medium low)(c2 is medium high)
3. If (iteration is low) and (CPBE is high) then (c1 is medium)(c2 is medium)
4. If (iteration is medium) and (CPBE is low) then (c1 is medium low)(c2 is high)
5. If (iteration is medium) and (CPBE is medium) then (c1 is medium)(c2 is high)
6. If (iteration is medium) and (CPBE is high) then (c1 is medium high)(c2 is low)
7. If (iteration is high) and (CPBE is low) then (c1 is high)(c2 is low)
8. If (iteration is high) and (CPBE is medium) then (c1 is medium high)(c2 is medium low)
9. If (iteration is high) and (CPBE is high) then (c1 is low)(c2 is medium low)

For designing the rules of fuzzy system, it was decided that in early iterations the PSO algorithm must explore and finally exploit.
These approaches usually start with large inertia values, which decrease over time to smaller values. Large values for w facilitate exploration, with increased diversity. A small w promotes local exploitation.

4. PSO controller tuning

The parameters of adaptive control law such as Γ_1, Γ_2, Γ_3, Γ_4, Λ_1 and k_1 is found using PSO.

All the parameters of controller are adjusted to minimize the fitness function based on the integral square of errors that is defined as follows:

$$f = \int_0^T \sum_{i=1}^2 e_i(t)^2 dt \qquad (22)$$

Where $e_i(t)$ is the value of tracking error and T is the control system running time.

5. Simulation results

The dynamics of a two links manipulator has been mentioned in section (2), so the element of this equation such as $M(q)$, $C\left(q, \dot{q}\right)$ and $G(q)$ are given as follows [4]:

$$\begin{pmatrix} \tau_1 \\ \tau_2 \end{pmatrix} = \begin{pmatrix} M_{11} & M_{12} \\ M_{21} & M_{22} \end{pmatrix} \begin{pmatrix} \ddot{q}_1 \\ \ddot{q}_2 \end{pmatrix} + \begin{pmatrix} -C\dot{q}_2 & -C\left(\dot{q}_1 + \dot{q}_2\right) \\ C\dot{q}_1 & 0 \end{pmatrix} \begin{pmatrix} \dot{q}_1 \\ \dot{q}_2 \end{pmatrix}, \qquad (23)$$

$G(q) = 0$

Where:

$$M_{11} = a_1 + 2a_3 \cos q_2 + 2a_4 \sin q_2 \qquad (24)$$

$$M_{12} = M_{21} = a_2 + a_3 \cos q_2 + a_4 \sin q_2 \qquad (25)$$

$$M_{22} = a_2 \qquad (26)$$

$$C = a_3 \sin q_2 - a_4 \cos q_2 \qquad (27)$$

$$a_1 = I_1 + m_1 l_{c1}^2 + I_e + m_e l_{ce}^2 + m_e l_1^2 \qquad (28)$$

$$a_2 = I_e + m_e l_{ce}^2 \qquad (29)$$

$$a_3 = m_e l_1 l_{ce} \cos \delta_e \qquad (30)$$

$$a_4 = m_e l_1 l_{ce} \sin \delta_e \qquad (31)$$

In the simulations, the below values have been used in the following order:

$$m_1 = 1, \; l_1 = 1, \; m_e = 2, \; \delta_e = \frac{\pi}{6}, \; I_1 = 0.12,$$

$$l_{c1} = 0.5, \; I_e = 0.25, \; l_{ce} = 0.6$$

The components of matrix of $Y(q, \dot{q}, \dot{q}_r, \ddot{q}_r)$ can be written explicitly:

$$Y_{11} = \ddot{q}_{r1}, \; Y_{12} = \ddot{q}_{r2}, \; Y_{21} = 0, \; Y_{22} = \ddot{q}_{r1} + \ddot{q}_{r2}$$

$$Y_{13} = \left(2\ddot{q}_{r1} + \ddot{q}_{r2}\right)\cos q_2 - \left(\dot{q}_2 \dot{q}_{r1} + \dot{q}_1 \dot{q}_{r2} + \dot{q}_2 \dot{q}_{r2}\right)\sin q_2$$

$$Y_{14} = \left(2q''_{r1} + q''_{r2}\right)\sin q_2 +$$
$$\left(q'_2 q'_{r1} + q'_1 q'_{r2} + q'_2 q'_{r2}\right)\cos q_2 \tag{32}$$

$$Y_{23} = q''_{r1}\cos q_2 + q'_1 q'_{r1}\sin q_2$$

$$Y_{24} = q''_{r1}\sin q_2 - q'_1 q'_{r1}\cos q_2$$

The desired trajectory is chosen as:

$$q_{d1}(t) = \frac{\pi}{6}\left(1 - \cos(2\pi t)\right)$$
$$q_{d2}(t) = \frac{\pi}{4}\left(1 - \cos(2\pi t)\right) \tag{33}$$

$$\Gamma = diag\begin{bmatrix}3.3 & 0.97 & 1.04 & 0.6\end{bmatrix}, \Lambda = 20I,$$
$$K = 100I$$

The controller parameters have been set with PSO, such as :

$$\Gamma = diag\begin{bmatrix}\Gamma_1 & \Gamma_2 & \Gamma_3 & \Gamma_4\end{bmatrix}, \Lambda = \Lambda_1 I, K = K_1 I$$

The searching ranges are set as follows:

$$0 \le \Gamma_1 \le 0.07, \qquad 0 \le \Gamma_2 \le 0.05, \qquad 0 \le \Gamma_3 \le 0.15,$$
$$0 \le \Gamma_4 \le 0.3, \ 0 \le \Lambda_1 \le 20, \ 0 \le K_1 \le 100$$

In all PSO algorithms, $c_1 = c_2 = 2$ [17], w decreases from 0.9 to 0.4, in NWD-PSO n=1.2 [18] and in IPSO n=1.5 [21], population size is set to 10 and maximum number of iteration is set to 50 and each algorithm runs 25 times.

Table 1. Results of comparison between LDW-PSO, NDW-PSO, IPSO, F-PSO.

Control parameters	Real value	LDW-PSO	NDW-PSO	IPSO	F-PSO
Γ_1	0.03	0.0595	0.0591	0.0420	0.0415
Γ_2	0.05	0.0500	0.0499	0.0482	0.0500
Γ_3	0.1	0.1499	0.1499	0.1499	0.1500
Γ_4	0.3	0.3000	0.2999	0.2388	0.2996
Λ_1	20	19.9996	19.9978	19.9986	19.9991
K_1	100.000	99.9987	99.9981	99.9960	99.9869

Table 2. Results of LDW-PSO, NDW-PSO, IPSO and F-PSO algorithm.

Algorithms	Best result	Mean result	Worst result	Std
LDW-PSO	0.0037074	0.0037089	0.0037173	2.5757×10^{-6}
NDW-PSO	0.0037074	0.0037090	0.0037154	2.1170×10^{-6}
IPSO	0.0037083	0.0037322	0.0038063	2.2897×10^{-5}
F-PSO	0.0037076	0.0037111	0.0037155	2.1454×10^{-6}

Table 3. Iteration and time required by LDW-PSO, NDW-PSO, IPSO and F-PSO.

Algorithms	Best result		Average result		Worst result	
	Iterations	Elapse time(s)	Iterations	Elapse time(s)	Iteration	Elapse time(s)
LDW-PSO	35	24228	41	24534	48	24591
NDW-PSO	30	22935	34	23216.7857	35	23456
IPSO	33	24571	45	24673	47	24696
F-PSO	28	27531	32	27561	35	27695

Table 1 exhibits the average of results obtained for adaptive controller parameters and table 2 shows the results ISE for LDW-PSO, NDW-PSO, IPSO and F-PSO, where each algorithm runs 25 times and table 3 shows iteration and necessary time to reach the best, mean and worst results.

Figures 1-6 confirm the success of optimization by F-PSO algorithm compared with the other algorithms for parameters of optimal controller $\Lambda_1, \Gamma_1, \Gamma_2, \Gamma_3, \Gamma_4, K_1$.

These figures are represented from iteration 1 to iteration 50. Figure 7 exhibits the convergence of the optimal ISE. It confirms the superiority of F-PSO algorithm in terms of convergence speed without the premature convergence problem.

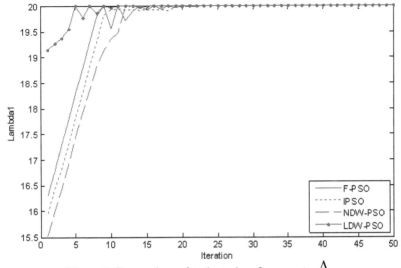

Figure 1. Comparison of trajectories of parameter Λ_1.

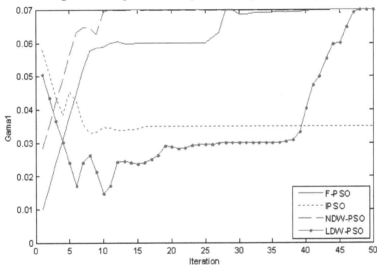

Figure 2. Comparison of trajectories of parameter Γ_1.

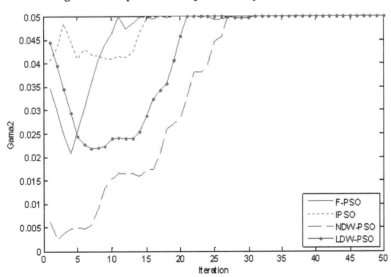

Figure 3. Comparison of trajectories of parameter Γ_2.

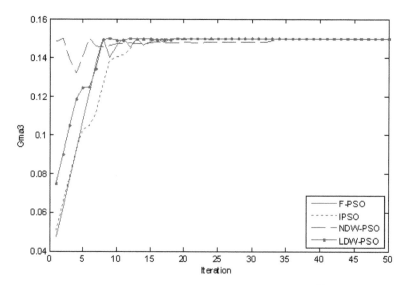

Figure 4. Comparison of trajectories of parameter Γ_3 .

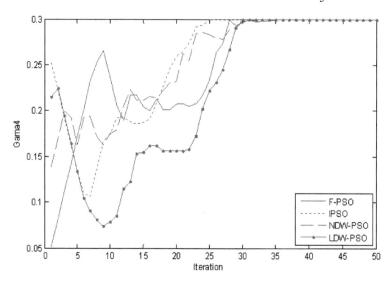

Figure 5. Comparison of trajectories of parameter Γ_4 .

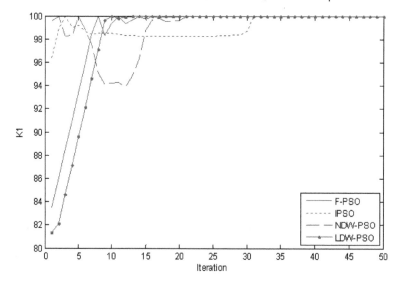

Figure 6. Comparison of trajectories of parameter K_1 .

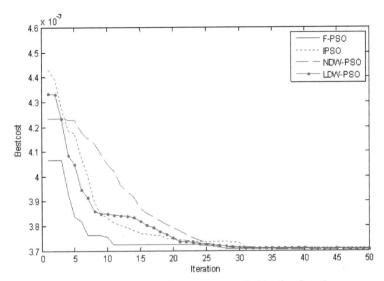

Figure 7. Comparison of convergence of objective function.

6. Conclusion

PSO has been efficient to design the adaptive controller by finding the optimal control parameters. The fuzzy system was proposed for adjusting the parameters for particle swarm optimization. It can improve the quality of result of method in the particle swarm optimization. The simulation results obtained from F-PSO, NDW-PSO, LDW-PSO and IPSO algorithms were compared . The simulation results also show the F–PSO has a better performance for purposes of parameter accuracy and convergence speed than the other algorithms.

References

[1] Alvarez-Ramirez, J., Cervantes, I. & Kelly, R. (2000). PID regulation of robot manipulators. stability and performance. System & Control Letters, vol. 41, pp. 73-83.

[2] Burkan, R. & Uzmay, I. (2005). A model of parameter adaptive law with time varying function for robot control. Applied Mathematical Modelling, vol. 29, pp. 361-371.

[3] Faieghi, M. R., Delavari, H. & Baleanu, D. (2012). A novel adaptive controller for two-degree of reedom polar robot with unknown perturbations. Commun Nonlinear SciNumer Simulate, vol. 17, pp. 1021-1030.

[4] Zeinali, M. & Notash, L. (2010). Adaptive sliding mode control with uncertainty estimator for robot manipulators. Mechanism and Machine Theory, vol. 45, pp. 80-90.

[5] Choi, Y., Chung, W. K. & Youm, Y. (2001). On the Optimal PID Performance Tuning for Robot Manipulators. IEEE/RSJ International Conference On Advanced Intelligent Robots and Systems, Maui, Hawaii, US, 2001.

[6] Wai, R.J., Tu, C. H. & Hsieh, K. Y. (2003). Design of Intelligent Optimal Tracking Control for Robot Manipulator. IEEE/ASME International Conference On Advanced Intelligent Mechatronics, 2003.

[7] Perez P, J., Perez, J. P., Soto, R., Flores, A., Rodriguez, F. & Meza, J. L. (2012). Trajectory Tracking Error Using PID Control Law for Two Link Robot Manipulator via Adaptive Neural Networks. Procedia Technology, vol. 3, pp. 139-146.

[8] Tomei, P. (1991). Adaptive PD controller for robot manipulators. IEEE Trans. Robot. Automat, vol. 7, pp. 565–570.

[9] Girirajkumae, S. M., Jayaraj, D. & Kishan, A. R. (2010). PSO based Tuning of a PID Controller for a High Performance Drilling Machine. International Journal of Computer Applications, vol. 1, pp. 0975-8887.

[10] Cao, S., Tu, J. & Liu, H. (2010). PSO Algorithm-Based Robust design of PID Controller for PMSM. Sixth International Conference on natural Computation, 2010.

[11] Chang, W. D. & Shih, S. P. (2010). PID controller design of nonlinear systems using an improved particle swarm optimization approach. Commun Nonlinear SciNumerSimulat, vol. 15, pp. 3632-3639.

[12] Sun, S., Zhang, J., W, J. & X, L. (2011). The Application of New Adaptive PSO in AGC and AFC Combination Control System. Procedia Engineering, vol. 16, pp. 702-707.

[13] Chen, S. M. & Dong, Y. F. (2011). Satellite Attitude Tracking Controller Optimization based on Particle Swarm Optimization. Procedia Engineering, vol. 15, pp. 526-530.

[14] Jaberipour, M., Khorram, E. & Karimi, B. (2011). Particle swarm algorithm for solving systems of nonlinear equations. Computers and Mathematics with Application, vol. 62, pp. 566-576.

[15] Modares, H. & Naghibi Sistani, M. B. (2011). Solving nonlinear optimal control problems using a hybrid IPSO-SQP algorithm. Engineering Application of Artificial Intelligence, vol. 24, pp. 476-484.

[16] Mehdi, h. & Boubaker, O. (2011). Position/force control optimized by Particle Swarm intelligence for constrained robotic manipulator. 11th International Conference on Intelligent System Design and Applications, 2011.

[17] Kennedy, J. & Eberhart, R. C. (1995). Particle swarm optimization. IEEE International Conference on Neural Networks, vol. 4, pp. 1942-1948 .

[18] Chatterjee, A. & Siarry, P. (2006). Nonlinear inertia weight variation for dynamic adaptation in particle swarm optimization, Computers and Operations research, vol. 33, no. 3, pp. 859-871.

[19] Shi, Y. and Eberhart, R. C. (1998a). Parameter selection in particle swarm optimization. Seventh Annual Conference on Evolutionary Programming, New York, pp. 591-600.

[20] Shi, Y. & Eberhart, R. C. (1998b). A modified particle swam optimizer. Conference on Evolutionary Computation, pp. 69-73.

[21] Modares, H., Alfi, A. & Fateh M. M. (2010). Parameter identification of chaotic dynamic systems through an improved particle swarm optimization, Expert Systems with Applications, vol. 37, pp. 3714-3720.

[22] Shi, Y. (2001). Fuzzy Adaptive Particle Swarm Optimization. Proceeding of the Congress on Evolutionary computation, vol. 1, pp. 101-106.

[23] Melin, P., Olivas, F., Castillo, O., Valdez, F., Soria, J. & Valdez, M. (2013). Optimal design of fuzzy classification system using PSO with dynamic parameter adaptation through fuzzy logic. Expert system with applications, vol. 40, pp. 3196-3206.

24

FDMG: Fault detection method by using genetic algorithm in clustered wireless sensor networks

A. Ghaffari[*] and S. Nobahary

Department of Computer Engineering, Tabriz branch, Islamic Azad University, Tabriz, Iran.

Corresponding author: a.ghaffari@iaut.ac.ir (A. Ghaffari).

Abstract

Wireless sensor networks (WSNs) consist of a large number of sensor nodes which are capable of sensing different environmental phenomena and sending the collected data to the base station or Sink. Since sensor nodes are made of cheap components and are deployed in remote and uncontrolled environments, they are prone to failure. Thus, maintaining a network with its proper functions even when undesired events occur is necessary and is called fault tolerance. Hence, fault management is essential in these networks. In this paper, a new method has been proposed with particular attention to fault tolerance and fault detection in WSN. The performance of the proposed method was simulated in MATLAB. The proposed method was based on majority vote, which can permanently detect faulty sensor nodes accurately. High accuracy and low false alarm rate helped exclude them from the network. To investigate the efficiency of the new method, the researchers compared it with Chen, Lee, and hybrid algorithms. Simulation results indicated that the proposed method has better performance in parameters such as detection accuracy (*DA*) and a false alarm rate (*FAR*) even with a large set of faulty sensor nodes.

Keywords: *Wireless Sensor Networks, Fault Detection, Genetic Algorithm, Fault Diagnosis, Clustering Algorithm.*

1. Introduction

Recent advancements in Micro-Electro-Mechanical Systems (MEMS) technology and wireless communication have promoted the emergence of a new generation technology which is called WSN. It consists of tiny, inexpensive sensors with limited processing and computing resources. These sensor nodes can sense, measure, and gather information from the environment. Hence, they have been used in many applications such as environmental monitoring, object tracking, agricultural lands, office buildings, industrial plants and military systems [1-3].

It is obvious that sensor networks are prone to failure which is mainly due to the fact that many applications require deploying sensors in harsh and contaminated environments such as battlefield. Fault detection and fault tolerance in wireless sensor networks have been investigated in the literature. Moreover, deployed sensor networks may suffer from many faults because of environmental impacts such as lightning, dust and moisture which can reduce the quality of wireless communications and divert sensors from their desirable operations. Moreover, hardware defects of sensors are related to cheap sensors prices which have low quality electronic components; such sensors are used in the construction of sensors which can negatively affect desirable network operations. Also, software bugs have such negative impacts on network operations[4]. These faults can be the cause of data failure and functional failures[5]. Data faults and failures result in inappropriate response of the network manager and faulty nodes bring about inaccurate routing by directing data through intermediate faulty nodes. Accordingly, it is essential to detect and manage faults in WSNs.

As mentioned above, due to the failure of network, there should be a kind of responsibility for avoiding failure so that network fault tolerance is guaranteed. In general, the first step in enhancing fault tolerance in a system is to try to use fault avoidance techniques so as to avoid damaging factors. To achieve this objective, one should use high-technology electronic devices, advanced equipment for designing, constructing and strict compliance of the design roles and testing stages. It should be noted that the first two cases, in particular, will increase the cost of production and is not operational for such networks. On the other hand, the two other cases only ensure reliability of performance accuracy for each sensor node in the construction stage and there is no guarantee for network operation against environmental factors. Consequently, fault avoidance techniques should be used in a network as well as other mechanisms so that network can continue to function properly. These mechanisms are referred to as fault tolerance techniques. The networks having the above-mentioned capability are known as fault-tolerant networks. In general, four types of redundancies, namely, hardware, software, information and time redundancy are used in the development of fault tolerant systems [6]. Using the first two redundancy types significantly increases the cost of production; hence, they are not appropriate for WSNs. In contrast, the other two redundancy types are used in some protocols which are proposed for these networks.

There are several sophisticated techniques and methods for detecting faults in WSNs. For instance, one highly powerful method, i.e. the majority vote method, is appropriate for detecting faults. This method makes use of genetic algorithms (GAs). GA is aimed at using natural evolution and a fitness value for each possible solution to the problem. The best GA choice and candidate is a representation of candidate solutions to the problem in (genotype).The initial population randomly produces a fitness function. It measures and compares each solution in the population; genetic algorithm operates the crossover and mutation functions to produce new Generation. Finally, the algorithm tunes parameters such as population size either finds the best data or finishes the time of execution, etc. Successful application of GAs in sensor network designs [7] has resulted in the development of several other GA-based application-specific approaches in WSN design mostly by the structure of a single fitness function [5,8,9]. Also, it has led to meditation optimality in the evaluation of fitness values[7].However, in the majority of these methods, very limited network characteristics are considered; hence, several requirements of application cases are not taken

into consideration in the performance measure of the algorithm.

However, in this paper, the researchers proposed a new method to solve the problem of majority vote. Moreover, it should be noted that by using GA, the proposed method can detect faulty sensors with high detection accuracy and low false alarm rate. In the proposed method, GA was used in sinking to select the best data and to define the status of each sensor node.

The rest of the paper is organized as follows: Section (2) provides a brief overview of fault detection methods in WSNs and related works; then in section 3, the proposed method was explained and network models are discussed in detail. The results of the simulation are mentioned and evaluated in section 4. Ultimately, section 5 sums up the findings, concludes the study and suggests directions for future works.

2. Related works

In this section, common and related algorithms and methods to fault detection literature are reviewed [10-14]. These methods use majority vote but they can't detect common failure nodes.

Chen et al.[15]have proposed a new distributed fault detection algorithm for wireless sensor networks. In this algorithm, data of sensors were compared twice to achieve a final decision on the status of sensors; moreover, four steps have to be taken and the improved majority voting was used. Two predetermined threshold values, marked up by θ_1 and θ_2, were used. Each sensor node compared its own sensed data with the data of neighbor nodes in the time stamp t; if the difference between them was greater than θ_1, the comparison would be repeated in the time stamp $t+1$; in case the difference was greater than θ_2, too, it was interpreted that data of this node was not similar to data of the neighbor nodes. In the next step, each sensor defined its own status as likely good (LG) if its own sensed data was similar to at least half of the neighbors' data. Otherwise, the sensor status would be defined as likely faulty (LF). In the next step, each sensor can determine its own final status according to the assumption that the sensor status is GOOD (GD) if it determined its status as LG in the previous step and more than half of the neighbors are LG. Then, sensors whose statuses are GD broadcast their status to their neighbors. A sensor node with an undetermined status can determine its status using the status of its neighbors. If a sensor node whose status is defined as LG and receives GD status from its neighbor node whose own sensed data is similar to the data of the sender of this message;

hence, it changes its status to *GD*. If a sensor whose status is defined as *LF* and receives faulty status from its neighbor whose own sensed data is similar to the data of the sender of this message, then it will change its status to faulty. The complexity of this algorithm is low and the probability of fault detection accuracy is very high. This algorithm only detects permanent faults while transient faults are ignored although these types of faults may occur in most of the sensor nodes.

Lee et al. [16] proposed a distributed fault detection algorithm for wireless sensor networks which is simple and highly accurate in detecting faulty nodes. This approach used time redundancy for increasing the tolerance of transient faults. In this method, two predetermined threshold values marked up by θ_1 and q were used. Every node compared its own sensed data with data from its neighbor nodes q times in order to determine whether its data are similar to the data of neighbors or not. In the next step, the sensor status would be defined as fault-free if its sensed data is similar to at least θ_1 of the data of neighbor nodes. Each sensor whose status is determined will broadcast its status to undetermined sensors so that they define their status. Simulation results in that study indicated that fault detection accuracy of this algorithm would decrease rapidly when the number of neighbor nodes was low but fault detection accuracy would increase when the number of neighbor nodes was high. The disadvantage of this algorithm is that it is not able to detect common mode failures.

As mentioned above, most fault detection algorithms [6, 16-20] in WSNs compare their own sensed data with the data of neighbor nodes. If their data is similar to at least half of the data sensed by neighbors, the cited sensor will be considered as fault-free. Comparison-based fault detection methods suffer from several deficiencies. They are unable to detect faulty nodes in remote areas where sensors do not have any availability to data of neighbors' nodes in their transceiver boards. The poor performance of algorithms in detecting common mode failures is another problem for these techniques.

With respect to the research gap highlighted above, in this paper, the researchers proposed a distributed method which is able to detect faulty nodes. To increase load balancing and lifetime of WSNs, different clustering algorithms are used. NHEEP[3](anew hybrid energy efficient partitioning approach for WSN clustering) is a clustering approach based on a partitioning technique in which the number of partitions are determined by the sink. After partitioning, each node can determine which partition is present. For electing a CH (cluster head) inside a partition, different parameters are considered such as position, distance of the nodes and the residual energy of nodes. NHEEP takes two important parameters into account for selecting cluster head node as follows:

Energy: Due to the lack of energy sources needed for regulating the lifetime of WSNs, energy is one of the most important parameters in research on WSNs. The residual energy is very important for the cluster head. Cluster head is negatively affected by high energy consumption of cluster members. Inasmuch as cluster head is responsible not only for gathering data from cluster members but also for processing data aggregation and data transmission to the sink; hence, its energy runs out very quickly. A qualified node for the cluster head is selected to ensure uninterrupted accomplishment of tasks. This node has more residual energy compared with others nodes.

Centrality: Sometimes the density of a node is high but the nodes which are around that node are only in one side of the mentioned node. When the nodes are in the central part of the area, they play an important role in network structure because the central nodes have an important role in transmitting data to the next step. Thus, it is preferable to have cluster heads in central neighborhood to maintain load balance.

In this algorithm, firstly, nodes identify their own clusters and then they try to select the best node in terms of high centrality and high remaining energy in each cluster as cluster head. In this algorithm, the cluster head collects the data of the cluster and sends it to the other cluster heads to send to the sink through multi-hop approach.

In the next section, the proposed fault detection algorithm is described. In this method, the network is clustered by using NHEEP [3] algorithm.

Then, in the stability phase, before the transmitting data to the cluster head, faulty sensors will be detected according to the fault detection algorithm. This fault detection phase is repeated in proportion to the existing noise in the operational area. In the time slot, fault detection process takes place, and data sensing and transmission will stop. After the mentioned time slot, the network continues its operation again.

3. Proposed method

In this section, fault model, variables and assumptions used in the proposed method are described.

Fault model:
In detecting WSN faults, nodes with faulty state and permanent communication faults are spotted. Since selfish sensor nodes with malfunctioning behavior are still capable of routing information, they could participate in the network operation. However, the sensor nodes with a permanent communication fault (including lack of power) are eliminated from the network [23-24].

Definitions:
The notations used in proposed fault detection algorithm are listed as follows:
- n: total number of sensor nodes distributed throughout the environment;
- M: number of clusters in the network;
- $L=[^N/_M]$: length of chromosomes;
- x_i: data of i-nodes;
- $|x_i - x_j|$: fitness function;

- θ_1: predetermined threshold value;
- R_r: the best selected gen among all gens

The proposed fault detection algorithm includes three phases: (a) setup and clustering process, (b) fault detection phase, and (c) Data transmission and updating phase. The above-mentioned three phases are described below.

3.1. Set up and clustering processes
In this phase, the deployed sensor nodes identify their neighbor nodes, create neighbor table and create clustering process. For creating the neighbor table, each sensor node sends a hello message at the beginning to identify its neighbors. Hello message includes the identification number of sensor nodes, node coordination and residual energy level of nodes. Figure 1 shows the structure of the hello packets as follows:

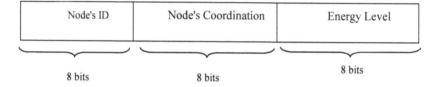

Node's ID	Node's Coordination	Energy Level
8 bits	8 bits	8 bits

Figure 1. Structure of HELLO message.

The neighbor nodes receiving the hello message respond to the sender node by sending echo message. This echo message includes the node's ID (Identifications), its distance to sink, and

energy level (residual energy) of neighbor nodes. Figure 2 represents the format and number of bits of response package message (echo packet) as follows:

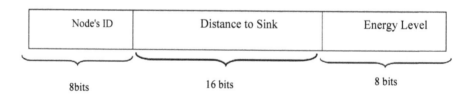

Node's ID	Distance to Sink	Energy Level
8bits	16 bits	8 bits

Figure 2. Structure of response (echo) message.

All nodes receive the parameters of their neighbor nodes and store them in the neighborhood table. At this stage, nodes automatically try to select a cluster and their cluster heads. Clustering operation in the proposed method was carried out with the partitioning algorithm which was described in the previous section. For selecting cluster heads, the proposed scheme took the following parameters into account: centrality and residual energy. After choosing cluster heads, cluster member nodes introduce themselves to the cluster head and practically justify their membership in the cluster. In the next step, the cluster members gather the information from the occurred events and send the data packets to the

sink node after data aggregation processing. Figure 3 depicts clustered WSN model with faulty sensor nodes, faulty cluster head, fault-free sensor nodes and fault-free cluster head nodes.

3.2. Fault detection phase
During the normal operation of network, nodes send their data to the cluster head. However, in the fault diagnosis and fault detection phase, each member node of the cluster sends data to nodes of each cluster head. Thus, cluster heads will select the best data of the clusters by applying genetic algorithm and sending them to the sink. Also, sink applies GA whose properties are determined in the following section. The best data is selected between cluster head data previously sent to sink

and the status of each cluster head is determined   by the sink.

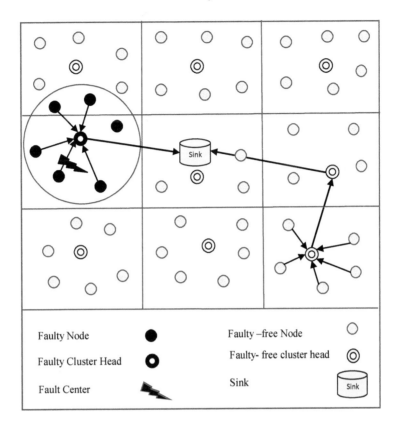

Figure 3. Wireless sensor network with fault-free and faulty nodes and cluster head.

The selected data of sink is broadcast as a message to all the cluster heads. Fault-free cluster heads can determine the status of the cluster nodes but faulty cluster heads should be changed and given to a healthy cluster head. Figure 4 depicts the structure and number of bits of a broadcast message. Cluster head with a faulty plate is detected by broadcasting messages to all members of the cluster to choose their cluster head node again. It is obvious that the choice of a new cluster head node is healthy. If 30% or less nodes on the cluster nodes as well-known nodes are allowed to join, the cluster nearby nodes is proportional to their distance.

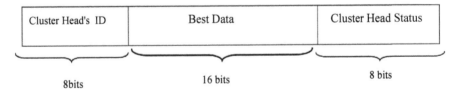

Figure 4. Structure of broadcast message.

Cluster head with a faulty plate is detected by broadcasting messages to all members of the cluster to choose their cluster head node again. It is obvious that the choice of a new cluster head node is healthy. If 30% or less nodes on the cluster nodes as well-known nodes are allowed to join, the cluster nearby nodes is proportional to their distance.

Before determining θ_1 parameter of member nodes, a definite threshold fitting data network is determined. If the dispute is declared as the best dispute in a particular node, it is greater than θ_1. Nodes will be regarded as faulty nodes; otherwise, the node is known to be healthy. The proposed method reveals that the decision about nodes' status and cluster heads are determined in the sink. Indeed, the method introduced in this paper is a combined approach for selecting the best data based on genetic algorithms.

In the first generation, a chromosome whose genes are real numbers and whose chromosome length is equal to the number of nodes in each cluster. Number of nodes in each cluster is denoted by the symbol L. Values of each gene is equal to the amounts of data sensed by each node. In the proposed algorithm, the number of generations is one thing and the fitness function is used between each gene and other genes of chromosome according to (1). Hence, the last gene will continue using the same gene L and each of the obtained data is gathered and placed in the W and generalizes the corresponding gene in an array according to (2).

Finally, the fitness of a gene (least amount of conflict with other genes) is the most as the genes in the chromosome (R_r) is selected.

$$F= |x_i - x_j | \qquad (1)$$
$$W_1=|x_1 - x_1 |+|x_1 - x_2 |+...+|x_1 - x_{L-1} |+|x_1 - x_L |$$
$$W_2=|x_2 - x_1 |+|x_2 - x_2 |+...+|x_2 - x_{L-1} |+|x_2 - x_L |$$

$$\vdots$$

$$W_L=|x_L - x_1 |+|x_L - x_2 |+...+|x_L - x_{L-1} |+|x_L - x_L | \qquad (2)$$

Figure 5 shows the chromosome of the best gene.

| W_1 | W_2 | ... | W_L |

Figure 5. The chromosome of the best gene.

For ensuring the accuracy of selecting correct data in each cluster, the algorithm repeats it 10 times to set chromosomes R_0, R_1,...,R_9.

Then, the highest fitness chromosome is selected. Repeating the fitness function diminishes the probability of transient fault occurrence in the network.

3.3. Data transmission and updating phase

Data transmission phase corresponds to network application based on event occurrence; alternatively, the sensed data collected to the cluster head node and it forwards the aggregated data to the sink.

Since faulty node detection consumes considerable energy, it is not used in all the stages of data collection. In each cluster, sensor nodes send data to the cluster head.

Cluster node controls, aggregates and sends data to the sink.

In the proposed algorithm, new cluster head will be selected if cluster head node is faulty or its battery is low. In this case, cluster members select a new cluster head. Figure 6 illustrates the pseudo code of the first and third stages.

Algorithm phase 1(layer 1)
1: Step 1: Each node S_i sets its status to H, send hello message to each node, and each node is neighbor sends reply message.
2:     Establish clusters and definite cluster head.
3:     Step 2: Fault detection done for first time (and in each R_r round)
4:       Each node S_i sends its data to CH_i(for example r=10)
5:         for k=1 to rs_i sends data to CH_i
6:           for j=1 to L do
7: $W_k= |s_i^k - s_j^k|$
8:             Best(i)=Min(W_i)
9:       Send Best(i) for each cluster to sink
10: for j=1 to $i$do
11: $W_i= |Best_i - Best_j|$
12:     Total Best=Min(W)
13: Each CH_i determines its status
14:         if $|X_{CH_i} - TotalBest| \leq \theta_1$ then $T_{CHi}=H$
15:           else $T_{CHi}=F$
16:       if $T_{CHi}=F$ then elect another CH_i
17: Each S_i determines its status
18:         if $|X_{S_i} - TotalBest| \leq \theta_1$ then $T_{Si}=H$
19:           else $T_{Si}=F$
20: Step 3: Send data to sink and update network status

Figure 6. Pseudo code of the first to third stages.

4. Simulation results
4.1. Network model

The proposed method was simulated in MATLAB software. n sensors were randomly deployed in $A*A(m^2)$ square area which was aimed at collecting data during each round. It was assumed that the sink was in the middle of the area with the coordinate of ($A/2$, $A/2$).The simulation was repeated in 1000 cycles and the simulation parameters were indicated in Table 1.The following two metrics, detection accuracy (DA) and false alarm rate (FAR) are used to evaluate the performance, where DA is defined as the ratio of the number of faulty sensor nodes detected to the total number of faulty nodes and FAR is the ratio of the number of fault-free sensor nodes diagnosed as faulty to the total number of fault-free nodes [23]. In this simulation and performance evaluation, nodes with some transient faults are treated as fault-free nodes [23].A simple model for radio hardware energy dissipation was used where the transmitter dissipates energy to run radio electronics, and power amplifier and the receiver dissipates energy to run the radio electronics.

Based on the model, the network had the following features:

- All nodes were uniformly distributed within a square area.
- Each node has a unique ID.
- Each node has a fixed location.

- All nodes can perform data aggregation.
- Transmission energy consumption was proportional to the distance of the nodes.

Both free space and multi-path fading channel models were used for the experiments of this study based on the distance between the transmitter and receiver. Thus, energy consumption for transmitting a packet was calculated for l bits over distance d by (3) as follows [21]:

$$E_{tx}(l, d) = E_{tx-elec}(l) + E_{tx-amp}(l)$$

$$= \begin{cases} E_{tx}(l,d) = l.E_{elec} + l.\varepsilon_{fs}d^2 & d < d_0 \\ l.E_{elec} + l.\varepsilon_{amp}.d^4 & d > d_0 d_0 \end{cases} \quad (3)$$

According to the above-mentioned energy consumption model, if the distance between sensor node and base station (BS)is less than a threshold d_0, as calculated by (4), the free space (f_s) model will be used; otherwise, the multi-path (mp) model will be used [21].The $d_0$parameter can be calculated as follows [21]:

$$d_0 = \sqrt{\frac{\varepsilon_{fs}}{\varepsilon_{amp}}} \quad (4)$$

Table 1 shows the values of ε_{fs} and ε_{amp}. Energy consumption for receiving a packet of l bits is calculated according to (5) [21] as follows:

$$E_{RX}(l) = E_{RX-elec}(l) = l.E_{elec} \quad (5)$$

The probability of faulty sensor nodes was assumed to be 0.10, 0.2, 0.3, 0.4 and 0.5. The number of included nodes was assumed to be 100 and 150, respectively.

Table 1. Simulation parameters.

Parameter	Value
Number of sensors	100, 150
Area	400×400 (m²)
Sink position	(200, 200)
d_0	87 m
Radio range	70 m
E_{elec}	50nj/bit
ε_{fs} (if destination to BS<=d_0)	10pj/bit/m²
ε_{amp} (if destination to BS >=d_0)	0.0013 pj/bit/m⁴
Initial energy	1j
E_{da} (Data aggregation energy)	10 nj/bit/packet
Packet size	4000 bits
Simulation repeat	1000 cycles

4.2. Simulation results and performance evaluation

The efficiency of the proposed method was evaluated and compared with Lee [16] and Chen [15] algorithms in terms of detection accuracy and false alarm rate parameters. Whereas DA was defined as the ratio of the number of detected faulty nodes to the total number of faulty nodes, FAR was defined as the ratio of the number of fault-free nodes that are detected as faulty node to the total number of fault-free nodes [22]. Table 2 compares the fault detection accuracy in the proposed scheme, Chen [15], Lee [16] and Hybrid [6] algorithms.

Table 2. Fault detection accuracy in the proposed method, Chen [15], Lee [16] and hybrid [6] algorithms.

Algorithms								
Chen [15]	Lee [16]	Hybrid [6]	Proposed	Chen [15]	Lee [16]	Hybrid [6]	Proposed	P
0.984	0.986	0.988	1	0.984	0.986	0.988	1	0.1
0.982	0.984	0.985	1	0.982	0.984	0.985	1	0.2
0.96	0.97	0.977	1	0.96	0.97	0.977	1	0.3
0.97	0.50	0.6	1	0.95	0.5	0.6	1	0.4
0	0	0	0.42	0	0	0.1	0.34	0.5
		n=150				n=100		

Figures 7 and 8 show the comparison of the proposed algorithm with the algorithms of Chen [15], Lee [16], and hybrid [6] respectively, in terms of detection accuracy and false alarm rate with 100 nodes in network.

When the probability of sensor failure was 0.1, the detection accuracies of Chen [15], Lee [16], and hybrid [6] algorithms were 0.986, 0.984, 0.988 and 0.986 respectively. However, the detection accuracy of the proposed algorithm was equal to

1.When the probability of the sensor failure was 0.25, the detection accuracies of Chen [15], Lee [16], and hybrid [6] algorithms were 0.975, 0.97, and 0.977, respectively. However, it should be noted that the detection accuracy of the proposed algorithm was equal to 0.981. When the probability of sensor failure was 0.25, the false alarm rate in Lee [16] and Chen [15] algorithms was 0.0018 and 0.0021, respectively. In contrast, the false alarm rate of the proposed algorithm was equal to 0.0013.

Figures 9 and 10 compare the proposed algorithm with that of Chen [15] and Lee [16] in terms of detection accuracy and false alarm rate when there were 150 nodes in the network.

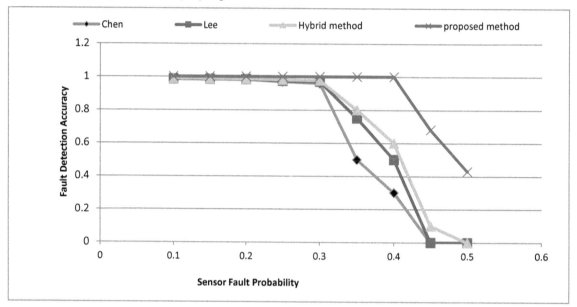

Figure 7. Fault detection accuracy when N=100.

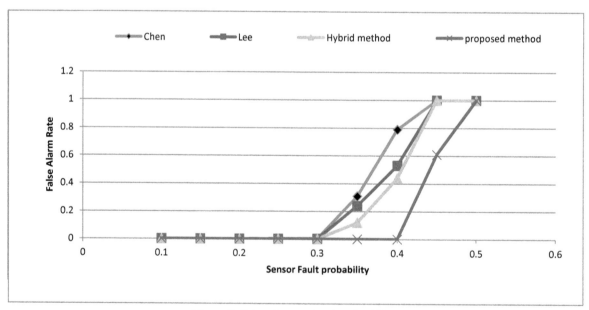

Figure 8. False alarm rate when N=100.

When the probability of sensor failure was 0.1, the detection accuracy in both Lee [16] and Chen [15] algorithms was 0.999. However, the detection accuracy of the proposed algorithm was equal to 1.

When the probability of the sensor failure was 0.25, the detection accuracy of Lee [16], Chen [15], and hybrid [6] algorithms were 0.993, 0.991, 0.991 and 0.994, respectively. Nevertheless, the detection accuracy of the proposed algorithm was equal to 0.994.

Similarly, when the probability of sensor failure was 0.15, then, the false alarm rate of Chen [15] algorithm was 0.0001. In contrast, the false alarm rate of Lee [16], hybrid [6] and the proposed algorithm was equal to zero.

When the probability of sensor failure was 0.25, the false alarm rate of Lee [16], Chen [15], and hybrid [6] algorithms were 0.0012, 0.0014, 0.0007and 0.0004, respectively but that of the proposed algorithm was equal to 0.0006. In other words, as the probability of sensor failure increases, the false alarm rate of the proposed algorithm was less than those of Lee [16] and Chen [15] algorithms. Based on figures 7 and 8, the researchers can draw the conclusion that the detection accuracy increases as the number of neighbors' increases but false alarm rate decreases. Furthermore, as the probability of sensor failure increases, detection accuracy of the proposed algorithm will be higher than those of Lee [16] and Chen [15] algorithms.

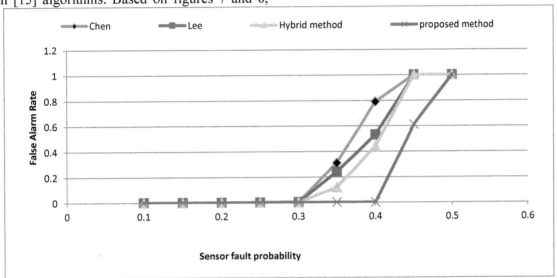

Figure 9. Fault alarm rate when N=150.

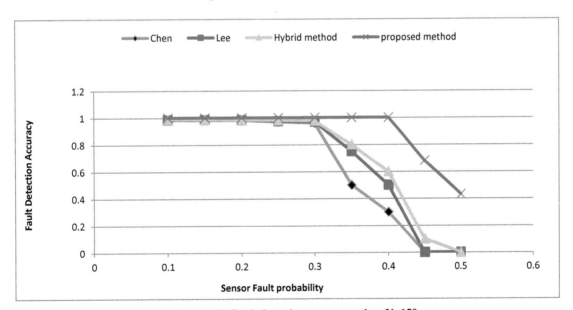

Figure 10. Fault detection accuracy when N=150.

5. Conclusion and directions for further research

Inasmuch as the failure rate of WSNs is remarkable, fault tolerance should be regarded as a significant attribute in these networks; this feature can be utilized to detect faulty nodes and emit them from the network. This paper presents a distributed fault detection algorithm for wireless sensor networks. In this paper, based on GAs, researchers proposed a new method for detecting faulty node. The proposed method was also intended to detect permanent faults in sensor nodes with an extremely high detection accuracy and low fault alarm rate in the network. The proposed algorithm is simple and detects faults in WSN with high accuracy. Faulty sensor nodes are identified based on comparisons between neighboring nodes and dissemination of the decision made at each node and each cluster. Simulation results revealed that the proposed method demonstrates better performance across parameters such as *DA* and *FAR* even when the number of faulty sensor nodes is high.

A direction for further research can use a combination of the method proposed in this paper with a learning automata technique for fault detection and network fault tolerance enhancement.

References

[1] Ian, F. A., Weilian, S., Sankarasubramaniam, Y. & Cayirci, E. (2002). Wireless sensor networks: a survey. Computer networks, vol. 38, pp. 393-422.

[2] Yick, J., Mukherjee, B. & Ghosal, D. (2008). Wireless sensor network survey. Computer networks, vol. 52, pp. 2292-2330, 2008.

[3] Babaei, S., B., Zekrizadeh N. & Nobahari, S. (2012). NHEEP: A New Hybrid Energy Efficient Partitioning Approach for Wireless Sensor Network Clustering. International Journal of Information and Electronics Engineering, vol. 2, pp. 323-327.

[4] Chenglin, Z., Xuebin, S., Songlin, S. & Ting, J. (2011). Fault diagnosis of sensor by chaos particle swarm optimization algorithm and support vector machine. Expert Systems with Applications, vol. 38, pp. 9908-9912.

[5] Warriach, E., Nguyen, T., Aiello, M. & Tei, K. (2012). Fault detection in wireless sensor networks: a hybrid approach. ACM/IEEE 11th International Conference onInformation Processing in Sensor Networks (IPSN), pp. 87-88.

[6] Warriach, E., Nguyen, T., Aiello, M. & Tei, K. (2012). A hybrid fault detection approach for context-aware wireless sensor networks. 2012 IEEE 9th International Conference onMobile Adhoc and Sensor Systems (MASS), pp. 281-289.

[7] Jourdan, D. & Weck, O. (2004). Layout optimization for a wireless sensor network using a multi-objective genetic algorithm. 2004-Spring. 2004 IEEE 59th Vehicular technology conference (VTC), pp. 2466-2470.

[8] Aldosari S., & Moura, J. (2004). Fusion in sensor networks with communication constraints. In Proceedings of the 3rd international symposium on Information processing in sensor networks, pp. 108-115, 2004.

[9] Mitchell, R. & Chen, R. (2014). survey of intrusion detection in wireless network applications. Computer Communications, vol. 42, pp. 1-23, 2014.

[10] Bari, A., Jaekel, A., Jiang, J. & Xu, Y. (2012). Design of fault tolerant wireless sensor networks satisfying survivability and lifetime requirements. Computer Communications, vol. 35, pp. 320-333.

[11] Ding, M., Chen, D., Xing, K. & Cheng, X. (2005). Localized fault-tolerant event boundary detection in sensor networks. 24th Annual Joint Conference of the IEEE Computer and Communications Societies. Proceedings IEEE in INFOCOM, 2005, pp. 902-913, 2005.

[12] Geeta, D., Nalini, N. & Biradar, R. C. (2013). Fault tolerance in wireless sensor network using hand-off and dynamic power adjustment approach. Journal of Network and Computer Applications, vol. 36, pp. 1174-1185.

[13] Jiang, P. (2009). A new method for node fault detection in wireless sensor networks. Sensors, vol. 9, pp. 1282-1294.

[14] Kaushik, B., Kaur, N. & Kohli, A. K. (2013). Achieving maximum reliability in fault tolerant network design for variable networks. Applied Soft Computing, vol. 13, pp. 3211-3224.

[15] Chen, J., Kher, S. & Somani, A. (2006). Distributed fault detection of wireless sensor networks. in Proceedings of the 2006 workshop on dependability issues in wireless ad hoc networks and sensor networks, pp. 65-72.

[16] Lee, S., Choe, H., Park, B., Song, Y. & Kim, C. (2011). LUCA: An energy-efficient unequal clustering algorithm using location information for wireless sensor networks. Wireless Personal Communications, vol. 56, pp. 715-731.

[17] Banerjee, I., Chanak, P., Rahaman, H. & Samanta, T. (2014). Effective fault detection and routing scheme for wireless sensor networks. Computers & Electrical Engineering, vol. 40, pp. 291-306.

[18] Cho, K., Jo, M., Kwon, T., Chen, H. & Lee, D. (2013). Classification and experimental analysis for clone detection approaches in wireless sensor networks. IEEE journal of Systems, vol. 7, pp. 26-35.

[19] Mahapatro, A. & Khilar, P. (2013). Fault diagnosis in wireless sensor networks: A survey. IEEECommunications Surveys & Tutorials, vol. 15, pp. 2000-2026.

[20] Xie, M. Hu, J., Han, S. & Chen, H. (2013). Scalable hypergrid k-NN-Based online anomaly detection in wireless sensor networks. IEEE Transactions onParallel and Distributed Systems, vol. 24, pp. 1661-1670.

[21] Heinzelman, W. B., Chandrakasan, A. P. & Balakrishnan, H. (2002). An application-specific protocol architecture for wireless microsensor networks. IEEE Transactions on Wireless Communications, vol. 1, pp. 660-670.

[22] Guo, S., Zhong, Z. & He, T. (2009). Find: faulty node detection for wireless sensor networks. In Proceedings of the 7th ACM conference on embedded networked sensor systems, pp. 253-266.

Permissions

All chapters in this book were first published in JAIDM, by Shahrood University of Technology; hereby published with permission under the Creative Commons Attribution License or equivalent. Every chapter published in this book has been scrutinized by our experts. Their significance has been extensively debated. The topics covered herein carry significant findings which will fuel the growth of the discipline. They may even be implemented as practical applications or may be referred to as a beginning point for another development.

The contributors of this book come from diverse backgrounds, making this book a truly international effort. This book will bring forth new frontiers with its revolutionizing research information and detailed analysis of the nascent developments around the world.

We would like to thank all the contributing authors for lending their expertise to make the book truly unique. They have played a crucial role in the development of this book. Without their invaluable contributions this book wouldn't have been possible. They have made vital efforts to compile up to date information on the varied aspects of this subject to make this book a valuable addition to the collection of many professionals and students.

This book was conceptualized with the vision of imparting up-to-date information and advanced data in this field. To ensure the same, a matchless editorial board was set up. Every individual on the board went through rigorous rounds of assessment to prove their worth. After which they invested a large part of their time researching and compiling the most relevant data for our readers.

The editorial board has been involved in producing this book since its inception. They have spent rigorous hours researching and exploring the diverse topics which have resulted in the successful publishing of this book. They have passed on their knowledge of decades through this book. To expedite this challenging task, the publisher supported the team at every step. A small team of assistant editors was also appointed to further simplify the editing procedure and attain best results for the readers.

Apart from the editorial board, the designing team has also invested a significant amount of their time in understanding the subject and creating the most relevant covers. They scrutinized every image to scout for the most suitable representation of the subject and create an appropriate cover for the book.

The publishing team has been an ardent support to the editorial, designing and production team. Their endless efforts to recruit the best for this project, has resulted in the accomplishment of this book. They are a veteran in the field of academics and their pool of knowledge is as vast as their experience in printing. Their expertise and guidance has proved useful at every step. Their uncompromising quality standards have made this book an exceptional effort. Their encouragement from time to time has been an inspiration for everyone.

The publisher and the editorial board hope that this book will prove to be a valuable piece of knowledge for researchers, students, practitioners and scholars across the globe.

List of Contributors

F. Safi-Esfahani, Sh. Rakian and M.-H. Nadimi-Shahraki
Faculty of Computer Engineering, Najafabad Branch, Islamic Azad University, Najafabad, Isfahan, Iran

L. Khalvati, M. Keshtgary and N. Rikhtegar
Department of Computer & Information Technology, Shiraz University of Technology, Shiraz, Iran

D. Koundal
University Institute of Engineering and Technology, Panjab University, Chandigarh, India

F. Alibakhshi
Control Department, Islamic Azad University South Tehran Branch, Tehran, Iran

M. Teshnehlab
Center of Excellence in Industrial Control, K.N. Toosi University, Tehran, Iran

M. Alibakhshi
Young Researchers & Elite Club, Borujerd Branch, Islamic Azad University, Borujerd, Iran

M. Mansouri
Intelligent System Laboratory (ISLAB), Electrical & Computer engineering department, K.N. Toosi University, Tehran, Iran

M. Aghaei and A. Dastfan
Electrical Engineering Department, University of Shahrood, Shahrood, Iran

M. Zahedi and A. Arjomandzadeh
School of Computer Engineering & Information Technology, University of Shahrood, Shahrood, Iran

A. Pakzad and B. Minaei Bidgoli
Department of Computer Engineering, Iran University of Science & Technology, Tehran, Iran

E. Golrasan and H. Sameti
Department of Computer Engineering, Sharif University of Technology, Tehran, Iran

D. Darabian, H. Marvi and M. Sharif Noughabi
Department of Electrical Engineering, University of Shahrood, Shahrood, Iran

S. A. Taher and M. Pakdel
Department of Electrical Engineering, University of Kashan, Kashan, Iran

M. M. Abravesh and H. Abravesh
Department of Electrical Engineering, Hadaf Institute of Higher Education, Sari, Iran

A. Sheikholeslami and M. Yazdani Asrami
Department of Electrical Engineering, Noshirvani University of Technology, Babol, Iran

R. Satpathy and J. Ratha
School of Life Sciences, Sambalpur University, Burla, Sambalpur, India

V. B. Konkimalla
Department of Biological Sciences, National Institute of Science Education & Research (NISER), Bhubaneswar, India

E. Ghandehari and F. Saadatjoo
Computer Engineering Department, Science and Art University, Yazd, Yazd, Iran

N. Bigdeli and H. Sadegh Lafmejani
EE Department, Imam Khomeini International University, Qazvin, Iran

F. Tatari and M. B. Naghibi-Sistani
Electrical Engineering Department, Ferdowsi university of Mashhad, Azadi square, Mashhad, Iran

A. Mesrikhani and M. Davoodi
Department of Computer Science & Information Technology, Institute for Advanced Studies in Basic Sciences (IASBS), Zanjan, Iran

M. A. Saadatjoo and S. M. Babamir
Department of Computer Engineering, University of Kashan, Kashan, Iran

Kh. Sadatnejad, S. Shiry Ghidary and M. rahmati
Computer Engineering & Information Technology, Amirkabir University of Technology, Tehran, Iran

S. Beiranvand and M. A. Z. Chahooki
Electrical & Computer Engineering Department, Yazd University, Yazd, Iran

A. Khosravi and A. Roshandel
Department of Electrical and Computer Engineering, Babol University of Technology, School of Computer Engineering

A.R. Alfi
Faculty of Electrical and Robatic Computer Engineering, Shahrood University of Technology, Iran

M. Heidari, M. Banejad and A. Hajizadeh
Shahrood University of Technology, Shahrood, Iran

M. AllamehAmiri, V. Derhami and M. Ghasemzadeh
Department of Electrical and Computer Engineering, Yazd University, Yazd, Iran

S. Asadi Amiri
Department of Computer Engineering, University of Shahrood Technology, Shahrood, Iran

E. Moudi
Department of Dental Maxillofacial Radiology, University of Medical Science Babol, Babol, Iran

F. Soleiman Nouri, M. Haddad Zarif and M. M. Fateh
Department of Electrical Engineering and Robotics, University of Shahrood, Iran

V. Khoshdel and A. Akbarzadeh
Center of Excellence on Soft Computing & Intelligent Information Processing, Mechanical Engineering Department, Ferdowsi University of Mashhad, Mashhad

E. Golpar-Rabooki
Department of Mathematics, University of Qom, Qom, Iran

S. Zarghamifar
Department of Computer Engineering, University of Qom, Qom, Iran

J. Rezaeenour
Department of Industrial Engineering, University of Qom, Qom, Iran

A. Ghaffari and S. Nobahary
Department of Computer Engineering, Tabriz branch, Islamic Azad University, Tabriz, Iran

Index

Printed in the USA
CPSIA information can be obtained
at www.ICGtesting.com
JSHW051431221024
72173JS00006B/1439